Swedish Cinema and
the Sexual Revolution

Swedish Cinema and the Sexual Revolution

Critical Essays

Edited by ELISABET BJÖRKLUND *and* MARIAH LARSSON

McFarland & Company, Inc., Publishers
Jefferson, North Carolina

LIBRARY OF CONGRESS CATALOGUING-IN-PUBLICATION DATA

Names: Björklund, Elisabet, 1983– editor. |
Larsson, Mariah, 1972– editor.
Title: Swedish cinema and the sexual revolution : critical essays /
edited by Elisabet Björklund and Mariah Larsson.
Description: Jefferson, N.C. : McFarland & Company, Inc., Publishers, 2016. |
Includes bibliographical references and index.
Identifiers: LCCN 2016025537 | ISBN 9781476665443
(softcover : acid free paper) ∞
Subjects: LCSH: Sex in motion pictures. | Erotic films—Sweden—
History—20th century. | Pornographic films—Sweden—History—
20th century. | Motion pictures—Censorship—Sweden.
Classification: LCC PN1995.9.S45 S94 2016 | DDC 791.43/653809485—dc23
LC record available at https://lccn.loc.gov/2016025537

BRITISH LIBRARY CATALOGUING DATA ARE AVAILABLE

**ISBN (print) 978-1-4766-6544-3
ISBN (ebook) 978-1-4766-2501-0**

© 2016 Elisabet Björklund and Mariah Larsson. All rights reserved

*No part of this book may be reproduced or transmitted in any form
or by any means, electronic or mechanical, including photocopying
or recording, or by any information storage and retrieval system,
without permission in writing from the publisher.*

Front cover: Harriet Andersson in the title role from the
1953 film *Sommaren med Monika* (*Summer with Monika*)
(Hallmark Productions/Photofest)

Printed in the United States of America

*McFarland & Company, Inc., Publishers
Box 6ɪɪ, Jeʾerson, North Carolina 28640
www.mcfarlandpub.com*

Table of Contents

Acknowledgments
    Elisabet Björklund *and* Mariah Larsson   vii

Introduction: Beyond Swedish Summers
    Elisabet Björklund *and* Mariah Larsson   1

I. Summertime Sensuality

The Story of a Bad Girl! *Summer with Monika*, Sexploitation and the Selling of Erotic Bergman in America
    Arne Lunde   11

It Started with a Kiss: Sexuality and Swedish Film in 1951
    Anders Marklund   21

II. Art, Sexploitation and Pornography

Pillow Talk, Swedish Style: *To Love*
    Anu Koivunen   37

Her Body, His Self: Authorship and Gender in *I Am Curious (Yellow)* and *I Am Curious (Blue)*
    Anders Wilhelm Åberg   49

Ann and Eve: A Filmmaker Strikes Back
    Bengt Bengtsson   61

A Porn of One's Own? Anne-Marie Berglund and *Weekend in Stockholm*
    Mariah Larsson   74

Come and Blow the Horn: Sound, Sex and Cultural Heritage
    Mats Björkin   86

III. Obscenity and Censorship

The Open Secret: Illegal Screenings of Pornographic Films for Public Audiences in Sweden, 1921–1943
    Tommy Gustafsson   101

491 and the Censorship Controversy
 LENA LENNERHED   116

The Limits of Sexual Depictions in the Late 1960s
 ELISABET BJÖRKLUND   126

IV. The Institutionalization of Sex in Sweden

Institutionalized Sexploitation? The Swedish Film Institute and Research on the Effects of Cinema in the 1960s
 PER VESTERLUND   141

P(owe)R, Sex and *Mad Men* Swedish Style—Or How the Personal Can Become the Political
 MAARET KOSKINEN   153

Egrets in the Porno Swamp: The Swedish Film Institute and Swedish Sin
 LARS DIURLIN   168

V. The American Reception of Swedish Sin

Illegally Blonde: Swedish Sin and Pornography in U.S. and Swedish Imaginations, 1955–1971
 KLARA ARNBERG *and* CARL MARKLUND   185

A Modicum of Social Value? The Critical and Legal Discussion of *I Am Curious (Yellow)* in America
 ULF JONAS BJÖRK   201

Many of Your Finer Nudie Films: Saga Film, Swedish National Cinema and Seventies Transnational Erotic Film
 KEVIN HEFFERNAN   216

About the Contributors   233
Index   235

Acknowledgments

ELISABET BJÖRKLUND *and* MARIAH LARSSON

A book such as this one cannot be made without the efforts of many. First of all, we would like to thank our contributors, who were patient when the process was slow and quick to respond when haste was necessary, and whose work has resulted in this volume. In addition, we are extremely grateful to Stefan Nylén at Studio S, Rickard Gramfors at Klubb Super 8, and Krister Collin at the Swedish Film Institute who aided us in tracking down images and transferring them into digital copies, and Leif Furhammar, who visited our workshop in Stockholm in December 2013 to talk about Harry Schein and Swedish film censorship.

We have had two workshops during this process, one at Stockholm University with the Swedish contributors, and another at University of Illinois, Urbana-Champaign, in February 2014, with the American contributors. These workshops were financed by the Strategic Funding of the Humanities and Social Sciences at Stockholm University. We would like to thank Anna Stenport for helping us arrange the workshop at University of Illinois.

The Wahlgren Foundation granted a generous scholarship to Elisabet Björklund for her work on the volume. Funding for the transfer of images into digital copies as well as various permissions was granted by Holger and Thyra Lauritzen's Foundation for Film Historical Research.

Finally, and as always, our deepest love and gratitude go to our families: Lasse and little Naima, and Olle, Albert, Martha, and Kinsey the dog.

Introduction
Beyond Swedish Summers

ELISABET BJÖRKLUND *and* MARIAH LARSSON

Several Swedish films and television series idealize the Swedish summer. The iconography is closely associated with nature: forests, rural landscapes, the archipelagos of Stockholm, Gothenburg, and Blekinge, lakes surrounded by trees and covered with water lilies, the warm sunlight that lasts late into evenings, patches of wild strawberries, birdsong, midsummer celebrations, fish angling, and so on. This is a long-standing trope that stretches back to Swedish silent cinema, continues through the provincial comedies and farces of the 1930s and through films depicting agrarian communities in the 1940s and 1950s; becomes even further romanticized in a string of children's film and television productions in the 1960s and 1970s and continues to this day.[1] Although it is in many ways such an exhausted trope that it might very well be called a cliché, it is so strongly connected to the "imagined community" of Sweden that its power to evoke strong feelings seems endless.[2]

The warmth and light of late spring and summer are also closely linked to a sense of eroticism. It is often said that March 22—nine months after Midsummer—is the day when most Swedes are born, but in fact, this varies from year to year.[3] Several films combined summer themes with romance, nudity, and/or sensuality—from the simple skinny dip in a lake or the sea as in *Bara en mor/Only a Mother* (Alf Sjöberg, 1949), to romantic and erotic adventures during the warm months of the year as in *Sommaren med Monika/Summer with Monika* (Ingmar Bergman, 1953), *Käre John/Dear John* (Lars Magnus Lindgren, 1964), *...som havets nakna vind/One Swedish Summer* (Ulf Palme, Gunnar Höglund, 1968), *Strandhugg i somras/*"Raid in the Summer" (Mikael Ekman, 1972). Films such as these utilized the strong emotional resonance of summer in the national imaginary, connecting nature in full bloom and the warm rays of life-giving sunlight to the naked human body.[4] They also represented a sexuality that played well not only within national borders but also abroad, something which quickly caught on and became a subject of parody in the film *I rök och dans* "Iu smoke and dance" (Yngve Gamlin and Bengt Blomgren) from 1954, in which two people take a nude swim and a subtitle comes up stating "for export." The joy with which Swedish people have embraced this stereotype of themselves even further testifies to how strong the sentiments are regarding summer in Sweden.

In this way, Swedish summers became symbolic, connoting a nature that encompasses more than striking landscapes and a celebration of warmth and light, that included the (sexual) bodies in that landscape. Sweden, sexuality, and cinema is a triad that has had a particular resonance abroad, and that still shows up frequently in popular culture and imagination.[5] From *Taxi Driver* (Martin Scorsese, 1976), via Woody Allen's description of his first viewing of *Summer with Monika* in his review of Ingmar Bergman's *Magic Lantern* (1988), to a mention of *I Am Curious (Yellow)* in *Mad Men* (season 7, 2014), references to dirty Swedish movies are abundant.[6]

With this book, we have gone beyond the iconic Swedish summer as well as the symbolic summer with the objective to further explore the reasons, the effects, the influences, and the reception of sexuality in Swedish cinema and, among other things, its implications for genre, gender, and nationality. The scholars contributing to this volume bring their particular areas of expertise to analyses of key films, but they have also found new archival material, made interviews, and gone behind the scenes of the Swedish Film Institute, which played a significant, albeit ambiguous, role during these years in attempting to bring down Swedish film censorship.

There was a relaxation of Swedish film censorship in the 1960s that had to do with a general liberalization in society—what has sometimes been termed the sexual revolution—but also with a few very specific films which "broke through the sex barrier."[7] Featuring female masturbation, casual intercourse, and hinted lesbian incest, Ingmar Bergman's *Tystnaden/The Silence* (1963) challenged the limits of censorship. Although *The Silence* was released with no cuts, the Bergman disciple Vilgot Sjöman caused a prolonged censorship process with his adaptation of Lars Görling's *491* (1964). Here, bestiality, homosexuality, and various sexual forms of abuse were portrayed with a raw intensity that proved too much for the Board, which disallowed the film for public screening. The decision was appealed to the government which settled on the compromise that the film would be released but with some alterations. That the government proved more liberal in relation to sex and sexual violence than the National Board of Film Censors (Statens biografbyrå) would set a precedent for the coming years, and may be regarded in the light of the close connections between Social Democracy and the Swedish Film Institute.

In 1965, the Danish-Swedish production *Jeg—en kvinde/Jag—en kvinna/I, a Woman*, directed by the skilled Mac Ahlberg and with Essy Persson in the lead, was released with no cuts. *I, a Woman* contained scenes of masturbation, semi-nudity, and discreetly simulated intercourse which firmly place it within a sexploitation/softcore framework. It had no apparent social commentary (as in *491*) and no artistic justification (as in the Bergman films). In 1967, Vilgot Sjöman released the first installment of the *Jag är nyfiken/I Am Curious*–films; in 1968, *Dom kallar oss mods/They Call Us Misfits* (Stefan Jarl and Jan Lindqvist) was allowed to show an authentic intercourse and the American sexploitation director Joe Sarno's first Sweden-produced film *Jag, en oskuld/Inga* premiered; and in 1969, *Ur kärlekens språk/Language of Love*, the first in a string of sex educational films directed by Torgny Wickman, screened the first close-ups of genitals and intercourse in a Swedish, theatrically distributed film. The process that can be said to have started already in the 1950s culminates with the removal of the obscenity clause in the penal code in 1971, in effect legalizing pornography. During the 1970s, Swedish film censorship concerned itself mainly with images of violence, which became more common in the wake of the Vietnam War, the changes in the U.S. from Production Code to rating system, and the European trash/mondo/horror wave. Explicit images of sex were censored only if they were connected to violence, and even this was to a certain extent dependent of the context of the film. Pornography was more regularly censored than mainstream film, and well-known directors were allowed greater freedom.

This part of Swedish film history can be said to be well known. However, the knowledge of this period is full of vague understandings and misconceptions. In addition, there is very little scholarly research on this phenomenon. Instead, previous historiography has been of a more popular character or written by fans.[8] The topic itself, with all its associations of sensationalism and trashiness, provides an effective obstacle to serious treatment and also results in a continuous reproduction of these misconceptions, like for instance that the film that Travis and Betsy visit during their date in *Taxi Driver* is the Swedish film *Language of Love*, when in fact the footage shown is from the American film *Sexual Freedom in Denmark* (John Lamb, 1970), although with a Swedish soundtrack.[9]

Accordingly, this edited volume goes beyond the myths and misconceptions. Our objective has been to look at sexuality in Swedish cinema from both sides of the Atlantic. The image of Sweden as "sinful" began in the U.S. with a *Time Magazine* article in the 1950s and became even further reinforced through cinema.[10] As described above, however, it was definitely not arbitrary and, in a complex way, Sweden began to—after having at first combated this reputation—embrace it and try to mold it to fit with Sweden's perception of itself as modern and progressive.[11] Contributions to this volume describe what happens in Sweden as well as what happens abroad, in particular in the U.S., and also how the relation between what is actually happening and how it is perceived is negotiated by Swedish film officials in the form of the Swedish Film Institute.

The reputation of Swedish sexuality has been said to have changed in the past fifteen years or so, after the passing in 1999 of the Sex Purchase Act, which prohibits the buying of sexual services and a vast campaign against trafficking of women for sexual purposes.[12] Nonetheless, from the release of *Summer with Monika* as *Monika—the Story of a Bad Girl!*, via the Milwaukee beer commercial featuring the Swedish bikini team, to the present day, Sweden's reputation for sexuality seems to remain, at least in the U.S.

Summertime Sensuality

In the 1950s, some films were seminal in making an impact regarding sexual representation, not only domestically but also abroad. In the first section of this book, two essays specifically deal with films from the 1950s. Arne Lunde describes what happened to Ingmar Bergman's *Summer with Monika* in its export context of the U.S. In America, *Summer with Monika* was illegally acquired and distributed in a re-edited and dubbed version on the exploitation film circuit by showman Kroger Babb, who had earlier made a fortune on postwar underground sex education films such as *Mom and Dad* (William Beaudine, 1945). Lunde reflects on the implications of this release, and of Bergman's later films, distributed by Janus film but still marketed with an emphasis on their adult content.

Shifting the perspective to a Swedish context, Anders Marklund discusses a trio of films that were identified by leading critics as the most important ones from 1951, all still internationally well-known Swedish films: Alf Sjöberg's *Fröken Julie/Miss Julie*, Ingmar Bergman's *Sommarlek/Summer Interlude*, and Arne Mattsson's *Hon dansade en sommar/One Summer of Happiness*. These films do not, however, represent only the second international breakthrough of Swedish cinema, but also the hesitating beginning of the franker depictions of sexuality that would follow during the coming decades.

Art, Sexploitation and Pornography

In the next section, four contributors deal with five different films. Anu Koivunen discusses Jörn Donner's second feature film, *Att älska/To Love* (1964), as a crossover between intimate chamber drama and sex comedy and, as such, a symptomatic media text signaling changes in the media landscape, in cultural distinctions and hierarchies, and in discourses on sexuality. While starting with a funeral scene, as a narrative about a young widow with a son, *To Love* quickly turns into a playful story about a couple's erotic games. Without any flirtation with porn aesthetics, the film is about sex and takes place mostly in the widow's bed or her bedroom, featuring scenes of play and games.

The Swedish director Vilgot Sjöman's cinematic diptych *Jag är nyfiken—gul/I Am Curious (Yellow)* (1967) and *Jag är nyfiken—blå/I Am Curious (Blue)* (1968) introduced a new vein of political and semi-documentary filmmaking in Swedish mainstream cinema, and were international sexploitation hits, due to their sexual content. Anders Wilhelm Åberg traces the complexities of real and implied cinematic authorship as they appear in the films, as well as in discussions in the press. Åberg argues that the common observation that Lena Nyman's creative contribution to the films has been systematically belittled and underrated may be linked to the fact that Sjöman consistently plays with the notion that she is a proxy for the male author-subject.

Bengt Bengtsson takes a closer look at Arne Mattsson, director of the emblematic *One Summer of Happiness*, but focuses on a much later film, *Ann och Eve—de erotiska/Ann and Eve* (1970). Arne Mattsson occupies an ambiguous space in Swedish film history: on the one hand a skillful director long held in high regard who, on the other, fell from grace and entered into a period of making sleazy and violent films. Bengtsson analyzes *Ann and Eve* as a film that, at first glance, seems like a typical Swedish sex export film, but is in fact an angry retribution on the film critics that Mattsson felt were persecuting him.

Mariah Larsson focuses on a unique figure in the Swedish pornscape of the 1970s: Anne-Marie Berglund, who wrote, directed, and starred in the porn film *Veckända i Stockholm/Weekend in Stockholm* (1976). In the credits, the film is described as a "short story by Anne-Marie Berglund," and Berglund would move on to poetry and novel writing. By now, she is a well-established author, the recipient of several national literary awards. Placing the film in the context of both women's filmmaking and the Swedish sex film wave, Larsson describes the background of *Weekend in Stockholm*, concluding with an analysis of the film.

In Sweden, the most famous porn film of the 1970s (or maybe ever) is *Fäbodjäntan/Come and Blow the Horn* from 1978, which is discussed by Mats Björkin. Paradoxically, this most Swedish of all porn films was directed by an American, Joseph W. Sarno. *Come and Blow the Horn* makes use of the full array of Swedish national insignia by utilizing the position of the *fäbod* (traditional summer farm) within the cultural history of Swedish region Dalarna, and Dalarna's role as a national ideal.

Obscenity and Censorship

The regulations surrounding depictions of sexuality on film in Sweden are discussed in detail in three essays in the third section. Tommy Gustafsson examines the pre-history to the development during the 1960s and 1970s by studying three trials on illegal screenings of porn films in Sweden in 1921, 1932, and 1943, shedding light on the little-known history of illegal pornographic films and their production, distribution, and exhibition.

Lena Lennerhed describes the debate and circumstances surrounding the seminal censorship process of Vilgot Sjöman's *491* (1964). Depicting homo- and heterosexual abuse, rape, and bestiality, the film was disallowed for public screening by the National Board of Film Censors. This decision was appealed and, in the end, the government decided to release the film with a few cuts. Nonetheless, the process spawned intense debate in Swedish society, with liberals, Social Democrats, and cinephiles arguing against censorship, and conservatives and Christian groups arguing against the film.

In Elisabet Björklund's contribution, the liberalization of film censorship is also in focus. In 1964 and 1965, two official inquiries were commissioned, investigating censorship and the borders for freedom of speech respectively. In 1969, the first inquiry proposed the abolishment of censorship, while the second proposed the legalization of pornography. The result was that pornography was decriminalized in 1971, while censorship was maintained. Björklund delves deeper into the discussions at the National Board of Film Censors in the 1960s and 1970s and the negotiations around sexual content in specific films.

The Institutionalization of Sex in Sweden

For a long time, the national historiography has treated the films produced during Sweden's "sex film wave" with contempt. It has been an underlying assumption that the films were made by less respected filmmakers and that "official" discourse on film in Sweden distanced itself from these films. In this section, three scholars take a closer look at how this discourse and people of power related to the increasing sexual explicitness of Swedish film in the 1960s.

Per Vesterlund explores the workings of the Film Research Group and Harry Schein, the founder of the Swedish Film Institute and creator of the Swedish film policy, and on-screen sexuality. In 1964, with the explicit ambition to liberalize film censorship, Schein initiated a group of scholars from different academic fields with the purpose of studying the effects of films on audiences. The aim of the research from Schein's point of view was crystal clear—films cannot be proven to cause damage. An important area of research was (of course) the impact of representations of sex on audiences.

Maaret Koskinen investigates Stockholm as a center for cultural and political capital and the blurred boundaries between personal and political power. Harry Schein was also personal friends with Prime Minister Olof Palme and Ingmar Bergman, then artistic director at Svensk Filmindustri. All three also wielded considerable media power and were often represented as men with looks, style, and women, not unlike the male protagonists of the TV series *Mad Men* (2007–2015). Through hitherto unpublished archive material, Koskinen explores Schein's role in this network of power in relation to cinema, and thus the degree to which at the time the personal was indeed blurred with the political.

By looking at the periodical *Film in Sweden*, commencing publication in 1965 and edited by Schein, Lars Diurlin uncovers a paradox in how the SFI positions itself at a stance of double standards, using means of nudity and sexual references to brand Swedish films more commercially viable for international buyers, and at the same time trying to curb the perception of Swedish films as immoral.

The American Reception of Swedish Sin

The reputation of Sweden abroad played into how these films were received, and vice versa—the films influenced the perception of Sweden. In this section, three contributions take on how Sweden and Swedish films were constructed in the U.S. reception. Klara Arnberg and Carl Marklund's essay focuses on the development of the notion of "Swedish sin" and how it increasingly became connected to the politics and content of pornography in Sweden and in the U.S. The article follows how Swedish politicians handled this imagination of Sweden as a sexual paradise (or maybe Gomorrah) and how it touched upon anxieties in both Sweden and the U.S. about gender and sexuality from the 1950s onwards, but also describes how the porn magazine *Private* used the notion of Swedish sin to market itself.

Ulf Jonas Björk discusses the American reception of Vilgot Sjöman's much canonized *I Am Curious (Yellow)* (1967) against the background of the changing U.S. legal definition of obscenity that began in the late 1950s. In a series of rulings from 1957 onwards, the U.S. Supreme Court instructed lower-court judges to consider in its entirety any work that was alleged to be obscene rather than to look only at sexually explicit passages, and also to balance sexual explicitness against the social, educational, and/or artistic value of the work at issue. Sjöman's film, a mixture of political satire and chronicle of a sexual affair and of fictional and documentary material, was in many ways an ideal test case for this new standard.

In the final essay, Kevin Heffernan traces out the relationship between a contested and ambivalent "Swedish" erotic cinema and the role of international finance and distribution in two of American director Joe Sarno's projects for Saga Film, *Butterfly* (1975) and *Come and Blow the Horn*. Heffernan argues that the Swedish sex films of the hardcore era exhibit contradictory, hybrid discourses of national identity, genre, and the star system. Through films produced in Sweden as well as investment in international production and distribution to both theatrical and ancillary markets, the Swedish film industry was vitally engaged with important changes in transnational adult cinema.

Notes

1. See for instance Per Olov Qvist, *Folkhemmets bilder: modernisering, motstånd och mentalitet i den svenska 30-talsfilmen* (Lund: Arkiv, 1995), Per Olov Qvist, *Jorden är vår arvedel: landsbygden i svensk spelfilm 1940–1959*. (PhD diss., Stockholm University, 1986), Tytti Soila, "Sweden," in *Nordic National Cinemas*, ed. Tytti Soila et al. (London: Routledge, 1998), 135–220, Anders Wilhelm Åberg, "Seacrow Island: Mediating Arcadian Space in the Folkhem Era and Beyond," *Regional Aesthetics: Locating Swedish Media*, ed. Erik Hedling et al. (Stockholm: Kungliga biblioteket, 2010), 125–140.
2. Benedict Anderson, *Imagined Communities: Reflections on the Origin and Spread of Nationalism* 2nd ed. (London/New York: Verso 1991).
3. Statistiska Centralbyrån has statistics on Sweden and the Swedish population. See http://www.scb.se/sv_/Hitta-statistik/Statistik-efter-amne/Befolkning/Befolkningens-sammansattning/Befolkningsstatistik/#c_li_196358, accessed 12 May 2015.
4. Soila, "Sweden," 177.
5. Eric Schaefer, "'I'll Take Sweden': The Shifting Discourse of the 'Sexy Nation' in Sexploitation Films," in *Sex Scene: Media and the Sexual Revolution*, ed. Eric Schaefer (Durham and London: Duke University Press, 2014), 207–234.
6. See Elisabet Björklund "'This is a dirty movie'—*Taxi Driver* and 'Swedish sin,'" *Journal of Scandinavian Cinema* 1:2 (2011), 163–176; Woody Allen, "Through a life darkly," *New York Times*, September 18, 1988, http://www.nytimes.com/1988/09/18/books/through-a-life-darkly.html. Accessed December 3, 2013.
7. See for instance Lena Lennerhed, *Frihet att njuta: Sexualdebatten i Sverige på 1960-talet*

(Stockholm: Norstedts, 1994), Gunnel Arrbäck, ed., *90 år av filmcensur: [något ur Statens biografbyrås historia 1911–2000]* (Stockholm: Statens biografbyrå, 2010); Erik Hedling, "Breaking the Swedish Sex Barrier: Painful lustfulness in Ingmar Bergman's *The Silence*," *Film International*, 6: 6 (2008): 17–27; Maaret Koskinen, *Ingmar Bergman's* The Silence: *Pictures in the Typewriter, Writings on the Screen* (Seattle: University of Washington Press, 2010); Anders Åberg, *Tabu: Filmaren Vilgot Sjöman* (Lund: Filmhäftet, 2010).
    8. See for instance Jack Stevenson, *Scandinavian Blue: The Erotic Cinema of Sweden and Denmark in the 1960s and 1970s* (Jefferson: McFarland, 2010); Daniel Ekeroth, *Swedish Sensationsfilms: A Clandestine History of Sex, Thrillers, and Kicker Cinema* transl. Magnus Henriksson (New York: Bazillion Points, 2011); *Magasin Defekt* 1995–1997; Klubb Super 8, http://klubbsuper8.com/?cat=9.
    9. This is discussed in Björklund, "'This Is a Dirty Movie.'"
    10. Schaefer, "'I'll Take Sweden.'" See also Klara Arnberg and Carl Marklund's contribution to this volume.
    11. Nikolas Glover and Carl Marklund. "Arabian Nights in the Midnight Sun? Exploring the temporal structure of sexual geographies." *Historisk Tidskrift* 3 (2009): 487–510.
    12. Mattias Andersson, *Porr—en bästsäljande historia* (Stockholm: Prisma, 2005). pp. 281–287.

REFERENCES

Åberg, Anders. *Tabu: filmaren Vilgot Sjöman*. Lund: Filmhäftet, 2001.
Åberg, Anders Wilhelm. "Seacrow Island: Mediating Arcadian Space in the Folkhem Era and Beyond." In *Regional Aesthetics: Locating Swedish Media*, edited by Erik Hedling, Olof Hedling and Mats Jönsson, 125–140. Stockholm: Kungliga biblioteket, 2010.
Allen, Woody. "Through a life darkly." *New York Times*, September 18, 1988. Accessed December 3, 2013. http://www.nytimes.com/1988/09/18/books/through-a-life-darkly.html.
Anderson, Benedict. *Imagined Communities: Reflections on the Origin and Spread of Nationalism* 2nd ed. London/New York: Verso, 1991.
Andersson, Mattias. *Porr—en bästsäljande historia*. Stockholm: Prisma, 2005.
Arrbäck, Gunnel, ed. *90 år av filmcensur: [något ur Statens biografbyrås historia 1911–2000]*. Stockholm: Statens biografbyrå, 2010.
Björklund, Elisabet. "'This is a dirty movie'—*Taxi Driver* and 'Swedish sin.'" *Journal of Scandinavian Cinema* 1:2 (2011): 163–176.
Ekeroth, Daniel. *Swedish Sensationsfilms: A Clandestine History of Sex, Thrillers, and Kicker Cinema*. Translated by Magnus Henriksson. New York: Bazillion Points, 2011.
Glover, Nikolas, and Carl Marklund. "Arabian Nights in the Midnight Sun? Exploring the temporal structure of sexual geographies." *Historisk Tidskrift* 3 (2009): 487–510.
Hedling, Erik. "Breaking the Swedish Sex Barrier: Painful lustfulness in Ingmar Bergman's *The Silence*." *Film International*, 6: 6 (2008): 17–27.
Klubb Super 8. http://klubbsuper8.com/?cat=9.
Koskinen, Maaret. *Ingmar Bergman's* The Silence: *Pictures in the Typewriter, Writings on the Screen*. Seattle: University of Washington Press, 2010.
Lennerhed, Lena. *Frihet att njuta: Sexualdebatten i Sverige på 1960-talet*. Stockholm: Norstedts, 1994.
Qvist, Per Olov. *Folkhemmets bilder: modernisering, motstånd och mentalitet i den svenska 30-talsfilmen*. Lund: Arkiv, 1995.
Qvist, Per Olov. *Jorden är vår arvedel: landsbygden i svensk spelfilm 1940–1959*. PhD diss., Stockholm University, 1986.
Schaefer, Eric. "'I'll Take Sweden': The Shifting Discourse of the 'Sexy Nation' in Sexploitation Films." In *Sex Scene: Media and the Sexual Revolution*, edited by Eric Schaefer, 207–234. Durham, NC: Duke University Press, 2014.
Soila, Tytti. "Sweden." In *Nordic National Cinemas*, edited by Tytti Soila, Astrid Söderbergh Widding and Gunnar Iversen, 135–220. London: Routledge, 1998.
Statistiska Centralbyrån. Accessed May 12, 2015. http://www.scb.se/sv_/Hitta-statistik/Statistik-efter-amne/Befolkning/Befolkningens-sammansattning/Befolkningsstatistik/#c_li_196358.
Stevenson, Jack. *Scandinavian Blue: The Erotic Cinema of Sweden and Denmark in the 1960s and 1970s*. Jefferson: McFarland, 2010.

I
Summertime Sensuality

The Story of a Bad Girl!
Summer with Monika, *Sexploitation* and the Selling of Erotic Bergman in America

ARNE LUNDE

As this essay will demonstrate, *Summer with Monika* and the selling of Ingmar Bergman films in America in the 1950s and 1960s consistently straddled the grey area between arthouse and grindhouse. Before Bergman was fully canonized as the most philosophically and grimly serious of all European auteurs, sexploitation and Swedish sin were a decisive part of his entry into the American film markets. There is no question that his early (pre–1955, say) films include a number of popular genre melodramas containing exploitation elements, including pre-marital sex, adultery, lesbianism, prostitution, drug use, juvenile delinquency, abortion, and suicide. Harriet Andersson's love-goddess nudity in *Sommaren med Monika/Summer with Monika* (1953) makes that film the flagship entry of what might be termed "erotic Bergman" in the fifties. But even beyond *Monika*, sexuality and eroticism (both overt and displaced) pervade virtually all the early Bergman films as an organizing principal. In a 1950s American exhibition market in which the Production Code was slowly beginning to fray and where the desire for an adult alternative to Hollywood censorship was growing, Bergman films helped fill the void.

High-culture prestige and low-culture sexploitation were inextricably intertwined in the selling and marketing of Bergman in America in the 1950s and early 1960s. The most compelling case study in this essay will be the aforementioned *Summer with Monika*. Harriet Andersson's nudity in an archipelago swimming scene (and the scene's reprise in a flashback at the film's end) made it the emblematic early Bergman eroticized film. *Summer with Monika* was illegally acquired and distributed in America in a re-edited and dubbed version titled *Monika: The Story of a Bad Girl!* Shorter by at least half an hour than the original version, the film was released on the exploitation film circuit by showman Kroger Babb. In the U.S. subsequently, the co-founders (Cyrus Harvey, Jr., and Bryant Haliday) of the arthouse distribution company Janus Films acquired the rights to *Summer of Monika* and to the Bergman catalogue. Kroger Babb, David Friedman, Janus Films, and other American distributors consistently saw and utilized an opportunity to sell both forbidden sex and edifying art together in one Swedish package. Sexploitation and erotic Bergman are a part of a reception story that has too often remained under the radar.

Only a handful of early Bergman films appear to have received much distribution in the U.S. until the mid–1950s. During the late 1940s (in the wake of the success of *Hets/Torment* in the U.S. in 1948), David O. Selznick offered to bring Alf Sjöberg and Ingmar Bergman to Hollywood to make a film version of Henrik Ibsen's play *Et dukkehjem/A Doll's House* (1879). Though both Swedes were well-paid to co-develop a workable script in Stockholm, the project ultimately came to nothing. The first Bergman-directed film to get much attention in the U.S. is *Skepp till Indialand/A Ship Bound for India* (1947), released in 1949 as *Frustration*. *The New York Times* review commented: "There is nothing on the screen of the Rialto theatre to warrant the cheap sensationalism of the poster display outside the house advertising 'Frustration,' a Swedish importation that is being distributed by Film Classics, Inc. 'Frustration' is simply a bad motion picture...."[1] As Daniel Humphrey notes in *Queer Bergman*, the film was cut by approximately 17 minutes and given a new chronology.[2]

The Swedish film that first established the genre of the Swedish erotic summer film was *Hon dansade en sommar/One Summer of Happiness* (1951), directed by Arne Mattsson (1919–1995). Based on the 1949 novel *Sommardansen/The Summer Dance* by Per Olof Ekström, this rural romance starred Ulla Jacobsson and Folke Sundquist as the class-crossed lovers. Although mostly a naturalistic melodrama about conformist social oppression in rural Sweden, the film became notorious abroad for the skinny-dipping of the lovers in a lake. As American grindhouse historians Eddie Muller and Daniel Faris have argued:

> Scandinavian skinny-dipping is what prepared America for Ingmar Bergman films. While the Italians romped al fresco amid the peasant shacks, the Swedes seemed to have a thing for naked plunges into the fjords. The trend started in 1951 with *One Summer of Happiness*, the tale of a young farm girl's idyllic summer of freedom, love, and budding sexuality—all of which is ended, Swedish-style, by a sudden motorcycle accident. Soon Swedish filmmakers realized that it was swimming scenes that ensured an overseas sale. When *I Rok och Dans* [sic] was released, the nude bathing scene was facetiously subtitled "For Export Only." Bergman's *Summer with Monika* (1953) contained the requisite nude shots of star Harriet Andersson, guaranteeing an eventual U.S. run in both arthouses and grindhouses.[3]

Yet in its European release, *One Summer of Happiness* competed for prestigious awards in major festivals. The film won the Golden Bear at the Second Berlin International Film Festival and was also nominated for the Palme d'Or at the 1952 Cannes Film Festival. *One Summer of Happiness* was not released in the U.S. until 1955 when the Times Film Corporation distributed it and where it opened in New York at the Little Carnegie cinema. In his *New York Times* review, critic Bosley Crowther emphasized that despite the lyrical tone of its title "It is rather a melancholy picture—tender and touching, to be sure, and warm with a bucolic beauty, but essentially tortured and sad—of a briefly partaken romance between a rich city boy and a country girl, brought together in an atmosphere of prudery on the farm of the boy's uncle."[4]

While Crowther's review makes little to no mention of the film's nudity or potentially salacious elements, the marketing by Times Film Corporation aggressively does. The sexploitation ingredients of the film were emphasized in the poster of the two naked leads embracing each other in the water, and by banner taglines like: "Recommended for Adults Only," "The picture everyone is talking about!," "I'm not ashamed.... I love you!," and "A Romance of Ecstasy!"[5]

Even before *One Summer of Happiness* reached the U.S. in 1955, however, a re-edited version of Bergman's *Sommarlek/Summer Interlude* (1951) had been released in 1954 under the title of *Illicit Interlude*. Shots of nude bathers had been inserted into Bergman's original version, but there are slightly conflicting accounts of where these nude bathing scenes might have been shot. Arthur Knight and Hollis Alpert report that the scenes were shot on a private lake in New Jersey and were likely inserted into the film by Gaston Hakim, the distributor, who hired an American director to shoot them.[6] According to the Bergman Archive website, however, *Illicit Interlude* "had freely and indulgently spliced in unrelated scenes of naked bathing filmed at a nudist colony on Long Island."[7]

Another consistent thread that emerges in the American publicity for *Illicit Interlude* is the selling of highbrow prestige together with lowbrow eroticized sensationalism in one package.

The film had its US premiere in 1954. It was given the somewhat seedy title "Illicit Interlude," and in the first version the distributor had freely and indulgently spliced in unrelated scenes of naked bathing filmed at a nudist colony on Long Island. One poster for the 1954 release of *Illicit Interlude* includes tag lines such as "The most intimate story ever told" and "Recommended for adults only!" But at the same time the poster emphasizes the appearance of "The Ballet Theatre of the Stockholm Royal Opera in Tschaikowsky's [sic] *Swan Lake*." In other publicity visuals, co-stars Maj-Britt Nilsson and Birger Malmsten are shown kneeling together in their bathing suits, while a naked woman stands at their right in profile. The film's publicity also included the following endorsement from the New York–based gossip columnist Walter Winchell: "This is an adult film. Young people under 17 years of age will not be admitted. An adult from Sweden is *Illicit Interlude* at the Plaza. Some of the dialog is more robust than Americans are used to. And there is a scene where the leading lady out–Hedy Lamarr's nude swimming in 'Ecstasy.'"[8]

In his *New York Times* review Bosley Crowther defended the film against its sexploitation release title as *Illicit Interlude*:

> There is something cheap and unpleasant about the title, "Illicit Interlude" as applied to the handsome Swedish picture that arrived at the Plaza yesterday. For this beautifully realized recount of a rhapsodic romance between a 15-year-old ballet dancer and an initially bashful young man gives a subtle and sensitive presentation of a strange, youthful affair, no more meriting the pornographic word "illicit" than is deserves to be labeled smut.[9]

The 1955 American sexploitation campaign for Bergman's 1953 *Summer with Monika* as *Monika: The Story of a Bad Girl!* remains the most fascinating case, however. As Eric Schaefer has documented, the Bergman film was released in the U.S. on the exploitation film circuit as *Monika: The Story of a Bad Girl!* by showman Kroger Babb (1906–1980). Babb's company Hallmark Productions had earlier made a fortune on postwar underground sex education films such as *Mom and Dad* (William Beaudine, 1944). Babb cut down *Summer with Monika*'s original 95-minute running time to 62 minutes, the crucial nude swim sequence was of course kept in, and the film was dubbed into what Babb called "American" English.[10]

In his 1990 memoir *A Youth in Babylon: Confessions of a Trash-Film King*, David F. Friedman (1923–2003), the so-called "Mighty Monarch of Exploitation," recounts the origins of *Monika: The Story of a Bad Girl!* in these words:

> Kroger Babb saw pronounced profit possibilities in Miss Andersson's bare behind by eschewing the artsy orbit and bringing the movie to the hoi polloi. He purchased the American theatrical rights from international film sales agents Arthur David and Gaston Hakim.... After concluding the deal with Davis and

Hakim, Babb, paying the $10,000 license fee, received an English-titled print and a dupe negative of *Sommaren med Monika*. The picture was filmed in black and white. It was also, excepting the soaked-skin sequences, long and lugubrious, running over 95 minutes in the original version. The English title, *A Summer with Monika*, wouldn't sell. It sounded like a Bible School vacation. Sitting in the cutting room with scissors and splicer, Babb trimmed the dreary, darkly photographed film to a mercifully short sixty-two minutes, sloughing Swedish symbolism but retaining, of course, the "money shot."[11]

Muller and Faris also claim that Babb had in 1955 acquired the U.S. rights to *Monika* from international film agent Gaston Hakim, an Egyptian-born Frenchman. According to IMDB, another figure, Jerald Intrator, was hired by Babb to shoot a few additional nude inserts for *Monika: The Story of a Bad Girl!*, as well as to supervise the U.S. dub and re-scoring by Les Baxter. Daniel Humphrey suspects that the nudity insert story is just an urban legend. No extra footage exists in the Kroger Babb *Monika* print that the Criterion collection possesses, and in an interview before he died, David Friedman told Humphrey that the Hallmark Films version of *Monika* had not added anything to the pre-existing Swedish footage.[12]

Humphrey has further dispelled other myths connected to the Babb-Friedman Hallmark version. The title that appears in the film itself is not actually *Monika: The Story of a Bad Girl!*, but simply *Monika*. The phrase "The Story of a Bad Girl!" is simply a tagline used on the posters and other advertising materials. Secondly, while Humphrey acknowledges that Babb did replace Erik Nordgren's original score with music by American composer-arranger Les Baxter, he notes that the score is not "jazzy" in the slightest. And again, Humphrey has demonstrated that the Hallmark cut actually features no added footage of any kind to "sex up" the material.[13]

The Hallmark version was dubbed with American voices, allowing audiences to not only avoid reading subtitles but also to hear the characters speak in familiar American idioms. Interestingly, Bergman's original has a scene in which Monika (Harriet Andersson) and Harry (Lars Ekborg) go a Stockholm cinema to see an American romance film called *Song of Love*. In Bergman's parody of a bland escapist Hollywood romance, the bland, Anglo-accented line readings of the couple on-screen could almost double for the vacuous, clichéd line readings in Babb's dubbed version. As noted above, Babb did erase Nordgren's original music score and substituted it with a music track written by exotica "lounge master" Les Baxter (1922–1996). Baxter released a large number of popular instrumental concept albums in the 1950s with titles such as *Taboo!*, *Caribbean Moonlight*, and *Ports of Pleasure*. In the 1960s he also wrote scores for exploitation B-picture studio AIP (American International Pictures), including several of Roger Corman's Edgar Allan Poe adaptations, teen beach films, and other drive-in horror offerings. Some of the publicity material for *Monika: The Story of a Bad Girl!* emphasizes that Baxter wrote the title song and musical score for the film.

Monika: The Story of a Bad Girl! was sold on the exploitation circuit with tag lines such as "Naughty and nineteen," "The Devil controls her by radar," "The Greatest! … and You'll Flip." One poster ad includes the copy: "FROM SWEDEN, native land of Garbo, comes a great new actress. Emotional, expressive, she's a girl of many moods and faces. MONIKA thought the warm rays of the sun and an ocean swim, would wash away her sins!"[14] Babb's Hallmark Productions released *Monika: The Story of a Bad Girl!* on a double bill together with *Mixed-Up Women*, a retitled reissue of Babb's *One Too Many* (1950). That film was directed by Erle C. Kenton and starred Ruth Warrick (best known for *Citizen Kane*) as a female alcoholic.

In *The Foreign Film Renaissance on American Screens, 1946–1973*, Tino Balio has traced the film's release as follows:

> Forgoing the New York launch, Jack Thomas, the distributor, opened *Monika* in Los Angeles at the downtown Orpheum and in nine Pacific Drive-ins on February 3, 1956. Ads: "She's Here!" and "Sweden's Answer to Marilyn Monroe!" Nowhere in the ads did Bergman's name appear…. The following day Morton Lippe, the Orpheum's manager, was arrested by the L.A. vice squad and the film was seized. Not long after that Thomas was tried and found guilty of selling a lewd and indecent film. He was sentenced to ninety days in a city jail and fined $750. Thomas appealed the decision. While awaiting the outcome, he opened the film in several Minneapolis drive-ins, accompanied by a similar ad campaign.[15]

The Criterion Collection website on *Summer with Monika* includes a trailer of the Kroger Babb version. Typical of the trailer's sensationalist ballyhoo are banner-lines such as "Filmed EXTRA-WIDE for Broad Screens! Filmed EXTRA-BOLD for Broad Minds!"[16] In one stroke this carney pitch deceptively appealed to spectators who might be seeking the emergent 1950s wide-screen process (which the conventional aspect ratio of the film did *not* deliver). Likewise it also flattered a supposedly liberal, tolerant, "broad-minded" audience in repressed Eisenhower America while hinting that they might also have broads (i.e., dames) on their minds. The film's advertising also capitalized on a recent *Time* magazine story: "Sin & Sweden."[17] Substituting the preposition "in" for the article's actual conjunction "and," the tagline stated that *Monika: The Story of a Bad Girl!* was "Based on the Time Magazine shocking story 'Sin in Sweden!'"

One of Bergman's greatest fans, writer-director Woody Allen, has famously claimed to have first discovered his Swedish idol through seeing *Summer with Monika* as a teenager. But it is difficult to ascertain when Allen might have seen the film and in which version. In his 1988 *New York Times* book review of Bergman's autobiographical memoir, *The Magic Lantern*, Allen wrote:

> Less than ennobling was the motive for seeing my first Ingmar Bergman movie. The facts were these: I was a teenager living in Brooklyn, and word had got around that there was a Swedish film coming to our local foreign film house in which a young woman swam completely naked. Rarely have I slept overnight on the curb to be the first on line for a movie, but when *Summer with Monika* opened at the Jewel in Flatbush, a young boy with red hair and black-rimmed glasses could be seen clubbing senior citizens to the floor in an effort to insure the choicest, unobstructed seat. I never knew who directed the film nor did I care, nor was I sensitive at that age to the power of the work itself—the irony, the tensions, the German Expressionist style with its poetic black- and-white photography and its erotic sado-masochistic undertones. I came away reliving only the moment Harriet Andersson disrobed, and although it was my first exposure to a director who I would come to believe was pound for pound the best of all filmmakers, I did not know it then.[18]

Even if Allen (who was born in 1934) did manage to see the 1955 release of *Monika: The Story of a Bad Girl!*, he would have been 21 years old and hardly still a teenager or "young boy" as he describes himself. More than likely, he saw the Janus release of *Summer with Monika* around 1960 when he was 26. But Allen's self-portrait as a horny adolescent bullying defenseless, elderly spectators for the best seat in the house makes for a much stronger visual joke. There also may be a sly self-identification with the young boy Antoine Doinel (Jean-Pierre Léaud) in François Truffaut's debut feature *Les Quatre Cents Coups/ The 400 Blows* (1959). Truffaut (who was 27 at the time) included an overt homage to *Summer with Monika* in the scene where his young alter ego Antoine and a friend steal a still photograph from outside a Paris film theater. That iconic cheesecake publicity still is of a radiant, tanned Monika basking in the sun with her sweater pulled down around her shoulders.

Janus Selling Bergman

The situation of unauthorized selling and mangling of Bergman's films in America was finally stopped and stabilized through a distribution deal between Svensk Filmindustri and Janus Films.

Janus was the 1956 co-creation of partners Cyrus Harvey, Jr. (1925–2011) and Bryant Haliday (1928–1996). As a Fulbright student for two years in Paris, Harvey allegedly spent far more time at the Cinémathèque française than at the Sorbonne. Later, as a part owner of the Brattle Theater in Cambridge, Massachusetts off of Harvard Square, he transformed the Brattle into an arthouse cinema. Haliday ran the 55th Street Playhouse in New York City. Seeing an opportunity in the art house movement beginning to take off, Harvey and Haliday named their new company after the two-faced Roman god Janus. As Harvey's widow reported in her husband's 2011 obituary "They named it that because they themselves were opposites. Bryant was gay and catholic. Cy was straight and Jewish. They really liked that."[19] Janus not only became an international distributor of Bergman's films in America but of masterworks of world cinema by Fellini, Kurosawa, and other major foreign directors as well. They sold the company in 1966 and it has since evolved into Criterion, the high-end Tiffany's of DVD distributors.

Tino Balio writes that it was the success of *Smiles of a Summer Night* that inspired Haliday and Harvey to acquire the U.S. distribution rights to Bergman's films and that the deal with SF was made in 1958. In building up the Bergman brand, Harvey hired the prominent publicity firm of Blowitz and Maskel. Under the new Janus banner, *Det sjunde inseglet/The Seventh Seal* (1957) opened at the Paris Theatre on October 13, 1958, and *Smultronstället/Wild Strawberries* (1957) at the Beekman on June 22, 1959.[20] He further relates that during October 1959 "as many as five Bergman films were playing simultaneously in New York's best art houses, setting a record for a foreign film director. In early 1960 Bergman made the cover of *Time* magazine—the first foreign filmmaker to do so since Leni Riefenstahl in 1936."[21] Yet Janus cagily continued to exploit the concept of Swedish sin in their marketing of the Bergman 1950s back catalogue through the urban arthouse venues as well as on the suburban drive-in circuit.

Although Janus is justly famous as the art cinema distributor of Bergman's films in America, Bergman's fifties persona was still so identified with artsy erotica and exploitation that Janus initially capitalized on that. The company, for example, marketed *Gycklarnas afton/Sawdust and Tinsel* (1953) as *The Naked Night* and sold *Kvinnors väntan/Waiting Women* (1952) as *Secrets of Women*, trading on the extra salaciousness suggested by those titles. But as Daniel Humphrey has documented, Janus merely further perpetuated such sexploitation titles when they purchased the Swedish rights to the Bergman catalogue in the late 1950s. *Gycklarnas afton*, for example, was first released as *The Naked Night* in the U.S. by Times Film Corporation in 1956.[22] For a period Janus continued to market *Summer Interlude* as *Illicit Interlude*, with one poster announcing it as "Starring May Britt and the Royal Stockholm Opera Ballet" and being "Ingmar Bergman's Most Personal Film."

Janus remained very alert to niche audiences for Bergman even outside the sexploitation market. In his book *Ghouls, Gimmicks, and Gold: Horror Films and the American Movie Business, 1953–1968*, Kevin Heffernan cites Janus trade ads in *Variety* that sold Bergman's *Ansiktet/The Face/The Magician* (1958) as a horror film. As he describes the company's cagey cross-marketing strategy:

Janus's release of Bergman's *The Magician* was initially aimed at both the art and horror markets.... Janus saw the sex-free Magician as a vehicle for breaking down the boundaries between mass and class entertainment in a wide release for Halloween 1959. Their newspaper ad for the film included a satanic looking Max Von Sydow gazing at the viewer from the right margin while bats flew across the top of the ad. The words "The Magician" appeared in ragged block letters identical to those used by the art departments of AIP and other distributors to promote horror movies.[23]

During the height of Bergman mania in America in the early 1960s, Janus thus appeared to market Bergman to several different target audiences. Bergman with subtitles to the urban arthouse sophisticates and Bergman dubbed into English for the suburbs and the youth-oriented drive-in market. Heffernan describes 1961 as a year in which "respected art distributor Janus Film's huge push to establish crossover popularity for its Ingmar Bergman catalog included an aggressive courting of the drive-in market for the Academy Award–winning *Jungfrukällan/Virgin Spring* ('We strongly recommend this film for adults only') and the retitled *Secrets of Women* and *Djävulens öga/The Devil's Eye*."[24]

Janus was not the only American distributor playing the sexploitation card with Bergman's newer films and back catalogue in the early 1960s. Joseph E. Levine's Embassy Pictures secured the rights to Bergman's *Fängelse/Prison*. Embassy released this 1949 film made for Lorens Marmstedt's Terrafilm studio thirteen years later in the U.S. as *The Devil's Wanton* (1962). The poster tagline stressed "Ingmar Bergman reflects on life, love, the Devil, and immortality...," while the art design and photo of Doris Svedlund subliminally suggested more "immorality" than immortality. Levine's Embassy Pictures also released another Terrafilm Bergman picture *Musik i mörker/Music in Darkness* (1948) as *Night is My Future* in this period.

Bergman's 1949 *Törst/Thirst* from SF also received a long-belated release in the U.S. Daniel Humphrey documents that it appeared in Washington, D.C., in mid-1956 under the distribution imprimatur of "Helen and Arthur Davis" and under the title *Thirst*. According to Humphrey, display ads in the August 30, 1956, edition of *The Washington Post* feature a clothed woman lying on her back under the quotation "I thirst for love.... I am so lonely for a man's touch." Among the advertisements' other provocative statements are "In a moment of thirst ... all of their morals, their passions, their loves, their desires ... bared!" ... "The film that dares to express the secrets of a woman's love-stared [sic] soul!" and "Share the intimate details of their private lives!"[25] Janus released *Thirst* in the early 1960s under the title *Three Strange Loves* and with the tagline "A Film You Must See With An Open Mind." Capitalizing on the popularity of Rod Serling's sci-fi-fantasy TV anthology series *The Twilight Zone* on CBS (1959–1964), one poster for *Three Strange Loves* further announced that "Ingmar Bergman Explores the Twilight Zone of Human Emotions." The poster's art design featured an expressionistic woodcut of three abstract sets of embracing couples hovering over a carpet.

Bergman's 1963 *Tystnaden/The Silence* brazenly challenged and helped reform the Swedish film censorship restrictions of its time. The trailer that Janus created for the American release of *The Silence* aggressively sold the sexploitation elements of the film, while barely referencing its modernist experimentation. Among American reviewer citations presented visually and quoted aloud in the Janus trailer is Judith Crist of *New York Herald-Tribune*: "NOT FOR THE PRUDISH. It demands maturity and sophistication from the viewer. There is no doubt that the film contains more sexuality than we have ever seen on screen." Wanda Hale of the *New York Daily News* is cited with "I COULDN'T BELIEVE MY EYES! On incest, self-defilement and nymphomania, this Bergman latest is the most shocking film I have ever seen." Maaret Koskinen has reproduced a full transcript of the Janus trailer voiceover by "an ominous, yet cultured male voice."²⁶

In their chapter on the marketing and reception of *Persona* (1966), Ingrid Stigsdotter and Tim Bergfelder discuss how the 1967 American release trailer was received at a 2003 Bergman retrospective at the National Film Theatre in the U.K.:

> ... the dramatic voice-over caused audible amusement in the auditorium, and one of the critical quotations appearing at the end of the trailer generated loud outbursts of laughter: "Haunting. Intense. A Monologue [sic] describes a bizarre sexual encounter with two boys on a beach. It is verbal stimulation" [*New York Times*].²⁷

As Stigsdotter and Bergfelder argue, for 21st-century London cinefile audiences such portentous voiceovers and sexual references "dubiously placed within the boundaries of high art rather than low culture, strikes a note of incongruity, and appears to be a stereotype of 1960s European art cinema marketing."²⁸

Conclusion

What is here termed "erotic Bergman" is a consistent thread in the director's long career, from the very beginning. Sex and eroticism abound in Bergman's films as a director and screenwriter from 1944 onwards. As a young bohemian in postwar Swedish cinema, Bergman consistently pushed the envelope, spicing popular genre melodramas with sexploitation elements. A number of early Bergman features both rattled and circumvented the Swedish censors of the era. Just to cite one example, in *Hets/Torment* (1944), for example, the photo still of Hollywood satyr Errol Flynn hovering over Bertha's just-off-screen bedroom seduction of Jan-Erik slyly confirms that the virginal young man is finally getting laid and is thus "In like Flynn." Early Bergman reads like a laundry list of sexploitation titillation and taboos: Stig Olin's gigolo in *Kris/Crisis* (1946), prostitution in *Det regnar på vår kärlek/It Rains on Our Love* (1946) and *Prison*, illegal abortion and suicide in *Hamnstad/Port of Call* (1948), nymphomania in *Till glädje/To Joy* (1950), lesbianism in *Thirst*, bare-breasted French cancan dancers in *Waiting Women*, to name a few. As Erik Hedling has documented, subversive jazz and swing music are also often tied to youth rebellion and liberated libidos for men and women alike in a number of these films.²⁹ And as the prior examples of *The Silence* and *Persona* make clear, even after his breakthrough as an international arthouse auteur, "erotic Bergman" tropes hardly disappear. The rapid-fire, semi-autobiographical opening montage of *Persona* includes an erect penis. And Bergman's jazz-age sex farce *För att inte tala om alla dessa kvinnor/All These Women* (1964), co-written with fellow satyr Erland Josephson, arguably contains Bergman's sexually crudest, most vulgar dialogue (a dirty-mouthed companion to the Wildean bon mots of *Smiles of a Summer Night*). Bergman in the seventies continues the pattern: the camera's voyeuristic lingering on the breast-fondling auto-eroticism of a female mental patient in *Ansikte mot ansikte/Face to Face* (1976); Liv Ullmann's Berlin cabaret harlot à la Marlene Dietrich in *Ormens ägg/The Serpent's Egg* (1977), and the violent murder and necrophiliac sodomization of a German prostitute in *Ur marionetternas liv/From the Life of the Marionettes* (1980). Sex and eroticism inform a good share of the Bergman canon, a fact not lost on American distributors who often added ballyhoo and savvy marketing to sexploitation elements already deep in the DNA of these Swedish imports.

NOTES

1. *The New York Times*, August 27, 1949, 7:3.
2. Daniel Humphrey, *Queer Bergman: Sexuality, Gender, and European Art Cinema* (Austin: University of Texas Press, 2013), 87.
3. Eddie Muller and Daniel Faris, *Grindhouse: The Forbidden World of "Adults Only" Cinema.* (New York: St. Martin's Griffin, 1996) 57.
4. Bosley Crowther. *The New York Times*, March 22, 1955, 35:2.
5. Muller and Faris, 57.
6. Arthur Knight, and Hollis Alpert, "The History of Sex in Cinema," *Playboy*, December 1966: 248.
7. http://ingmarbergman.se/en/production/summer-interlude.
8. https://www.criterion.com/current/posts/2312-illicit-interlude
9. Bosley Crowther, *The New York Times*, October 27, 1954, 32:6.
10. Eric Schaefer, *"Bold! Daring! Shocking! True!": A History of Exploitation Films, 1919–1959* (Durham: Duke U. Press, 1999), 335.
11. David F. Friedman, *A Youth in Babylon: Confessions of a Trash-Film King.* Buffalo (NY: Prometheus Books, 1990), 101
12. Daniel Humphrey, "Ingmar Bergman Outside the Box: *Summer with Monika* as American Drive-In Movie" (paper presented at the Society for Cinema and Media Studies conference, Fairmont Queen Elizabeth Hotel, Montreal, Canada, March 29, 2015).
13. Ibid.
14. Reproduced in Muller and Faris, *Grindhouse*, 57.
15. Tino Balio, *The Foreign Film Renaissance on American Screens, 1946–1973* (Madison: University of Wisconsin Press, 2010), 131–132.
16. "*Monika* Trailer: For 'Broad Minds' Only!" https://www.criterion.com/current/posts/2332-monika-trailer-for-broad-minds-only.
17. Joe David Brown, "Sin & Sweden," *Time*, April 25, 1955, 65:17, 31.
18. Woody Allen, "Through a Life Darkly," *New York Times* book review, September 18, 1988. https://www.nytimes.com/books/98/12/06/specials/bergman-magic.html
19. *The New York Times*, April 16, 2011.
20. Balio, *The Foreign Film Renaissance*, 133.
21. Balio, *The Foreign Film Renaissance*, 130.
22. Humphrey, "Ingmar Bergman Outside the Box."
23. Heffernan, Kevin, *Ghouls, Gimmicks, and Gold: Horror Films and the American Movie Business, 1953–1968.* (Durham: Duke University Press, 2004), 119–120.
24. Heffernan, *Ghouls, Gimmicks, and Gold*, 119.
25. Humphrey, *Queer Bergman*, 50–51.
26. Maaret Koskinen, *Ingmar Bergman's The Silence: Pictures in the Typewriter, Writings on the Screen* (Seattle: University of Washington Press, 2010), 151–152.
27. Ingrid Stigsdotter and Tim Bergfelder, "Studying Cross-Cultural Marketing and Reception: Ingmar Bergman's *Persona* (1966)" in *The New Film History: Sources, Methods, Approaches*, ed. James Chapman et al. (New York: Palgrave Macmillan, 2007), 215–228, 223.
28. Ibid., 224.
29. Erik Hedling, "Music, lust and modernity: Jazz in the films of Ingmar Bergman" *The Soundtrack*, 4:2 (2011): 89–99.

REFERENCES

Allen, Woody. "Through a Life Darkly." *The New York Times*, September 18, 1988. https://www.nytimes.com/books/98/12/06/specials/bergman-magic.html.
Balio, Tino. *The Foreign Film Renaissance on American Screens, 1946–1973.* Madison: University of Wisconsin Press, 2010.
The Criterion Collection. "*Monika* Trailer: For 'Broad Minds' Only!" https://www.criterion.com/current/posts/2332-monika-trailer-for-broad-minds-only.
_____. "Illicit Interlude." https://www.criterion.com/current/posts/2312-illicit-interlude.
Brown, Joe David. "Sin & Sweden." *Time*, April 25, 1955.
Crowther, Bosley. *The New York Times*, March 22, 1955.

_____. *The New York Times*, October 27, 1954.
Friedman, David F. *A Youth in Babylon: Confessions of a Trash-Film King*. Buffalo, NY: Prometheus Books, 1990.
Hedling, Erik. "Music, lust and modernity: Jazz in the films of Ingmar Bergman." *The Soundtrack*, 4:2 (2011): 89–99.
Heffernan, Kevin. *Ghouls, Gimmicks, and Gold: Horror Films and the American Movie Business, 1953–1968*. Durham and London: Duke University Press, 2004.
Humphrey, Daniel. "Ingmar Bergman Outside the Box: *Summer with Monika* as American Drive-In Movie." Paper presented at the Society for Cinema and Media Studies conference, Fairmont Queen Elizabeth Hotel, Montreal, Canada, March 29, 2015.
_____. *Queer Bergman: Sexuality, Gender, and European Art Cinema*. Austin: University of Texas Press, 2013.
The Ingmar Bergman Foundation. "Summer Interlude." http://ingmarbergman.se/en/production/summer-interlude.
Knight, Arthur, and Hollis Alpert. "The History of Sex in Cinema." *Playboy*, December, 1966.
Koskinen, Maaret. *Ingmar Bergman's The Silence: Pictures in the Typewriter, Writings on the Screen*. Seattle: University of Washington Press, 2010.
Muller, Eddie, and Daniel Faris. *Grindhouse: The Forbidden World of "Adults Only" Cinema*. New York: St. Martin's Griffin, 1996.
The New York Times, April 16, 2011.
The New York Times, August 27, 1949.
Schaefer, Eric. *"Bold! Daring! Shocking! True!": A History of Exploitation Films, 1919–1959*. Durham, NC: Duke University Press, 1999.
Stigsdotter, Ingrid, and Tim Bergfelder. "Studying Cross-Cultural Marketing and Reception: Ingmar Bergman's *Persona* (1966)." In *The New Film History: Sources, Methods, Approaches*, edited by James Chapman et al., 215–228. New York: Palgrave Macmillan, 2007
Weber, Bruce. "Cyrus Harvey, an Extravagant Entrepreneur, Dies at 85." *New York Times*, April 16, 2011.

It Started with a Kiss
Sexuality and Swedish Film in 1951

ANDERS MARKLUND

When the trade journal *Biografbladet* asked leading critics to assess Swedish films of 1951, three films were clearly identified as the year's best achievements: Alf Sjöberg's *Fröken Julie/Miss Julie,* a formally advanced and Cannes-winning adaptation of August Strindberg's battle of the sexes-play; Ingmar Bergman's *Sommarlek/Summer Interlude,* an early masterpiece of a leading auteur; and Arne Mattsson's *Hon dansade en sommar/One Summer of Happiness,* a film whose nudity and almost "explicit" sex scene were part of the film's outstanding success in Swedish as well as in international cinemas.[1] All three films still belong to a modest canon of internationally known Swedish films and are good representatives of the second international breakthrough of Swedish cinema (after the so called "Golden Age" between 1917 and 1925). While quality, international success, and canonization are important, I will use these three 1951 films for a different, though not entirely separate, discussion concerning the hesitant beginnings of franker cinematic representations of sexuality that would follow during the coming decades. As Eric Schaefer has shown, these would eventually position Sweden (together with Denmark) as the top "nation-of-the-naughty" towards the end of the 1960s.[2]

My aim here is to discern the narrative and aesthetic norms governing filmmakers' representations of sexual encounters in the early 1950s. At this time sexual representations still resorted to what Linda Williams has cleverly termed "kisses and ellipses," i.e., letting kisses hint at sex while avoiding further, more explicit, representations.[3] Both *Miss Julie* and *Summer Interlude* include sex scenes that are skillful and interesting variations of the kisses and ellipsis strategy. Still, they do not push the boundaries of sexual explicitness in the way *One Summer of Happiness* does with its ground-breaking nude sex scene. For viewers today, Mattsson's aesthetic choices appear as nothing more than a mild transgression, but contrasting Mattsson's work with the two other films and observing the film's strategy of containing any potential criticism of being exploitative or sensationalist, it becomes clear how carefully even the smallest transgression had to be prepared at this time.

Doyen film critic Nils Petter Sundgren opens his televised history of sexuality in Swedish film—*Från pussar till porr* (1994)—with *One Summer of Happiness* and its iconic images of the young couple splashing in a lake and later lying down together in the grass, naked and clearly about to make love. These images—never before seen in a mainstream film and consequently used for movie posters both in Sweden and internationally—would help pave the way for ever more explicit representations of sexuality. Still, in an interview on Sundgren's program Mattsson himself downplays the originality of this sex scene, suggesting that it was merely motivated by a sense of realism: "I used to believe people were naked when they had sex...." However, Mattsson's seemingly natural choice to show a nude sex scene is certainly not as straightforward as he suggests, and needs to be studied in greater detail. Why, one may ask, had he not made this choice in his earlier films? Both *Rötägg/Bad Seed* (1946) and *När kärleken kom till byn/When Love Came to the Village* (1950), for example, respect established norms, using darkness to obscure what is happening and never even hinting at the removal of any clothes. Furthermore, why had no other filmmaker done so before *One Summer of Happiness*?

In order to frame these questions, David Bordwell's work on historical poetics is helpful. Bordwell understands that a filmmaker's work is not only governed by his or her own ideas and creativity, but also guided by a range of "constructional options" available at a given historical moment.[4] A filmmaker's particular choice is influenced by an "*institutional* dimension of practice [which] forms the horizon of what is permitted and encouraged at particular moments," something which also includes "tacit aesthetic assumptions."[5] Given the three films' success, with both audiences and critics, it is clear that Bergman's, Sjöberg's, and Mattsson's choices regarding sexual representation fit within the Swedish horizon of 1951 in terms of what was permitted and encouraged. The task here will be to outline how the filmmakers found options within this paradigm that were both fresh and functional, and to demonstrate how Mattsson found a way to extend the horizon towards more explicit sexual representations.

In her volume *Screening Sex*, Linda Williams discusses the constructional options regarding representations of sex, and how these have evolved throughout (American) film history. The book's title foregrounds a key tool in Williams' analysis of sexual representation, namely "the double meaning of the verb *to screen* as both revelation and concealment."[6] Thus, screening does not only involve "to reveal on a screen," but also "to shelter or protect with or as a screen"—a dualism that allows her to study screen sex as a "constructed, mediated, performed act" in which "every revelation is also a concealment that leaves something to the imagination."[7] As will become clear, Mattsson's film is anything but an unmediated representation of real life sexuality—it carefully balances a sense of frankness with respect for accepted norms.

The earliest phase in the representation of sex, before the development towards ever more explicit sex scenes took off during the decades following World War II, was to use kisses. As Sidney Gottlieb has observed in his study of kisses in Hitchcock's films: "The kiss is also traditionally the most explicit and yet still allowable—that is to say, publicly performable and viewable—signifier of sexual activity."[8] This is perhaps especially true for Williams' discussion on kisses, since her volume concerns American cinema, for a long time under the influence of the so-called Production Code, or Hays' Code, and its chaste and detailed regulations of filmic representation. Williams devotes her first chapter to kisses, since this was "the screen's first sex act" and would remain so in the context of U.S. mainstream cinema until the late 1960s when foreign films, not least from Sweden, had become so influential that it was necessary to discontinue this form of internal censorship.[9]

The primary concerns here are aesthetic and narrative norms for kisses and sex in films, but the introduction also stressed the films' critical success, since this is a significant part of the wider institutional dimension of practice mentioned by Bordwell. Although it is not possible to establish a causal connection, it appears evident that the tentative changes discussed here relate to institutional (and wider social) changes regarding sexuality. It is beyond the scope of this article to explore this in any detail, but in order to establish the discourse I will introduce deliberations made by the Swedish censorship committee (considering changes in film censorship, work initiated in 1949 and completed in 1951). In a key passage, the committee's report paves the way for less rigid censorship, at least under certain circumstances:

> The Committee has [...] carefully considered the risk that censorship based mainly on mental hygienic principles may conflict with artistic values of films and contribute to a mediocrity that is not desirable. It thus becomes inevitable that censorship in its assessment takes some account of the artistic quality of the films.[10]

This open-minded view determines the principle that "films and film scenes should not be evaluated only on account of which elements they formally contain, but mainly by their contexts and aims."[11] The committee tentatively establishes a distinction between films that "aim towards deepening the understanding of people" and films which may be "aesthetically appealing and stimulating but primarily characterized as diversion."[12] While both Sjöberg's and Bergman's films rather clearly belong among the valuable films, it is equally clear that the melodramatic story in *One Summer of Happiness* would be more at risk of being called a diversion and thus in greater need of constructing an appropriate narrative and moral context for the transgressive images. Since my discussion considers such scenes and elements that could fall under the censorship rules—scenes that extend the established representation of sexuality—I will suggest that *One Summer of Happiness* carefully establishes enough valuable contextual elements to allow the film to pass censorship uncut.[13]

The following discussion will rather quickly move from *Summer Interlude* to *Miss Julie*, and finally to a somewhat longer discussion on *One Summer of Happiness*.

Summer Interlude's *Verbal Outspokenness*

Based on an idea first formulated at the age of eighteen, *Summer Interlude* would become Ingmar Bergman's critical breakthrough in Sweden.[14] Through a fairly elaborate flashback structure, the film tells the story of a summer romance between the young ballet dancer Marie and Henrik, a young man who, just like Marie, spends the summer in the Stockholm archipelago. Their romance has a tragic ending; Henrik dies after hitting a rock while diving from the cliffs.

About halfway into the film, the first and only sex scene occurs. It is a good example of a traditional, but also somewhat elegant, way to screen away from the sex. Marie and Henrik have quickly become close. They have a relaxed and open dialogue about the pleasures of kissing (which neither appears to have tried before), Henrik says he loves her, and they almost kiss, when Marie surprisingly turns away and they instead continue their friendly talk. Playfully establishing their closeness and the thought of greater intimacy, Bergman prepares the viewer for the sexual union in the scene to follow—a strategy of suspension, as we will see, also used by Mattsson in *One Summer of Happiness*.

In the evening the couple arrives at the manor of Marie's aunt Elisabet and uncle

Erland where she stays during the summer. They go upstairs to her dance studio. Because of the earlier depicted closeness of their relationship, and their almost-kiss, it is well motivated that she asks: "I think we should kiss now. Don't you think so, too?" He agrees, and they kiss. Their kiss is one of those kisses, also described by Williams, which does not suggest any further sexual passions: they do not embrace, hardly even move, and the camera remains distant and immobile. Indeed, Bergman avoids any passion, instead casting the scene in a laid back, matter-of-fact mold. As we will see, Mattsson also refrains from displaying passion in *One Summer of Happiness*' sex scene, a scene that very well could have been the most passionate scene of the film. It appears that the sexual frankness and explicitness of the two films require a decoupling of sex and passion.

Narrating the sex scene, Bergman uses images of Henrik's dog Gruffman to create two ellipses which allow him to disregard parts of the couple's growing intimacy. From the initial, immobile kiss there is a dissolve to Gruffman, looking somewhat sad noticing that his master's attention lies elsewhere. The camera lingers a while before it pans left to reveal Marie and Henrik now lying on the floor kissing. This first dog-dissolve moves Marie and Henrik into close-up and a horizontal position. Such a position would already be too daring by Hollywood's Hays' code standards, but it can be seen, briefly, in several other Swedish films from these years. Marie and Henrik are for a moment reminded of the external world and of what they are doing, by the sounds of Marie's aunt and uncle talking on the stairs and attempting to open the door. As they lie down again the camera leaves their renewed kissing for a pan back to Gruffman and a series of dissolves of the night landscape outside. The series ends with the sun shining through the room's window; it is morning and they have made love.

Bergman frames the ellipsis in a way that makes it perfectly clear what has happened, and that foregrounds it as sweet and natural. With the image still on the sunlit window, Marie's hand reaches up in the foreground, is caressed by Henrik's hand, and we hear them talking on the floor, below the frame. Marie giggles: "Now you have a mistress. How does that feel?" Their talk covers some of their, mostly Henrik's, top-of-the-head thoughts—ranging from "but we will get married," and "actually, I was really scared [about making love]," to him being hungry.

Williams discusses how overtly sex can and must be signaled, and how much the audience must read into the images. In her main example, *Casablanca* (Michael Curtiz, 1942), it is not at all clear whether the characters Ilse and Rick have sex. Rather, Williams shows how the scene excels in being vague. After the ellipsis, Ilse and Rick talk about quite other matters, certainly not about sex as in Bergman's film. They are fully dressed, and there are no other signs around of lovemaking.[15]

There are also limits to Bergman's representation. It is as if he feels that the constructional options for displaying sex do not allow him to go further. After the ellipsis, Bergman plays a little game with the couple's nakedness. With an image showing only the (naked) caressing hands and parts of the arms, and with dialogue about them now being lovers, Bergman lets the viewer *assume* that they are now naked. Somewhat surprisingly, when they later stand up, they are both fully dressed. Had it not been for the explicit dialogue, this would have been a cryptic scene just like the one in *Casablanca*. Thus, one can say that while Bergman's film is very open and straightforward in its discussion of sex and represents it as acceptable, it seems clear that there are also constraints, for example on combining this sexual openness with passion and nudity.

Miss Julie's *Symbolic Montage*

Alf Sjöberg had recently staged August Strindberg's naturalistic play *Fröken Julie/Miss Julie* (1888) at the Royal Dramatic Theatre in Stockholm when he was asked if he would not also want to adapt it to the screen for Sandrews.[16] Sjöberg constructed the passionate and dangerous midsummer game of love between a count's daughter, Julie, and the servant Jean, in a temporally complex way (even more so than Bergman's *Summer Interlude*). The film was enthusiastically received, winning the Grand Prize at the Cannes film festival in 1951.

It is reasonable to suggest that there are two sex scenes in *Miss Julie*. Both meticulously avoid anything visually or verbally explicit and instead let viewers figure out what might be going on. The first scene will be only briefly mentioned. Julie, and the viewer, sees a farm hand and a maid laughing and hugging in the hay in a barn. It is quite clear what is going on, but soon the viewer can observe only Julie's shocked reaction as she cannot stop looking. The screenplay describes it as: "Close-up of Julie. This is news to her, imprisoned and horrified her eyes dilate."[17] The brief scene introduces Julie to carnal love, and the viewer to the film's sex theme.

The second sex scene is of fundamental importance, marking a radical turning point in Julie and Jean's relationship, and thus in the story. It is clear that Sjöberg searched for a way to remain true to Strindberg's original play while simultaneously creating a scene with great intensity. His solution is to fill the ellipsis following Julie and Jean's kiss with a sequence of metaphoric images—images that may be read (or may not, depending on the viewer) as a very graphic sex depiction. The solution is quite distinct from more traditional sex ellipses with a fade-out fade-in as in *Casablanca*, a series of dissolving landscape images as in Bergman's *Summer Interlude,* and so on. Sjöberg does not merely visualize the passing of time, but also what happens during that time.

It is interesting to note that the images just before and just after the ellipsis are really very traditional: a passionate kiss before the ellipsis (although, according to the original play, it is meant to show Julie fainting, rather than being passionately kissed) and afterwards the two characters leaving the bedroom and adjusting their clothes.

The situation before the ellipsis may very well be read in a way not suggested by the dialogue, in which Jean proposes to shoot anyone entering the room. Julie says that he should rather shoot her, directs the gun to her mouth, and then she faints. One could, however, equally well interpret his gun in a more phallic way, and the last shot before the ellipsis as an intimate embrace.

Again, the series of images that follows may simply just illustrate the happy midsummer festivities mentioned in Strindberg's play. However, for a viewer with a lively Freudian fantasy or, like Sjöberg, interested in psychoanalysis and Soviet intellectual montage, they may also be read symbolically.[18] The series includes dancing though a tunnel, tapping of beer, dancing back and forth, raised salute shots, and the final images, following the salute shots, showing how a beer keg is emptied with the pouring beer superimposed over persons hurrying out of a doorway. Should these images be translated to non-symbolic actions, the scene would have been pornographic.

It is hard to imagine Sjöberg choosing more explicit and less symbolical images, even if he would have been able to. Still, it is quite evident that he had carefully considered how, within existing constraints, he could create a sex scene that would suggest details of intercourse. In a symbolic way, Sjöberg went far beyond what the constructional options of the time allowed.

One Summer of Happiness

One Summer of Happiness is an adaptation of Per Olof Ekström's novel *Sommardansen,* published in 1949. The screenplay, written by Vladimir Semitov in cooperation with Olle Hellbom, was directed by Arne Mattsson for Nordisk Tonefilm. The film premiered in December 1951 and was an immediate and extraordinary success, winning, for example, the Golden Bear at the Berlin film festival in 1952.

One Summer of Happiness is part of a new cycle of films gaining importance during the 1940s, films characterized by Per Olov Qvist as "dramatizations of contemporary countryside issues" since they are concerned with "problems having to do with rural and community development at large, such as depopulation and changes in the social structure" where there is a clear rural-urban conflict.[19] Within this context, Mattsson's film contains a harsh criticism of a rigid and destructive mentality, most critically represented by a generally outdated portrait of a village vicar who is unable to respond to secularization, developing youth culture or indeed the modernization and urbanization of society. In this changing countryside and world, the film focuses on the love between Kerstin and Göran, who simultaneously embody the distinction between the traditional and the new, and between the countryside and the modern, urban society. (Kerstin is associated with tradition and the countryside, Göran with modernity and urbanity.) This relationship story drives the narrative, and its unprecedented depiction of intimacy would generate widespread interest in the film.

What interests me here is the motif of kisses, and how it is used in the film as a significant device for characterization, for the development of the relationship story, and in particular and more concretely for the increasing intimacy between Kerstin and Göran. The analysis is informed by Gottlieb's discussion on Hitchcock's films, and how "linked series of kisses throughout a film [...] dramatize complex character formations and changing relationships."[20] Gottlieb's observation that there is a tremendously "close connection between kissing and telling in Hitchcock" is, as we will see, equally true in Mattsson's film.[21] In fact, *One Summer of Happiness* is structured around a series of kisses that can be characterized as (1) attempted stealing of kiss, (2) reciprocal, relationship-confirming kiss, (3) intimate and passionate kiss interrupted, (4) a series of kisses leading to sex, and finally, (5) public kissing acknowledging their relationship. As may be sensed already, these kisses are not only a storytelling device, but also a central part of the film's articulation of fairly traditional values regarding sex and romance.

Undesired Kisses

During the midsummer night festivities Kerstin and Göran have become quite close, and all is fine and well until he kisses her.[22] He turns her face towards his and kisses her on the mouth, whereupon she turns away, slaps him, and exclaims "Fool! Why did you have to ruin everything when it was so beautiful?" as she runs away. Such a scene is common enough in films from this time—there is even an example in Sjöberg's *Miss Julie,* when Jean first kisses Julie and promptly gets slapped. These actions reflect both a gendered double standard, and a real enough challenge to know when the time is right for a kiss. The logic is well articulated in Georg Theslöf's etiquette books (published 25 years earlier, but seemingly still topical at the time). Had Göran read Theslöf's advice for men he would have known that: "The lady must therefore first vigorously reject any attempt to kisses. Still, the man keeps trying. She then protests less energetically [...] And that is the end of that matter. After the first 'violent kiss' ten reconciliation kisses follow,"[23] whereas Kerstin properly follows Theslöf's advice for women: "There are some imprudent youths who consider themselves irresistible and after a few hours' acquaintance 'steal' a kiss. This is the only case in which even the most feminine among women could, or rather *should*, resort to physical violence: a (slight) slap is the only response to such clumsiness."[24]

Göran's kiss and Kerstin's slap should be seen as not only a matter of prescribed etiquette, but also mark an important evaluation of the situation and a significant transition in their relationship. In her study of films with a "first-love-plot," to which Mattsson's film belongs, where kisses are the first phase of intimacy, Anette Kaufmann notes that the first kiss signals the transition into the world of adult sexuality.[25] This obviously makes the kiss more sensitive. When Göran "ruins everything when it was so beautiful," Kerstin articulates a different understanding of the beauty of the situation and the appropriate level of intimacy. Göran trespasses boundaries drawn by society and internalized by Kerstin.

Kerstin's resistance suspends the relationship story, but does not end it. In fact, they will re-establish and soon enough move beyond what they had before his kiss. In a more general discussion about impermissible touching and the resulting feelings of disgust and indignation, William Ian Miller suggests that "not unattractive people"—like Göran in this case—have a benefit, with

> their unpermitted touchings processed as if they were proper requests for permission for the touching taking place. Such a touching is the first escalation in the ritual of courtship, and [...] a request to consider the prospect of the ultimate sexual touching.[26]

Accordingly, since Göran is constructed as attractive, his clandestine kiss may trigger an initial resistance, but it also activates thoughts—both in Kerstin and in viewers—about a later sexual union.

As Gottlieb pointed out, kisses are used for characterization. In addition to Göran and Kerstin's kiss, there are two other situations around this point of the film that involve kissing and that also help characterize Kerstin and Göran. First, after a dance a few scenes earlier, another girl wants to kiss Göran. The screenplay captures intentions and reactions, describing how "[s]he closes her eyes and pouts her lips for a kiss. He regards her with indifference."[27] In contrast to this obtrusive girl, Kerstin is appropriately chaste and also respects the male privilege of taking the initiative when it comes to intimacy. It also clarifies—much more so than did the original novel—that Göran is not interested in only playing around with girls, and kissing them, but that he is specifically attracted to Kerstin. Second, a few scenes later, another young man who is interested in Kerstin, Nisse, "has locked her arms behind her back and tries to kiss her, and she tosses and turns her body in order to escape" when Göran arrives, intervenes, and claims that "It is beneath my dignity to use violence to kiss girls!," before the two young men begin to fight.[28] Although Göran also kissed Kerstin against her will, Nisse's attempt is more clearly inappropriate; it is violent and, unlike Göran, Nisse has no reason to believe that Kerstin has any feelings for him. The contrast with Nisse's crude behavior, which also allows Göran to protect a somewhat vulnerable Kerstin, rehabilitates Göran and lends him an air of gentlemanliness.

Confirming Love—Nothing Else

The next kiss in the film's relationship story signals the reconciliation between Kerstin and Göran and a confirmation of their relationship. The dialogue clarifies that Kerstin has no reason to be jealous—which she was—and that Göran's feelings for her are indeed genuine. After that, Kerstin affirms her feelings for Göran, and allows him to kiss her: "Then he pulls her close to him and kisses her and this time she lies softly in his arms."[29]

The kiss does not suggest any further sexual activities. The scene functions to establish Kerstin and Göran's mutual and genuine feelings of romantic love, and the kiss serves as an appropriate punctuation to this achievement.[30] To suggest a sexual attraction at this point would confuse the characters' motivations, which here belong within a sphere of a romantic relationship, not a sexual one. Mattsson's staging carefully restrains any sign of passion, and ascertains that the kiss is a punctuation (to the confirmation of love and relationship) and not an ellipsis (leaving out sexual intimacy). Kerstin and Göran remain immobile, like statues, during the kiss. The visual weight of the couple kissing is diminished, first by a tracking shot reducing their size within the frame, and then by a dissolve to a distant view foregrounding the picturesque postcard-like landscape of the following scene. In many ways the kiss resembles the one from *Summer Interlude*—immobility, dissolves—but here without any hinting at sex. It is a kiss to which Hays would not object; by no means lustful.

If the narrative purpose of this scene and kiss was to foreground genuine feelings of love, the task ahead for Mattsson is to prepare the viewer for the couple's sexual union, both by clarifying the attraction and passion and by making this morally acceptable. Kisses help him achieve this; first in a sequence that makes sex a very tangible possibility, then in a tri-partite sequence leading to their lovemaking.

Establishing Sexual Desire

With their first reciprocal kiss, Kerstin and Göran reached a new stage in their relationship. Next time they kiss a new degree of intimacy is reached. After a lovely evening Göran has taken Kerstin home. He should be leaving when Kerstin asks him in; there is sudden rain and thunder, and she is scared and also worried about him. Once inside they kiss intensely and would probably have done much more, had they not been interrupted by Kerstin's aunt, causing Göran to sneak out the window. The scene may be titillating on its own, but it also contributes to the forward movement of the story—the interrupted kissing has established sexual desire and leaves the viewer to anticipate their union.

Two strategies employed should be pointed out here. The first is the use of a standard, or ritual, situation developing organically. The scene starts with one of the "conventional and predictable moments" for kisses, in this case a parting kiss which is "not highly charged."[31] However, and as Anette Kaufmann has noted, such "kiss-rituals" are sometimes used in films to overcome bodily distance and speed up intimacies.[32] In this case, it is not only the ritualized kiss but also the sudden change in weather that leads the way to intimacies later in the scene. The rain and thunder give Kerstin a plausible excuse to invite Göran into the house and, as a consequence, to the intense kissing that follows. As we will also see later in the film's sex scene, Mattsson downplays internal motivation and consequently also individual responsibility. One may note that a similar strategy is used also in *Miss Julie*, where Julie and Jean are more or less forced by the chasing crowd to hide in his bedroom where they end up making love, and in *Summer Interlude*, where Marie and Henrik very consciously decide to kiss, but where Bergman never suggests a similar decision about making love. Kisses may be expected as part of a ritual or even planned, but sex simply appears to happen, facilitated by external forces.

The second strategy used by Mattsson regards the blending of dialogue foregrounding social and sexual norms, and the simultaneous disregard of these norms. The dialogue may appear somewhat silly and artificial, but nevertheless neatly illustrates a Foucauldian internalization of rules. When Göran wonders "what would they do if they saw me here?" Kerstin responds that "they would lock me up in a tower where you could not reach me," and they continue talking in a similar fashion. The dialogue, however, is well-aligned with the film's theme of young love versus old-fashioned norms and values. Furthermore, their words highlight the very tangible risk of being caught, with severe consequences, thus adding suspense to the scene.[33]

Their voicing of norms is contrasted with a series of increasingly intimate non-verbal behaviors. They kiss, Göran places his hand on Kerstin's breast, she places her hand on top of his (and presses it harder, rather than removing it[34]), Göran starts kissing her neck, and before he gets any further, they are interrupted. This time the kissing is not interrupted because of their own (Kerstin's) internalized norms, but by Kerstin's aunt and the social norms she polices.[35] It is a well-known trope to introduce something that interrupts behaviors that might otherwise lead too far, too soon. Sometimes this interruption will be permanent. On other occasions it is rather a way to tease the viewer by delaying the action and preparing the viewer by suggesting what might be about to happen.[36] Here, the unfinished kissing creates another delay in their relationship story, just as it did in Bergman's *Summer Interlude*. Also, just like in Bergman's film, the next time we meet the lovers it is time for the actual sex scene. It is thus clear that film kissing is not only, or even primarily, aiming for social verisimilitude, but that it is a carefully constructed device used for distinct narrative, thematic, and affective purposes.

A Small Contribution to More Explicit Onscreen Sex Scenes

The next set of kisses will eventually lead to the film's sex scene, a sex scene with naked bodies, horizontal position, enough light and sufficient hints as to the couple's intentions. The audience can be in no doubt as to what is going on. In significant ways the staging is not dissimilar to that discussed by Williams regarding Mike Nichols's much later film *The Graduate* (1967), which she considers to be "the major pioneer in screening sex for the transition out of the [Hays'] Code." Williams uses the film to discuss carnal knowledge and delineates what Bordwell might have seen as the constructional options available. Williams observes that Nichols' film

> forges a trope that would prove very popular in mainstream American cinema as a "tasteful," discreetly concealing, way of suggesting carnal knowledge. Carnal knowledge is thus *revealed* (we are certain the couple does have sex, there is no coy fade-out or narrative obfuscation such as that in *Casablanca*) and *concealed* (we are not asked to confront the visual fact of genital action).[37]

Although there is (verbal) meandering going on also in *The Graduate* before the couple has sex, it is particularly elaborate in *One Summer of Happiness*. Three phases structure the sequence—each with its own kisses.

In the first phase Kerstin and Göran meet again after a long separation arranged by her puritan relatives as a response to Kerstin and Göran's intimate kissing earlier. After a standard reuniting trope (he opens his arms, she hugs him, he kisses her) a brief dialogue follows—"Do you like me?" etc.—clarifying that they really care about each other, before they kiss again. At this point of the film, intimate touch is clearly appropriate, also to Kerstin.

The second phase, in which they suddenly find themselves naked in the water, is particularly interesting since it foregrounds a spontaneity that reduces their agency regarding the intimacy that will follow.[38] Göran's fairly innocent question whether they should swim, and Kerstin's answer that they should see who is quickest into the water, adding speed and playfulness, motivates the removal of their clothes without necessarily suggesting any erotic intentions. The playful thrust is underscored by joyful traditional folk music.

What started out in a playful mood soon changes to a romantic, or perhaps rather melancholic, mood. The music introduces a contemplative tone, as Kerstin and Göran stop playing and splashing and become quite still. They approach each other, kiss in a serious and almost devout way, before he takes her in his arms and carries her out of the water to the grassy meadow.

The film is well-known for its nudity—and indeed Kerstin and Göran are nude—but it is obvious that the film still respects norms for what can actually be shown. While they are in the water, long shots are used, except for a medium shot while they are partly hidden behind reeds. Also, no key lights are used and with the setting sun behind them little is visible other than their silhouettes. Later, as they lie in the meadow, the immobile medium close-up shot centers on their faces, but extends the frame enough to reveal Kerstin's naked breast. Mattsson may have taken the cue from two earlier films, Bjarne Henning-Jensen's Danish *Ditte menneskebarn/Ditte—Child of Man* (1946) and Sjöberg's *Bara en mor/Only a Mother* (1949), each showing a woman bathing naked. Although these women are sexually active in the films—indeed this is quite important to the films' themes—these nude scenes are not inserted into a lovemaking context. This is, however, what Mattsson does and what he himself claimed to see as so natural in the interview with Sundgren.

The third phase begins when Kerstin and Göran are already lying down and ends with a quick pan away when they kiss and are about to make love—followed by an ellipsis to another day. Before this pan, however, Mattsson lets them share both words and kisses, adding both meaning and tenderness to the scene. Göran first says that he will never forget her, and then that he wishes to remain in the village, with her, instead of returning to the city (and a modern life as an engineer, as his father wishes): "I'm staying here. I'll stay with you forever." In the concluding lines Göran asks if she knows what they are getting into, to which Kerstin responds that she likes him so very much. Thus, before they have sex, Mattsson establishes a frame (again) clarifying that this is a lasting relationship based on reciprocal love between consenting adults.[39]

It should be noted that throughout this melancholic-romantic sequence Mattsson downplays Göran and Kerstin's passion, both compared to the earlier scene in her home and with other about-to-make-love scenes in films of this time. In fact, the most passionate moves in the scene are those performed by the camera as it very quickly pans away and by the music as it gains force directly after the last line and they kiss. It is possible that Mattsson felt that he could not have it both ways, both displaying an unprecedented degree of nudity (in the context of lovemaking), and displaying intense passion. Thus, when Mattsson evokes verisimilitude, saying that he used to believe that people were naked when they had sex, this is primarily restricted to nakedness. Every other element is carefully designed to frame the nude sexuality within a non-sensationalist mood and context—a strategy well aligned with the Censorship Committee's regard for "deepening the understanding of people" as opposed to merely "appealing and stimulating" scenes.

The Final Curtain

Throughout the film the romantic storyline has been complemented with one in which a youth group struggles to set up a play. Once Kerstin and Göran have confirmed their relationship—love, sexuality and commitment—the film's final sequences stage (literally) a more public confirmation directly after the play's premiere.

After the performance, Kerstin and Göran kiss behind the curtains when a mischievous person opens the curtains again, thus making their kiss as well as their relationship public. Kerstin initially feels exposed and wants to run away but realizes that she does not have to—she can commit to their relationship and no longer fears the moral restraints voiced by some persons close to her. Further, the audience's cheerful and supportive response signals that their love and relationship is accepted by this community. Most explicitly and importantly, this is formulated by Göran's uncle, who acts as the moral center in the film, when he turns towards the camera and exclaims "you couldn't ask for a happier ending."

One Summer of Happiness could have ended with this kiss. The traditional end-kiss has been a widely accepted and very popular convention since the early days of feature filmmaking. Here, however, the staged happiness and public acceptance of their love lasts only a little while, before Kerstin is killed in an accident.

Not only Kerstin dies in the three films discussed here. It is almost a bit frightening to note that in each of the films one of the lovers dies: Kerstin, Miss Julie, and Henrik. It is almost as if the films adhered to the Hays' code's standards of punishing illegitimate sex (unmarried, in these cases) and daring sex scenes. Another and probably more likely explanation has to do with the films' slant towards the emerging art cinema. Avoiding a simplistic happy ending and instead staging a tragedy lends the films an air of seriousness, of quality, and of artistic merit. The films avoid being "primarily characterized as diversion" and should thus be rewarded greater freedom in exploring the constructional options for representing sexuality, at least according to the new standards proposed by the Film Committee.

It is therefore not surprising to see further explorations taking place within rather serious stories—beginning with Bergman's *Sommaren med Monika/ Summer with Monika* (1953), shot the following summer and quite likely encouraged by Mattsson's successful nude representation in *One summer of Happiness*, and continuing on quite a different level in the early 1960s, with films such as Bergman's *Tystnaden/The Silence* (1963).

This study has pursued a line of inquiry suggested by Bordwell, with the ambition to better understand the gradual development of conventions and constructional options—in this case within the very narrow topic of sex representations in feature films, and in particular the conventional use of kisses and ellipsis. It has detailed which constructional options were available to filmmakers in Sweden in 1951 and how one film extended those conventions just a little bit. Although one still comprehends the socially controlled constraints governing several narrative and aesthetic choices, with *One summer of Happiness* Mattsson managed to go a bit further than others had done before.

Notes

1. "De främsta filmerna säsongen 1951–52," *Biografbladet*, 4 (1952): 19–27.
2. Eric Schaefer, "'I'll Take Sweden': The Shifting Discourse of the 'Sexy Nation' in Sexploitation Films," in *Sex Scene: Media and the Sexual Revolution*, ed. Eric Schaefer (Durham and London: Duke University Press, 2014), 207–234.
3. Linda Williams, *Screening sex* (Durham and London: Duke University Press, 2008).
4. David Bordwell, *Poetics of Cinema* (New York and London: Routledge, 2008), 27.
5. Bordwell, *Poetics of Cinema*, 28.
6. Williams, *Screening sex*, 2.
7. Williams, *Screening sex*, 2.
8. Sidney Gottlieb, "Hitchcock and the Art of the Kiss: A Preliminary Survey," *Hitchcock Annual*, 6 (1997): 69.
9. Williams, *Screening sex*, 26.
10. All translations in this article are mine. SOU 1951:16, 1949 års filmkommitté, *Filmcensuren: Betänkande I* (Stockholm: Ecklesiastikdepartementet, 1951), 14.
11. SOU 1951:16, 14.
12. SOU 1951:16, 14.
13. Regarding censorship, Mattsson's film was allowed from age 15 (the highest age limit), just as the ones by Bergman and Sjöberg.
14. Birgitta Steene, *Ingmar Bergman: A Reference Guide* (Amsterdam: Amsterdam University Press, 2005), 195.
15. Williams, *Screening sex*, 34–40.
16. Gunnar Lundin, *Filmregi Alf Sjöberg* (Lund: Wallin and Dalholm Boktryckeri, 1979), 99.
17. I will use some verbalizations taken from screenplays when they capture the ideas to be communicated by the film. "Fröken Julie," screenplay accessible at the library of the Swedish Film Institute, 17.
18. It should be noted that Strindberg certainly encouraged a symbolic *mise-en-scène*, since his play foregrounded a folk song, "Det kommo två fruar från skogen" containing traditional, but not particularly obvious, sexual symbols. See Tommy Olofsson, "Att tappa sin sko eller bli våt om foten. Fröken Julie, Askungen och Träskomannen." *Tidskrift för classiska studier*, 1 (2011), 126–131. In his foreword to *Miss Julie* Strindberg writes that the singing people "use already existing material, which may attain a double meaning" and that the "words do not hit their target spot-on, but approximately." August Strindberg, *Fröken Julie* (Stockholm: Jos. Seligmanns förlag, 1888), XX, http://www.dramawebben.se/sites/default/files/StrindbergA_FrokenJulie-ocr_0.pdf. One of the symbols in the song, the wreath, is also used in Sjöberg's staging. Strindberg also handed down the overall festive activities—including playing music, dancing, and drinking—taking place outside the room where Jean and Julie hide (and make love), but Sjöberg has made the sexual connotations more distinct.
19. Per Olov Qvist, *Jorden är vår arvedel: landsbygden i svensk spelfilm 1940–1959* (Uppsala: Filmhäftet, 1986), 30–31.
20. Gottlieb, "Hitchcock and the Art of the Kiss," 73.
21. Gottlieb, "Hitchcock and the Art of the Kiss," 74.
22. It should be pointed out that all three films discussed here use a summer setting, and to some degree also foreground the symbolism of a life-affirming summer (vs. autumn), and that two of them prominently include the Swedish midsummer celebration, associated with love and lust.
23. Georg Theslöf, *Mannen i sino prydno* (Helsingfors: H Schildts förlag, 1925), 62.
24. Georg Theslöf, *Kvinnan i sino prydno* (Helsingfors: H Schildts förlag, 1926), 60–61.
25. Anette Kaufmann, *Der Liebesfilm: Spielregeln eines Filmgenres* (Konstanz: UVK, 2007), 113.

26. William Ian Miller, *The Anatomy of Disgust* (Cambridge, Mass. and London: Harvard University Press, 1997), 65–66.

27. "Sommardansen" (andra scenario), Script I, screenplay accessible at the library of the Swedish Film Institute, 42.

28. "Sommardansen," 70.

29. "Sommardansen," 100. The verbal negotiation is reflected in their body language. True to norms of male initiative and female resistance, Göran approaches Kerstin three times during their dialogue, seeking eye contact, and holding her shoulders. Each time she moves away, and only when she knows that he loves her, and only her, do they kiss in a reciprocal kiss.

30. Cfr. Williams, *Screening sex*, 35.

31. Gottlieb, "Hitchcock and the Art of the Kiss."

32. Kaufmann, *Der Liebesfilm*, 113.

33. Stories drawing on norms regarding what behaviors are forbidden or taboo are briefly discussed by Kaufmann. Kaufmann, *Der Liebesfilm*, 119.

34. This distinction (and non-verbal affirmation) can be observed both in literary works, such as Swedish classic *Doktor Glas* as well as in films. Hjalmar Söderberg, *Doktor Glas* (Stockholm: Albert Bonniers Förlag, 1905). Linda Williams notes this regarding *Casablanca*: "Hard bodily pressure, which Ilsa returns, signaled by her placement of her own hand over his, constitutes the essence of this 'big kiss,'" see Williams, *Screening sex*, 37.

35. In both the book and the screenplay, Kerstin is much more reluctant, "but when his hands despite all silent vows began straying she stiffened and pushed them away. 'No, not like that, I do not dare....'" Per Olof Ekström, *Sommardansen* (Stockholm: LT:s förlag, 1949), 292. In the screenplay she says "no" and "she backs away into the corner," see "Sommardansen," 107. Most likely, Kerstin's hesitation is removed in order to make the following sex scene appear better motivated and more consequential.

36. See, i.e. David Bordwell, *Narration in the Fiction Film*, London: Routledge, 1985), 38, 55–56.

37. Williams, *Screening sex*, 82.

38. Spontaneity is frequently captured in Ekström's novel, with "suddenly" being a key word used several times to indicate a quick shift which the author seems unable or unwilling to explore in greater detail.

39. As Williams observes regarding one of the otherwise hottest Hollywood kisses at this time—in *It's a Wonderful Life* (Frank Capra 1946), a film that to some degree also mirrors *One Summer of Happiness*' contrast between traditional countryside/small-town life and education and the outside world—more intimacy is accepted for a loving couple that intends to get married: "A kiss between sweethearts that leads directly to marriage can hardly be called taboo [but without the prospect of marriage the kiss has to be more contained]" Williams, *Screening sex*, 42.

REFERENCES

Bordwell, David. *Narration in the Fiction Film*. London: Routledge, 1985.
_____. *Poetics of Cinema*. New York: Routledge, 2008.
Ekström, Per Olof. *Sommardansen*. Stockholm: L.T's förlag, 1949.
"De främsta filmerna säsongen 1951–52." *Biografbladet*, no. 4 (1952): 19–27.
"Fröken Julie," screenplay accessible at the library of Svenska filminstitutet.
Gottlieb, Sidney. "Hitchcock and the Art of the Kiss: A Preliminary Survey." *Hitchcock Annual*, 6 (1997).
Kaufmann, Anette. *Der Liebesfilm: Spielregeln eines Filmgenres*. Konstanz: UVK, 2007.
Lundin, Gunnar. *Filmregi Alf Sjöberg*. Lund: Wallin & Dalholm Boktryckeri, 1979.
Miller, William Ian. *The Anatomy of Disgust*. Cambridge: Harvard University Press, 1997.
Olofsson, Tommy. "Att tappa sin sko eller bli våt om foten. Fröken Julie, Askungen och Träskomannen." *Tidskrift för classiska studier*, 1 (2011): 126–131.
Qvist, Per Olov. *Jorden är vår arvedel: landsbygden i svensk spelfilm 1940–1959*. Ph.D. diss., Stockholm University, 1986.
Schaefer, Eric. "'I'll Take Sweden': The Shifting Discourse of the 'Sexy Nation' in Sexploitation Films." In *Sex Scene: Media and the Sexual Revolution*, edited by Eric Schaefer, 207–234. Durham, NC: Duke University Press, 2014.
Söderberg, Hjalmar. *Doktor Glas*. Stockholm: Albert Bonniers Förlag, 1905.

34   I. Summertime Sensuality

"Sommardansen" (andra scenario), Script I, screenplay accessible at the library of Svenska filminstitutet.
SOU 1951:16, 1949 års filmkommitté. *Filmcensuren: Betänkande I*. Stockholm: Ecklesiastikdepartementet, 1951.
Steene, Birgitta. *Ingmar Bergman: A Reference Guide*. Amsterdam: Amsterdam University Press, 2005.
Strindberg, August, *Fröken Julie*. Stockholm: Jos. Seligmanns förlag, 1888. http://www.dramawebben.se/sites/default/files/StrindbergA_FrokenJulie-ocr_0.pdf.
Theslöf, Georg. *Mannen i sino prydno*. Helsingfors: H Schildts förlag, 1925.
Theslöf, Georg. *Kvinnan i sin prydne*. Helsingfors: H Schildts förlag, 1926.
Williams, Linda. *Screening sex*. Durham, NC: Duke University Press, 2008.

II

Art, Sexploitation and Pornography

Pillow Talk, Swedish Style
To Love

ANU KOIVUNEN

In December 1965, film journal *Chaplin* published an article discussing how love is represented in Swedish films. While sexual relations were, as the international film world since *Hon dansade en sommar/One Summer of Happiness* (Arne Mattson, 1951) expected, a central topic in many Swedish films, the article concluded that sexual liberalism had not resulted in positive but, rather, in strikingly negative descriptions of sexual relations. Instead of "sensualism, joy of play, refinement, striptease, and all the pleasures of seduction and expression," feelings of disgust, guilt, and threat were overrepresented in Swedish film depictions of sex. As a "brave" exception in the genre of "a man, a woman and a bed" and an attempt to represent love as "desire, joy and fulfilment (*förlösning*)," the article named Jörn Donner's *Att älska/To Love* (1964). While criticizing the film for failing to fully reach its objectives, the article nevertheless praised its distinctive ambitions.[1]

The very same year, a similar analysis of sex as gloom not only in Swedish but also in Scandinavian cinema more generally was presented in a Danish book on "erotica in film." Here, too, the call was for "an alternative to Bergman's portrayal of sexuality, an alternative to a (purely) intellectual understanding of erotic physics, this guilt-ridden and repressed sexuality rendered in dark shades."[2] What the authors, Ove Brusendorff and Poul Malmkjær, asked for was "more films that present sex as a jubilation, as fun, liberating, inspiring and healthy, films that send the message that sex is not a burden but can be a value in and of itself, that sex without eternal love and faithfulness can be a nice way to pass the time."[3] While Brusendorff and Malmkjær mainly discussed Ingmar Bergman's films in their chapter on "groundswell of nudity" in Scandinavian cinema, a more recent overview of the subject, Jack Stevenson's *Scandinavian Blue: The Erotic Cinema of Sweden and Denmark in the 1960s and 1970s*, names *To Love* as answer to Brusendorff's and Malmkjær's call:

> Here a woman loses her husband in a car accident but goes on to find love in the arms of a younger man with whom she experiences an ideal erotic relationship. Their physical enthusiasm for each other is obvious and sex is depicted as life-affirming and fun. For the first time in her life the woman feels confidence and value as an erotic being, and this helps to keep the couple grounded when the mundane realities of life once again intrude.[4]

This description echoes the very first PR-articles published in Swedish press about *To Love* as "a comedy in chamber drama tone with an erotic Pygmalion-motif" and as a film in which Harriet Andersson plays a widow who "is inhibited and bound, but becomes liberated through her new love [...], an experienced man with Don Juan–characteristics."⁵ While "erotic" appears to be a keyword here, a study of the film's promotion (PR-plans, authorial correspondence, advertisements, posters, and trailers) as well as its critical reception in Sweden and abroad demonstrates, however, that *To Love* was not produced as a sex film but was, rather, intended as an art film. Indeed, as argued in this essay, *To Love* marks a moment when the two categories actually seem inseparable in Swedish cinema, illustrating and testifying to what in recent scholarship has been identified as a productive yet understudied alliance between European art cinema and the nebulous categories of adult film or sexploitation cinema.⁶ The sexual revolution being, as Eric Schaefer has suggested, a media phenomenon, cinema too was put on "the sex scene" or, rather, its always already implicated role as an important agent in the "rise of the public sex" was now in full view. As a result, "[i]n movies characters no longer got married. Now they got laid. Movies no longer had a big love scene; they now had a sex scene."⁷

While Swedish cinema since the 1950s and the notion of "Swedish sin"⁸ can be identified as a key factor in this development, sexuality and the question of public decency and censorship were also debated in the Swedish public sphere. As Lena Lennerhed has demonstrated, sexuality was a key discussion topic in Swedish media during the first half of the 1960s. "Sex liberals" demanded free abortion, free access to pornography, more and new kinds of sex education in schools, as well as a revision of non-normative sexual practices ("deviations"), and these debates engendered legislative reforms during the decade.⁹ In fact, the year 1963 seems a turning point as it featured both the unprecedented international success of *Tystnaden/The Silence* (1963) by Ingmar Bergman, a success that "cannot entirely be put to [its] artistic qualities" but also to its sensational depiction of intercourse and masturbation, and the initial banning of *491* by Vilgot Sjöman that launched a heated debate on film censorship in Sweden, resulting in the film eventually being released in a cut version.¹⁰ *To Love* hence entered a public sphere where "the sex wall had been crushed," to use the expression coined around the premiere of *The Silence*— the sense of public codes and conceptions undergoing transformation.¹¹ Furthermore, it entered a schizophrenic film culture where modernist notions of film art and auteurship both collided and interacted with the mediatized "sex scene."

In what follows, I explore *To Love* as a cross-over between art cinema and sex comedy, and as such a symptomatic media text signaling the changing place of cinema in the media landscape, in cultural distinctions and hierarchies, as well as in changing discourses on sexuality. First, I trace marketing strategies and critical reception in Sweden; second, I discuss the interpretive framings offered by the then contemporary festival circuit in Venice and New York—and the subsequent U.S. reception. Finally, I return to the key question posed by the film's title and its aesthetics: the relationship between love and sex in the film.

A Speculation in Sex?

To Love was the second feature film by Jörn Donner, a Finnish-born, Swedish-speaking novelist, essayist, and film critic who in 1962 had turned to filmmaking. Having won the Venice film festival debut film prize, Opera Prima Vista, for his first feature, *En söndag i September/A Sunday in September* in 1963, Donner was considered a rising star in Swedish cinema, an auteur-to-be and one of the potential heirs to Ingmar Bergman, alongside Vilgot Sjöman and Bo Widerberg. While having received bad Swedish reviews for his debut film, the Venice prize and successful foreign sales together with Donner's already established position as a public intellectual with a distinctive critical voice in Swedish cultural life heightened the expectations for his second feature film. In Sweden, therefore, the publicity surrounding the film was as much about Jörn Donner as a person—a public figure promising "Donnerwetter," the German word for thunderstorm—as it was about the film itself.[12] One of the first longer interviews with him in a major Swedish weekly magazine was tellingly titled "Here comes Donner the Great."[13]

According to a PR-plan by the production company Sandrews, *To Love* was to be marketed as a comedy, and this was to be repeated "constantly." The ambition was to reframe Jörn Donner—whose debut film *A Sunday in September* had been criticized as gloomy and pessimistic—as a film director with a sense of humor. The theme of the film was, however, summarized in a non-comic tone: "*To Love*, a film about sensual love, about being liberated through love, a young widow who falls in love with an international travel agency clerk and discovers her dignity as a woman."[14] Harriet Andersson was as an international star naturally considered a major marketing asset for the film, but also Jörn Donner was thought of as "a name that sells."[15] In 1963, furthermore, Jörn Donner and Harriet Andersson had come out in Swedish popular press as a celebrity couple.[16]

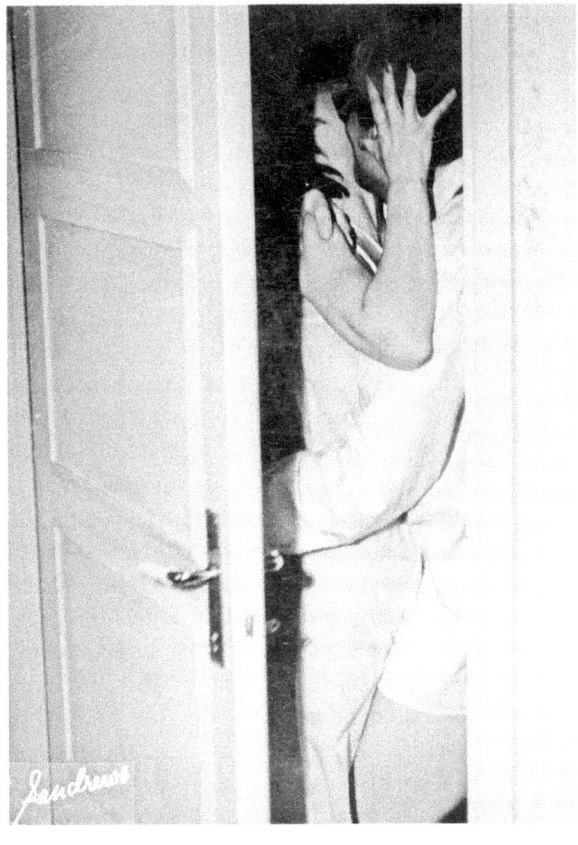

"To Love—that is fun!" Harriet Andersson as Louise in *To Love* (Jörn Donner, 1964). Courtesy of Jörn Donner.

To Love turned out not to be a critical success in Sweden, even if it was generally deemed a better film than Donner's debut. As a director, Donner was described as a scenographer or as one who thinks in images, and reviewers devoting attention to the aesthetics of the film evoked European contemporary filmmakers such as Godard and Antonioni as references.[17] However, while cast by PR-materials, in interviews and reviews as an auteur, a filmmaker with a personal vision (to quote the English title of Jörn Donner's 1962 monograph on Ingmar Bergman's films[18]) the Swedish press also explicitly confronted Donner about "speculating in sex." Preceding the premiere, an extensive interview in Swedish daily *Expressen* featured a blown-up publicity still of the loving couple, a peek of Louise (Harriet Andersson) and Fredrik (Zbigniew Cybulski) having sex in a closet, and a sensation-seeking title: "To Love—that is fun!"[19] Six smaller stills featured Harriet Andersson in black underwear and as a striptease dancer in a dream sequence.

In the interview Donner rejected the labeling of *To Love* as "a speculation in sex." Responding to a comment on how "a couple of acts of sexual intercourse in *The Silence* resulted in the biggest sales success in Swedish film history," Donner states that in his film "Louise and Fredrik play poker, they talk, they do crossword puzzles and read books." In this interview, as a gesture of rejection of Bergmanian aesthetics, Donner describes his film as featuring "a happy kiss" distinctive in Swedish film where "most loving couples find it boring or anxiety-ridden to make love." While acknowledging the existing international market for "Swedish sin," Donner refutes any notion of his film being pornographic: "The story about Louise and Fredrik is a new one at least in the sense that it shows love that is victorious instead of losing itself in pain."[20]

New Wave to "Exploitation Film with Taste"

To Love was submitted and accepted as the official Swedish entry to the main competition in Venice in 1964. A study of Jörn Donner's correspondence shows how important this admission was for the filmmaker and production company, alongside with invitations to the New York Film Festival and London Film Festival as well as a screening at La Cinémathèque Française in Paris. It appears that there were competing efforts to include *491* by Vilgot Sjöman in the Venice festival programming, but the Swedish quota was filled with *To Love* and *För att inte tala om alla dessa kvinnor/All These Women* by Ingmar Bergman outside the competition.[21]

To Love was successfully sold to many countries, and the international sales and exportability were publicized as merits by the Swedish press.[22] As for the critical reception of *To Love*, the Italian festival context offered the most explicit and self-evident framing of the film in terms of art cinema and of Donner as an auteur in the European New Wave sense of the concept. Swedish press reported how Donner took the center stage at a press conference, responding to journalists' questions in English, French, and Italian, distancing himself from Swedish film in general and Ingmar Bergman in particular.[23] While dividing opinions and described also as a disappointment, long reviews in Italian newspapers offered meticulous interpretations of *To Love*, framing it as a film worth contemplation and scrutiny—sometimes to the surprise of the Swedish journalists reporting from the Venice film festival.[24] Following the festival screening, Italian newspapers alerted readers to "the liberated woman in an anti–Bergman film" and described a film that challenged the notion of love in a marriage, juxtaposing love and marriage, suggesting them as mutually exclusive. Meanwhile many reviewers were disappointed in the film, describing it as being about nothing more than "eating, sleeping and loving."[25] That the Swedish entry to the competition featured a "bed as the protagonist," preaching "authentic sexual and emotional emancipation" and "a civilization of the bed," was interpreted as symptomatic of either the liberal sex education in Sweden or the quality of social problems in a welfare state, or explained as expressing the coldness of the Swedes.[26] The reviewers noted how social security does not seem to equal emotional security.

Sex, as discussed in the Italian public reception, was a matter of philosophy and politics. In the context of a film festival with an academic approach to cinema, such a conception appeared as self-evident. As argued by Geneviève Sellier, it was indeed the French New Wave films rather than the mainstream productions of the post-war era that "invented a cinema where amorous and sexual relations" were explored "as explicitly as was permitted under the censorship of the time."²⁷ For the New Wave directors, love and sex acquired a political meaning, and sex scenes were offered as a critique of public morality and hypocrisy. In this framing, love was represented as "an ultimate risk" which "must give meaning to one's life or die," and passion acquired "a transcendental value."²⁸

In Italian reviews, as well as in many subsequent assessments of festival screenings elsewhere, *To Love* was ascribed intertextual references beyond Bergman: French New Wave, Antonioni, and Fellini.²⁹ Some identified Alain Resnais's *Hiroshima, Mon Amour* (1959) as the visual inspiration for "sculptural" love-making scenes, some discussed Donner's style as similar or different from Godard or Louis Malle.³⁰ However, as Andrew Sarris alluded in his review for *Village Voice* in conjunction with the New York Film Festival, the framings of art cinema and sex film overlapped: "For us deep thinkers, Jörn Donner's pleasant exercise in erotic communication is not without a certain minor charm. For the boys in the back room, Harriet Andersson burns up the screen."³¹

In the promotion of the New York Film Festival, *To Love* was introduced as a film by "a protégé of Ingmar Bergman," but also as "sexplicit" film "whose sex scenes raised European eyebrows," and "a bedroom tour de force which is gay and frivolous."³² With screenings at Lincoln Center's Philharmonic Hall, the festival catered to art audiences with films that, in the words of the program director Richard Roud, "can only be classified as difficult," but it also signaled "a shift in audience tastes" to favor "more mature products," including "quality foreign films."³³ The New York Film Festival, then, can be seen as one of the sites symptomatic of and generating what Justin Wyatt has described as the "formation of the adult market segment" in the U.S.³⁴ The overlap of art film and sex film was evident in the critical framings of *To Love*. *New York Times* referred to *Lady Chatterley's Lover*, calling the film "saucy" and fixated on frivolity, stirring up the "hep and blasé" New York film audience.³⁵ The partnership of European art cinema and sexploitation was evident in a characterization of *To Love* as "more of a one-track study of sex than anything seen in this country since *The Lovers*."³⁶ What is there more than sex asked since, "after their first date he and the widow spend their time primarily in her bedroom, in and under and around the bed, in closets, in a chest, cavorting, playing patty-cake and talking about how grand sex is."³⁷ In *Time*, the reviewer called Donner a "priapic" with a narrative where the main characters are "bouncing around on her bed, and for the 80 minutes they hardly ever leave it—except to hurry over and bounce around his bed. Sometimes they bounce all over the floor. Sometimes they bounce blindfolded."³⁸ Importantly for the overlap of art film and sex film, in the festival publicity "sexplicitness" was not only ascribed to the Swedish entry, but also to *La Femme est une femme/A Woman Is a Woman* by Jean-Luc Godard. Indeed, a *Time* article coupled the two, a story of "an orgiastic courtship" and "a salute to life, liberty and off-beat movies" together under the subheading of "sex."³⁹

Whereas on-screen sex in the European film context was associated with the aesthetic and thematic doxa of the French New Wave, in the U.S. film market it was viewed as—sex. To read reviews of *To Love* following its repertoire release in November 1964, is to recognize the dilemma of film reviewers of the time: how to approach and make sense of the emerging mediatized "sex scene."⁴⁰ "Evidently the Swedes think the greatest invention since the Stone Age is the bed," Wanda Hale opened her film review in *Daily News*, concluding that "the Swedes are the world's foremost practitioners of free love." While critical of *To Love*, calling it "a bore" and "distasteful," the review simultaneously reads as an advertisement of Swedish sin, framing *To Love* as a sex film: "there is an hour-and-a-half of it in 'To Love,' give or take a few moments for eating and talking." Not merely a film *about* but also *with* sex: "Louise and Fredrik lock themselves in the bedroom of her apartment where her latent talent for love making is awakened beyond her wildest hopes by an experienced teacher who is a master at the art. When not indulging in the protracted debauchery, the debauchees leave the bed to satisfy the other appetite and after a bite to eat and champagne they run happily back to bed." The review was entitled "It's Sex, Sex and More Sex."[41]

In *Variety*, the generic classification of *To Love* was discussed in the harsh terms of marketability and "sales points," thus making explicit the formation of the adult market underway. The film was described as "a quality entry about a widow who becomes merry" which "has exploitable angles": a "combo of arty story and development and tastefully handled but nevertheless exploitable love scenes set it up for this parlay."[42] The film's "unhypocritical" portrayal of sex—"documented in a completely honest, unleering manner though in great detail, taking up about 80% of the pic—is cited as resulting in a "rarity, the exploitation film with taste."[43]

The notion of "exploitation film with taste" flaunted the overlap between art cinema and sex film, which also entailed constant definitional boundary work in relation to pornography. Opinions were divided as to whether *To Love* was voyeuristic or not, whether it was a "Peeping Tom movie" or in fact succeeded in avoiding voyeurism.[44] Some considered Donner's material pornographic, referring to it as suitable for "a certain type of post card,"[45] some thought *To Love* invoked the same question as *491* by Vilgot Sjöman: "the great, thumping issue here is whether you'd have your blue movies shown in public or privately."[46]

Woman as the Subject of "Pure" Sexual Ethics

Echoing the promotional framing, *To Love* was repeatedly characterized as "erotic comedy," "bedroom comedy," and "sex comedy," but—as is typical of the general New Wave rhetoric of film as art and as such non-generic—discussed without any association with contemporary films in these genres.[47] A film historical reference and generic association was provided by the fact that *To Love* was dedicated to the Finnish-Swedish silent film director Mauritz Stiller, but not much was made of this connection in the public framings. However, a small article published in *Chaplin* the same year suggested that Stiller's film *Erotikon* (1920) be reviewed as a forerunner to later comedies of manner by filmmakers such as Ernst Lubitsch and Billy Wilder.[48] While *To Love* was not mentioned here, it can be speculated whether invoking such a legacy might have been an authorial intention behind Donner's dedication. Films such as *Sabrina* (Billy Wilder 1954), *The Seven Year Itch* (Billy Wilder 1955), and *The Apartment* (Billy Wilder 1960), identified by *Chaplin* as a generic lineage descending from Stiller, would indeed serve as a rich generic context for *To Love* that aimed for "happy kisses" and a light-handed, non-moralizing style.

Even thematically and structurally, there are connections to fifties romantic comedies: the emphasis on play and games in Louise's and Fredrik's interaction evokes *Pillow Talk* (Michael Gordon 1959) and the famous battle of the sexes between a "career girl with only work on her mind and bachelor songwriter with only sex on his mind."[49] However, while *Pillow Talk* concludes in the formation of a nuclear family, an allusion to a successful romance leading to a reproductive future, *To Love* is strikingly different. As openly revealed in PR-publicity, the film ends in a situation where the Don Juan–like Fredrik would like to give up his initially cherished bachelorhood and get married, whereas Louise has now discovered a new life as a bachelorette and is unwilling to return to wifehood.

In the Swedish context *To Love* is hence associated with a debate on sexual morals started in 1962 by Kristina Ahlmark-Michanek with her book that coined the notion of "sex for the sake of friendship" (*för vänskaps skull*). This book, which is said to have started the sex debates in Sweden, took issue with sex education in schools in which sex and love were firmly attached together and where the difference between active male and passive female sexuality was taken for granted. Ahlmark-Michanek became the voice of moral relativism, an advocator of a "pure" sexual morality and "physical compatibility" (*köttets sympati*) and, importantly, a critic of the "worship of virginity" (*jungfrutro*) by which she referred to a notion of female sexuality as something to be protected and regulated.[50] Indicating the power of cinema as an agent in the rising of "public" sex, Ahlmark-Michanek was initially inspired by *La Vérité/The Truth* (Clouzot, 1961) in which she saw Brigitte Bardot's character, a woman accused of having killed her lover, as representative of "pure sexual morality." Ahlmark-Michanek's book became a bestseller and was subsequently filmed in 1965 by Hans Abramson with no less than Harriet Andersson in the main role.

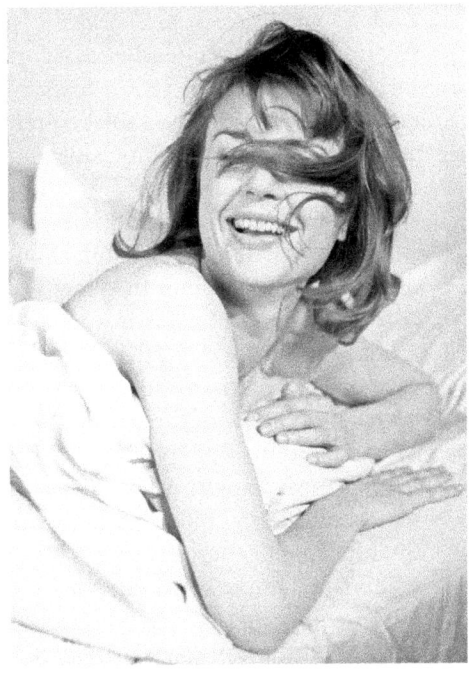

A light-handed, non-moralizing style. Harriet Andersson as Louise in *To Love* (Jörn Donner, 1964). Courtesy of Jörn Donner.

In the light of this Swedish discussion, the approach of *To Love* to sex invokes the notion of sex "for the sake of friendship," even if this connection was never explicitly made in the Swedish public reception. A recurrent critique of *To Love* focused, in Italy and the U.S. but also in Sweden, on the film being just about sex and nothing more.[51] Some saw the film as also failing in its attempt to "to tell about joy, sensuality and love" with "precisely joy, sensuality and love,"[52] or to portray "how natural and nice it can be to love."[53] For others, the film appeared as "a lively romp around the boudoir and around the rationalization of erotica," portrayed in an "attractively life-enhancing" or "surprisingly warm-hearted and humorous fashion."[54]

Whether *To Love* succeeded in its attempted celebration of sensuality or not, the film is highly interesting as one which both aspired to the aesthetic doxa of the French New Wave and the authorial status that this doxa seemed to provide—and took issue with this legacy—in two important senses. First, *To Love* lacks the characteristic sense of transcendental urgency as it features no romantic or tragic seriousness. Instead, being a comedy, it maintains a distanced, non-psychological, and ironic distance to the main characters. Love or sex, this film states, is not about politics or transcendence but about pleasure, and Louise explicitly refuses to discuss politics or social issues when visited by a friend who is a Social Democrat woman activist. On the contrary, as the promotional framing of the film underlined—alongside all spectacular close-ups of Harriet Andersson in bed—the film's narration foregrounded a sense of everydayness. The lovers indeed stay in the bedroom, and the bed remains the key site of this chamber drama, but rather than offering ninety minutes of on-screen sex as one might conclude from many U.S. reviews and sensational review titles, the film shows the couple talking, playing, reading, eating, and spending non-eventful time, as well as having sex.

Second, while being a film about a couple, *To Love* features a female protagonist and not a male hero who in the New Wave fashion often was an alter ego of the filmmaker. As a protagonist, Louise is a wife who turns into a bachelorette and, notably, without tragic consequences. Rather than Madame Bovary, then, as some Italian reviewers suggested, this "merry widow" reads as a version of Ahlmark-Michanek's subject of pure sexual morality or of the single girl as a figure of new ethics of pleasure and a key emblem of the 1960s rise of "public" sex. In a bestseller published in 1962, the same year as Ahlmark-Michanek's book, Helen Gurley Brown famously coined the notion of "single" when envisioning modern women free from the sexual constraints and social mores of their mothers' generation.[55] It is no coincidence that the Social Democrat woman activist who visits Louise is named Nora: as a gesture of generational distinction, the naming both invokes and rejects the protagonist of Henrik Ibsen's *Et dukkehjem/A Doll House* (1879) and the connoted origins of modern feminism.[56] Feminism was nonetheless an significant context for *To Love*. Even if not employed in the PR framings, it was there as a context for production and reception.[57] In this film, importantly, Harriet Andersson, the eroticized icon of "Swedish sin," was transformed into a sexual subject and cast as a subject of desire beyond love and marriage.

In this manner and on many levels, *To Love* both employed and rejected the legacy of "Swedish sin"—as it did with the contemporary phenomenon of the New Wave. Looking at the film's PR-framings and critical reception, its identity appears as fundamentally torn between art cinema and sex film. As such, this paper has suggested, it was highly symptomatic of wider transformations of the public sphere and the meeting of cinema culture and the mediatized sex scene both in Sweden and elsewhere. Furthermore, despite Jörn Donner's insistence on *To Love* being an apolitical film, in hindsight it also seems an example of contemporary debates of sexual politics, supporting and circulating a sex-radical agenda. Most radically, however, the film revised the conventional plot of *Pillow Talk* and gave the bachelorette a new kind of happy ending.

NOTES

1. Leif Krantz, "Kärlek på svenska," *Chaplin* 59 (1965): 458–460. These and all subsequent English translations of quotes from Swedish, Danish, and Italian are mine.
2. Ove Brusendorff and Poul Malmkjær, *Erotik i filmen: Den nøgne bølge* (Copenhagen: Thaning and Appels, 1965), 74. Cited and translated in Jack Stevenson, *Scandinavian Blue. The Erotic Cinema of Sweden and Denmark in the 1960s and 1970s* (Jefferson, NC and London: McFarland and Company, Inc., 2010), 57.
3. Brusendorff and Malmkjær, *Erotik i filmen*, 74, cited and translated in Stevenson, *Scandinavian Blue*, 57.
4. Stevenson, *Scandinavian Blue*, 57.
5. "Erotiskt Pygmalionmotiv i Jörn Donners nya film," *Dagens Nyheter* November 21, 1963.
6. Kevin Heffernan, "Prurient (Dis)interest: The American Release and Reception of *I Am Curious (Yellow)*," in *Sex Scene: Media and the Sexual Revolution*, ed. Eric Schaefer (Durham and London: Duke University Press, 2014), 105–125; David Andrews, *Theorizing Art Cinemas. Foreign, Cult, Avant-Garde, and Beyond* (Austin: University of Texas Press, 2013), 58–63.

7. Eric Schaefer, "Sex Seen: 1968 and Rise of 'Public' Sex," in *Sex Scene: Media and the Sexual Revolution*, ed. Eric Schaefer (Durham and London: Duke University Press, 2014), 8.

8. Frederick Hale, "'Time' for Sex in Sweden: Enhancing the Myth of the 'Swedish Sin' during the 1950s," *Scandinavian Studies* 75:3 (2003): 351–374; Elisabet Björklund, "'This is a dirty movie'— *Taxi Driver* and 'Swedish sin,'" *Journal of Scandinavian Cinema* 1:2 (2011): 163–176; Susanna Paasonen, "Smutty Swedes: Sex films, pornography and 'good sex,'" in *Tainted Love: Screening Sexual Perversities*, eds. Darren Kerr and Donna Pederby (London: I.B. Tauris, forthcoming 2016).

9. Lena Lennerhed, *Frihet att njuta. Sexualdebatten i Sverige på 1960-talet* (Stockholm: Norstedts, 1994).

10. Lennerhed, *Frihet att njuta*, 171–188. For the characterization of *The Silence*, see Jan Holmberg, "Bergman and Sweden," http://ingmarbergman.se/en/universe/bergman-and-sweden, last modified May 19, 2012.

11. Lennerhed, *Frihet att njuta*, 170, quoting Alf Montán from *Expressen* September 15, 1963.

12. Carro Bergkvist, "Premiärmåndag med varning för Donnerwetter," *Aftonbladet*, August 10, 1964.

13. Bengt Michanek, "Här kommer Donner den Store," *Vecko-Journalen*, January 4, 1963.

14. Unpublished document: David Bonnier, "PR-plan för Jörn Donners Att älska," Stockholm May 5, 1964.

15. Bonnier, "PR-plan."

16. Jörn Donner, "Mitt porträtt av Harriet," *Idun: Vecko-Journalen*, April 15, 1963; Åke Cato, "Nu gifter vi oss!," *Expressen*, April 15, 1963; Gunnar Oldin, "Jörn, Harriet och jag," *Nya Folket i Bild*, April 9–15; Monica Zak, "Jörn, han är mjuk och ömsint," *Damernas Värld*, July 11, 1963; Ragnvi Gylder, "Jörn, sa' Harriet," *Svensk Damtidning*, November 13, 1963

17. Bo Johan Hultman, "Att älska," *Chaplin* 48, 6 (1964); Mauritz Edström, "Donners lektion i kärlek," *Dagens Nyheter*, August 11, 1964; Björn Norström, "Donners Att älska komedi med blytyngd," *Stockholms-Tidningen*, August 11, 1964; Jurgen Schildt, "Lite bättre den här gången," *Aftonbladet*, August 11, 1964; Jonas Cornell, review of *Att älska*, *Bonniers Litterära Magasin* 7 (1964).

18. Jörn Donner, *The Personal Vision of Ingmar Bergman*, English translation by Holger Lundbergh (Bloomington: Indiana University Press, 1964).

19. Alf Montán, "Att älska—det är roligt!," *Expressen*, August 2, 1964.

20. Montán, "Att älska—det är roligt!"

21. Camillo Bassetto to Jörn Donner, May 15, 1964.

22. Göran Sellgren, "Narrarna skäller men Donners kärlekslektioner har blivit en god affär," *Göteborgs-Tidningen*, August 13, 1964; Mauritz Edström, "Donner säljer i Venedig," *Dagens Nyheter*, August 31, 1964; Carl Henrik Svenstedt, "Donners festivalbidrag fick kraftiga applåder," *Svenska Dagbladet*, August 31, 1964.

23. Carl Henrik Svenstedt, "Donners festivalbidrag fick kraftiga applåder," *Svenska Dagbladet*, August 31, 1964; "Ingen succé för Donner," *Aftonbladet*, August 31, 1964.

24. For example, Bengt Idestam-Almquist, "Sverige syns och hörs bäst på hela festivalen," *Stockholms-Tidningen*, September 2, 1964.

25. "Una donna libera in un film anti–Bergman," *La Notte*, August 31–September 1, 1964; Gian Luigi Rondi, "Non salvano Amare due grandi interpreti," *Il Tempo*, August 31, 1964; Alberico Sala, "Un furiosi idillio che finisce ned nulla," *Correre d'informazione*, August 31, 1964; Francesco Dorigo, "Immoralità e vuoto nello svedese Amare," *L'Italia del Lunedì*, August 31, 1964; Giovanni Grazzini, "Una vedova impara ad Amare ned film svedese di Donner," *Corriere della Sera*, August 31, 1964.

26. Leo Pestelli, "Un letto è il protagonista del film presentato dalla Svezia al festival," *Stampa Sera*, August 31–September 1, 1964; Aldo Scagnetti, "La voglia di vivere," *Paese Sera*, August 31, 1964; Giovanni Grazzini, "Una vedova impara ad 'Amare' ned film svedese di Donner," *Corriere della Sera*, August 31, 1964; Dario Zanelli, "Come consolare una giovane vedova," *Il Resto del Carlino*, August 31, 1964; Alberico Sala, "Un furiosi idillio che finisce ned nulla," *Correre d'informazione*, August 31, 1964; Luigi Giliberto, "Amare: il chiodo degli svedesi," *Il Gazzettino del Lunedì*, August 31, 1964.

27. Geneviève Sellier, *Masculine Singular: French New Wave Cinema*, transl. Kristin Ross (Durham and London: Duke University Press, 2008), 6.

28. Sellier, *Masculine Singular*, 96.

29. Dario Zanelli, "Come consolare una giovane vedova," *Il Resto del Carlino*, August 31, 1964; Aldo Scagnetti, "La voglia di vivere," *Paese Sera*, August 31, 1964; G.B. Cavallaro, "Copia il suo maestro e Antonioni ma aridamente," *L'avvenire d'Italia*, August 31, 1964.

30. John Coleman, "Not to Speak about Bergman," *New Statesman*, August 21, 1964, 255–256; Klaus Rifbjerg, "Den varme enke," *Politiken*, October 1, 1964; Richard Gertner, "To Love," *Motion Picture Herald*, 2/1965.

31. Andrew Sarris, "Films," *The Village Voice*, September 17, 1964.

32. Eugene Archer, "World Fare for New York Film Festival," *New York Times*, August 2, 1964; Joseph Gelmis, "New York Film Festival is Ready to Roll," *Newsday*, September 11, 1964; Joseph Gelmis, "City's Film Festival Has an Assured Role," *Newsday*, November 29, 1964; "Cinema: Festival in New York," *Time*, September 25, 1964.

33. "Art movies pack the house," *Business Week*, September 19, 1964; Carol Brightman, "Hollywood vs. 'Camp,'" *The New Leader*, September 28, 1964.

34. Justin Wyatt, "Selling 'Atrocious Sexual Behavior': Revising Sexualities in the Marketplace for Adult Film of the 1960s," in *Swinging the Single. Representing the Sexuality in the 1960s*, ed. by Hilary Radner and Moya Luckett (Minneapolis and London: University of Minnesota Press, 1999), 105–132.

35. Bosley Crowther, "Film Festival: Nimble Swedish Frolic…," *New York Times*, September 23, 1964.

36. Article on New York Film Festival, The *Independent Film Journal*, October 3, 1964.

37. Judith Christ, "The New Movies," *New York Herald Tribune*, November 25, 1964.

38. "Pipsqueak Plautus," *Time*, December 4, 1964.

39. "Cinema: Festival in New York," *Time*, September 25, 1964. For a comparison of Donner with Godard, see also Cynthia Grenier, "Sweden's 'To Love' Stars," *New York Herald Tribune*, September 2, 1964.

40. Raymond Haberski, Jr., "Critics and the Sex Scene," *Sex Scene: Media and the Sexual Revolution*, edited by Eric Schaefer (Durham: Duke University Press, 2014), 383–406

41. Wanda Hale, "'To Love'—It's Sex, Sex and More Sex," *Daily News*, November 25, 1964.

42. Hawk., "To Love," *Variety*, September 9, 1964.

43. Hawk., "To Love."

44. Wanda Hale, "'To Love'—It's Sex, Sex and More Sex," *Daily News*, November 25, 1964; Brendan Gill, "To Love," *New Yorker*, November 28, 1964; Mandel Herbstam, "To Love," *The Film Daily*, November 24, 1964. Brendan Gill, "To Love," *New Yorker*, November 28, 1964; Mandel Herbstam, "To Love," *The Film Daily*, November 24, 1964.

45. Alton Cook, "Nonstop Embraces Make 'To Love' Tedious Film," *New York Telegram and Sun*, November 25, 1964.

46. John Coleman, "Not to Speak about Bergman," *New Statesman*, August 21, 1964, 255–256.

47. "Et erotisk lystspil. Premiere på At Elske i Carlton," *Politiken*, September 30, 1964; Richard Gertner, "To Love," *Motion Picture Herald*, 2/1965.

48. T.M. Erotikon, *Chaplin* 50, 6:7 November (1964): 328.

49. Steven Cohan, *Masked Men. Masculinity and the Movies in the Fifties* (Bloomington: Indiana University Press, 1997).

50. Lennerhed, *Frihet att njuta*, 99–111.

51. Lasse Bergström, "Lysande prestation av Harriet Andersson," *Expressen*, August 11, 1964; Carl-Eric Nordberg, "Att älska," *Vi*, 34 (1964).

52. Anne-Marie Vyth, "Sängspel utan kättja," *Filmrutan* 3 (1964).

53. Erland Törngren, "Donner—blindbock i kärlek," *Arbetet* 34 (1964),

54. Bosley Crowther, "After the Festival," *The New York Times*, October 4, 1964; Brendan Gill, "To Love," *New Yorker*, November 28, 1964; Bo Johan Hultman, "Att älska," *Chaplin* 48 (1964): 16.

55. Helen Gurley Brown, *Sex and the Single Girl* (New York: Random House, 1962). On the 1960s media phenomenon, see in Hilary Radner, "Queering the girl," in *Swinging the Single. Representing the Sexuality in the 1960s*, ed. by Hilary Radner and Moya Luckett (Minneapolis and London: University of Minnesota Press, 1999).

56. Louise was criticized as a reactionary female character by Carl-Eric Nordberg, "Att älska," *Vi*, 34/1964.

57. "Den modige Donner," *Aftonbladet*, May 31, 1964.

REFERENCES

Andrews, David. *Theorizing Art Cinemas. Foreign, Cult, Avant-Garde, and Beyond*. Austin: University of Texas Press, 2013.

Archer, Eugene. "World Fare for New York Film Festival." *New York Times*, August 2, 1964.
"Art movies pack the house." *Business Week*, September 19, 1964.
Article on New York Film Festival. The *Independent Film Journal*, October 3, 1964.
Bergkvist, Carro. "Premiärmåndag med varning för Donnerwetter." *Aftonbladet*, August 10, 1964.
Bergström, Lasse. "Lysande prestation av Harriet Andersson." *Expressen*, August 11, 1964.
Björklund, Elisabet. "'This is a dirty movie'—*Taxi Driver* and 'Swedish sin.'" *Journal of Scandinavian Cinema* 1:2 (2011): 163–176.
Bonnier, David. "PR-plan för Jörn Donners Att älska." Unpublished document. Stockholm May 5, 1964.
Brightman, Carol. "Hollywood vs. 'Camp.'" *The New Leader*, September 28, 1964.
Cato, Åke. "Nu gifter vi oss!" *Expressen*, April 15, 1963.
Cavallaro, G.B. "Copia il suo maestro e Antonioni ma aridamente." *L'avvenire d'Italia*,
Christ, Judith. "The New Movies." *New York Herald Tribune*, November 25, 1964.
"Cinema: Festival in New York." *Time*, September 25, 1964.
Cohan, Steven. *Masked Men. Masculinity and the Movies in the Fifties*. Bloomington: Indiana University Press, 1997.
Coleman, John. "Not to Speak about Bergman." *New Statesman*, August 21, 1964.
Cook, Alton. "Nonstop Embraces Make 'To Love' Tedious Film." *New York Telegram and Sun*, November 25, 1964.
Cornell, Jonas. Review of *Att älska*. *Bonniers Litterära Magasin* 7 (1964).
Crowther, Bosley "After the Festival." *The New York Times*, October 4, 1964.
_____. "Film Festival: Nimble Swedish Frolic…," *New York Times*, September 23, 1964.
"Una donna libera in un film anti–Bergman." *La Notte*, August 31–September 1, 1964.
Donner, Jörn. "Mitt porträtt av Harriet." *Idun: Vecko-Journalen*, April 15, 1963.
_____. *The Personal Vision of Ingmar Bergman*. Translated by Holger Lundbergh. Bloomington: Indiana University Press, 1964.
Dorigo, Francesco. "Immoralità e vuoto nello svedese Amare." *L'Italia del Lunedi*, August 31, 1964.
Edström, Mauritz. "Donner säljer i Venedig." *Dagens Nyheter*, August 31, 1964.
_____. "Donners lektion i kärlek." *Dagens Nyheter*, August 11, 1964.
Erotikon, T.M. *Chaplin* 50, 6:7 November (1964): 328.
"Et erotisk lystspil. Premiere på At Elske i Carlton." *Politiken*, September 30, 1964.
"Erotiskt Pygmalionmotiv i Jörn Donners nya film." *Dagens Nyheter*, November 21, 1963.
Gelmis, Joseph. "City's Film Festival Has an Assured Role." *Newsday*, November 29, 1964.
_____. "New York Film Festival is Ready to Roll." *Newsday*, September 11, 1964.
Gertner, Richard. "To Love." *Motion Picture Herald*, 2/1965.
Giliberto, Luigi. "Amare: il chiodo degli svedesi." *Il Gazzettino del Lunedi*, August 31, 1964.
Gill, Brendan. "To Love." *New Yorker*, November 28, 1964.
Grazzini, Giovanni. "Una vedova impara ad 'Amare' ned film svedese di Donner." *Corriere della Sera*, August 31, 1964.
Grenier, Cynthia. "Sweden's 'To Love' Stars." *New York Herald Tribune*, September 2, 1964.
Gurley Brown, Helen. *Sex and the Single Girl*. New York: Random House, 1962.
Gylder, Ragnvi. "Jörn, sa' Harriet." *Svensk Damtidning*, November 13, 1963.
Haberski Jr., Raymond. "Critics and the Sex Scene." In *Sex Scene: Media and the Sexual Revolution*, edited by Eric Schaefer, 383–406. Durham: Duke University Press, 2014.
Hale, Frederick. "'Time' for Sex in Sweden: Enhancing the Myth of the 'Swedish Sin' during the 1950s." *Scandinavian Studies* 75:3 (2003): 351–374.
Hale, Wanda. "'To Love'—It's Sex, Sex and More Sex." *Daily News*, November 25, 1964.
Hawk. "To Love." *Variety*, September 9, 1964.
Heffernan, Kevin. "Prurient (Dis)interest: The American Release and Reception of *I Am Curious (Yellow)*." In *Sex Scene: Media and the Sexual Revolution*, edited by Eric Schaefer, 105–125. Durham and London: Duke University Press, 2014.
Herbstam, Mandel. "To Love." *The Film Daily*, November 24, 1964.
Holmberg, Jan. "Bergman and Sweden." http://ingmarbergman.se/en/universe/bergman-and-sweden, last modified May 19, 2012.
Hultman, Bo Johan. "Att älska." *Chaplin* 48, 16 (1964).
Idestam-Almquist, Bengt. "Sverige syns och hörs bäst på hela festivalen." *Stockholms-Tidningen*, September 2, 1964.

II. Art, Sexploitation and Pornography

"Ingen succé för Donner." *Aftonbladet*, August 31, 1964.
Lennerhed, Lena. *Frihet att njuta. Sexualdebatten i Sverige på 1960-talet.* Stockholm: Norstedts, 1994.
Michanek, Bengt. "Här kommer Donner den Store." *Vecko-Journalen*, January 4, 1963.
"Den modige Donner." *Aftonbladet*, May 31, 1964.
Montán, Alf. "Att älska—det är roligt!" *Expressen*, August 2, 1964.
Nordberg, Carl-Eric. "Att älska." *Vi*, 34 (1964).
Norström, Björn. "Donners Att älska komedi med blytyngd." *Stockholms-Tidningen*, August 11, 1964.
Oldin, Gunnar. "Jörn, Harriet och jag." *Nya Folket i Bild*, April 9–15.
Paasonen, Susanna. "Smutty Swedes: Sex films, Pornography and 'Good Sex.'" In *Tainted Love: Screening Sexual Perversities*, edited by Darren Kerr and Donna Pederby. London: I.B. Tauris, 2015.
Pestelli, Leo. "Un letto è il protagonista del film presentato dalla Svezia al festival." *Stampa Sera*, August 31–September 1, 1964.
"Pipsqueak Plautus." *Time*, December 4, 1964.
Radner, Hilary. "Queering the Girl." In *Swinging the Single. Representing the Sexuality in the 1960s*, edited by Hilary Radner and Moya Luckett. Minneapolis: University of Minnesota Press, 1999.
Rifbjerg, Klaus. "Den varme enke." *Politiken*, October 1, 1964.
Rondi, Gian Luigi. "Non salvano Amare due grandi interpreti." *Il Tempo*, August 31, 1964.
Sala, Alberico. "Un furiosi idillio che finisce ned nulla." *Correre d'informazione*, August 31, 1964.
Sarris, Andrew. "Films." *The Village Voice*, September 17, 1964.
Scagnetti, Aldo. "La voglia di vivere." *Paese Sera*, August 31, 1964.
Schaefer, Eric. "Sex Seen: 1968 and Rise of 'Public' Sex." In *Sex Scene: Media and the Sexual Revolution*, edited by Eric Schaefer, 1–22. Durham, NC: Duke University Press, 2014.
Schildt, Jurgen. "Lite bättre den här gången." *Aftonbladet*, August 11, 1964.
Sellgren, Göran. "Narrarna skäller men Donners kärlekslektioner har blivit en god affär."
Sellier, Geneviève. *Masculine Singular: French New Wave Cinema.* Translated by Kristin Ross. Durham, NC: Duke University Press, 2008.
Stevenson, Jack. *Scandinavian Blue. The Erotic Cinema of Sweden and Denmark in the 1960s and 1970s.* Jefferson, NC: McFarland, 2010.
Svenstedt, Carl Henrik. "Donners festivalbidrag fick kraftiga applåder." *Svenska Dagbladet*, August 31, 1964.
Törngren, Erland. "Donner—blindbock i kärlek." *Arbetet* 34 (1964).
Vyth, Anne-Marie. "Sängspel utan kättja." *Filmrutan* 3 (1964).
Wyatt, Justin. "Selling 'Atrocious Sexual Behavior': Revising Sexualities in the Marketplace for Adult Film of the 1960s." In *Swinging the Single. Representing the Sexuality in the 1960s*, edited by Hilary Radner and Moya Luckett, 105–132. Minneapolis: University of Minnesota Press, 1999.
Zak, Monica. "Jörn, han är mjuk och ömsint." *Damernas Värld*, July 11, 1963.
Zanelli, Dario. "Come consolare una giovane vedova." *Il Resto del Carlino*, August 31, 1964.

Her Body, His Self
Authorship and Gender in I Am Curious (Yellow) *and* I Am Curious (Blue)

ANDERS WILHELM ÅBERG

I Am Curious (Yellow) (Vilgot Sjöman, 1967) was a sexploitation hit with worldwide blockbuster appeal in the late 1960s, more so than its less famous and somewhat more somber companion piece *I Am Curious (Blue)* (Vilgot Sjöman, 1968). The two films contained numerous softcore scenes of sexual intercourse, and generously displayed the bodies of the lead actors, especially the star Lena Nyman, in full frontal nudity. The declared rationale behind the making of the films was to challenge the praxis of film censorship in Sweden, especially the censorship of sexual material.[1] Indeed, the director Vilgot Sjöman's claim to fame and, more to the point, the film's historical significance on a larger scale, remains tied to his role as a trailblazer for commercial, hardcore pornography. Especially *I Am Curious (Yellow)* tends to be commemorated as an emblem of the sexual liberation of the 1960s. However, the two *Curious* films—and the sex portrayed in them—were actually relevant to at least four main issues that are also thematically central to the films themselves: sex, politics, cinematic authorship, and authenticity. Internationally the *Curious* films were mainly discussed in terms of pornography and artistic freedom of expression, for example in the U.S.[2] The initial Swedish reception focused on the political efficacy of the films and their novel use of reflexivity in conjunction with a semi-documentary style. In this context the debate concerned, among other things, questions of authenticity versus ironic reflexivity, the real versus the fictional, authorship, and the body, specifically the female body of the lead actress Lena Nyman.

A few of the contemporary Swedish debaters made keen observations that brought these themes together. In an essay on the *Curious* films in the prestigious literary journal *Bonniers Litterära Magasin* shortly after the release of *I Am Curious (Blue)*, Göran O Eriksson elegantly remarked: "The curious one is Sjöman himself. And behind the question he has Lena vary throughout these two films—'What is the truth about Sweden?'—stands out a more private: 'What is the truth about my curiosity?'"[3] In a similar vein, Kerstin Vinterhed wrote an opinion piece in the national daily newspaper *Dagens Nyheter* where she questioned the substance of the film's portrait of a contemporary, politically engaged woman. The headline of the article snappily summarizes the gist of her—more nuanced—argument: "If Lena Nyman is Vilgot Sjöman's mouthpiece—Why isn't she a man?"[4] The answer to this question goes a long way in explicating the authorial position(s) at stake in the *Curious* project.

In this chapter, I will demonstrate, in contrast to common perceptions of the *Curious* films, the crucial significance of real and implied cinematic authorship in the films as well as in the debate. In addition, I will argue that the common observation, that Lena Nyman's creative contribution to the films has been systematically belittled and underrated, may be linked to the fact that Sjöman consistently plays with the notion that she is a proxy for the male author-subject. In the films, an intricate thematic of splitting and merging is foregrounded, blurring the boundaries between different (more or less "real") versions of "Lena Nyman" and "Vilgot Sjöman." This makes the authenticity of the films difficult to assess. The effect of these mechanisms is simultaneously amplified and obscured by the *Curious* films' *prima facie* status as "sex films." While Sjöman's "sexualism" in the films is concrete and substantial in terms of nudity and sexual acts, he also works with a fundamentally Freudian psycho-sexual dynamic that frames political as well as authorial efficacy in terms of classical perversions and complexes. In conclusion, I will suggest that this intricate thematic structure and sexual overkill threatens to undermine the political urgency of the films.

The Curious *Project*

In Vilgot Sjöman's development as a filmmaker, the *Curious* films are a watershed. He had a background as a literary author of, among other works, several novels in the 1940s and the 1950s. He was also a journalist and film critic, and at the end of the 1950s he oriented himself towards film as a medium of artistic expression, initially as a scriptwriter. Under the tutelage of his long-time friend and mentor, Ingmar Bergman, Sjöman learned to direct. His first film, *Älskarinnan/The Mistress* (1962), was received as part of a small but clearly visible "New Wave" of self-proclaimed Swedish auteurs.

Sjöman's second film *491* (1964) caused quite a stir due to its elements of sexually explicit imagery, foul language, and realistic violence.[5] It was hotly debated as a high profile censorship case in Sweden and elsewhere, which cemented a public image of Sjöman as a sincere, albeit audacious director pushing the limits of artistic freedom of expression. Critics often made note of the decidedly Bergmanesque flavor of Sjöman's subsequent films.[6] But especially in retrospect, Sjöman himself thought of the *Curious* project as a break with Bergman's themes and aesthetics, a father-rebellion of sorts.[7] This autobiographical theme was also hinted at in a published diary accounting for the making of the *Curious* films: *Jag var nyfiken: Dagbok med mig själv/I Was Curious: Diary with myself* (1967).[8] The title alludes to Sjöman's published diary/reportage from the filming of *Nattvardsgästerna/Winter Light* (Ingmar Bergman, 1963), which was called *L136: Dagbok med Ingmar Bergman/L136: Diary with Ingmar Bergman* (1963).

What I refer to here as "The *Curious* Project" consists of at least three texts: The two feature films and the diary. I would argue that other texts and comments, especially by Sjöman himself, could be considered as parts of a continuous artistic project. It seems obvious, for example, that Sjöman considered the partly published trial records from the obscenity trial in New York in 1968 as furthering the discourse on sex, politics, and authenticity that is already a vital part of the films and the journal, thereby adding another layer, as it were, to a highly reflexive construct.⁹ Here though, I will focus mainly on the three core texts.

As narrated by the diary, the *Curious* films were conceived as a form of alternative filmmaking in the vein of *cinéma vérité*. Sjöman wanted to work largely without a script, aiming for a "kaleidoscopical" portrait of Sweden in 1966. A document called the kitchen midden contained briefly sketched ideas or situations (fictional as well as "real" staged events, such as interviews or interventions), and that was all that existed by way of a script during shooting. Sjöman also wanted to stage a collaborative work process, where the actors and the small crew were invited to contribute ideas for the kitchen midden, and for improvised scenes. The storyline of the film(s)—the decision to make two films was arrived at during editing—was loosely about a young girl, Lena (Lena Nyman), her life and political activism in contemporary Sweden, and her love affair with a young man, Börje (Börje Ahlstedt). One of the major creative efforts of the actors resided in what Sjöman liked to call a psycho-dramatic method, through which they were encouraged to incorporate situations and feelings from their own lives in improvised scenes. During the shooting a frame story was introduced, focusing on the relationship and tensions between the director Vilgot (Vilgot Sjöman) and the actress Lena (Lena Nyman), but also providing glimpses of the psycho-dramatic method.

The *Curious* project is a complex, reflexive, and ironic structure. The resulting two films are not, as one might expect, easily understood within a prequel-sequel template. Rather, the two films narrate different parts of continuous story lines, and therefore start and end at roughly the same point in the narrative(s). They are, as Sjöman put it in the diary "parallel films."¹⁰ The two parallel films trace two main story lines, one about the girl Lena, one a frame story about the actress Lena. Somewhat confusingly, all characters appearing at different levels of the story have the same name as the actors playing them, and they play characters with clear similarities to their real life persona. This is especially true in the frame story, but as far as Lena Nyman is concerned also to some extent in the story about Lena, the girl. The introduction of autobiographical story material further serves to blur and complicate the relationship between fiction and reality. For example: Lena Nyman and Vilgot Sjöman had in fact briefly been lovers during and after the shooting of *491*, in which she starred, and *I Am Curious (Blue)* contains footage alluding to the reception of *I Am Curious (Yellow)*, among other things of actual letters addressed to Sjöman and/or Nyman.

The diary itself was always intended for publication; therefore it is not private or intimate, but should rather be considered as a literary product with certain functions. Indeed, the publication of diaries accounting for film productions was a fad. Sjöman's Bergman-book was quite a success, and other books in a similar diary format were published in Sweden around the time of *I Was Curious*, for example François Truffaut's diary from the making of *Fahrenheit 451* (1966). The generic, overall function of the diary from a film production is the manifestation of filmmaking as a serious artistic process worth chronicling. Also, it gives access to the vision of the auteur and the aesthetic and practical crossroads leading to the completed, cinematic work of art.

I Was Curious has some rather specific functions vis-à-vis the *Curious* films. One concerns authenticity: Of course, the diary has the personal, "true" voice of the director, and it also contains brief excerpts from Lena Nyman's diary, lending credence to the idea of a collective process. The diary also contains quite a lot of explanatory discourse on the ambitions and working methods of the project. However, many of these entries are in the mode of the confession, where Sjöman laments the difficulties to fulfill these ambitions. He pleads his guilt that, in fact, he has trouble with the overall structure of the film—known only to himself among the crew, and very vaguely at that—and therefore, he interferes with the material provided by actors, and subjects their efforts to his own artistic agenda. Of course, these confessions also have the cardinal function of claiming authorship. It is no accident that the diary is titled *I Was Curious*, not *We Were Curious*.

Akin to this claiming of authorship, is the function to attempt to control meaning. On the most basic level, this amounts to providing the reader/prospective spectator or critic with a kind of user's guide, explaining the film-within-a-film structure, and the "parallel films," but also the intentions and considerations behind other aspects of the films such as the inclusion of sex scenes, specific themes and motifs, and technical challenges. There is also an autobiographical aspect that makes the reader privy to certain traits in Sjöman's experience of the world, other people and himself. He portrays himself as privately and professionally jealous, sexually inhibited, grumpy, slightly dishonest, and as a self-proclaimed hypochondriac and masochist (in general rather than specifically sexual terms, as someone who is pessimistic, berates himself, and is prone to excessive self-criticism). This, I would suggest, invites comparison with the portrait of the director in the frame story, and it also seems to offer a precise interpretative frame to this portrait.

Sjöman and the Psychoanalytic Imagination

In a letter to Swedish author Gunnel Vallquist, Sjöman once confessed that he had been so embittered that his old friend and fellow author Lars Forssell had called his novels "Handbooks in Freud," that he considered retiring as a writer: "Damned world. Damned world of literature."[11] The comment had obviously offended him, since it maliciously suggested that Sjöman's work was faddish and formulaic.

Sjöman's early criticism and literary work do in fact return consistently to themes and motifs recurrent in psychoanalytic theory, such as infantile fixations (particularly insufficiently resolved oedipal conflict), neurotic symptomology, perversion, and projection. Above all, Sjöman is profoundly symptomatic in his outlook on life and art. In a clipbook of criticism and essays published in the aftermath of the *Curious* project, *Surdegen/The Sourdough* (1969), Sjöman coined the thesis of the unavoidability of autobiography: "Reviews are autobiography. Reporting, interviews, essays in comparative literature—it is all disguised autobiography/…/take anyone who writes about books, people, art, films … they only talk about themselves, just the damn same! Year in and year out."[12] Naturally, in this instance, Sjöman is proving his own point by actually speaking about himself.

This tendency creates a duality in Sjöman's work, a profound sense of self-consciousness. The implicit author of Sjöman's literary texts, for example, is always preoccupied with his own status and point of view, as well as with the extent to which the real author is "really" speaking about some more or less secret (possibly shameful) aspect of himself. This manifests itself in meta-fictional commentary, for example in the form of a character mirroring or commenting on the manipulations of the implicit author. On a thematic level, the problem is treated through the motifs of communication and miscommunication, centering on the, in Sjöman, deeply ironic position of the subject: only able to "speak about itself," and similarly tied to a psychologically defined frame of understanding (others), or point of view, almost to the point of solipsism.¹³

Sjöman's most sustained and poetic formulation of an artistic credo infused by psychoanalysis appears in his book on Hollywood from 1961. There he writes:

> All art exists on the borders of taboo.
> It is created near them; and it pleads with them.
> It is created near them, like those animals born at the water's edge, at the boundary between land and sea. In the water dwells the floating and shapeless; on land form rules, the fixed and complete [...]
> The function of art, the magic of the dolls, becomes quite incomprehensible if one does not accept the concept of a subconscious—discernible like the bottom of the sea through shallow clear water, but unreachable as soon as it deepens. In the unconscious rule the suppressed desires torpedoed by everyday life, dreams forbidden by society. Every society forbids certain behaviors; our competitive society forbids, as we know, revenge, hatred, aggression, bad sportsmanship, selfishness, lovelessness; and it has determined that sexuality is permitted certain expressions but not others. And what does a human do with what she is not allowed to feel? Everything the rules deem taboo? While legitimate impulses make their way to land, to daylight and everyday life, the forbidden ones sink back into the sea, as dreams, swaying phantasmagorias. But they are not eradicated, as we know.
> The boundary between the legitimate and the taboo lies at the water's edge.
> There art is born.¹⁴

This is presented as a psychological critique of the Hollywood Production Code, explaining why the code is not consistent with true and profound artistic expression. It is safe to say, though, that Sjöman is actually laying out a personal poetics, "speaking about himself," as it were. This quote neatly prefigures the director Sjöman's subject choices, his preferred character psychology, and his stance on film as art and on its relationship to the spectator. And, centrally, it captures his view on political, sexual, social, and religious behavior, that they are essentially an expression (a symptom) of repressed, ultimately infantile impulses.

In the latter part of Sjöman's career, this poetics and the development of his work are more openly associated with autobiography, including the four-volume series of autobiographical novels about Linus, and three volumes of "anti-memoirs." Finally Sjöman, a few years before his death, published *Facit till mina böcker och filmer/A Key to my Books and Films* (2004), aiming to uncover, once and for all, the "real" motivations behind his work, the "secrets."

In this sketchily presented evolution, where a psychoanalytically informed poetics is a constant, paired with a tendency to gradually approach and *openly* treat secret "real" material—previously hidden, coded, hinted at—of acute personal significance, the *Curious* project is a breakthrough. It is an attempt to invite the spectator into the creative process and to present a layered, ironic self-portrait that plays with Sjöman's public persona as something of a celebrity. Hence, I would argue that the fundamental and tightly wound duality of the *Curious* project, its dynamics of hiding and showing, of openness versus control in aesthetic form, is indicative of the sheer effort on Sjöman's part to create an authorial subject that he can bear to present to the public.

Vilgot and Lena

In Annika Persson's recent biography of Lena Nyman, she claims—quoting extensively from Nyman's private notes and diaries—that Nyman's contribution to the *Curious* films was substantial: "If the political stuff is Vilgot Sjöman's, all the personal stuff is Lena's."¹⁵

She bears this out by pointing to obvious connections and parallels between Lena in the film and the real life actress, Lena Nyman. Persson wishes to place creative credit where credit is due, and she pointedly remarks on the inequality between Sjöman and Nyman, especially the fact that Sjöman retained very substantial royalties from the films over the years, whereas the co-creators, first and foremost Lena Nyman and Börje Ahlstedt, received only a fixed, relatively small one-time fee for their participation.[16]

Persson also highlights that Nyman took a personal blow from the reception of *I Am Curious (Blue)*. Some male critics and commentators made blatantly sexist and ungenerous remarks. Nils Beyer wrote: "It's also a pity that Lena Nyman is not as cute naked as she is dressed. One did not think much about her fat ass in the last film, since then it had the appeal of a novelty [...]."[17] One of Sweden's most renowned authors, Artur Lundkvist, just about to enter the Swedish Academy at the time, is quoted as saying: "I actually pity Lena Nyman. She's better with her clothes on. One is almost disgusted by her when she is naked."[18] This resulted in a bizarre debate about Nyman's body, where Lundkvist qualified his statements with the enigmatic dictum: "I call for the intelligent body. Lena Nyman's is soulless, a bit stupid."[19] In Persson's account of Nyman's life, this is not simply unfair, but fateful, since Nyman during her first years in film and theatre worked with Sjöman on several occasions while she developed bulimic eating disorders, and a lifelong addiction to alcohol and psychotropic drugs. Nyman was, according to Persson, never content with her body—a body exploited, as it were, by Sjöman in several films, and thereafter dubiously debated in public.

Of course, it is easy to sympathize with Persson's ambitions to properly recognize Lena Nyman's status as an authorial subject of the *Curious* project. Nyman's sheer effort and her "responsibility"—in the eyes of Lundkvist and others—especially for the relative failure of *I Am Curious (Blue)* seems to validate these claims for (more) credit. However, the rhetoric of the *Curious* project tends to undermine Lena's (the actress portrayed in the frame story, as well as the girl in the film-within-the-film) authorial position, and even a clear sense of self-contained subjectivity on her part.

The plot(s) of the *Curious* films is a bit difficult to summarize briefly. In the frame story, Lena and Vilgot are lovers. He is quite jealous, she teases him, flirts with the other actors and so on. He sulks, and sometimes takes his revenge by "tormenting" her as a director. But there are also moments of fun, engagement, and tenderness, when they watch rushes, or when Vilgot explains what he wants with the film or in a scene. Eventually, Lena hooks up with Börje (the actor in the frame story) and Vilgot and Lena break up in the last scenes. This is a reversal of the events in the story about Lena, the girl. She is a political activist engaged in various interviews and interventions together with her friends Ulla and Magnus, forming the vaguely organized "Nyman's Institute." She meets Börje, a car salesman, and they become lovers. There are also scenes that depict Lena's relationship with her father, and of her having a fling with an older man, Hans. Lena takes a trip to various parts of Sweden (both north and south). She meets different people, and she continually conducts interviews and raises questions about contemporary society. Eventually, it is discovered that she and Börje have scabies. They break up and are treated for the disease.

Even in a very detailed blow-by-blow account of "what happens" in the parallel films, it is quite difficult to construct a clear timeline and a causally (or logically) linked chain of events, and there are certainly plot holes that are explained by the production process, lack of script, and overall cinematic mode of articulation.

The complex structure of splitting and mirroring the authorial position in the *Curious* project is most clearly present in the form of the director in the frame story and the author of the diary. As noted, however, contemporary reviewers commented on Lena's function as a proxy or mouthpiece for her director. They may very well have been primed to this conclusion by the diary, which most reviewers seem to have read around the opening of *I Am Curious (Yellow)*, since it is more or less obliquely referenced in several reviews and in the debate following the release of the film. In the diary Sjöman claims that he "hides" behind his actors, and describes how he uses them to sneak his "dream luggage" past his "inner controllers."[20]

One trait in the figure(s) of Lena that is constantly foregrounded is her childishness, as if her curiosity is that of a child. This motif is emphasized in the first scenes of *I Am Curious (Yellow)*. Lena and Vilgot cuddle in an elevator, on their way to Vilgot's flat. A woman appears and throws them a deprecatory glance. When the woman leaves Lena sighs: "Pheew, I thought it was my mom," Later, she is about to spend the night at Vilgot's. While he is preparing for the night, she falls asleep in his bed, clutching a teddy bear. Vilgot sits down beside her, removes the teddy bear and starts to put several pairs of glasses on Lena's sleeping face. When he removes the glasses, her eyes open wide. They tumble on the bed, and Lena pulls his beard. This is reminiscent of the Pygmalion myth. Vilgot blows life into his creation, and it is a child.

In the rest of the parallel films, Lena wears at least eight different pairs of glasses in a number of scenes. The glasses are a complex and contradictory symbol in this context. They point to the fact that she is in a sense in disguise. The glasses are also evidence that her vision is distorted; her sight needs to be guided by someone else (Vilgot, putting the glasses on her). At the same time, and reversely, glasses are of course tools for heightened vision, a tool of the curious and investigative, like the microscope or the camera. Finally, the glasses point to a parallelism or identity between Vilgot and Lena: both look (curiously) on the world through a system of lenses.

Lena's and Vilgot's similarity in this respect is counterbalanced by traits in the film that highlight their complementarity. They are, for example, the subjects of opposite impulses. Understood through a psychoanalytical frame of reference, Vilgot initially represents the sadistic father figure, looking at Lena with voyeuristic delight during the takes. Her demeanor—naked or in various disguises—is a corresponding expression of her exhibitionistic, feminine (therefore "constitutional") masochism.[21] However, this gender-coded dualism (active/passive, looking/looked-at, dominance/submission) is frequently challenged and reversed. Vilgot activates Lena's aggressions in the frame story, as does Börje in the film-within-the-film. Eventually, the Lena character(s) appears as complex, not just a curious child, but also a voyeur filled with oedipal fear and guilt over the sexually tainted aggressiveness she discovers in herself.

Father figures abound in the films, as do, to a lesser extent, mother figures. The Oedipal aspects of Lena's relationship with actual or vicarious fathers and mothers are treated straightforwardly. For example, the primal scene is clearly alluded to in a scene in *I Am Curious (Blue)*. When instructing Lena, Vilgot asks her to imagine that she is a very small child watching her parents. We see the parents speak softly but inaudibly and caress each other. Suddenly the mood changes, the father becomes angry, curses and shakes the mother by her arms. The quarrel ends in an embrace. Vilgot urges Lena to watch the parents through the viewfinder of the film camera. There she sees them, now naked, engaging in intercourse. The composition of the image of Lena and Vilgot, which alternates with the images of the parents, simultaneously suggests merging and splitting of the voyeuristic subject in this fantasy scenario. Much in the same way that Ingmar Bergman famously uses images of faces partly covering each other in *Persona* (1966) to suggest merging subjectivities, Sjöman positions Lena and Vilgot as sharing the subjective point of view of the child. At the same time, the split of this subject position is highlighted, which invites us to imagine this as *one* subject, historically divided, one adult, experienced part of the subject coexisting with, or harboring the memory of another, earlier, infantile and "innocent" part.

This scene seems to be an almost literal interpretation of the primal scene, as imagined by Freud in several texts since the 1890s.[22] Lena's (on all levels of the *Curious* project) relationships with father- and mother figures are all more or less humorously resonant of the Freudian speculations on the Oedipus complex and its presumed relationship to adult manifestations of neurosis and sexual behavior. Even Freud himself is jokingly referred to in one scene as a kind of theoretical or spiritual father figure, along with Karl Marx; the Spanish dictator Francisco Franco figures as a symbolic evil father. This is manifested also on the level of the project that consists of the diary, perhaps especially there. In an attempt, apparently, to control meaning or simply to provide interpretative keys to the prospective audience, Sjöman reflects on the motif of Lena's three father figures. He also specifically invites comparison between the sexually charged, symbolic father-daughter dyads and his own real life experiences. Referring in the diary to a girlfriend called "Kerstin," he relates how their breakup mimics the scenes between him and Lena, rather than the opposite: life imitating art. In an entry dated a few weeks after the

The primal scene à la Vilgot Sjöman. Lena Nyman and Vilgot Sjöman in *I Am Curious (Blue)* (Vilgot Sjöman, 1968). © 1968 Sandrew AB. Still photographer: Kenneth Skogsberg/Walter Hirsch.

breakup he muses: "Happy girl [Kerstin] has passed the test for her driving license, and wants praise. What seemed to be man and woman, that was father and daughter?"[23]

However, Sjöman, I would argue, does not content himself with symbolically occupying the position of the father. The curious, infantile subject is also associated with the film's director in more or less subtle ways, some of them related above. Other instances are more difficult to decode, or were at the time, for example that quite a lot of story material, Annika Persson's claims to the contrary notwithstanding, is actually as consistent with Sjöman's life, as it might be with Nyman's. The portrait of Lena's drunk of a father, the working class milieu, the preoccupation with Franco and Spain and other details as well, are tied to Sjöman's autobiography as well as consistently reiterated in his later work. This opens the possibility to interpret Lena at least partly as a fictionalized version of Sjöman, akin to the boy Linus of Sjöman's autobiographical series (whose father is a drunk, who has a relationship with a much older woman, who is engaged in the issue of fascism in Spain, etc.). Linus is obviously and undeniably a portrait of Sjöman himself in a way that Lena is not. However, the parallels between the characters cannot be accidental, and are, perhaps, highlighted also by the similarity of their names.

The articulation of the authorial subject of the *Curious* project, much as the construction of the narratives about Lena, and Lena and Vilgot, is carried out kaleidoscopically, and in shifting moods (jokingly, sincerely tender and erotic, violent and dramatic). Overall, one can discern a trajectory in this articulation from the first scenes in *Yellow* to the last scenes in *Blue*. In such a reading of the films—a reading sensitive to the "story" about the authorial subject—a meta-fictional level appears that is hidden, as it were, among the many meta-fictional layers of the *Curious* project. In the opening of *Yellow*, Vilgot (the director) wakes up the child (Lena). Their eyes meet and a connection is established between them. He disguises the child with glasses, but thereby he also blesses it with clarity of vision. The films then show the child's situation in the infantile state as well as the nascent and painful insights into the conditions and limitations of this state. Finally, in the end of *Blue* we return to the hospital introduced at the end of *Yellow*. We see Lena mount a gynecological chair. The gynecologist is brusque. He takes a smear test and then inspects her vagina with a tubular speculum. Vilgot is off screen, but from the corresponding scene in *Yellow*, we know that he watches with voyeuristic and sadistic delight. The examination becomes a dense image of the ambivalent infantile subject. On the one hand, it is sadistic, examining, castrating, invading the Other with a dominating gaze and a mechanical extension of the eye. On the other hand it is punished, tied to a chair, ripped open and vulnerable in a classical position of masochistic submission and humiliation. The director and the child, the director that is the child captured in an image that sums up the dilemma of psychosexual infantilism. It also self-referentially shows that the films themselves are a part of this dynamic. The director examines himself with a sadistic gaze—Freud would probably say: the gaze of the superego—on his cruelty, imperfections, and inhibitions. Then he masochistically puts this self-portrait on display as a public spectacle. The masochistic aspect of the enterprise is amplified by the meticulous control exerted by the director over his staged humiliation.

To answer Kerstin Vinterhed's question—why isn't she a man?—by saying that it is because a man would not end up in a gynecological chair in the finale would be to overstate the case. Nonetheless, Lena's gender makes her position as an object of a sadistic director's male gaze "natural." As one part of a bipartite infantile subject that assumes both masculine and feminine positions, and in accordance with the heterosexual norm, she can display the masochistic behavior conventionally associated with femininity.[24] This feminine position has not been the prerogative of female characters in Sjöman's other work. In the script to the film *Siesta Samba*, that was never produced, Sjöman introduces the cartoonist Alexander Twijk, no doubt an ironically treated version of the authorial subject. The first scene is a dream. Almost in a manner of baring the device of the *Curious* project, Sjöman lets Twijk mount a gynecological chair and spread his legs, high up in the air. He wakes up screaming. This scene picks up on Sjöman's motif of the infantile subject in the very first line of *Siesta Samba*: "A pencil draws the image of an infant ... who looks more and more like an old man."[25] This cartoon character turns out to be Twijk. Within the span of a few pages of script, Sjöman repeats and distils the movement of the *Curious* project: from the birth of the authorial subject to its final humiliation. It is not clear what Lena (on any fictional level), let alone the real life actress Lena Nyman, has to do with this movement, if anything. Except, perhaps, as a proxy.

Conclusion: Sexualist or Socialist?

In a classical text about the problem of masochism, Freud writes: "Conscience and morality have arisen through the overcoming, the desexualisation, of the Oedipus complex; but through moral masochism morality becomes sexualized once more, the Oedipus complex is revived and the way is opened for a regression from morality to the Oedipus complex."[26] The *Curious* project is, on one essential level, a masochistic portrait of its authorial subject. The director Sjöman in the frame story and the narrator Sjöman in the diary are characterized by their shortcomings, their ignorance, cruelty, voyeurism, jealousy, and general lack of amiability. The curiosity on display is surrounded with moral decrepitude. The sheer exhibitionism—especially on Sjöman's part—of the films and the diary that was noted by many critics, consists of making this decrepitude a public spectacle. This, again, is a typical masochistic trait.[27] The films do in fact, as we have seen, relate the regressive movement back to the Oedipus complex.

In reviews and debates about the *Curious* films in Sweden, were noted the exhibitionism, the preoccupation with sex—which some critics regarded as somewhat lame and overdone—and a certain lack of clarity regarding the films' political stance or analysis. In particular, critics aligned with the political left found the brew difficult to stomach.[28] In a published editorial conversation about *I Am Curious (Yellow)*, Jonas Sima ponders whether Sjöman should be considered a "sexualist" or a socialist. He argues that Sjöman's goal may have been primarily to tear down sexual taboos, not to reform, let alone revolutionize, society.[29] It is true that the films challenged taboos on sexually explicit representation, especially outside Sweden.[30] However, Sjöman appeared as a "sexualist" on a psychological level, since the films are fixated on the birth throes of adult sexuality. This Freudian brand of "sexualism" also challenged taboos, in particular Sjöman's artistic taboo on actually displaying that the things that "every society forbids" were present in the authorial subject, in himself. Taboos, Sjöman seems to say, are not just there to keep the demonized Other in place, but are crucially active on a personal, psychosexual level; they are there to stop infantile impulses from rising and expressing themselves in the adult subject. The candor with which Sjöman used himself as an example may not have shocked contemporary reviewers, but several did claim that the masochistically tainted exhibitionism of the project thwarted its political ambitions, at least to some degree.[31]

Finally, it would be a misreading to align the *Curious* project and Sjöman's oeuvre too readily with the sexual liberation of the 1960s and the discourse of the time on the liberalization of the individual from restraining conventions (or taboos). This might seem counterintuitive, since Sjöman's films of the period are clear-cut cases of works advancing, in particular, the freedom to treat sexuality candidly. However, Sjöman's brand of Freudianism has its edge on the throat of the infantile subject. Its return and workings in the adult subject are invariably tragic. In Sjöman's oeuvre the incomplete adult is reprehensible, his or her actions are misled, their paths lost; they are weak, gullible, or perverse. Sjöman, in fact, cherishes repression of infantile impulses. Heroism in Sjöman consists of trying to avoid acting "like a child," however difficult or even impossible that might be. Pre-Oedipal "innocence" is hell. That is why Lena's attempts at political activism and sexual freedom end in punishment and tears.

NOTES

1. The censorship agency, Statens Biografbyrå, is satirized in a scene in *I Am Curious (Yellow)*. See also Vilgot Sjöman, *Jag var nyfiken: Dagbok med mig själv* (Stockholm: PAN/Norstedts, 1967), 86.
2. Edward De Grazia and Roger K. Newman, *Banned Films: Movies, Censors and the First Amendment* (New York and London: R.R. Bowker Company, 1982), 298–300.
3. Göran O Eriksson, "Ett barn i Sverige," *Bonniers Litterära Magasin* 4 (1968): 311.
4. Kerstin Vinterhed, "Varför är hon inte karl?," *Dagens Nyheter* October 21, 1967. All quotes from non-English sources are translated by me, unless otherwise indicated.
5. Lena Lennerhed's chapter in this volume.
6. For example in: Göran O. Eriksson, "Klänningen Sjömans tvångströja," *Stockholmstidningen*, October 6, 1964; Lasse Bergström, "Syskonbädd tänder Sjöman," *Expressen*, March 1, 1966; Jurgen Schildt, "Stilfullt, kräset, balanserat," *Aftonbladet*, March 1, 1966.
7. Vilgot Sjöman, *Jag var nyfiken*, 97f. Vilgot Sjöman, *Oskuld förlorad*, (Stockholm: Författarförlaget, 1988), 39.
8. Vilgot Sjöman, *Jag var nyfiken*, 5–6 and 22.
9. See Vilgot Sjöman, *I Am Curious (Yellow): A Film by Vilgot Sjöman* (New York: Grove Press, 1968), 234–243.
10. Sjöman, *Jag var nyfiken*, 185.
11. Quoted in Vilgot Sjöman, *Mitt personregister: Urval 97* (Stockholm: Natur och Kultur, 1997), 326.
12. Vilgot Sjöman, *Surdegen: Svårt med könet, Gud, dikten. Essäer m.m.* (Stockholm: PAN/Norstedts, 1969), 3.
13. An extended analysis of Sjöman's three first novels that bears this out can be found in Anders Åberg, *Tabu: Filmaren Vilgot Sjöman* (Lund: Filmhäftet, 2001), 38–54.
14. Vilgot Sjöman, *I Hollywood* (Stockholm: Norstedts, 1961), 251.
15. Annika Persson, *Jag vill ju vara fri: En bok om Lena Nyman* (Stockholm: Norstedts, 2013), 94.
16. Persson, *Jag vill ju vara fri*, 81 and 90–91.
17. Nils Beyer, "Nyfiken—Ljusblått," *Arbetet*, March 12, 1968.
18. Artur Lundkvist quoted in Annette Kullenberg, "Jag tycker synd om Lena Nyman," *Se* 11 (1968): 17.
19. Quoted in Persson, *Jag vill ju vara fri*, 102.
20. Sjöman, *Jag var nyfiken*, 102–103 and 162.
21. This refers to Freud's assessment that "feminine masochism" is constitutional in women. See Sigmund Freud, "The economic problem of masochism," in *The Standard Edition of the Complete Psychological Works of Sigmund Freud*, volume XIX, ed. James Strachey (London: Hogarth, 1962 [1924]), 159–170.
22. Cf. Sigmund Freud, "From the history of an infantile neurosis," in *The Standard Edition of the Complete Psychological Works of Sigmund Freud*, volume XVII, ed. James Strachey (London: Hogarth, 1955 [1918]), 1–122.
23. Sjöman, *Jag var nyfiken*, 176.

24. Cf. Carol Clover, *Men, Women, and Chainsaws: Gender in the Modern Horror Film* (Princeton, NJ: Princeton University Press, 1992), 21–64.
25. Vilgot Sjöman, *Originalmanuskriptet till den aldrig inspelade Siesta Samba* (Gothenburg: Print on demand, 1997 [1975]), 417 [The manuscript starts with p. 414].
26. Freud, "The economic problem of masochism," 169.
27. C.f. Theodor Reik, *Masochism in Modern Man* (New York: Farrar, Straus and Company, 1949 [1941]), 72–83.
28. Anders Åberg, "The Reception of Vilgot Sjöman's *Curious* Films," in *Swedish Film: An Introduction and Reader*, ed. Mariah Larsson and Anders Marklund (Lund: Nordic Academic Press, 2010 [2001]) 243–249.
29. Stig Björkman, Torsten Manns and Jonas Sima, "Sjöman och Sverige," *Chaplin* 76 (1967): 296.
30. Ulf Jonas Björk's chapter in this volume.
31. Among them, some of the most influential critics and/or voices in the cultural debate, such as: Bo Strömstedt, "Sjöman and Nyman," *Expressen*, October 10, 1967, Eriksson, "Ett barn i Sverige," 311, and Jurgen Schildt, "Vilgot Sjöman beskriver sig," *Aftonbladet*, November 18, 1967.

References

Åberg, Anders. "The Reception of Vilgot Sjöman's *Curious* Films." In *Swedish Film: An Introduction and Reader*, edited by Mariah Larsson and Anders Marklund, 243–249. Lund: Nordic Academic Press, 2010 [2001].
_____. *Tabu: Filmaren Vilgot Sjöman*. Lund: Filmhäftet, 2001.
Bergström, Lasse. "Syskonbädd tänder Sjöman." *Expressen*, March 1, 1966.
Beyer, Nils. "Nyfiken—Ljusblått." *Arbetet*, March 12, 1968.
Björkman, Stig, Torsten Manns and Jonas Sima. "Sjöman och Sverige." *Chaplin* 76 (1967).
Clover, Carol. *Men, Women, and Chainsaws: Gender in the Modern Horror Film*. Princeton, NJ: Princeton University Press, 1992.
De Grazia, Edward, and Roger K. Newman. *Banned Films: Movies, Censors & the First Amendment*. New York: R.R. Bowker Company, 1982.
Eriksson, Göran O. "Ett barn i Sverige." *Bonniers Litterära Magasin* 4 (1968).
_____. "Klänningen Sjömans tvångströja." *Stockholmstidningen*, October 6, 1964.
Freud, Sigmund. "From the history of an infantile neurosis." In *The Standard Edition of the Complete Psychological Works of Sigmund Freud*, volume XVII, edited by James Strachey, 1–122. London: Hogarth, 1955 [1918].
_____. "The economic problem of masochism." In *The Standard Edition of the Complete Psychological Works of Sigmund Freud*, volume XIX, edited by James Strachey, 159–170. London: Hogarth, 1962 [1924].
Kullenberg, Annette. "Jag tycker synd om Lena Nyman." *Se* 11 (1968).
Persson, Annika. *Jag vill ju vara fri: En bok om Lena Nyman*. Stockholm: Norstedts, 2013.
Reik, Theodor. *Masochism in Modern Man*. New York: Farrar, Straus and Company, 1949 [1941].
Schildt, Jurgen. "Stilfullt, kräset, balanserat." *Aftonbladet*, March 1, 1966.
_____. "Vilgot Sjöman beskriver sig." *Aftonbladet*, November 18, 1967.
Sjöman, Vilgot. *I Am Curious (Yellow): A Film by Vilgot Sjöman*. New York: Grove Press, 1968.
_____. *I Hollywood*. Stockholm: Norstedts, 1961.
_____. *Jag var nyfiken: Dagbok med mig själv*. Stockholm: PAN/Norstedts, 1967.
_____. *Mitt personregister: Urval 97*. Stockholm: Natur och Kultur, 1997.
_____. *Originalmanuskriptet till den aldrig inspelade Siesta Samba*. Gothenburg: Print on demand, 1997 [1975].
_____. *Oskuld förlorad*. Stockholm: Författarförlaget, 1988.
_____. *Surdegen: Svårt med könet, Gud, dikten. Essäer m.m.* Stockholm: PAN/Norstedts, 1969.
Strömstedt, Bo. "Sjöman & Nyman." *Expressen*, October 10, 1967.
Vinterhed, Kerstin. "Varför är hon inte karl?" *Dagens Nyheter* October 21, 1967.

Ann and Eve
A Filmmaker Strikes Back

BENGT BENGTSSON

Ann och Eve—de erotiska—Ann and Eve (Arne Mattsson, 1970) begins with a dream sequence. Defenseless, the director, Amos Matthews (Birger Malmsten), is executed in cold blood by the malevolent film critic Ann (Gio Petré), in the middle of a circus ring. After this symbolic image of a director's vulnerability, we follow Ann and her younger, innocent friend Eve (Marie Liljedahl) on a vacation to the Mediterranean. Here, they engage in a number of sexual relations with mainly local talent.

Amos Matthews is an obvious alter ego for the director of the film, Arne Mattsson (1919–1995). Mattsson was one of Sweden's most prolific film directors with a long and varying career encompassing approximately sixty feature films. In the 1940s and 1950s, he had gained critical recognition and commercial success through most notably the acclaimed *Hon dansade en sommar/One Summer of Happiness* (1951), but also films such as the artistic endeavor *Kärlekens bröd/The Bread of Love* (1953) and his skillfully directed crime films. By the end of the 1960s, however, his career was all but shattered, not least due to the unfavorable and sometimes scathing reception of his films by Swedish film critics. This had to do with a change in the film cultural climate. In Sweden, as in many other countries at around the same time, the second part of the 1960s was a turning point in relation to how film was regarded as an art form.[1] The critical climate was radical and inclined towards auteur films and art cinema, which created a generation gap dividing the younger generation of intellectually and artistically oriented filmmakers making films with a social or political edge from an older generation of established and skillful directors who found the new climate difficult to adjust to.

Consequently, during the 1960s, the critical reception of Mattsson became increasingly harsh. To a new and younger generation of film critics and reviewers—who preferred to praise artistically inventive auteur films from abroad—Mattsson's visually striking and expressive films appeared obsolete. The light comedies he intermittently made often received even less favorable reviews and, with a few exceptions, Mattsson's films in the 1960s met with near-unanimous vehemence by the Stockholm reviewers, who found them speculative and cinematically overloaded.

Instead of entering into debate or dialogue with the film critics, Mattsson chose to strike back at his detractors through his own film. *Ann and Eve*, its director, and its reception thus form an interesting case study from a transitional period in (Swedish) film history. In addition, *Ann and Eve* provides a bleak contrast to Mattsson's international breakthrough, *One Summer of Happiness* with its sensuous celebration of young love and life-affirming representation of sexuality. This chapter concerns itself with how Mattsson made use of the sexploitation film to reach out with his message, and with how *Ann and Eve* demonstrates a director's view of the relationship between filmmaking and film criticism. The focus lies on two significant themes in the film: an attack on the "mob" of Swedish film critics and the satire of overindulgent pseudo-interpretations of art films by these same critics.

Stylistically, *Ann and Eve* is a quite typical sexploitation film. It has explicit sex scenes and a fair share of female nudity, but there are no graphic close-ups of genitals as in hardcore pornography. The film's themes are expressed in particular through the character of Ann, a film critic who has, together with some colleagues, pursued Amos Matthews in a smear campaign that eventually concludes with Matthews committing suicide in his despair.

A Has-Been...

During the 1960s, it became apparent that Arne Mattsson was regarded as a has-been in contemporary Swedish film culture. After the initiation of a new film policy and the establishment of the Swedish Film Institute in 1963, a film climate had developed that first and foremost favored auteurs, while it became progressively more difficult for skillful craftsmen such as Mattsson to be taken seriously.[2] Several other professionally practiced filmmakers, who without any greater personal vision simply made the best of other people's screenplays or original works, stopped making films or ended up working for smaller film companies with dubious reputations. As inventive formal devices in the spirit of the French new wave and art cinema modernism became à la mode, contemporary film criticism embraced radical and socially conscious themes. In hindsight, Arne Mattsson himself observed that he had been out of touch with the times:

> There were new producers. There were new directors. There were new reviewers. Everything became like new. Everything old was wrong. Everything was so terribly wrong. [...] The twenty-two year-olds were going to make their films. [...] Social and intellectual film had a heyday in that century [*sic*] that came. Entertainment was reprehensible then. As soon as people even smiled a little in a theater, it was reprehensible. Entertainment was crap.[3]

In interviews and articles, Mattsson commented on the recurring criticism that he placed film technique and craftsmanship before a personal vision: "People think that a doctor should master his instruments—as well as a musician. Why should not a film director need to do so? An artist should be able to master his means of expression."[4]

...Who Tried to Keep Up

In 1967, Arne Mattsson nevertheless attempted to adjust to the current climate. The year before, he had had a critical success with the historical murder and incest drama *Yngsjömordet/Woman of Darkness* (1966), produced by Svensk Filmindustri. *Woman of Darkness* attracted quite an audience and also received a quality award from the Swedish Film Institute.[5] Now, he wanted to become less dependent and to gain more control over his own production by producing his own films. Consequently, he started the company A-produktion which was intended to function as a Swedish United Artists, where filmmakers ventured their own capital in their own productions. At A-produktion he made three feature films: *Mördaren—en helt vanlig person/The Murderer—a Perfectly Ordinary Person* (1967), a psychological drama about how all people could become potential murderers, was trashed and ridiculed by critics, whereupon Mattsson claimed that the critics had not understood that he was making fun of his own crime stereotypes in a conscious self-parody.[6]

The subsequent *Den onda cirkeln/The Vicious Circle* (1967) was a heavy and fateful drama about eternal evil, shot on Gotland. The film received a series of scornful reviews and several critics complained about its obvious Ingmar Bergman-emulations.[7]

Bamse/Bamse—the Teddy Bear (1968) was a tragic love drama with an intricate narrative structure including various levels of time in the style of Alf Sjöberg's *Fröken Julie/Miss Julie* (1951). Made with apparent stylistic inspiration from the French new wave, *Bamse* is a color film whose aesthetics and themes bring to mind Claude Lelouch's *Un Homme et une femme/A Man and a Woman* (1966) and Bo Widerberg's *Elvira Madigan* (1967). According to Mattsson, he put a lot of himself into the film,[8] but by contemporary critics it was regarded as superficial, uninteresting, and full of "weekly magazine drama."[9]

Accordingly, when Mattsson in 1969 began to film *Ann and Eve*, he had made at least two more ambitious films, in cinematic styles that usually worked well with contemporary critics—but for which he received no sympathy. After these setbacks (to a large extent financed by himself) he was apparently almost broke. In one interview he claimed to have been close to committing suicide in his despair, but that the coincidental visit of a person delivering oil to his home had stopped him.[10]

In 1968, he moved temporarily to Spain, in part because producers, according to himself, no longer dared to give him work. In Mattsson's view, he had reached a point where both he and producers realized that it did not matter what kind of film he made—it would still be panned by the critics.[11]

Arne Mattsson v. Film Criticism

The comedy *Sommar och syndare/Summers and Sinners* (1960) was by Mattsson himself, in hindsight, regarded as a turning point. Basically everyone disparaged it, the film was used on Swedish public radio as an example of bad contemporary Swedish film, whereby the distributor and some of the cast also denounced it.[12]

The following year there was a minor stylistic debate concerning the Maria Lang adaptation *Ljuvlig är sommarnatten /Lovely Is the Summer Night* (1961). Veteran film critic Robin Hood (pseudonym for Bengt Idestam-Almquist) wrote an article titled "Trashed for no reason," defending Mattsson and his film aesthetics.[13] However, the new, younger generation of critics did not respond. The only one who found the subject relevant and met Robin Hood with opposition was another veteran of film criticism, Nils Beyer. Beyer claimed that Mattsson "cultivates a kind of art for art's own sake—and his style is fully formed long before he gets his hands on the material. In this manner, he uses violence to force his style on to the content instead of letting content determine the style."[14]

Sometimes the negative critical reception advanced beyond simply crushing words in reviews. For instance, after the unanimously panned fiasco with the Viking farce *Här kommer bärsärkarna/The Wild Vikings* (1965), Leif Furhammar analyzed the film and Mattsson's artistic profile in a long, in-depth, and ironic essay in the film journal *Filmrutan*. The essay concluded with the ambiguous wording: "It is doubtful whether we have had any film that has stretched so deeply towards the bottom of a subject since the 1930s."[15]

Mattsson was hurt by the critique. "You get sad. When they write crap about you. There are those who say that they don't care about reviews, but that's not right, because of course you do," he observed in 1991. "But of course, I know that I have, at some times, made too many films, even made some definitely bad films," he admitted in an article in 1968.[16]

In spite of the harsh reviews and other attacks on him, Mattsson did not, on the whole, defend himself in any public debate with critics. Compared to the new generation of filmmakers, for instance Bo Widerberg and Vilgot Sjöman, who occasionally wrote in daily newspapers and film journals, Mattsson was an outsider. He belonged to an older generation of filmmakers and did not have that position in contemporary public life. When asked in interviews, he complained about unappreciative reviewers. With *Ann and Eve*, however, he found a way to have his say in the matter. His intentions with the film were made explicit in various interviews during its production:

> Regard this film as an assault on Swedish film reviewers! They have haunted me for many years—now I strike back. [...] The film is thus an attack on the critics of Stockholm, who have hounded me for many years. You who write in the papers always get the last word. Now I have used the only option that is available to me: I made a film about the persecution of me. In my case, the issue has not been objective criticism of my films. Everything I have made has been poison, crap, and wretchedness according to the so-called expertise. It went as far as people in the business making bets about what the reviewers would say about my films.[17]

The Evil Journalist or Critic in Other Films

There are some predecessors in Swedish film with regards to striking back at film criticism. Ingmar Bergman made a metaphorical assault in *Smultronstället/Wild Strawberries* (1957), in which the pathetically quarrelling couple who have a car accident quite obviously were modeled on the journalist and reviewer Stig Ahlgren (who wrote in for instance *Veckojournalen*) and his wife, the writer and former actress Birgit Tengroth. A related theme is Vergerus, a recurring figure in Bergman's gallery of characters. One example is the skeptic played by Gunnar Björnstrand in *Ansiktet/The Magician* (1958), who Bergman himself admitted was a veiled malicious portrayal of Harry Schein, at the time film critic for the literary journal *BLM* (Bonniers Litterära Magasin). Bergman also criticizes the myth of the artist and grandiloquent critics in the Fellini-like comedy *För att inte tala om alla dessa kvinnor/All These Women* (1964).

Another Swedish example is Torbjörn Axelman's *Kameleonterna/The Chameleons* (1969) that was shot at around the same time as Mattsson's film. Axelman had also, after several successes on television, had an unfavorable reception of his feature films and felt that he was thwarted by the Swedish Film Institute. His payback had a broader scope and was directed against not only the narrow-minded film critics in the Swedish backwater, but the entire film establishment with cynical film producers, naive actors, and the power-hungry Swedish Film Institute. Among other things, the film satirized the autocratic managing director of the Institute, Harry Schein.

Internationally, there are film portrayals of more or less cynical theater critics in

Citizen Kane (Orson Welles, 1941) and in *All About Eve* (Joseph L. Mankiewicz, 1950), as well as in the morbid horror film *Theater of Blood* (Douglas Hickox, 1973), in which the wronged theater actor played by Vincent Price executes the critics who have previously trashed him. A film director meets his critics in Fellini's *8½* (Federico Fellini, 1963), but this is no negative portrayal of critics but rather a self-criticism directed at the filmmaker himself. A more common cliché is the ruthless, cynical gossip columnist, as in *Ace in the Hole* (Billy Wilder, 1950) and *Sweet Smell of Success* (Alexander Mackendrick, 1957). To some extent, the character of Ann in *Ann and Eve* can be regarded as a further development of this stereotype.

Thematically, *Ann and Eve* followed in the tracks of a string of similar Swedish sexploitation films from the late 1960s, films that often were made as international co-productions—most often in financial collaborations with the U.S. or West Germany.[18] Such films were stable export commodities to American and European grindhouse or second-rate cinemas during these years when the myth of Swedish sin had a high currency and hardcore pornography had not yet overtaken sexploitation.

The production company, Omega Film, had previously had commercial success with some of Joe Sarno's Swedish excursions: *Jag, en oskuld/Inga* (1968) and *Kvinnolek/To Ingrid, My Love, Lisa/Yes, Count the Possibilities* (1969). The former featured, in the title role, the Swedish dancer and model Marie Liljedahl who "possessed an innocence and freshness that was unusual for the majority of sexploitation starlets."[19] Liljedahl played the young and innocent Eve in Mattsson's film, whereas Gio Petré performed the role of Ann. Petré had been one of Mattsson's recurring actresses since the crime film *Mannekäng i rött/Mannequin in Red* (1958), but had more recently performed in the softcore *Jag— en kvinna 2/I, a Woman, Part II* (1968), produced by Omega Film's competitor Minerva Film.

Ann and Eve: *Murder and Mediterranean Sex*

After the initial symbolic shooting of Amos Matthews in the circus ring, we follow Ann and her friend Eve on their vacation and sexual exploits at a Yugoslavian resort.[20] Ann is the driving force behind these exploits—she is skeptical of Eve's idea to remain chaste until her upcoming wedding and urges her to have sexual adventures. To her joy, Ann encounters the famous art cinema director Francesco (Francisco Rabal) at a local party, but he is unmoved by her admiration and remains cold towards her. At the same time, Eve has ritual-like sex with a lesbian night club singer, an event that afterwards provokes Ann's anger.

During the vacation, Ann tells the story of her ongoing, long-lasting smear campaign against the director Amos Matthews. Matthews is Ann's former lover—"the best lover I've ever had"—whom she broke up with after a misunderstanding, believing that he had left her for another, younger woman. This is why she began the smear campaign, aided by a group of similarly insidious film critics, but she continued even after she realized that she had been deceived by a female rival. Eve questions her motivations, and also asks why she writes her reviews under a male pseudonym.

Unexpectedly, Ann receives a message from Sweden that Matthews has committed suicide. Shaken, she steps up on the stage of a local restaurant and performs as an homage the deceased's favorite song "Det gör detsamma var du stupar, kavaljer" ("It doesn't matter

66   II. Art, Sexploitation and Pornography

where you fall, cavalier").[21] She is conscience-stricken and seized with remorse, and states sadly: "It wasn't suicide—it was murder. We were a small group that killed him."

The "Mob" of Critics Under Attack

As mentioned, there are two notable themes in the film: on the one hand the assault on the Swedish "mob" of critics, and on the other the satire of overindulgent pseudo-interpretations by the same critics.

The mob-like coalition of film critics is basically depicted through Ann's description of the organization and purpose of the group and her discussions about it in detailed conversations with Eve. This group of film critics—"the clique"—is purposefully driving Matthews to his death:

> The whole thing was too far advanced to stop it. The group we had formed had found someone to destroy, someone to kill in order to show their own power. We kept writing bad reviews of his works. I wrote once: "Amos Matthews should realize that his films are outdated, tired and meaningless. Goodbye, Amos!" [...] But we don't confine ourselves only to his professional activities; we attack even his personal life. Though it has nothing to do with his filmmaking, we do everything we can to ruin his reputation, to destroy his nerves and to kill him. The clique has decided to kill Amos and that's the way it is. There's no way out for him.

Innocence destroyed. Marie Liljedahl as Eve in *Ann and Eve* (Arne Mattsson, 1970). Courtesy of Studio S.

Ann and Eve are juxtaposed, with Ann as the active part and Eve the passive one. Ann embodies *film criticism* in general—that she uses a male pseudonym possibly underlines that she represents the whole corpus of critics. At the same time, Eve can be regarded as a symbol for *Swedish film*. She is exploited, soiled, humiliated, and eventually becomes pregnant—in contrast to Ann's chosen childlessness. Already from the beginning, the calculating Ann intends to pull Eve down from her pedestal of sexual virtue and make her as unsentimentally hypocritical as is Ann herself. She urges her to have sex with various local acquaintances and encourages her to ignore her fiancé and the upcoming wedding.

The final obliteration of Eve's innocence is completed towards the end of the film in a strange and ambiguous sequence on a truck bed, where a number of Italian workers play cards over Eve and proceed to have sex with her, one by one, in what seems like a group rape. Eve's symbolic status as Swedish film is also implied by her appearance in Amos Matthews' posthumous production *The Emperor's New Clothes*, screened at the Venice film festival at the end of the film. Here, she performs (among other things) an inner monologue about her erotic experiences.

This "film-in-the-film" begins like a kind of affected, fragmented art cinema parody, but continues with a trailer with quotes from reviews—clearly referring to the film critics of Stockholm. Rather than the film, these quotes seem to review Eve's personal character:

> "...AN EXAMPLE TO YOUNG WOMEN OF TODAY! m.a.o. swanstedt DAILY NEWS"
> "...SUPERBLY UNSPOILED!! m. hed WEEKLY CHRONICLE"
> "...SO YOUNG, SO REAL, SO ADMIRABLE!!! Jörgen Schön, B.A."
> "...YOU CAN POSITIVELY FEEL HER FRESHNESS!!!! Jonathan Suori, PRESSWEEK"[22]

That these named critics have got her character all wrong—and see her as a prime example of the Swedish woman—reflects the actual critics' own misleading image of Swedish film.

In addition, one can note that Ann in the color and style of her hair looks quite a lot like the well-known intellectual Marianne Höök. Höök had a public persona as an emancipated, open, and modern woman of the 1960s. Moreover, she was a good friend of Harry Schein and frequently appeared with the inner circles of the Swedish cultural elite. In this way, the film targets not only film critics, but also the Swedish Film Institute, the cultural establishment, and the contemporary film climate.

Art Cinema and the Emperor's New Clothes

The second theme of the film is the satire of how critics fall for incomprehensible symbols and contrived cinematic devices in "difficult" films. Mattsson illustrates this through Ann's encounter with the celebrated, artistic director Francesco—who seems like a mix between Federico Fellini and Michelangelo Antonioni. Ann meets him first at the Yugoslavian resort and then later at the Venice film festival. This director, pronounced a genius by critics, rejects Ann's and her colleagues' praise and explains his contempt for their in-depth interpretations of his complex films—interpretations that find intentions at which he never aimed.

When Ann ingratiatingly states that "your films are always so artistically clean—you never speculate commercially when you make a film," Francesco responds with sarcasm:

> My dear, commercial films are always speculations. If you don't understand that, it's a shame that you've chosen to be a film critic. You either speculate that a film will be popular and there will be crowds, or that someone like yourself will like it, and praise it as an artistic film and make it possible to get an award at a film festival. But don't forget one thing: a filmmaker exists for the public, not for you. The words you print don't mean a thing in the final analysis, the public's alive and you're not.

Ann, however, holds her ground and comments on a scene of running water in Francesco's film *The Sun*:

> When you made that drain-water picture it must have meant something to you—and you didn't want to admit it later. When we saw that picture we understood what you wanted to express. We understood the significance. Oh yes, by the way—it was a marvelous symbolism in just that scene....

According to Francesco, this scene ended up in the film by coincidence. He replies:

68　II. Art, Sexploitation and Pornography

Francesco functions as a spokesperson for Arne Mattsson's views. Francisco Rabal as Francesco and Gio Petré as Ann in *Ann and Eve* (Arne Mattsson, 1970). Courtesy of Studio S.

> People don't look at films like critics do. There is no similarity between what you've written and what I intended. [...] You'll go on interpreting things to show what a smart critic you are, how brilliant you are, to the public. [...] All the same, with complete honesty, I must frankly say I'm disgusted by your asininity, your stupid little film interpretations. But that won't stop you, I know that. You keep on. And the next time at Cannes or Venice when you interpret my work, I know you'll praise it. You write brilliantly, in spite of the fact that you've been unable to understand the film at all. And I will appropriate your praise, and in public conceal my contempt for you and your kind. Goodbye!

Here, Francesco functions as a spokesperson for the opinions Arne Mattsson expressed in contemporary interviews and articles, such as in *Film & Bio* 1968:

> The audience has an instinct for good films. Obviously, I don't mean that the best films are always the ones that are the most successful with the audience. But film is an art form for the large audience, and it is the audience that decides the fate of a film.[...] Certainly, it is never fun to get bad reviews, but there is nothing more unbearable than an empty movie theater.[23]

Using a successful art film director as a spokesperson creates a minor imbalance in Mattsson's defense of audience-friendly entertainment film. This imbalance is resolved by Francesco's experience of self-doubt and his explicit wish that he himself could direct a film that would make people laugh. At the Venice Film Festival at the conclusion of the film, Francesco's latest production *The Emperor's New Clothes* is screened to general praise, but so is Amos Matthews' posthumous film with the same title. Francesco shows up at the screening of Matthews' film and laughs at the film's depiction of sanctimony.

In the final sequence of *Ann and Eve* Francesco walks naked down a street. On the soundtrack we hear voices expressing various admiring superlatives: "Brilliant!" "Fantastically directed and performed!" "A symbol of the relief felt afterward by the perpetrator of a compulsive act!" "So society-oriented and at the same time so detached from the world!" But the celebratory comments are deflated by a child's words: "But he's got nothing on!"[24]

Intention and Speculation

In *Ann and Eve*, Arne Mattsson thus presents different but quite concrete accusations against contemporary Swedish film criticism: Critics do not understand how to appreciate professional skill, good craftsmanship, and films that aim to entertain without any radical or social implications. They are easily deceived by artistic profundity that provides them with the potential to interpret widely and groundlessly without any respect for the director's intentions. And there really is a Swedish "mob" of critics that functions as a community and that had, together, agreed to trash his films.

According to Mattsson, there was reason to believe these ideas about the Swedish "mob" of critics, because the same devastating phrases could show up in several different reviews at the same time.[25] In a number of interviews he made statements about this clique: "The film is a very harsh attack on one of the nastiest phenomena I know. That awful contempt that the clique of critics show towards films that aim to be entertaining. To filmmakers with ambitions of entertainment, these critics use a language as if they were guilty of murder."[26]

Notwithstanding that Mattsson's film can be regarded as a speculative sex film typical of its time, *Ann and Eve* uses erotic scenes foremost as a means to communicate its critical message. On the whole, sexuality appears as a destructive force in the film. Ann's hatred of Amos Matthews is an expression of her jealousy and compensation for her erotic frustration. In addition, sexuality becomes a way of soiling Eve; it characterizes the women and becomes a significant element in the power play between them.

In many ways, *Ann and Eve* diverge from contemporary, similar films. Rarely does a sexploitation film provide such a bleak, anxiety-ridden, and dark image of sexuality and erotics. Hence, the film also differs

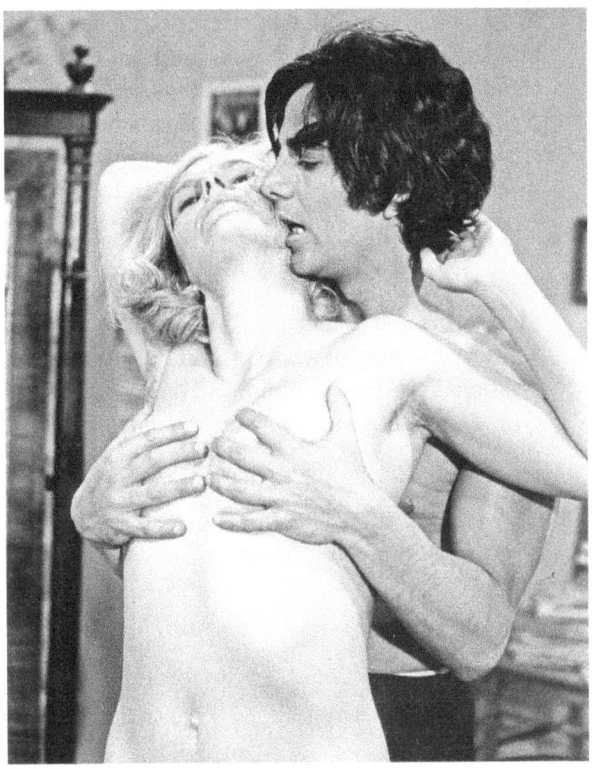

Sexuality as a destructive force. Gio Petré as Ann and Julián Mateos as the hotel porter in *Ann and Eve* (Arne Mattsson, 1970). Courtesy of Studio S.

quite remarkably from *One Summer of Happiness*, which, although ending tragically, seems to revel lyrically in the young couple's sensual awakening.

The contemporaneous Scandinavian sexploitation film often made emancipation a significant theme. Sexuality in these films functioned as a tool for liberation and self-realization.[27] The set-up of *Ann and Eve*, with two attractive Swedish women who go on vacation to the Mediterranean, seems perfect for a tale of emancipation—but instead, *Ann and Eve* aligns itself with a long tradition of anxiety-filled representations of sexuality in Swedish art cinema.

Already in 1965, Leif Krantz discussed the phenomenon of anxiety-ridden sex in Swedish films in the film journal *Chaplin*, and exemplified "the in Sweden so stubborn connection between sexual acts and impressions of awfulness and discomfort" with Ingmar Bergman's *Tystnaden/The Silence* (1963) and Vilgot Sjöman's *491* (1964). Krantz asks: "Can it be a coincidence that almost every Swedish film director portrays love as something repulsive or as a threat. [...] Why do they not speculate in light-heartedness, release, sexual happiness without any clouds of doom?"[28]

Persecution or Paranoia?

Ann and Eve premiered in Cannes in 1970, where distribution rights to the film were sold to a number of countries. In reports from the festival and reviews from the premiere in Stockholm the following year, Swedish critics were scathing and completely bewildered by Mattsson's accusations of a "mob" of critics and falsely profound reviewers: "After this film, I find the Mattsson case merely tragic," observed Hanserik Hjertén in *Dagens Nyheter*.[29] "It is very serious if this is how Mattsson experiences his situation. Paranoia is always serious," Leif Dahlström wrote in *Expressen*.[30] "At the request of Jörgen Schön in the newspaper BA [...] I, however, feel compelled to provide an impartial disclaimer: Arne Mattsson is not the victim of personal 'persecution,' but a victim of his own films after 1960," Jurgen Schildt stated in *Aftonbladet*.[31]

As expected, *Ann and Eve* did not initiate any debates about the relationship between filmmakers and film critics. No one seemed to find Mattsson's attack justified. Only Jurgen Schildt took note of Mattsson's claim that film critics would find profound messages and symbolism without ground—an opinion that was rejected without any further discussion. One single reviewer, Elisabeth Sörenson in *Svenska Dagbladet*, saw a streak of hope in the film:

> Let us now hope that Mattsson, when he has had the opportunity to speak his mind, can move on and leave behind the impasse in which bitterness has placed him. In that case, this by itself completely dead film, will have served a purpose.[...] Come on, Arne Mattsson, and knock out the critics with a Film instead of an act of revenge![32]

This, however, was a hope in vain. Mattsson's career continued quite dismally.

Commercial Success but Professional Suicide

From a wider perspective, *Ann and Eve* was not only an attack on film criticism, but moreover reflected a general sense of being an outsider in a society and film culture in which Mattsson felt alienated.

Within the national film industry, this discourse of public debate had a great influence since the inception of the Swedish Film Institute and the new film policy implemented in 1963. Conditions for production changed with the new goals of stimulating so called "quality film." Quality film was conceptualized as auteur-directed art films, which were thus privileged before the solidly crafted films by an older generation of directors. Filmmakers such as Hasse Ekman did not fit in with this new production environment and left the industry during the first half of the 1960s. Others tried to adapt to the new climate. Gunnar Höglund and Torgny Wickman, both of them experienced as industrial filmmakers, ventured into the production of sex films with for instance ... *som havets nakna vind/As the Naked Wind from the Sea/One Swedish Summer* (1968) and *Ur kärlekens språk/Language of Love* (1969) respectively.

Accordingly, when Arne Mattsson made *Ann and Eve*, he probably had a sense of having little left to lose. Previously his films, albeit made for the large audience, had to some extent been dependent on a good reception in the papers. As a sexploitation film, *Ann and Eve* belonged to an undergrowth of film that relied more on successful promotion than good reviews,[33] whereas art films are included in a cultural circulation with festival screenings, national support of artistic directors, attention from critics and an audience that is open to unconventional narrative devices.[34]

By moving into sexploitation, Mattsson could ignore the institutional framework of Swedish film criticism and instead focus on the international sexploitation market. Simultaneously, he could make fun of art cinema and its admirers. Several statements Mattsson made around the time of the release of *Ann and Eve* underline his serious ambition to begin making films abroad:

> Because it is so wrong in Sweden right now to be a story-teller, an entertainer, I will have to turn to other parts of the world. [...] Right now only drugs, whoring, and long exposition about little asocial Charlie are accepted as representative of Swedish society. There should be room for other topics.[35]

In spite of the commercial success of *Ann and Eve*, no new international career came out of it. Offers were conspicuously absent and Mattsson's next project was the violent thriller *Smutsiga fingrar/Dirty Fingers* (1973) in collaboration with Inge Ivarson, his old companion from low-budget company Bison Film in the 1960s. It would be five years before his next feature film, *Mannen i skuggan/Black Sun* (1978), and to support himself Mattsson spent the years in between making commercials for Hitachi and other companies. In hindsight, Mattsson observed that for his part the cinematic assault on Swedish critics had, in fact, boomeranged:

> *Ann and Eve* was, so to speak, a suicide. And I was actually quite aware that I was committing it. I was rabid with the Swedish critics. I thought I would be able to get my revenge, but I couldn't. [...] It was a suicide that had very dire consequences for me. Because after that I couldn't make films in Sweden for a very long time. [...] I had to become housebroken first. I was not housebroken in Sweden above all. And I was forced to stay here as well. In 1973, I didn't make anything.[36]

Nevertheless, after well-publicized and attention-drawing troubles with censorship, *Ann and Eve* made more than 18 million dollars at the U.S. box office.[37] In its U.S. promotion, its Swedish origin and the previous achievements of its two female leads were emphasized in the tag line: "Just when you thought you'd seen it all ... the love animals of *Inga* and *I, a Woman, Part II* trade secrets."[38] Mattsson himself had a share in the profits, and afterwards he claimed: "The only good thing about this film is that it gave me some good money. [...] It was a great success across the world. Not because of what

I say about the reviewers, absolutely not, but there were erotic scenes in it that people hadn't seen before. Their jaws dropped."[39] However, no serious discussion about film criticism and its relation to filmmakers came out of Mattsson's foray into exploitation. Critics still have the last word—a condition that this film did not change.

NOTES

1. For discussions of the changing Swedish film climate in the 1960s, see for instance Anders Åberg, *Tabu: Filmaren Vilgot Sjöman* (Lund: Filmhäftet förlag, 2001); Cecilia Mörner, *Vissa visioner: Tendenser i svensk biografdistribuerad långfilm 1967–1972* (PhD diss., Stockholm University, 2000); Mariah Larsson, *Skenet som bedrog: Mai Zetterling och det svenska sextiotalet* (Lund: Sekel bokförlag, 2006). For a more general description of the changing perception of cinema in Europe, see for instance David Bordwell, *Narration in the fiction film* (London: Methuen, 1985).
2. With the new film policy, films received financial support in relation to their "quality." See Per Vesterlund's and Lars Diurlin's respective contributions to this volume.
3. From an interview in 1991 for a planned book by Stina Klemming, co-worker on several of Arne Mattsson's later films. The interview transcript is kept in the archive at the Swedish Film Institute.
4. Lars-Olof Löthwall: "Arne Mattsson och kritikerna," *Chaplin* 7 (1970).
5. The income from ticket sales at 1.8 million SEK were supplemented with 318,000 SEK in quality support and loss compensation from the Swedish Film Institute. *Svensk filmografi 6: 1960–1969*, ed. Jörn Donner (Stockholm: Svenska filminstitutet, 1977), 36.
6. According to an interview in *Arbetet*, February 6, 1967.
7. An overview of the reception can be found in *Svensk filmografi 6*, 343c.
8. Klemming.
9. An overview of the reception can be found in *Svensk filmografi 6*, 427c.
10. According to interview in *Helsingborgs Dagblad*, June 12, 1970.
11. Bengt Bengtsson, Interview with Arne Mattsson, February 28, 1985.
12. Alf Montán, "Bottenfilm. Ekonomisk spekulation" *Expressen*, September 28, 1960.
13. Bengt Idestam-Almquist, "Utskälld utan skäl," *Stockholm-Tidningen*, August 29, 1961.
14. Nils Beyer "Mattssons skötesynd," *Stockholm-Tidningen*, September 1, 1961.
15. Leif Furhammar: "Matsson-film [sic] bryter med konventioner," *Filmrutan* 1 (1965).
16. Arne Mattsson, "Verkligheten är inte enkel ens på film!," *Film & Bio* 9 (1968).
17. Interview in *Aftonbladet*, March 23, 1970. See also interview in *Arbetet*, January 23, 1970.
18. See for instance Mariah Larsson, "Practice Makes Perfect? The Production of the Swedish Sex Film in the 1970s" in *Film International* special issue Making Movies in Europe, 6 (2010), 40–49.
19. Eric Schaefer: "'I'll take Sweden': the shifting discourse of the 'sexy nation' in sexploitation films," in *Sex Scene: Media and the sexual revolution*, ed. Eric Schaefer (Durham and London: Duke University Press, 2014), 219.
20. The main part of the film is shot in what today is Croatia.
21. An unfinished and unpublished memoir manuscript by Arne Mattsson has the same title. In the archive of the Swedish Film Institute.
22. These names are clearly modeled on Stockholm critics, such as Mauritz Edström, *Dagens Nyheter*, Jurgen Schildt, *AB/Aftonbladet* and Jonas Sima, *Expressen*.
23. Arne Mattsson, "Verkligheten är inte enkel ens på film!," *Film & Bio*, 9 (1968).
24. Mattsson had for a long time been skeptical of what he regarded as overindulgent interpretations of films. Already in his comedy *Kyssen på kryssen/The Kiss on the Cruise* (1951), he ridicules intellectual filmmakers and critics, personified in an esoteric scholar who makes an exaggeratedly profound interpretation of a film.
25. Klemming.
26. Tony Kaplan: "Hämnd för dåliga recensioner. Mattson klipper till." *Arbetet*, January 23. 1970. See also Lars-Olof Löthwall: "Arne Mattsson och kritikerna." *Chaplin* 7 (1970)
27. Schaefer, "'I'll Take Sweden,'" 207 and 215c.
28. Leif Krantz, "Kärlek på svenska," *Chaplin*, 9 (1965).
29. Hanserik Hjertén, "Obehaglig klagovisa av Mattsson" *Dagens Nyheter*, August 17, 1971.
30. Leif Dahlström, "Tjatig sexfilm av Arne Mattsson." *Expressen*, August 17, 1971.
31. Jurgen Schildt, "Arne Mattsson i suckarnas dal..." *Aftonbladet*, August 17, 1971.

32. Elisabeth Sörenson, "En regissörs hämnd" *Svenska Dagbladet*, August 17, 1971.
33. Raymond J Haberski Jr highlights some exceptions, like for instance Andy Warhol's *Fuck/Blue Movie* (1969) and censored films such as Vilgot Sjöman's *Jag är nyfiken—gul/I Am Curious (Yellow)* (1967), in "Critics and the Sex Scene," *Sex Scene: Media and the sexual revolution*, ed. Eric Schaefer (Durham and London: Duke University Press, 2014), 386–391.
34. David Bordwell, *Narration in the Fiction Film* (London: Methuen, 1985), 228–233.
35. Lars-Olof Löthwall, "Arne Mattsson och kritikerna," *Chaplin*, 7 (1970). See also Tony Kaplan, "Hämnd för dåliga recensioner. Mattson klipper till." *Arbetet*, January 23, 1970.
36. Klemming, 129, 138.
37. At least according to the Internet Movie Database, imdb.com.
38. Schaefer, "'I'll Take Sweden,'" 228.
39. Klemming, 138, 128.

REFERENCES

Åberg, Anders. *Tabu: Filmaren Vilgot Sjöman*. Lund: Filmhäftet, 2001.
Beyer, Nils. "Mattssons skötesynd." *Stockholm-Tidningen*, September 1, 1961.
Bordwell, David. *Narration in the Fiction Film*. London: Methuen, 1985.
Dahlström, Leif. "Tjatig sexfilm av Arne Mattsson." *Expressen*, August 17, 1971.
Donner, Jörn, ed. *Svensk filmografi 6: 1960–1969*. Stockholm: Svenska filminstitutet, 1977.
Furhammar, Leif. "Matsson-film bryter med konventioner." *Filmrutan* 1 (1965): 31–32.
Haberski, Raymond, Jr. "Critics and the Sex Scene." In *Sex Scene: Media and the Sexual Revolution*, edited by Eric Schaefer. Durham, NC: Duke University Press, 2014.
Hjertén, Hanserik. "Obehaglig klagovisa av Mattssson." *Dagens Nyheter*, August 17, 1971.
Idestam-Almquist, Bengt. "Utskälld utan skäl." *Stockholm-Tidningen*, August 29, 1961.
Kaplan, Tony. "Hämnd för dåliga recensioner. Mattson klipper till." *Arbetet*, January 23, 1970.
Krantz, Leif. "Kärlek på svenska." *Chaplin* 9 (1965).
"Kyssen på kryssen." Screenplay. Archive of Uppsala Filmstudio [Uppsala Film Society].
Larsson, Mariah. "Practice Makes Perfect? The Production of the Swedish Sex Film in the 1970s." *Film International* special issue, *Making Movies in Europe*, 6 (2010): 40–49.
_____. *Skenet som bedrog: Mai Zetterling och det svenska sextiotalet*. Lund: Sekel bokförlag, 2006.
Löthwall, Lars-Olof. "Arne Mattsson och kritikerna." *Chaplin* 7 (1970): 325–326.
Mattsson, Arne. "Det gör detsamma var du stupar, kavaljer." Unfinished and unpublished memoir manuscript. Archive of the Swedish Film Institute.
_____. "Verkligheten är inte enkel ens på film!" *Film & Bio 9* (1968): 36.
_____. Interview by Bengt Bengtsson, February 28, 1985. The recording is kept by the author.
Montán, Alf. "Bottenfilm. Ekonomisk spekulation." *Expressen*, September 28, 1960.
Mörner, Cecilia. *Vissa visioner: Tendenser i svensk biografdistribuerad långfilm 1967–1972*. Ph.D. diss., Stockholm University, 2000.
Schaefer, Eric. "'I'll take Sweden': The Shifting Discourse of the 'Sexy Nation' In Sexploitation Films." In *Sex Scene: Media and the Sexual Revolution*, edited by Eric Schaefer. Durham, NC: Duke University Press, 2014.
Schildt, Jurgen. "Arne Mattsson i suckarnas dal..." *Aftonbladet*, August 17, 1971.
Sörensen, Elisabet. "En regissörs hämnd." *Svenska Dagbladet*, August 17, 1971.

A Porn of One's Own?
Anne-Marie Berglund and Weekend in Stockholm

MARIAH LARSSON

In the 1970s, pornographic film was still colored by its earlier terms of production and consumption as illicit stag films for primarily a male audience. Although a few feminists and consciousness-raising groups demonstrated some degree of curiosity about the emancipatory potential of representing sexuality on screen, this curiosity did not, in Sweden, lead to any further explorations. Quite early on, the Swedish feminist movement established a harsh policy on pornography—it was regarded not only as a capitalist and patriarchal exploitation of women and sexuality for profit, but as the "most extreme deformed variety of oppression" of patriarchy, in effect teaching men to treat women as objects and making women feel bad about themselves.[1]

However, as Klara Arnberg has demonstrated regarding the pornographic press in Sweden 1950–1972, the feminist dictum that porn is made by men, for men, can be questioned. Comparing the number of women entrepreneurs in early Swedish porn publishing with the number of women in publishing in general, it seems that they were proportionally more common within pornographic publishing. Since the ratio of women to men was very small in the general publishing industry, the somewhat larger share of women in porn publishing does not mean that there was a large number of them. Nonetheless, Arnberg notes that "a number of women played important entrepreneurial roles in making pornography a mass-market commodity by challenging the obscenity regulations before the 1971 decriminalization of pornographic publishing in Sweden."[2]

Arnberg argues that women's entrepreneurship within porn publishing followed a general pattern of women getting involved with small-scale businesses where the threshold to entering is lower. Accordingly, the production of theatrically released, feature length hardcore pornographic films cannot be readily compared to the publishing of comparatively cheap magazines with "dirty pictures," since the cost involved—even for low-budget productions—was significantly higher. In 1970s Sweden, there was only one such film directed by a woman. Anne-Marie Berglund wrote, starred in, and directed *Veckända i Stockholm/Weekend in Stockholm* in the mid–1970s. Berglund had performed in two other pornographic films, as an extra in the Swedish *Sams/Swedish Family Games* (Calvin Floyd, 1974), and in the Danish Zodiac-film *I løvens tegn/In the Sign of the Lion* (Werner Hedman, 1976), but *Weekend in Stockholm* seems to have been her own venture;

in the credits the film is described as "A short story by Anne-Marie Berglund" (she would continue on to writing poetry and novels).

This essay sets Berglund's film against the backdrop of women's cinema and the pornographic film. During the 1970s, women filmmakers within mainstream (non-pornographic) cinema were beginning to gain a small foothold, inspired by the feminist movement as well as cultivated (albeit under resistance) through the various film schools that had been established in the 1960s.[3] However, although sexuality could well be explored by women filmmakers on-screen, as evidenced by for instance Mai Zetterling's *Nattlek/ Night Games* (1966), Liliana Cavani's *Il portiere di notti/The Night Porter* (1974), or Nelly Kaplan's *Nea* (1976), Berglund does not fit into the category of European women directors or avant-garde or, for that matter, experimental filmmakers, due to her choice of genre (hardcore porn) and format (theatrically released 35mm). Still, I would argue that her film, seen in relation to Berglund's career as a whole, blurs the boundary between pornography and art by connecting hardcore porn to poetry and short story prose.

The Swedish Porn Film Until 1976

In 1971, pornography was legalized in Sweden. Already during the late 1960s, however, films with quite explicit sexual content had been produced and released, from *Jag— en kvinde/Jag—en kvinna/I, a Woman* (Mac Ahlberg, 1965) and *Jag, en oskuld/Inga* (Joe Sarno, 1968) to the first of the *Language of Love*-films, *Ur kärlekens språk/Language of Love* (Torgny Wickman, 1969), which would be the first theatrically released 35mm film in Sweden to show—albeit educationally and scientifically framed—close-ups of sexual intercourse.[4] As several pieces in this volume point out, the "sex barrier" was broken by established film directors including Ingmar Bergman, but there was also a conscious attempt at dismantling the Swedish film censorship in general, orchestrated by no less than Harry Schein, the CEO of the Swedish Film Institute.[5] Nevertheless, the institution of film censorship would remain until 2011, whereas the clause in the penal code that forbade obscene material was removed in 1971.

The immediate results of this legalization are debatable. Many testified that porn became ubiquitous and even those who had previously been in favor of removing the obscenity clause from the penal code lamented the development that took place in the first few years of the 1970s.[6] In the mid–1970s, there was already a resistance to pornography that had several disparate parties: social workers, police officers, and politicians who found that the establishments where porn films as well as other sexual entertainment were on offer were also breeding places for crime, debasement, and prostitution; women who took offense by the loud advertising for such places and for other commodities such as porn and men's magazines; journalists who reported about sleazy destitution and titillating sex scandals; and feminists who understood the production as well as the consumption of porn as exploitation and a reification of women.[7] The Christian groups that had protested sexually explicit representations in the 1960s, however, became less visible during the 1970s, but were still active.

The sense of pornography invading public space came, however, to a large extent from the sex stores, sex clubs, and porn cinemas where pornographic films were screened and from the pornographic press and men's magazines, rather than from the production of Swedish sex films. Although the Swedish production of sexually explicit feature films for theatrical release during this decade totaled approximately one fifth of the entire domestic film production, this number needs to be set in relation to the fact that the 1970s was not a very prolific decade for the national cinema.[8] In all, around 200 films were made. Of these, around forty were, in various ways, sexually explicit.

These sexually explicit feature films were very different from each other.[9] Some were sex comedies, quite discreet in how much sex they showed, but with a lot of nudity and innuendo. Others were sex educational sequels to the successful *Language of Love* from 1969, or "social problem" films, similar to the American exploitation films described by Eric Schaefer.[10] Again others were soft-core with a narrative/number structure but without graphic close-ups of penetration, while still others were hardcore. Not infrequently, hardcore inserts with body doubles were used, and such versions of the films could be made both for export and for domestic release. There were also genre hybrid films including Bo A. Vibenius' *Thriller—en grym film/Thriller—A Cruel Picture/They Call Her One-Eye* (1974), which combined a rape-revenge narrative with, in some versions, hard-core inserts like described above, and whose combination of sex and violence caused the National Board of Film Censors to ban it from public screening. A string of films produced by Inge Ivarson and directed by Mac Ahlberg might be described as attempts to make "quality porn"—comparatively high budget productions based on literary, erotic classics and with an international cast—*Flossie* (1974), *Justine och Juliette/Justine and Juliette* (1975), *Bel Ami* (1976), and *Molly—familjeflickan/Molly* (1977), whereas others were more cheaply made.[11]

Approximately half of the forty sexually explicit films were hardcore in their Swedish release. One was written and directed by a woman. If there is any point to statistics with such low numbers, one could say that one out of twenty films, or 5 percent, of the hardcore porn films for theatrical release were female-directed. This can be compared to around 10 percent of all feature-length films for theatrical release, although this number is problematic in itself since some of these films were documentaries that were co-directed by a man and a woman.

Women Directors

Ever since the women's movement within film and film studies began to interrogate moving images and gender in the early 1970s, one of the issues at stake has been the notion of women filmmakers.[12] Within popular genre cinema as well as within the festival fare, women directors are rare, but although the main focus within the auteur-centered film studies for a long time has been women directors, the scope has widened and now includes female producers, screenwriters, and cinematographers as well.[13] The issue concerns statistics—how large a percentage of films are directed by women? What were their budgets and how much did they make at the box office? How often is a film festival opened with a film by a woman? How many awards do such films win? Other questions raised by the issue of women filmmakers deal with cinematic language and modes of representations—Do women make films differently and in that case how and why? Will gender equality in film improve with more women directors? Does a woman director have to be a feminist filmmaker?[14] Archival research has been devoted to finding women behind the camera during the silent era through the Women Film Pioneers Project, and another project deals with Nordic women filmmakers.[15] It is worth noting that during the silent era, there were comparatively more women involved in film production than after the breakthrough of sound, and the statistics concerning popular genre film has since then not really improved.[16] Within various European film institutions—like the Swedish Film Institute—efforts have been and are made to increase the number of women filmmakers.[17]

During the 1970s and 1980s, a small but significant number of women directors began appearing within especially the European art cinema.[18] Many of these came out of some kind of involvement with the feminist movement, and many of them had also gone to the various film schools that were established during the post-war years. If film industries previously had functioned based on a kind of apprentice system—in which a homosocial, predominantly male network provided both training and opportunities for filmmaking—these film schools created new kinds of networks, as well as enabled young directors to make their first films.[19] In addition, feminist networks and associations and film festivals specifically organized around films directed by women (in for instance New York and Toronto) began appearing in the 1970s. Various chapters of what would become Women in Film and Television International were established from 1973 and onwards and the network Women Make Movies in 1972.[20]

Within pornographic film, this development was later and somewhat different, both because of the fraught relationship between the women's movement and pornography and because of its primarily commercial circuit of production and consumption. With distribution and exhibition often in areas with a lower degree of access for women,[21] consumption of pornography remained a mainly male tradition, which in its turn influenced production. Although films such as *Deep Throat* (Gerard Damiano, 1972) and the Danish *Bedside* and *Zodiac* films reached a wider audience of both men and women, it is undoubtedly so that the majority of pornographic films had a majority male audience.

In the U.S., Candida Royalle began her production of Femme films in 1984, directed towards women and couples, and other pornographers have followed suit, including Puzzy Power (the subsidiary of Lars von Trier's Zentropa) in the late 1990s, Anna Span in the early 2000s, and Erika Lust a few years later. Another direction has been taken in queer, lesbian, and feminist porn in which an exploration of female and queer sexuality through moving images is part of a simultaneously theoretical and activist project.[22]

Consequently, Berglund's film cannot function as an illustrative example of any "movement" of the 1970s. As a hard-core porn film directed by a woman, *Weekend in Stockholm* is quite unique in 1970s Sweden.

Anne-Marie Berglund as Poet, Writer ... Pornographer?

Anne-Marie Berglund has a working-class background, something which is pointed out in articles on her literary work.[23] She was born in Finland in 1952, and moved to Sweden with her family when she was five. In 1977, her first collection of poetry (*Luftberusningen*/"Air intoxication") was published, and by now she is a well-established author, the recipient of several national literary awards, although her latest publication is from 2005.

The theme of sexuality in Berglund's works is often brought up by scholars, but they do not always seem to know how to deal with it. For instance, Katarina Davidsson observes that "Berglund sings praise to physical love, but sexual encounters often turn into an empty, soulless act [---] Berglund early on received the epithet of the poetess of sexuality and ecstasy because she wrote so-called 'erotic' poetry. Whatever that means."[24] Sexuality, in Berglund's writings, is regarded as something which holds a promise that is rarely fulfilled, that "dies in a mechanic movement, where dirt and refuse is all that is left of a human being."[25] Even when discussing Berglund's linguistic terms, the "indolently posed slut-thinking" is mentioned in passing.[26] Short stories by Berglund are included in two collections of women's erotic writing from the 1990s. One of these texts is an original short story in the form of a diary about a man in a hotel who becomes erotically entangled with the cleaning woman, her daughter, and a young man.[27] The other one, titled "A Dog Does It Better," is taken from one of Berglund's own collections and is very short. A woman is picked up by a stranger who promises to perform cunnilingus on her. As the title implies, he does not perform it very well.[28]

There is an interesting paradox in Berglund's works, since the scholars who have written about her usually are feminist, literary scholars and as such not likely to be interested in this one film, which still can be understood through Berglund's oeuvre as a whole. There is a handful of articles on Berglund, and she is commented on in connection to women's literature, where her poems and prose are regarded as part of the "confessional" literature that was a strong tendency in women's writing in the 1970s.[29] In an article in *Tidskrift för genusvetenskap*, Kajsa Widegren and Linnea Isberg reject that understanding of Berglund in order to instead read her works as "a struggle for and with the power of words." Through a spectrum of girlhood theory, by which they see girlhood—and Berglund's girl characters—as (in) a nomadic state, they analyze her writing with no mention of her filmmaking.[30]

One exception to this exclusion of Berglund's film is an article by Carl-Mikael Edenborg, historian of ideas, in the literary journal *Res Publica* from 1999.[31] Edenborg devotes a relatively large part of his article to *Weekend in Stockholm* and another film, *Orfelias erotiska uppfostran/L'Éducation d'Orphélie* (1981), to which Berglund—according to Edenborg—does the (Swedish) voice-over.[32] Edenborg reads the narration, aesthetics, and point-of-view of *Weekend in Stockholm* as highly "Berglundian," while the porn scenes are regarded as monotonous and "grey."[33] Even the non-glamorous settings of the film (the friend's apartment, a wintry Stockholm), are described as going against the porn cliché and aligning itself with Berglund's general universe. The female lead—described as shy, clumsy, and girlish—is also related to Berglund's main characters in later poems and short stories.

Weekend in Stockholm

One of the interesting things about *Weekend in Stockholm* is how far removed it is from a later canon of Scandinavian feminist pornography, such as the commercially produced Puzzy Power films (*Constance*, Knud Vesterskov, 1998; *Pink Prison*, Lisbeth Lyughøf, 1999; and *HotMen CoolBoyz*, Knud Vesterskov, 2000) or the collective and political work *Dirty Diaries* (2009). Its very ordinariness makes it stand out. *Weekend in Stockholm* follows a typical narrative: a young woman, Marie, comes to Stockholm to visit a friend and has a sexual awakening. Its mode of narration, too, is both simple and typical—there is very little direct sound or dialogue in the film, but mainly the voice-over of Berglund. Voice-overs are used frequently in Swedish 1970s porn films, both soft-core and hardcore, as in, for instance, *Flossie*, narrated by Jack Frank who plays the main character, and *Den k ... familjen/Happy Family* (Heinrich Arlach, 1976), narrated by Marie Forså. Berglund's soft and delicate voice actually resembles the girlish timbre of Forså a bit, thereby also conforming to the general mode of female voice-overs in Swedish porn at the time.

Although likely motivated by a low budget and a need for simplicity, the choice of voice-over and little direct sound results in a strong privileging of Berglund's own narrative as the character Marie. She describes, interprets, and explains to us what happens and how she feels about it. Instead of being met at the train station by her friend, it is the friend's boyfriend who picks up Marie, and she describes a kind of tension between them. Later, at night, she hears the couple having sex and she gets out of bed, watches them and masturbates, and then joins them. The next day, Kent, a friend of the couple, comes along. They visit an old porn cinema (Fenix) where they watch *Buried Treasure*, the by now famous animated porn film from the late 1920s, but they also have sex.[34] When the young woman leaves Stockholm, she thinks back upon the weekend with joy, hoping to see Kent again.

The film was produced by GeBe Film AB, a distribution company owned by Gösta Friberg and Bernt Elmquist that produced four films in the 1970s: one short, *Fången/ "Imprisoned"* (1975), *Weekend in Stockholm*, and two hardcore Joe Sarno films, *Kärleksön/Love's Island"* (1977) and *Fäbodjäntan/Come and Blow the Horn* (1978), and brought funding to other film projects.[35] Anne-Marie Berglund, as mentioned, wrote, directed, and starred in the film together with Norwegian-born Knud Jörgensen, who had performed in a handful of Danish and Swedish porn films in the 1970s. Berglund and Jörgensen might have met during the shooting of *In the Sign of the Lion* in which they both performed, but Jörgensen's most famous role (at least in Sweden) would probably be as the farmhand in *Come and Blow the Horn*. The cinematographer, Torbjörn Lindqvist, would also work on *Come and Blow the Horn*. The other actors in the film are unknown. It is quite clearly a small production, unlike the more lavish films produced by Inge Ivarson and more in line with *Happy Family* and the hardcore Sarno films, but it still falls, production-wise, quite clearly into the genre of hard-core pornography: the production company, the cinematographer, and at least one performer did regular hard-core porn.

There is another interesting paradox in relation to Berglund's film and her later, literary works. Although sexuality is a dominant theme in her poetry and prose, as evidenced by scholars and critics and mentioned above, it is rarely portrayed as something positive, whereas the film has a desirous curiosity, a cautiously happy tone, and an upbeat ending. This can perhaps be explained by generic conventions—porn is expected to have an affirmative view of sex, in which sex is always good but can become even better, whereas poetry and short story prose are forms that almost demand introspection and reflection, questioning and ambivalence. According to *Nordic Women's Literature*, Berglund's women characters "seek confirmation through a destructive, often violent, sexuality."[36] Davidsson writes that "for this writer, free love becomes an *imperative* and thereby something that basically limits—more of an anti-bourgeois principle than any particular acting out of desires."[37] The sexuality in *Weekend in Stockholm* is not destructive or violent, nor does it limit the main character. Rather, it liberates. Although initially presented as something slightly threatening, this feeling gives way as Berglund's character, Marie, becomes bolder throughout the film. During the drive from the train station, her friend's boyfriend touches her legs while driving and kisses her in an oak grove during an excursion from

80　II. Art, Sexploitation and Pornography

the car. She puts off his caresses, but feels something bewilderingly exhilarating about the kiss, and during dinner with the friend the boyfriend fondles her under the table, which is presented in a comedic manner. Nevertheless, all initiatives taken by the man are averted, whereas later at night she undresses and masturbates in her room, hears the couple making love, and gets up to watch. This time, she herself feels—according to the voice-over—emboldened by her own desire, and takes the initiative to watch the other two. Through the opened door, she looks on while the couple is having sex on the bed until she receives an invitation to join. Although she does await this invitation, her own agency—urged on by the strange sense of lust and desire that has been awakened during the day and while she has been listening in on the couple's intimacy—is underscored in this scene, as she openly gazes upon the couple through the door that she has opened.

Then again, female sexual agency and female voyeurism is not unusual in pornography and can be found in a number of the Swedish-produced films of the time, such as in *Flossie* or *Molly*. A recurring trope within pornography is the peeping Tom (or Jane), but with the slight difference that, in this film, the gazing upon the mating couple (the Freudian primal scene) is done quite overtly. The atmosphere, for Marie, has gradually built up to a point where she is led by her own desires and unhindered by her shyness.

In generic porn humor fashion (à la Harry Reems in *Deep Throat*), the boyfriend becomes exhausted by the attentions of two such demanding women and calls his friend Kent. The next day, they go together for a wintry walk in a park. In the voice-over, Berglund's character describes how she feels about Kent, and how she begins to imagine his naked body, and how she finally gets a chance to kiss him. Here, again, the initiative of the woman is underlined but, interestingly, in the voice-over rather than in the images,

Emboldened by her own desire. Anne-Marie Berglund as Marie in *Weekend in Stockholm* (Anne-Marie Berglund, 1976). Courtesy of Klubb Super 8.

which depict a traditionally acted kissing/seduction scene: the girl leans back towards a tree and Kent leans over her and kisses her.

The interlude at the porn cinema Fenix shows not your standard hard-core porn fare, but a legendary animated film. *Buried Treasure*—or *Eveready Harton in Buried Treasure*, or *Pecker Island*—is a humorous, animated, silent film, most probably from 1928 or 1929.[38] Here, Eveready, "the most famous animated porn character from the silent era," lives in a fraught but passionate relationship with his gigantic and unruly penis which literally has a life of its own.[39] The penis "runs off on its own, gets bent and has to be pounded back into shape, goes after a woman but accidentally fucks a man, and runs into the business end of a cactus, among other, often painful mishaps."[40] All of these mishaps are not shown in *Weekend in Stockholm*, but the scene at Fenix runs for around five minutes and shots of the two couples in the cinema seats are interspersed with shots from the film, of which we thus see quite a bit. Whether the choice of *Buried Treasure* is intentional or not is hard to say—it might be that it simply was that film that was being shown at Fenix at the time, but most likely it was part of a longer, non-stop program of films which means that the filmmaker could have chosen another part of that program. However, regardless of how consciously chosen that particular screening was, *Buried Treasure* adds a sense of crude, joyful bawdiness to *Weekend in Stockholm*, in particular as the main characters are shown to be laughing their heads off as well as becoming aroused by the film. In addition, Constance Penley describes in connection to *Buried Treasure* a certain theme common to a bawdy tradition that is expressed in both songs and stag films, namely "male humiliation" caused by "the penis run amok."[41]

Thereby, *Weekend in Stockholm* includes, in a metafilmic moment, scenes from a narrative of humorously uncontrollable masculine sexual desire, where the penis is conceived of both as a troublesome child and as the most cherished male appendix. As such, it presents an interesting juxtaposition to the more cautiously poetic sexual awakening of the main character, Marie, but also an indication of the world she is becoming initiated into as she begins her sexual adventures. If *Weekend in Stockholm* is, somehow, about recently aroused female desire and tentative but promising forays into the world of sexuality, *Buried Treasure* is about a world where sexuality (and the penis) is a constant; a relentless and mostly unsuccessful hunt for intercourse.

Although they make out during the scene in the porn cinema, the actual sex scene between Marie and Kent is delayed until later that night, after champagne and some dancing in the apartment of Marie's friend. Here it is Marie who takes Kent's hand and brings him into her bedroom. The scene begins with fellatio and continues on to vaginal penetration, accompanied by romantic instrumental music. Afterwards, they take a walk through the Stockholm dawn, while Berglund's voice-over describes her experience. "The ice had just broken," she says in a blatantly symbolic phrase, as we see the waters of Stockholm in the poetic light of the rising sun. Edenborg observes: "There is a sense of miracle, of a *favorable destiny*, over what happens; in particular in the first episode with the strange excursion to the grove of oak trees and in the one with the walk through the dawn. By a combination of lucky coincidence and will power, the girl experiences an adventure that is both nice in all its shabbiness and teaches her something."[42]

There is a final sex scene, between Kent, Marie, and what appears to be Kent's bisexual girlfriend, and then Marie leaves on the train. In a circular fashion, the film ends like it started, with Marie on the train with Stockholm passing by the window outside.

A Porn of One's Own?

Anne-Marie Berglund's directorial venture might seem timely. Coming of age just at the break between the sex-liberal 1960s and the 1970s of legalized pornography and anti-porn feminism, Berglund could be regarded as one individual in the (small but significant) wave of women directors within European cinema in the 1970s and 1980s. *Weekend in Stockholm* might also be regarded as an attempt by a young feminist to explore a previously oppressed and inhibited female sexuality, with the goal of liberation and empowerment. However, none of these explanatory models really work. Berglund's film is unique, not only because it is the only woman-directed porn film in Sweden in the 1970s, but also because Berglund herself did not continue making such films—apart from the voice-over to *L'Éducation d'Orphélie*—or any films at all, for that matter.

In relation to her further career, the film's uniqueness becomes even more extrapolated. Although sexuality continued to be significant in Berglund's work, poetry as such seems to be as far removed from pornography in the cultural sphere as can possibly be. As Peter Lehman notes "Porn [...] has led to a new polarization: art/no art. Or, the old opposition can be rephrased as high art/popular culture in which case we now have culture/porn. In other words, what is presumably some form of culture and value is opposed to unregenerate porn that lacks any redeeming value. Indeed, not only does it lack value, it threatens all values."[43] Although literary and feminist scholars who have studied Berglund's poetry and prose may have known about this film,[44] they have in that case chosen to disregard it since it cannot really be fathomed within her work as a serious author—accepted by literary critics, recipient of several awards—but also, perhaps, as a woman writer. As Lehman goes on to argue, however, the stark opposition between pornography and art or pornography and culture is misleading.[45] Not only is the border between the two categories blurred, it is also not uncommon for artists—experimental, avant-garde, surrealist—to be interested in bodies and sexuality, like for instance Kenneth Anger, Andy Warhol, or Nelly Kaplan. Although Berglund's film is not a perfect fit within any of the current or eventual movements except the Swedish sex film wave, *Weekend in Stockholm*, read through Berglund's persona, blurs the distinctions between art and porn.

Notes

1. Editorial in *Kvinnobulletinen*, 3–4, 1973, p. 3.
2. Klara Arnberg, "For Men, by Men? Women's Business Activities in the Pornographic Press Compared to the Overall Publishing Industry in Sweden 1950–1972" in *NORA—Nordic Journal of Feminist and Gender Research*, 21:1 (2013): 21–40, 22.
3. See B Ruby Rich, *Chick Flicks: Theories and Memories of the Feminist Film Movement* (Durham, NC: Duke University Press, 1998); and Tytti Soila, "Sweden," in *Nordic National Cinemas*, ed. Astrid Söderbergh Widding et al. (London: Routledge, 1998), 206–208.
4. Elisabet Björklund, *The Most Delicate Subject: A History of Sex Education Films in Sweden* (PhD diss., Lund University, 2012), 153–200.
5. See Per Vesterlund's and Maaret Koskinen's respective contributions to this volume.
6. See for instance Hans Nestius, *I last och lust: sexuella bilder förr och nu*, Stockholm: Prisma, 1982.
7. See Klara Arnberg, *Motsättningarnas marknad: den pornografiska pressens kommersiella genombrott och regleringen av pornografi i Sverige 1950–1980* (Lund: Sekel bokförlag, 2010), 277–279, and Mariah Larsson, "Contested Pleasures," in *Swedish Film: An Introduction and Reader*, eds Mariah Larsson and Anders Marklund (Lund: Nordic Academic Press, 2010), 205–213.
8. Leif Furhammar, *Filmen i Sverige—en historia i tio kapitel och en fortsättning*, third edition (Stockholm: Dialogos förlag and Svenska filminstitutet, 2003). Cf. Mariah Larsson, "Drawing the Line: Generic Boundaries of the Pornographic Film in Early 1970s Sweden," in Conference Proceed-

ings from NorLit Conference, eds. Magnus Ullén et al (Linköping: Linköping University Electronic Press, 2009-2010); Mariah Larsson, "Practice Makes Perfect? The Production of the Swedish Sex Film in the 1970s," *Film International* special issue Making Movies in Europe, 8:6, 2010: 40-49; Klara Arnberg and Mariah Larsson, "Benefits of the In-Between: Swedish Men's Magazines and Sex Films 1965-1975," *Sexuality and Culture*, June 2013, 18,:2, 2013: 310-330. See also Mariah Larsson, *The Swedish Porn Scene* (Bristol: Intellect, forthcoming).

9. Larsson, "Drawing the Line."
10. Eric Schaefer, *"Bold! Daring! Shocking! True!": A History of Exploitation Films, 1919-1959* (Durham: Duke University Press, 1999).
11. Mariah Larsson, "Practice Makes Perfect?"
12. See e.g. Alison Butler, *Women's Cinema: The Contested Screen* (London and New York: Wallflower Press, 2002); Jacqueline Levitin, Judith Plessis and Valerie Raoul (eds.), *Women Filmmakers: Refocusing* (Vancouver and Toronto: UCB Press, 2003).
13. See e.g. Martha M Lauzen, "The Celluloid Ceiling: Behind-the-Scenes Employment of Women on the Top 250 Films of 2014" (San Diego State University, 2015). The Celluloid Ceiling Report is issued annually from Center for the Study of Women in Television and Film at San Diego State University.
14. See e.g. Butler, *Women's Cinema*; Levitin, Plessis and Raoul, *Women Filmmakers*; Lucy Fischer, *Shot/Countershot: Film Tradition and Women's Cinema* (Princeton, New Jersey: Princeton University Press, 2014 [1989]).
15. Women Film Pioneers Project, https://wfpp.cdrs.columbia.edu/; Nordic Women Film http://nordicwomenfilm.com/.
16. Lauzen, "The Celluloid Ceiling."
17. See § 6 in the film agreement for 2013, Filmavtalet 2013, http://www.sfi.se/Documents/Filmavtalet/Filmavtalet/2013%20%C3%A5rs%20filmavtal.pdf, p. 2.
18. See Barbara Koenig Quart, *Women Directors: The Emergence of a New Cinema* (New York and London: Praeger, 1989).
19. Soila, "Sweden," 206-208.
20. Rich, *Chick Flicks*.
21. Jane Juffer, *At Home with Pornography: Women, Sex, and Everyday Life* (New York: New York University Press, 1998).
22. Ingrid Ryberg, *Imagining Safe Space: The Politics of Queer, Feminist and Lesbian Pornography* (PhD diss., Stockholm: Stockholm University, 2012). Available online http://urn.kb.se/resolve?urn=urn:nbn:se:su:diva-68789
23. See for instance Thomas Nydahl, "Den livslånga resan bort från klaustrofobin," essay and interview in Nydahl, *Politisk geografi: prosavandringar i sju städer: med tre kompletterande samtal om liv och litteratur med Anne-Marie Berglund, Gabriela Melinescu och Suzanne Brøgger* (Hallaryd: Occident, 2002), 103-115; and Carl-Mikael Edenborg, "Är vi alls intressanta? Att läsa Anne-Marie Berglund som pornograf, illusionist och desillusionist; något om noveller och att göra snedsteg," *Res Publica*, 35-36 (1999), 183-200.
24. Katarina Davidsson, "Flykten från vanligheten. Anne-Marie Berglunds författarskap," *Horisont*, 42:5/6 (1995): 22-27, 25 (my translation).
25. Nydahl, "Den livslånga resan," 114 (my translation).
26. Horace Engdahl, "Sju läsningar i 80-talet," *BLM* 4 (1987), 250-257, 250 (my translation).
27. Anne-Marie Berglund, "Vita eftermiddagar i Alfabetet (från A till O)" in *Sex kvinnors lusta: en erotisk bok* ed. Birgitta Stenberg (Stockholm: Månpocket, 1994), 9-36.
28. Anne-Marie Berglund, "En hund gör det bättre" (from *Dam med dåligt rykte på sin vanliga runda*, Stockholm: Alba, 1991), in *Erotiska berättelser (från Agnes von Krusenstjerna till Anne-Marie Berglund)*, ed. Magnus Palm (Stockholm: Bonnier Alba, 1994), 203-208.
29. Lena Malmberg, "Att skriva sig fri," *Nordic Women's Literature*, http://nordicwomensliterature.net/sv/article/att-skriva-sig-fri (my translation).
30. Kajsa Widegren and Linnea Isberg, "Perversa flickfantasier: Anne-Marie Berglunds textlekar, rumsligheter och ironier," *Tidskrift för genusvetenskap*, 2-3 (2013): 88-109, quote from p. 90 (my translation).
31. Edenborg, "Är vi alls intressanta?" 183-200.
32. *Orfelias erotiska uppfostran/L'Éducation d'Orphélie* is produced by Ulrich Geismar Productions and Les films de Michel Ricaud in what seems to be a French/Swedish collaboration.

33. Edenborg, "Är vi alls intressanta?," 189.
34. See Constance Penley, "Crackers and Whackers: The White Trashing of Porn," in *Porn Studies* ed. Linda Williams (Durham and London: Duke University Press, 2004), 309–331, 317.
35. *Come and Blow the Horn* is discussed at length by Mats Björkin in his contribution to this volume, and more briefly in Kevin Heffernan's contribution.
36. Malmberg, "Att skriva sig fri."
37. Davidsson, "Flykten från vanligheten," 26.
38. According to Amos Vogel's *Film as a Subversive Art* (London: Weidenfeld and Nicolson, 1974), it is from 1925, whereas later sources date it to 1928–1933 (Constance Penley), 1928 (José B Capino) or 1929 (internet movie database).
39. José B Capino, "Filthy Funnies: Notes on the Body in Animated Pornography," *Animated Journal* 12: 1, 2004: 53–71, 53.
40. Penley, "Crackers and Whackers," 317.
41. Penley, "Crackers and Whackers," 316–317.
42. Edenborg, "Är vi alls intressanta?," 189.
43. Peter Lehman, "Introduction: 'A Dirty Little Secret'—Why Teach and Study Pornography?" in (ed.), *Pornography: Film and Culture*, ed. Peter Lehman (New Brunswick, NJ, and London: Rutgers University Press), 2006, 1–21, 4.
44. Even before the internet revolution, and the subsequent dissemination of information, Berglund's film was listed in Lars Åhlander (ed.), *Svensk filmografi 7: 1970–1979* (Stockholm: Svenska filminstitutet/Norstedts 1989), 319.
45. Lehman, "Introduction," 5–10.

REFERENCES

Åhlander Lars, ed. *Svensk filmografi 7: 1970–1979*. Stockholm: Svenska filminstitutet/Norstedts, 1989.
Arnberg, Klara. "For Men, by Men? Women's Business Activities in the Pornographic Press Compared to the Overall Publishing Industry in Sweden 1950–1972." *NORA—Nordic Journal of Feminist and Gender Research*, 21:1 (2013): 21–40.
Arnberg, Klara. *Motsättningarnas marknad: den pornografiska pressens kommersiella genombrott och regleringen av pornografi i Sverige 1950–1980*. Lund: Sekel bokförlag, 2010.
Arnberg, Klara, and Mariah Larsson. "Benefits of the In-Between: Swedish Men's Magazines and Sex Films 1965–1975." *Sexuality & Culture*, June 2013, 18:2 (2013): 310–330.
Berglund, Anne-Marie. "En hund gör det bättre" (from *Dam med dåligt rykte på sin vanliga runda*, Stockholm: Alba, 1991). In *Erotiska berättelser (från Agnes von Krusenstjerna till Anne-Marie Berglund)*, edited by Magnus Palm. Stockholm: Bonnier Alba, 1994.
_____. "Vita eftermiddagar i Alfabetet (från A till O)." In *Sex kvinnors lusta: en erotisk bok* edited by Birgitta Stenberg. Stockholm: Månpocket, 1994.
Björklund, Elisabet. *The Most Delicate Subject: A History of Sex Education Films in Sweden*. Ph.D. diss., Lund University, 2012.
Butler, Alison. *Women's Cinema: The Contested Screen*. London: Wallflower Press, 2002.
Capino, José B. "Filthy Funnies: Notes on the Body in Animated Pornography." *Animated Journal* 12: 1 (2004): 53–71.
Davidsson, Katarina. "Flykten från vanligheten. Anne-Marie Berglunds författarskap." *Horisont*, 42:5/6 (1995): 22–27.
Edenborg, Carl-Mikael. "Är vi alls intressanta? Att läsa Anne-Marie Berglund som pornograf, illusionist och desillusionist; något om noveller och att göra snedsteg." *Res Publica*, 35–36 (1999): 183–200.
Editorial in *Kvinnobulletinen*, 3–4 (1973).
Engdahl, Horace. "Sju läsningar i 80-talet." *BLM* 4 (1987), 250–257.
Filmavtalet 2013. http://www.sfi.se/Documents/Filmavtalet/Filmavtalet/2013%20%C3%A5rs%20film avtal.pdf.
Fischer, Lucy. *Shot/Countershot: Film Tradition and Women's Cinema*. Princeton, New Jersey: Princeton University Press, 2014 [1989].
Furhammar, Leif. *Filmen i Sverige—en historia i tio kapitel och en fortsättning*, third edition. Stockholm: Dialogos Förlag and Svenska filminstitutet, 2003.
Juffer, Jane. *At Home with Pornography: Women, Sex, and Everyday Life*. New York: New York University Press, 1998.

Koenig Quart, Barbara. *Women Directors: The Emergence of a New Cinema.* New York: Praeger, 1989.
Larsson, Mariah. "Contested Pleasures." In *Swedish Film: An Introduction and Reader*, edited by Mariah Larsson and Anders Marklund. Lund: Nordic Academic Press, 2010.
_____. "Drawing the Line: Generic Boundaries of the Pornographic Film in Early 1970s Sweden." In *Conference Proceedings from NorLit Conference*, edited by Magnus Ullén, et al. Linköping: Linköping University Electronic Press, 2009–2010.
_____. "Practice Makes Perfect? The Production of the Swedish Sex Film in the 1970s." *Film International* special issue Making Movies in Europe, 8:6 (2010): 40–49.
_____. *The Swedish Porn Scene.* Bristol: Intellect (forthcoming).
Lauzen, Martha M. *The Celluloid Ceiling: Behind-the-Scenes Employment of Women on the Top 250 Films of 2014.* San Diego: San Diego State University, 2015.
Lehman, Peter. "Introduction: 'A Dirty Little Secret'—Why Teach and Study Pornography?" In *Pornography: Film and Culture*, edited by Peter Lehman. New Brunswick, NJ, & London: Rutgers University Press, 2006.
Levitin, Jacqueline, Judith Plessis and Valerie Raoul, eds. *Women Filmmakers: Refocusing.* Vancouver: UCB Press, 2003.
Malmberg, Lena. "Att skriva sig fri." *Nordic Women's Literature.* http://nordicwomensliterature.net/sv/article/att-skriva-sig-fri.
Nestius, Hans. *I last och lust: sexuella bilder förr och nu.* Stockholm: Prisma, 1982.
Nordic Women Film. http://nordicwomenfilm.com/.
Nydahl, Thomas. "Den livslånga resan bort från klaustrofobin." In *Politisk geografi: prosavandringar i sju städer: med tre kompletterande samtal om liv och litteratur med Anne-Marie Berglund, Gabriela Melinescu och Suzanne Brøgger*, edited by Thomas Nydahl. Hallaryd: Occident, 2002.
Penley, Constance. "Crackers and Whackers: The White Trashing of Porn." In *Porn Studies*, edited by Linda Williams. Durham, NC: Duke University Press, 2004.
Rich, B. Ruby. *Chick Flicks: Theories and Memories of the Feminist Film Movement.* Durham, NC: Duke University Press, 1998.
Ryberg, Ingrid. *Imagining Safe Space: The Politics of Queer, Feminist and Lesbian Pornography.* Ph.D. diss., Stockholm: Stockholm University, 2012. Available online http://urn.kb.se/resolve?urn=urn:nbn:se:su:diva-68789.
Schaefer, Eric. *"Bold! Daring! Shocking! True!": A History of Exploitation Films, 1919–1959.* Durham, NC: Duke University Press, 1999.
Soila, Tytti. "Sweden." In *Nordic National Cinemas*, edited by Tytti Soila, Astrid Söderbergh Widding & Gunnar Iversen, 135–220. London: Routledge, 1998.
Vogel, Amos. *Film as a Subversive Art.* London: Weidenfeld & Nicolson, 1974.
Widegren, Kajsa, and Linnea Isberg. "Perversa flickfantasier: Anne-Marie Berglunds textlekar, rumsligheter och ironier." *Tidskrift för genusvetenskap* 2-3 (2013): 88–109.
Women Film Pioneers Project. https://wfpp.cdrs.columbia.edu/.

Come and Blow the Horn
Sound, Sex and Cultural Heritage

MATS BJÖRKIN

Introduction

Joseph W. Sarno's *Fäbodjäntan/Come and Blow the Horn* (1978) has become emblematic of the end of Swedish pornographic film for cinema audiences. Discussions of the film seem to have focused on three things: the pastoral environment (in the Swedish region of Dalarna), the connection between women, sexuality, and nature, and that the film is quite bad.

Ever since Arne Mattsson's *Hon dansade en sommar/One Summer of Happiness* (1951), erotic frivolity, beautiful nature, and more or less independent women have been important ingredients in what has been regarded as "Swedish" in Swedish film.[1] Since the so-called "golden age" of Swedish silent cinema during the late 1910s and early 1920s, with directors such as Victor Sjöström and Mauritz Stiller, through 1940s romanticizing of Swedish rural life in films including Gustaf Edgren's *Driver dagg, faller regn/Rain Follows the Dew* (1946), nature has been used not only as a setting but as a more or less active function in movies. *Come and Blow the Horn* takes this history further.

The narrative of the film is quite simple. Monika (Leena Hiltunen credited as Leena), the modern "fäbodjänta" (originally referring to a herding girl in mid- and northern Sweden, more correctly called *vallkulla*) has a horn, once found in an old Viking grave. The horn has magical properties. When blown into, all women who hear the sound become sexually aroused. Monika uses the horn to attack bigotry and make the situation in the small village friendlier. Especially targeted are Björn Johansson (Tomas), a missionary, and his wife Agneta (Marie Bergman credited as Marie), a stereotyped sexually inhibited puritanical woman. Of course, Monika in the end "liberates" the missionary and his wife, as well as Monika's friend Britt (Anita Berglund as Anita), and Britt's mother who in the film has no name (played by the pseudonym Anne). The film begins with Monika playfully seducing the farm hand Olle (Knud Jörgensen as Knut). Here Monika is presented as a young, a bit childish, sexually liberated 1970s woman. Soon we will realize that Monika is playing a game with the villagers, using the magical horn and thus developing, or helping to develop, their inner desires. As soon as the horn enters the story, we realize that Monika is a mischievous playmaster. Her friend Britt is the only one Monika tries to convince, verbally, that the horn actually works. Britt refuses to believe it, even if we in the audience notice that the horn does affect her. The first real "victim" of the horn is Britt's mother, a very correct and traditional mother living in a neat and tidy home, who before the entry of the horn is seemingly attracted to the farm hand Olle. Monika, who closely watches the result of her play, fails at persuading Britt that her mother had sex with Olle because Monika blew the horn. We soon realize that the missionary Björn and his wife Agneta are the real targets, and that the effect of the horn is gradually improving. Britt's mother, though, is obviously easier to affect and a bit after the midpoint of the narrative she helps herself, in Olle's absence, with a giant sausage, a typical regional kind of sausage called *falukorv* (named after the Dalarna regional capital town, Falun). Being the probably most well-known scene of the film, it combines the effect of the horn with a regional, and at the same time typically Swedish, food tradition. In what follows almost everyone has some kind of sexual relationship with the others (with the exception that the men never have sex with each other). The last turning-point of the film is when Britt's mother takes the horn. Thus Monika has succeeded; when the housewife is temporarily taking over as playmaster, Monika can play her other role as the sexually liberated farm girl. The "fäbodjänta" has proven that she controls the herd. The season is over: Thomas and Agneta leave for missionary work in the Philippines; Britt leaves with her boyfriend Karl (played by pseudonym Arne) to the neighboring region of Värmland; Britt's mother, Olle, and Monika are staying, obviously with Monika in charge.

The film seems to have been quite successful. It was shown in cinemas around Sweden during the autumn of 1978, had some international releases, and gained cult status in Sweden during the 1990s, together with a handful of erotic, violent, or just "bad" films that all film students and arthouse cinema-goers with "alternative" taste had seen (or at least were supposed to have seen). So why bother with a film that most cult film fans and aficionados of old pornographic films who actually have seen it find boring, ugly, and not very arousing? It is not the most successful Swedish pornographic film. It is not the first or last of something, even if it is one of the last pornographic feature films made for cinematic release in Sweden. Although something of a domestic porn star, Leena Hiltunen was not one of the most iconic figures of 1970s Swedish porn and sexploitation.

My interest in the film lies rather in how it negotiates certain national and regional features that at the time had almost disappeared from Swedish films and were not about to reappear until more than a decade later, most visible in Colin Nutley's *Änglagård/House of Angels* (Colin Nutley, 1992). It is a bit curious that both films, the most "Swedish" Swedish films of the last forty years have been made by foreigners: Colin Nutley is British, Joseph Sarno was American.

According to the Swedish Film Institute database, Sarno had made eight films in Sweden before *Come and Blow the Horn*. From 1968 on, he made soft-core films with established actors, but gradually the films became more explicit. The reduced market for soft porn and gradual increase of hard-core porn seem to have been a general trend in Sweden during the 1970s. In the biographic documentary *The Sarnos: A Life in Dirty Movies* (Wiktor Eriksson, 2013), *Come and Blow the Horn* is not mentioned at all, obviously because Sarno preferred to emphasize a nostalgic view of an "early" pornographic history, before hard-core porn. The documentary's focus on soft porn nostalgia and the aesthetic ambitions of Sarno resulted in what Mariah Larsson describes as a feminization of Sarno's films.[2] When considering this and the established view of Sarno being influenced by the Swedish landscape and Ingmar Bergman, it is not surprising that *Come and*

Blow the Horn does not fit in a (re)writing of the history of Sarno as a filmmaker. The interesting thing with *Come and Blow the Horn* is not "Joe Sarno"—it is "Sweden," because the film says something particular about a specific environment, at a specific time.

Sweden and the Fäbod

Come and Blow the Horn uses a nationally well-known cultural environment, the *fäbod*, in a very particular Swedish region, Dalarna, which together with use of sound traditions connected to the *fäbod*, constitute an intriguing interpretation of Swedishness—through sex. The essay discusses each of these aspects with examples from the film, and how the film succeeds in mixing those references with other cultural expressions that have been key to the formation of Dalarna and the *fäbod* as part of the Swedish cultural heritage.

First we need the scene: the "fäbod" (literally "animal shed"). The basic idea of *fäbod* is of farmers who during the summer, due to lack of sufficient pasturage, take their cattle with them, moving from one pasture to the next. Each haying area, which was used every year, had sheds for cattle and for herders. The herders were all women who thereby lived isolated, but quite independently, with the cattle during summer. The *fäbod* culture declined during the mid–20th century, but it had been a living culture in the northern parts of Sweden at least since the 16th century. The practice of women living alone in nature with cattle, in forests with wild animals such as bears and wolves, as well as male hunters and outlaws, has been a popular ground for erotic fantasies expressed in wide spread folk tales and local stories, but also appropriated by Ibsen in *Peer Gynt*. Even the origins of *fäbod* life are, in a way, sexualized. It is sometimes argued that one of the reasons why herding at the *fäbod* was conducted by women is a law from 1686 prohibiting men from working as shepherds, due to the risk of them having sex with the animals.[3]

In *Come and Blow the Horn* it is not Monika who takes care of the animals, it is a hunky guy, Olle. When dressed, he is constantly wearing typical 1970s blue suspender jeans with a yellow T-shirt (similar in color to the Swedish flag). Olle obviously has good hands with animals, and sometimes comments—to the cows—about how the interest of the cow compares with the interest of the women. He also seems to be Monika's closest ally. He is the first one she has sex with in the film, and is still at the *fäbod* by the end of the movie.

Fäbod life was common in the less inhabited central and northern parts of Sweden, which also were the most mythical areas of Sweden. They were geographically close enough, still culturally distant, to southern urban areas for the creation of strange ideas about them. More important is that as the interest in tourism grew in the late 19th century, these same areas became the most popular destinations for recreational travelling and experiencing nature. These areas were, and are, dominated by deep forests and farmlands. They were agricultural societies without the old aristocracy that owned most land in the southern part of Sweden. The nature, the natural resources, the beauty of the landscape, and the independence of the people living there became central to the creation of a national identity during the second half of the 19th century. Understanding of the area reflected the double meanings of "landscape" in Scandinavian and Germanic languages: on the one hand a term for a picturesque view of natural scenery, on the other hand the designation of a geopolitical territory, a region.⁴ The importance of Dalarna is both picturesque and geopolitical and, as we will see, also auditory. In the center of this nationalist discourse was the region with largest number of *fäbod*, Dalarna.

The film takes place during midsummer in Dalarna, but without any distinct visual or musical references to traditional Dalarna midsummer celebration. Rather, what we hear and see in the film is a combination of references to 20th century national visual stereotypes and a late 19th century nationalistic romanticization of Dalarna. This is hardly surprising, since no other Swedish region has been so idealized and romanticized. Already in the late 19th century, Dalarna became a sort of national symbol, "a Swedish Ideal."⁵ The image of Dalarna was based on an economic and moral conservatism as opposed to the ongoing industrialization of the southern part of Sweden. Dalarna was the peaceful and harmonic *arcadia*, which served as a gauge of national sentiments. It became a resort for distracted urban people, searching for a "real" Swedish home.⁶

Even if most characters only reside in the small village for the summer, when the minister and his wife are leaving—liberated by Monika and her horn—for missionary work in the Philippines, they know what their real home is or, thanks to Monika and her horn, what it has become.

Nation, Landscape and History

Perhaps the most elaborate description of Dalarna as a real Swedish home can be found in a book from 1937 by cultural historian (and later film and TV producer) Gustaf Näsström, *Dalarna som svenskt ideal* [Dalarna as Swedish ideal].⁷ He deals with three major themes: political and economic history from medieval times to the early modern era, literary and artistic representational strategies of the 19th and early 20th centuries, and, third, the work of Artur Hazelius. Hazelius was the founding father of two cultural history institutions in Stockholm: the outdoor museum Skansen, and the Nordic Museum, the museum of Swedish history and folk culture of the modern era. Hazelius' idea was to preserve disappearing rural life, which among other things resulted in outdoor museums with folk life tableaux, whole environments including objects and wax figures. The first Swedish outdoor museum, Skansen in Stockholm (opened 1891), was intended to preserve a view of a disappearing countryside for the urban population, where pre-industrial rural life and nature could be seen as an urban distraction, and to give the city a potential to incorporate a multiplicity of places. They gave the audience not only knowledge of the past, but also training in a way of perception.⁸

The relation between Dalarna and Skansen is particularly important for the 20th century conception of national identity. No other Swedish landscape has had the same role in the creation of national myths, or even nationally recognized regional myths. When tourism became a broader phenomenon, Dalarna was one of the most popular destinations, particularly the area around lake Siljan. The *fäbod* areas north and west of Siljan became accessible and, in representations, extremely widespread images of "authentic" Swedish landscapes. But, by then, as Näsström writes, the tourists must have become disappointed.⁹ The blowing of birch-bark horns at the distant blue mountains only occurred in advertisements for Sweden—and at Skansen.

It is not surprising, however, that the perhaps most atypical Swedish region became the ideal landscape. Dalarna was relatively more prosperous than the rest of Sweden, perhaps because it was less hierarchical (the land was owned by the farmers, not by the nobility as in the south) and had a much smaller rural proletariat. It had everything that both old rural Sweden and new industrial Sweden lacked: not only beautiful nature and rich natural resources, but also a small-scale economy, local self-determination, and personal freedom. That was certainly a good ideal.[10] The *fäbod* became a popular subject for folkloristic researchers as well as an obligatory stop on tourist's tours around the province. This tourist trend was extremely bourgeois, already at the time accused of being commercialized and theatrical, but—which is important in comparison with other forms of tourism around 1900—it involved no wildlife romanticism. The nature was important, of course, but only as an environment of the *fäbod* life.

The world outside *Come and Blow the Horn* is more or less absent. The 1970s is present though clothing, hairstyles, home décor, and cars. This is how modern tourists want to spend their holidays—a mix of authenticity, modern values, and a closeness to nature. Not a search for the wild and untouched, just a sense of being included in the well-known Swedish landscape. Generally speaking the Swedish landscape has for centuries conveyed a particular sense of "Swedishness," based on the foundations of the nation's wealth (the forests, mountains, and rivers), and a sense that this foundation has created a specific Swedish consciousness. Accordingly, it can be understood as a constituting factor in the imagined community, in Benedict Anderson's words, that developed during the 19th century in Sweden.[11] Nature and landscape have been particularly important since the 18th century. In the tradition from Carolus Linnaeus, the eighteenth-century biologist, most well-known for the sexual system and his taxonomical organization of nature, Swedish connectedness to nature can be described as a combination of natural sublimity (descriptions of the beauty and magnificence of nature in his travel narratives) and scientific systemization (the taxonomical system). Industrialization enhanced the economic value of natural resources, and, at the same time, demystified and threatened to destroy the same foundations of industrial growth, something Hazelius tried to counteract through his creation of Skansen.[12]

Hazelius also had another motivation for praising Dalarna. Many sources tell about Hazelius' fascination with women from Dalarna, the *dalkulla* [pl. dalkullor]. Literary critic Fredrik Böök, in a speech to Hazelius, described him as "You, the knight of all *dalkullor!*"[13] This could have been just an anecdotal curiosity, but it is such a profound part of the relationship between Dalarna and Skansen that it deserves to be taken seriously. Hazelius helped spread the erotic undertones of the image of *fäbod* women. Thus Hazelius included sexuality in his historical-geographical endeavor. This could, a bit exaggerated, be expressed as a "geo-sexual" movement from the mother (in the center), through the male traveler, to the sexualized adult woman (in the periphery).

The Swedish tourist movement, which in the 1880s and 1890s among other things supported increasing tourism from other countries, became at the turn of the century a more nationalist project. In the Linnaean tradition, the tourist movement wanted to teach the Swedish people to appreciate (and honor) their native land, by way of extensive knowledge of nature. In the early 1920s, the president of the national tourist organization talked about the entire country as an outdoor museum (as Linnaeus had described nature as the perfect natural history museum).[14] But the country-as-museum can also be seen as a result of a modern, urban way of perception, an idea that the tourist can experience only a representation. An antidote to this was the alleged authenticity of *fäbod* life. On the other hand, the growing interest in environmental issues during the 1960s did not result in a new interest in *fäbod* life, probably because it was too connected to the national romanticism of the 19th century, rather than its much longer tradition.

An interesting case for comparison is a comedy from 1971, *Sound of Näverlur* by Torbjörn Lindqvist, who later would become the cinematographer of *Come and Blow the Horn*. The film was made as a satire of the tourist industry of Dalarna. Here Dalarna becomes not a museum of a national ideal, but rather a museum of contemporary (1960s) stereotypes, and commercially motivated uses of these stereotypes. Every reference to tradition looks superficial and is made fun of.

Cultural Heritage

In the 1970s, *fäbod* culture again became the focus of attention. The *fäbod* was about to disappear. The early 20th century was in Sweden, as in many other European countries, an era of rapid urbanization, reinforced by the postwar Social Democratic ideology of modernization and rationality. Agriculture was more or less seen as an area of production, rather than a lifestyle with long traditions. The women working at the *fäbod* became older, and the younger generation was no longer interested. Nevertheless, the 1970s was also a decade of a new romanticism of nature and rural life. Young people, primarily artists and intellectuals, left the cities for a so-called "green wave" life in the countryside. This was a trend founded in modern environmentalism rather than in an interest in old "environmental" forms of farming. The concern for the *fäbod* thereby did not originate in the new "green" movement, but like half a century earlier, in ethnography. In 1976 and 1977, a couple of seminars and publications emerged that documented contemporary *fäbod* culture, its history, and its (problematic) future.[15] The main threat was modern agricultural policy, the large-scale economy, and, as at the beginning of the century, tourists. This time it was not the bourgeois travelers from the cities that were the problem, but the "green wavers" and the selling of *fäbodar* as summer houses. A combination of the two was very common, which resulted in a kind of rural gentrification.

Even changes in political and industrial economy affected *fäbod* culture. From more than 700 municipalities in Sweden in the early 1950s the local governing system was changed into less than 300 political areas. Local policy became, in one sense, more large-scale; on the other hand these new larger municipalities had more self-governance than in the earlier system. The economy changed. Many of the old industrial sectors, such as mining and the steel industry, forestry and logging—the industries that had kept Dalarna prosperous—went through a major crisis. Large restructurings of these sectors radically changed conditions for many areas of Sweden, and particularly so for Dalarna. Tourism became more important than ever. In the *fäbod* areas, the most important potential tourist attraction was the *fäbod*. Even for local authorities, the transformation of *fäbod* to summer house was a potential problem. It was good to have the "permanent" tourists in their summer houses, but it was even better to have a large flow of new tourists, consuming cultural history and locally produced goods and services.

Both local authorities and the state saw the importance of enhancing interest in cultural history. Many old buildings and sites were restored, documented, and incorporated in tourist information. A new form of cultural tourism emerged among other forms of tourism. Many of the old *fäbodar* thus became popular tourist attractions.

The *fäbod* in *Come and Blow the Horn* is a radical contrast both to the houses of

92 II. Art, Sexploitation and Pornography

Britt and her mother, and the missionary couple, as well as the village church. On the other hand it seems to be spatially quite close. The *fäbod* as an exception close to the modern village was an experience 1970s tourists encountered all the time. At least those who did not want the longer journey to the more genuine *fäbodar* in the north of Dalarna and beyond. The combination of Hazelius romanticization and eroticization of *fäbod* life, green wave life of the 1970s and the interest in cultural history brings us back to *Come and Blow the Horn*, and another feature of the 1970s. The interest in folk music grew rapidly in the 1970s, particularly the *fäbod* music.

Sounds of the Fäbod

The work at the *fäbod* had over the centuries become very rational and well organized. In the center of everything were the cattle (cows, sheep, and goats). The working day was organized around their needs. The semi-nomadic life was motivated by access of pasturage but also, of course, by the ownership of land used. Knowledge transfer from one generation to the next therefore focused much on means and methods of communication. Instead of modern communications, people at the *fäbod* used the human voice and musical instruments, most importantly lurs and horns.

Very early on lurs and horns were in the *fäbod* area regarded as female instruments. The sounds of cattle, human voices, lurs and horns are frequently described by (male) travelers visiting from the south. Certain sounds connected to the life of the *fäbod* can therefore be said to have a long history of potential sexual/erotic connotation.

During the era of national romanticism in the mid and late 19th century the sounds, and music, of the *fäbod* became emblematic of the origins of Swedish music. One of the many people who became fascinated by the *fäbod* music was the composer of the Swedish national anthem, Richard Dybeck. When the knowledge of *fäbod* music seemed to disappear around 1900, many attempts to strengthen the tradition were made. For example, Anders Zorn, perhaps the most well-known painter of the era (and the Swedish

Monika blows the horn. Leena Hiltunen in *Come and Blow the Horn* (Joe Sarno, 1978). Courtesy of Studio S.

painter that today is sold for the highest prices at international auctions for his full-bodied naked young women (*dalkullor*) in farming or nature surroundings) arranged competitions and helped organize a revival for *fäbod* music (albeit distanced from its original use). Again, with the connection to Anders Zorn and contemporary, more or less pornographic, or erotic, painting, the *fäbod* is circumscribed with sexualized discourses.

Consequently, the pastoral opening scene of an early summer morning, the forest, the meadows and the enclosed sheep pen with bleats of the sheep, the traditional old-fashioned *fäbod* style wooden houses, and the frivolous Monika playing with Olle is the Zorn environment transformed or translated into modern imagery, modern clothing, and modern ideals of female bodies, far from Zorn's voluptuous women. The accompanying music, as well, is translated into an accordion playing a waltz from the standard repertoire of the late 19th through 20th century rural popular entertainment.

Here the choice of music in the film becomes particularly ingenious. Instead of using traditional folk music, old-time dance music is used, which although based on traditional forms, is primarily a mix of 19th century European dance music traditions. For example, the film opens with a waltz, about halfway through the film we hear a somewhat quicker waltz, and the film ends with Swedish old-time dance music form called *hambo*. Old-time dance was, and still is, an important activity at Skansen, and it has during the 20th century been, and still is, a key part of cultural heritage discourses in Sweden.

Fäbod music is by and large a pragmatic form of musical communication between people and animals, and between people. The characteristic, and very strong, vocal techniques, that depending on topographic conditions could be heard more than ten kilometers, were used to keep the herd together and control its direction and speed, and to communicate with other herders, sometimes kilometers away. In sum, it was a system of important information as well as for gossip.[16]

Most important, though, is the use of sound (vocal or instrumental) for "remote" control of animals and people. Most of the time it was directed toward collectives, but often also individuals. The herding girl was always the "sender," the active, controlling part in this communication system, though constantly reacting to feedback from the "receivers" (whether a cow or another herding girl). The herding at the *fäbod* seems to have been a multi-sensual interplay, including also smell and taste (through different herbs and salt which were used to control the animals). Swedish ethnographer Sigurd Erixon even called it a "folk (or, vernacular) telegraphy."[17]

Within sight, the human contact and (normal) voice was the most frequent means of communication. For longer distances the special song technique, *kulning* (sometimes designated *longköuk*), and instruments had to be used. And, it is at long distances that the "mysterious" sound of the *fäbod* aroused so much interest from 19th century travelers (tourists as well as ethnographers). Both *longköuk* and instruments were used for purposes of attracting (keeping the herd together) or repelling (keeping wolves and bears away from the herd).[18]

For attracting sounds, fine songs and melodies were used, while screams, terrible sounds from horns and lurs, non-music, were used to scare animals.[19] The horn Monika uses in *Come and Blow the Horn* has nothing to do with the horns used at the *fäbod* but is actually closer to the repelling uses of sounds.[20] On the other hand, the effect created by Monika's horn is rather of the kind that could be connected to more attractive uses of sounds. In relation to the historical use of sounds at the *fäbod* it is useful to look at the communicative uses of the horn as a "remote control" rather than at the kind of instrument used. In *Come and Blow the Horn* the horn is said to be from the Viking age (early medieval times), thereby connecting to another historical discourse. But the remote control function is more than obvious. The main function of the horn is to make women sexually aroused from a distance.

The erotic engagement in *fäbod* life was also dependent on the double effect of both voice and instrument. Sounds used to attract the herd also attracted the bear. Here, men had another position in relation to predators. Male hunters were always regarded as a danger to the animals, while women were understood as having a closer link to animals (and nature) and were thereby exposed to the dangers of nature in ways that men were not. Animals were also often said to have "human" ways of reacting to the world, maybe for the purpose of making the cattle seem closer to human beings, and to explain, and perhaps demystify, the danger of bears and wolves.

The women of the *fäbod* did not carry weapons—they used only fire as protection, and, according to the legends, another, surprising method of defense: If a bear came too close, the woman sometimes lifted her skirts and showed herself naked to the bear, which was supposed to become "ashamed" and leave. In a discourse that looked upon both the herding woman and the wild animal as primarily sexual beings (in lieu of the more forbidden "couple" man/cow) sexuality was both a weapon and potential cause of trouble. Many folk songs talk about the herding girl being attacked by "twelve robbers [*rövare*]," which also was a nickname for the bear that was supposed to be as strong as twelve men.[21]

In *Come and Blow the Horn*, it is Olle who has a good hand with the animals, particularly the cows. He rarely talks, his main mode of expression is instead through sex. Perhaps Olle is a bear, domesticated by Monika, and brought into human relationship by Britt's mother. Or, it might be that Monika, and later Britt's mother, are using sex to prevent him from getting intimate with the cows.

In *fäbod* culture, most communication and information was carried by sounds. Monika is only using speech—she is constantly criticized for talking too much—and the horn, but no singing. There are stories that describe how young women learn wonderful songs and melodies from a supernatural being, the female *rånda*. These stories cor-

Monika as "näcken." Leena Hiltunen in *Come and Blow the Horn* (Joe Sarno, 1978). Courtesy of Studio S.

respond to the ones about how male musicians learn from *näcken* (the neck, the evil spirit of the water) with the difference that the men actively seek help in ritualized forms, while the women just happen to learn from the *rånda* living in the vicinities of the *fäbod*. The music at the *fäbod* was thereby considered less advanced, more of music for work and leisure where the sounds, in a physical-auditory sense, are emphasized (Johnson 1986).

The uses of both voice and instrument were also important for communication with supernatural beings. Many of the stories are, again, of sexual nature: such as that of the herding woman who was forced to celebrate a troll wedding, only to be rescued at the last moment by her fiancé. Supernatural phenomena in *fäbod* culture seem to be primarily auditory. They were rarely seen, but heard, and here the *fäbod* women were said to be more receptive than other people.[22] The *fäbod* thereby, both in its real as well as in its magical sense, was an auditory, pragmatic culture, sometimes eroticized by 19th and early 20th century scientific and popular discourses.

Conclusion

Joe Sarno's *Come and Blow the Horn* makes use of the full array of national insignia through the position of the *fäbod* within the cultural history of Dalarna and its role as a national ideal. Not in its details, but in its basic feature, the woman who uses a magical horn to arouse female desire with the purpose of connecting to both real nature (sexuality) and real culture (*fäbod* life). But Monika is at the same time a modern woman, someone who has moved to a *fäbod* no longer in use. She is an orphan, who just has happened to be placed in this environment. What Sarno did was perhaps worse than the worst possible scenario of the contemporary ethnographers: a complete mix-up of cultural history and popular representations of cultural history. Even worse, the film mixed, and perhaps revealed, the complex web of gender relations that involves a (male) sexualization of a pre-industrial culture of (relatively) independent women. To draw the conclusion even further: in order to really reveal the consequences of urbanization and modern tourism, environmentalism, folk culturalism, and nationalism, we need a hard-core pornographic aesthetics that brutally unveils all layers of art *and* scholarship, of history and myth. What remains is men watching a woman with good relations to animals, nature and history, affecting women by blowing a horn. The *fäbod* is not really a fäbod, but a small farm close to a small village. Monika says she might have Sami (the Nordic indigenous people) background, information with no further effect on the story. The horn, the prime communication tool of the traditional *fäbod* is here not made of horn, but metal (bronze), and is supposed to be a Viking horn, while Dalarna has very limited connection to Viking culture. The music is not *fäbod* music, but 19th and 20th century old-style dance music. But the landscape is there, the meadows, the forest, the small river, the old houses, sunny days, short light nights of Swedish midsummer times. And so the modern "vallkulla," the "fäbodjänta" of the Swedish title of the film, as mischievous playmaster playing a wicked game in order to liberate sexually repressed neighbors, with her "remote control," the horn instead of the voice. The modern "vallkulla," the "fäbodjänta" is combining speech with the bronze horn, discourse and technology, to take the bull by the horn. Old traditions are combined with "modern traditions" in order to fit in with the changing perceptions of the nation and its history. That is what Dalarna has been to Sweden since the 19th century. Cinematographically speaking, Joe Sarno's *Come and Blow the Horn* is a Swedish ideal—everything together, and more.

NOTES

1. Olof Hedling and Mariah Larsson, "National Boundaries? Notes on the Pornographic Film in Sweden in the 1970s," in *Media, Culture and Identity in Europe*, eds. Savaş Arslan et al. (Istanbul: Bahçeşehir University Press, 2009), 274.
2. Mariah Larsson, "Joe Sarno and Historiography: Some thoughts on *The Sarnos: A Life in Dirty Movies*," *Journal of Scandinavian Cinema*, 3:2 (2013): 101–105.
3. Kerstin Brorson, *Sing the Cows Home: The remarkable herdswomen of Sweden* (Seattle: Welcome Press, 1985), 8.
4. Karen Wonders, *Habitat Dioramas: Illusions of Wilderness in Museums of Natural History* (Uppsala: Acta Universitatis Upsaliensis, 1993), 83–96.
5. Ulf Sporrong, "The Province of Dalecarlia (Dalarna): Heartland or Anomaly?," in *Nordic Landscapes: Region and Belonging on the Northern Edge of Europe*, eds. Michael Jones and Kenneth R. Olwig (Minneapolis: University of Minnesota Press, 2008), 192.
6. Karl-Erik Forsslund, *Med Dalälven från källorna till havet* 1:2 (Stockholm, 1919).
7. Gustaf Näsström, *Dalarna som svenskt ideal* (Stockholm: Wahlström and Widstrand, 1937).
8. Mark B. Sandberg, "Effigy and Narrative: Looking into the Nineteenth-Century Folk Museum," in *Cinema and the Invention of Modern Life*, eds. Leo Charney and Vanessa R. Schwartz (Berkeley, Los Angeles, London: University of California Press, 1995), 349–50.
9. Näsström, *Dalarna som svenskt ideal*, 63.
10. Karin Johannisson, "Det sköna i det vilda: En aspekt på naturen som resurs," in *Paradiset och vildmarken: Studier kring synen på naturen och naturresurserna*, ed. Tore Frängsmyr (Stockholm: Liber Förlag 1984), 69.
11. Benedict Anderson, *Imagined Communities*, 2nd ed. (London/New York: Verso 1991), 6–7.
12. Wonders, *Habitat Dioramas*, 83–96.
13. Fredrik Böök, quoted in Näsström, *Dalarna som svenskt ideal*, 61.
14. Wonders, *Habitat Dioramas*, 46.
15. For example Göran Rosander ed., *Nordiskt fäbodväsen: Förhandlingar vid fäbodseminarium i Älvdalen, Dalarna, 1-3 sept 1976* (Stockholm: Nordiska musset, 1976).
16. Anna Johnson, "Sången i skogen—skogen i sången," in *Folkmusikboken*, eds. Jan Ling et al. (Stockholm: Prisma 1980), 79.
17. Sigurd Erixon, "Folklig telegrafering," *Svenska kulturbilder*, Ny Följd. 4, eds. Sigurd Erixon and Sigurd Wallin (Stockholm: Skoglunds Bokförlag, 1935), 36–39.
18. Cf. Åsa Nyman, "Lurar, horn och lockrop," in *Fäbodar*, ed. Hans Lidman (Stockholm: LT, 1963); and Jan Ling, 1964. *Svensk folkmusik: bondens musik i helg och söcken* (Stockholm: Prisma, 1964).
19. Birgit Kjellström, "'Harpor, Lurar, Nyckelgigor ... Kärngar, Drängiar, Bönder, Pijgor' Om folkliga instrument," in *Folkmusikboken*, eds. Jan Ling et al. (Stockholm: Prisma, 1980), 198.
20. Gunnar Ternhag, "Horn och lur—två vallinstrument," in *Nordiskt fäbodväsen: Förhandlingar vid fäbodseminarium i Älvdalen, Dalarna, 1-3 sept 1976*, ed. Gunnar Rosander (Stockholm: Nordiska musset, 1997) 68–71.
21. Anna Johnson, *Sången i skogen: Studier kring den svenska fäbodmusiken* (Phd diss. Uppsala University, 1986), 190.
22. Ibid., 199.

REFERENCES

Anderson, Benedict. *Imagined Communities*, 2nd ed. London: Verso 1991.
Brorson, Kerstin. *Sing the Cows Home: The Remarkable Herdswomen of Sweden*. Seattle: Welcome Press, 1985.
Erixon, Sigurd. "Folklig telegrafering." In *Svenska kulturbilder*, Ny Följd, 4. Edited by Sigurd Erixon. Stockholm: Skoglunds Bokförlag, 1935.
Forsslund, Karl-Erik. *Med Dalälven från källorna till havet*, 1:2. Stockholm, 1919.
Hedling, Olof, and Mariah Larsson. "National Boundaries? Notes on the Pornographic Film in Sweden in the 1970s." In *Media, Culture and Identity in Europe*, edited by Savaş Arslan, Defne Karaosmanağlu, and Süheyla Kirca Schroeder. Istanbul: Bahçeşehir University Press, 2009.

Johannisson, Karin. "Det sköna i det vilda: En aspekt på naturen som resurs." In *Paradiset och vildmarken: Studier kring synen på naturen och naturresurserna*, edited by Tore Frängsmyr. Stockholm: Liber Förlag 1984.

Johnson, Anna. "Sången i skogen—skogen i sången." In *Folkmusikboken*, edited by Jan Ling, et al. Stockholm: Prisma, 1980.

Johnson, Anna. *Sången i skogen: Studier kring den svenska fäbodmusiken*. Ph.D. diss., Uppsala University, 1986.

Kjellström, Birgit. "'Harpor, Lurar, Nyckelgijgor ... Kärngar, Drängiar, Bönder, Pijgor' Om folkliga instrument." In *Folkmusikboken*, edited by Jan Ling, et al. Stockholm: Prisma, 1980.

Larsson, Mariah. "Joe Sarno and Historiography: Some thoughts on *The Sarnos: A Life in Dirty Movies*." *Journal of Scandinavian Cinema*, 3:2 (2013): 101–105.

Ling, Jan. *Svensk folkmusik: bondens musik i helg och söcken*. Stockholm: Prisma, 1964.

Näsström, Gustaf. *Dalarna som svenskt ideal*. Stockholm: Wahlström & Widstrand, 1937.

Nyman, Åsa. "Lurar, horn och lockrop." In *Fäbodar*, edited by Hans Lidman. Stockholm: LT, 1963.

Rosander, Göran, ed. *Nordiskt fäbodväsen: Förhandlingar vid fäbodseminarium i Älvdalen, Dalarna, 1–3 sept 1976*. Stockholm: Nordiska museet, 1976.

Sandberg, Mark B. "Effigy and Narrative: Looking into the Nineteenth-Century Folk Museum." In *Cinema and the Invention of Modern Life*, edited by Leo Charney and Vanessa R. Schwartz. Berkeley: University of California Press, 1995.

Sporrong, Ulf. "The Province of Dalecarlia (Dalarna): Heartland or Anomaly?" In *Nordic Landscapes: Region and Belonging on the Northern Edge of Europe*, edited by Michael Jones and Kenneth R. Olwig. Minneapolis: University of Minnesota Press, 2008.

Ternhag, Gunnar. "Horn och lur—två vallinstrument." In *Nordiskt fäbodväsen: Förhandlingar vid fäbodseminarium i Älvdalen, Dalarna, 1–3 sept 1976*, edited by Gunnar Rosander. Stockholm: Nordiska museet, 1997.

Wonders, Karen. *Habitat Dioramas: Illusions of Wilderness in Museums of Natural History*. Uppsala: Acta Universitatis Upsaliensis, 1993.

III

Obscenity and Censorship

The Open Secret
Illegal Screenings of Pornographic Films for Public Audiences in Sweden, 1921–1943

TOMMY GUSTAFSSON

As in other western countries, pornography in all its forms was illegal in Sweden during the first decades of the 20th century. To publicly screen a pornographic film was a criminalized act that could lead to up to two years imprisonment. Despite this, screenings of films with pornographic content occurred in Sweden well before the legalization of pornography in the early 1970s, even as early as in the 1910s and 1920s. However, one outcome of this precarious legal situation is that most of the history of the early pornographic film is surrounded by a hush-hush mentality, legally and morally, that hampers a historical reconstruction of the distribution situation and screening contexts in Sweden, as elsewhere. There is hardly any information about who made these films, how they were made, or how they were imported, distributed, and screened.

American film scholar Linda Williams describes these early porn films as *stag films*, short silent films with a rudimentary narrative that depicted variations of scenes of sexual intercourse. She describes the viewing context for the stag film where the (illegal) film, together with a projector and a projection screen, was brought out on private and special occasions where only men had access, such as stag parties.[1] This holds an implicit class perspective, since the purchase of the 16mm equipment introduced in the 1920s was priced at such a high level that hardly anyone outside of the "leisure classes" could afford it. Eric Schaefer notes that it was with the introduction of 8mm equipment in 1932 that prices become more reasonable, but it would take until after the war before this home movie format became available to "everyone." In addition, Schaefer points to another important class aspect. The fact that these films primarily were purchased and viewed by middle-class and wealthier men meant that these films attracted little attention from censors and prosecutors, mainly because they seldom fell into the hands of children, women, minorities, and members of the working-class—the main groups of the middle-class' concern and fear.[2]

Besides the private viewing situation for the stag film there were several additional viewing contexts for this type of film. Schaefer mentions traveling road shows and traveling "stag masters" in the U.S.,[3] and in France, for example, these hard-core films were shown at brothels.[4] In Sweden, the phenomenon of stag films existed,[5] but what is more seldom described in international literature is the secret and illegal screenings of pornographic films at regular cinemas or other public venues after hours.

In this essay I will describe three different examples of secret but at the same time semi-public screenings of pornographic films that occurred in Sweden, by examining three court cases from between 1921 and 1943. The assumption is that this type of secret screening was unusual but not as exceptional as one perhaps is led to believe by the near silence in previous research. In fact, I will give evidence for the existence of informal distribution systems for illegal films, which had the ability to circulate for years without being reported to the authorities. I will also discuss the production and origin of pornographic films and how, for example, the strong cultural notion of "French films" was used to deceive the police and the Swedish legal system.

Moreover, the question of class is imperative for the analysis since these semi-secret screenings of illegal porn films shattered the protecting class barrier that surrounded the private sphere of the stag film where audiences most likely consisted of male middle-class spectators who could afford to pay for a private screening. The legal attention that these screenings attracted is therefore connected to the fact that the audiences were predominately composed of members from the working-class. Another fact that will be revealed by this study is that the producers, distributors, and exhibitors of these porn films belonged to the lower middle-class and the working-class, who seemingly were protected when they screened films in the private sphere of a middle-class home but who were considerably more vulnerable when they catered to their own classes in secret but public venues.

The three court cases concerned illegal screenings of pornographic films for public audiences in 1921, 1932, and 1943. They have been located by a thorough search in Swedish trade papers for film distribution and exhibition, where disciplinary actions and strongly worded condemnations against the perpetrators, and against pornography, were part of the film industry's self-regulation and self-defense during a time in which the film medium itself was under constant attack and censorship.[6] Although these three cases most certainly are not the only ones, the low figure nevertheless gives an indication of how extraordinary it was for pornographic screenings to be reported to the authorities.

1921: The Open Secret

The first trial took place on April 5, 1922, at Örbyhus District Court. A cinema owner, Karl Kaeyér (age 36) living in Gävle, was charged for showing films without an appropriate permit, and for the screening of a film on three occasions in 1921 that broke the law in the penal code about decency and morality.[7]

The procedure began on November 4, 1921, when a report was submitted to Gävle's police department by the district police superintendent and public prosecutor of Oland district who claimed that Kaeyér had "for a male audience, demonstrated a forbidden, very lewd film, showing among other things sexual intercourse between a man and a woman, and also sexual offense committed between two women." This led to an initial police interrogation with Kaeyér on November 8, where he confessed everything at the same time as he claimed that he in fact had not committed the offense since he had rented the locations and had a permit for public screenings issued by the county clerk. The permit, it turned out, was valid for only a single occasion in 1920, while Kaeyér had interpreted it as an ongoing permit for the last one and a half years. When asked about the immoral film, he claimed that it could not be prohibited since the film had not been reviewed by a censor. The film had been screened without any admission fee after the ordinary show ended at 9:30 p.m. "at the request of a few men in the village," according to Kaeyér.[8]

During questioning it transpired that the film, which was approximately ten minutes long and "probably filmed in America," was not Kaeyér's, but that he had borrowed it from the owner of Cinema Rivoli in Gävle. The owner had in turn supposedly obtained the film from "Werldsfilm Ltd." in Stockholm, and the film had for four years been in circulation for after-hours screenings.[9]

On March 25, 1922, the prosecutor of Dannemora district reported Kaeyér for another two film screenings held on September 23 and 25, 1921. A second interrogation is thus held with Kaeyér where he repeats his initial position. What is added in the form of a defense is a precision of the stratification of audiences. Now it is said that "only adult male persons that Kayer [sic] personally invited" had access to the screenings. The two extra screenings, which started at 10 p.m. and 10:30 p.m. respectively, are also said to have been attended by twenty to thirty men. When asked about the permit, Kaeyér stated that he had rented the premises and therefore had permission to screen the "funny film."[10] What emerges here is a defense built on the principle of private parties, that is, the notion that a personal invitation equated membership in a closed association where, for example, banned films were allowed to be screened as an exception to the law.[11] The question was whether these extra screenings could be labeled as private parties, and if the illegal "funny film" thereby became legal to screen.

The data seemingly confirm what has previously been known about stag films when it comes to the length of the film and that only men had access to it. But the record also confirms the existence of a secret distribution method in which a film could circulate for four years in a relatively small geographic area without interference from the authorities. And this despite the fact that the "secret" must have been known by a larger number of people than what can reasonably be considered an initiated circle.

As a result of the remarkable consistency of the testimonies during the trial, the defense's attempt to invoke the principle of private parties failed. Nonetheless, put together, the testimonies for the prosecutor and the defense give a detailed account of how the previously little-known "secret" screenings of pornographic films actually worked in small-town Sweden and what reactions these screenings spawned.

The prosecutor produced three witnesses who had attended the screening at the Temperance Society's house in Gimo on September 24. Two of the witnesses had heard a rumor that an extra screening was to be held in the sobriety house and went there out of curiosity. One of them had learned of it the day before while the other had "coincidentally" been told about it during a visit to Gimo's general store the same day. Only the third witness had been invited by Kaeyér personally "a few weeks before the 24th."[12] The prosecutor also presented written testimonies from five witnesses who had attended the screening at the Temperance Hall in Örbyhus on September 25, and they had similar recollections: three had been invited by Kaeyér, two the day before, and one had been asked to stay after the regular screening. The other two had unknowingly visited the regular show and then been told by a friend that afterwards would appear "a funny film," so they stayed.[13] The defense submitted a collective testimony for the show in Gimo that was signed by twenty-nine men who all claimed that they had been invited personally, while the testimony for the screening in Örbyhus was signed by the caretaker who stated that he, on behalf of Kaeyér, had "told acquaintances of Mr. Kaeyér" they were invited to "see an erotic film after the ordinary show."[14]

Guided by the testimonies, it appears that the extra screening, and what would be shown there, was an open secret in the sense that the invitations travelled mouth-to-mouth which meant that far more people than Kaeyér's acquaintances, though allegedly still only men, got news of the screening and subsequently showed up to watch the film. The screening in Gimo was reported to have been visited by as many as seventy to eighty persons, while the number for the show in Örbyhus oscillated between twenty-five and forty. Regardless of whether the testimonies came from the defendant's or the plaintiff's side it was, over and over again, emphasized that only adult males had been admitted.[15]

However, that these screenings were an open secret that only men knew about can be questioned. The image of secrecy and men who sneaked into the various venues under the cover of night fails if one looks at the actual viewing context. For example, the extra screenings were always placed directly after the public screenings which had a mixed audience of men, women, and children. After the regular show everybody left the cinema and the doors were closed. Outside, a number of men who had not seen the regular show waited, and when children, women, and, presumably, some of the men went home, others stayed for the additional screening.[16] In the case of Gimo, it was about seventy to eighty men who waited outside the temperance lodge and thereby the open secret becomes very open. It is, in other words, quite unlikely that those who went home, especially the women, could have been completely unaware of what would happen so late in the evening.

In addition to this, the testimonies regarding Gimo state that when the doors opened again for the extra screening, women still lingered outside the premises. Nobody invited the men who waited outside and no one controlled them as they went inside. As one witness stated, "but no women had, this time, entered" the cinema, which reveals that women had—perhaps inadvertently, perhaps out of curiosity—tried to get in to previous secret screenings. And before the show began, a slightly inebriated Kaeyér had discovered and thrown out two underage boys.[17]

In Gimo, the lights had been lit when the men went in and sat down, while the same procedure commenced in darkness in Örbyhus.[18] The screenings always, however, took place in complete darkness. The film that was screened consisted of a variety of sex scenes according to this, the most detailed testimony:

> The film that was exhibited had shown men and women who had practiced sexual intercourse with each other, as well as two naked women; one of whom had put on a device, similar to the male reproductive organ, after which the two women had sexual intercourse with each other[...]. At one point during the show [...] we had heard [Kaeyér], who apparently was up on the balcony where the projector was placed, exclaim: "Laugh now, you rogues," but the audience had remained silent. When the light [...] came on again, one in the audience had discovered his 20 year old son and they had been "ashamed both for themselves and for himself" that they attended the screening.[19]

As we have seen, the illegal porn film was described as both a "funny film" and an "erotic film" in interrogations and testimonies. Based on the described viewing context and the reactions that the film raised one could ask which function the pornographic film had in this particular context. While the private viewing context for stag films, according to some scholars, holds an educational element in which men learn about sex through a collective ritual, others say that the function of pornography, that is, to be used for masturbation, has remained constant regardless of media or historical context.[20] On the one hand, it is difficult to even imagine that the screenings in Österbybruk, Gimo, and Örbyhus had masturbation as its main objective. On the other hand, and despite the fact that it could be months, if not years, between the screenings, there could be a possible educational value present. Due to the legal regulations and the great lack of sex education at the time, is it likely that these films had a great and lingering impression on their audiences, who probably had individual moments in the film etched into memory and perhaps used these pictures to masturbate to later.

However, the pornographic element ought to be downplayed at the expense of the audiences' experience of excitement and curiosity that the film screening induced, surrounded as it was by secrecy and perhaps knowledge of the act's illegality. The term "funny film" and the drunken Kaeyér's shout to the crowd that they should laugh can therefore be interpreted as a way to deal with the shame of doing something morally wrong or forbidden in front of other people. The feeling of shame, together with inexperience and perhaps even the shock of seeing these explicit sexual acts also makes it easier to understand the strong repudiations that the witnesses conjured, describing the film as "filth."[21]

The legal condemnation was even harsher. Örbyhus District Court sentenced Kaeyér to two months in prison for having shown a film which "must be deemed to have offended decency and morality, so that danger of others' seduction has arisen." He was also sentenced to pay fifty crowns[22] in fines for not having a valid permit for cinema exhibition, which was turned into another eight days in prison.[23] The verdict must be considered to be severe, but not harsh enough for the trade paper *Biografbladet* which asserted that "it is regretful that the caning punishment is abolished."[24] Otherwise a peculiar silence surrounded the event, both locally and nationally. The two local newspapers, *Gävle Dagblad* and *Arbetarbladet*, published a brief press release a few days after the trial, but nothing else.[25] *Biografbladet*, however, reports that another cinema owner in Gävle—probably the owner of the film in question—had been called in for questioning by the police after accusations that he had screened film "after hours in front of a 'full house,' where also ladies had been present."[26] This accusation seems, however, to have disappeared. There is no further reporting about it in *Biografbladet* or in the local newspapers during 1922.

1932: Homemade

The second trial took place on November 3, 1932, at the Stockholm City Court. A photographer, Per Trygve Jerneman (Age 36), and a Miss Hilma Martina Pettersson (age 46), were charged for showing films without appropriate permissions, and for the screening of films on three occasions in 1932 that broke the penal code for decency and morality.

The process started on September 23, 1932, when a man, who wanted to stay anonymous, entered a police station in Stockholm and reported that an indecent film was to be shown at the banquet hall at a Housekeeping school located on Klara Södra Kyrkogata later the same evening. The anonymous man left two tickets for the evening's show that was to start at 11:15 p.m. The tickets were labeled "The M. L. Club 3 Crowns."[27]

Two police constables in civilian clothes named Liljeson and Roos were ordered to "go to the address to be able to do a closer inspection of the film's nature." As they approached the address an unknown man opened the street door without asking who they were and let them in. The constables continued to the 4th floor where the school was located. A woman let them in but did not ask them for the tickets, and they hung their clothes in the hall and entered the banquet hall where around thirty people, of whom three were women, sat on Windsor chairs in front of a white screen. When Liljeson and Roos took their seats the light was turned down and the show, presented in four parts, began.

> The first part had the title "Sample without Value." This film had shown a naked woman, who had done a number of gymnastic movements, at the same time as she diligently had exposed her genitals. This part had gone on for about ten minutes.
>
> The second part had the title, "The Association away with Men." This film had shown two naked women on an ottoman. The women had embraced and kissed each other on various parts of their bodies. Moreover, they had tried to satisfy their sexual desire by licking and using fingers on each other's genitals while rubbing. Later, the women had consumed a glass of wine, and one of them had poured out the content on the other's genitals, after which she licked the genitals. After that the women seemed to be exhausted, lying on the ottoman but then continued in the before-mentioned manner, embracing and licking each other. Next the film had shown a close-up of a woman's genitals, wherein fingers entered in and out. This part had gone on for about 20 minutes.
>
> The third part had the title, "On the Erotic Ottoman." This part had begun with a fully dressed man and a woman sitting on an ottoman, eagerly embracing and kissing each other. After a short while they had undressed and started to have intercourse on the ottoman while in different positions. The man and the woman had alternately lain on their back with the other on top. On one occasion the man was lying on his back while the woman straddles his genitals. She had entered the male organ into her genitals, and then moved her body up and down. Simultaneously one could read the inter-title, "Ride, ride, jerk off."[28] After that the man had lain down on his backs on the ottoman while the woman laid down next to him. Both were seemingly exhausted. After a while, however, the woman had with one hand taken hold of the male organ, rubbing it, but the male organ had not hardened, wherefore the woman had put it in her mouth and licked it. The male organ had then hardened, and they had intercourse once again. At various moments during this part, which went on for about 20 minutes, close-ups had been shown of both the woman's and the man's genitals.
>
> The fourth part had shown two naked women and a naked man, all lying on an ottoman. One of the women had put the male organ in her mouth at the same time as the other woman licked her female organ. The first woman had at the same time rubbed her hand on the other woman's genitals. Once the man had had sexual intercourse with one of the women, at the same time as the other woman had spit in her hand and then rubbed the male organ as it went in and out of the other woman's genitals. This part went on for about 10 minutes.[29]

The detailed police report then states that the audience members were between twenty and forty years old, and that the audience "expressed their satisfaction on several occasions by shouting loudly and laughing." Once again we have this connection to laughing and shouting at what are obviously hard-core pornographic films. Liljeson and Roos also confirm that three women attended the screening, and during the interrogations it turns out that women had also attended the other two screenings in what is usually believed to be a through-and-through male environment.[30]

Miss Pettersson, who had rented out the banquet hall, was questioned by the police and she said that the defendant, Mr. Jerneman, had approached her in order to rent the banquet hall for the screening of films for "theater people" on September 16. She agreed to that, not knowing what films were to be shown, and was paid the amount of fifteen crowns. At 11 p.m. the same evening, around twenty-five unknown men turned up and one hour later they left after the screening. Jerneman had contacted Miss Petterson a few days later, wanting to rent the banquet hall again for two screenings on the 23rd. Miss Petterson agreed, got twenty crowns, and this time around fifty men turned up for the first screening at 9 p.m. and then another twenty-five to thirty men for the second at 11 p.m. that is, the screening that was monitored by constables Liljeson and Roos. Miss Pettersson had on all three occasions been at the Housekeeping school premises, but had not herself seen the films in question.[31]

Jerneman was called in for questioning by the police on September 29, and he confessed and took sole responsibility for everything, but at the same time he also referred to the same principle as Kaeyér had done in 1921, namely that of private parties. Like Kaeyér, Jerneman felt that he had invited only "male peers" and acquaintances from his previous work places, the amusement park Gröna Lund, and he also mentions a string of Stockholm theaters: Mosebacke Teater, Circusteatern, and Vasateatern. The fact that he sold tickets was explained to be a consequence of having to cover his own expenses. The amount on the printed tickets, three crowns, is downplayed, as Jerneman claims that he in reality only charged between one and two crowns in admission, generating after expenses a profit of fifty crowns altogether. It is also Jerneman who mentions that women attended the various screenings, one of whom was a "fiancée of a male visitor" and the three women at the last screening were "acquaintances" of Jerneman's.[32]

When asked about the films Jerneman told a story about how he, as he worked at Gröna Lund in the summer of 1932, had been approached by a sailor who wanted to sell a "French film" to him for seventy crowns. Jerneman saw the film and decided to buy it. As he got it, the film was divided into three parts, but Jerneman edited it into four parts, and later the company Nerliens Fotografiska Magasin in Stockholm added Swedish inter-titles.[33]

As with the porn film with allegedly American origin, bought from the somewhat mysterious company "Werldsfilm Ltd." in Stockholm in the former case, Jerneman's acquisition of the "French film" points to a most irregular underground distribution system, so unbelievable that it in fact was untrue. That Kaeyér loosely referred to the borrowed film as "American" is in fact based on the same type of cultural stereotyping—that is, the notion of American popular culture as inferior and dangerous—as the older notion of "French cards" and "French films" as equated with "French sin," just like Swedish films later became a material symptom of the notion of "Swedish sin."[34]

A week later Jerneman was again called in for questioning by the police because a rumor had started saying that the "French film" was in fact made in Stockholm. Jerneman, who was said to be "erotically orientated by nature," revoked his previous story and confessed that he had made the four films himself. In May 1932 Jerneman had bought a used film camera for one hundred crowns, and sometime during the summer he had gotten drunk in his apartment together with a male actor and two women he knew. Jerneman suggested that they make an erotic film and the others agreed. Jerneman handled the camera and the man and the two women acted out the scenes described above. Jerneman had developed the film himself and just to show how elaborate the "forgery" was, Jerneman then drew and affixed a fake French trademark to the film before he handed in the film to Nerliens Fotografiska Magasin for the inter-titles.[35]

Now the actor, who was called an "extra" by the police, and the two women were called in for questioning. The actor had known Jerneman for two years and was acquainted with the two women. He told the police that he became intoxicated together with the women and Jerneman in the latter's apartment on a Sunday in July. Jerneman had suggested that, "as an experiment," they should make a film, but the actor stressed that neither he nor the women received any remuneration for their participation. Nor had Jerneman said anything about his plans to screen the film for other people. The actor, however, did acknowledge his presence at the third screening at the Housekeeping school, but told the police that he afterwards had "protested that Jerneman had shown the films."[36]

The two women, in their turn, told a similar story. They had gotten "very drunk" and thought that the film was for "private use." Neither they nor the actor were to receive any compensation for the filming, and they stressed that none of them had gotten any reimbursement after Jerneman's screenings. One of the women also denied that she was "beset with perverse inclinations, and asserted that her behavior during the filming of the movie had been the outcome of Jerneman's instructions."[37]

The three screenings had a combined audience of around a hundred people and through the different testimonies it transpires that many came from, or worked within, the entertainment and theater sphere, which traditionally has had a more open-minded attitude toward what has been considered deviant behaviors and activities. This is something that is emphasized in a petition signed by seventeen men who had attended one of the screenings, mostly actors and artists but there is also a typographer and a hairdresser represented. The petition was handed in as moral evidence by the defense in the form of a numbered list that, among other things, assured that no one had been under the age of eighteen and that the payment had been made only to cover the direct costs. One item on the list read:

> 7/ according to my definite opinion, the display of images could not be said to constitute an event that hurts the decency and morality of society, partly because the general public did not have access, partly because the images of the depicted subjects are familiar to any normal person who has reached adulthood, who therefore cannot take offense at them.[38]

The Stockholm City Court nevertheless did not agree with this relaxed view on decency and morality, and Jerneman was sentenced to one month in prison for having screened films that broke the law on decency and morality. Miss Pettersson was sentenced for having leased premises for the illegal screenings to pay a fine of one hundred crowns.[39] The audience and the actors in the porn films were not indicted.

However, the story does not end here. Jerneman appealed the verdict on the grounds that the screenings were private, and brought the case to the Svea Court of Appeals, where the original verdict was upheld, and then also to the Supreme Court which judged the case the same: Jerneman had "severely offended decency and morality, so that danger of other's seduction has arisen." The court also stated that even though "the screenings were not, strictly speaking, public; they nevertheless were public with regard to the conditions of entry provided."[40]

1943: The Opportunity

The third trial took place on May 11, 1943, at the Stockholm City Court. This time there were four defendants: the engineer Emil Sigfrid Wallin (age 40), the projectionist Axel Hakon Pettersson (age 27), cinema owner Karl Helge Söderström (age 31), and the white collar worker Ergon Percy Weidenhayn (age 38), who were all charged with screening of films on three occasions in 1943 that broke the penal code for decency and morality.

The trial started on March 11, 1943, when a man phoned Dick Lidblom, editor of the Stockholm daily paper *Social-Demokraten*, and asked if he knew that there was going to be an illegal screening of German propaganda films later that evening. The man left an address and Lidblom went to Västmannagatan and located a line outside one of the street doors. Lidblom stood in line and found out that a person called Söderström had rented the premises and that a man called "Veidenham or something similar" had "circulated a list where the workers at the workshop Automobilpalatset" could sign up for the screening at the price of 2.50 crowns. Lidbolm then managed to pass by the doorman, who scratched names off a list, without paying and entered Blå Salen where "around 250 people were seated, whereof about 30 were in uniform, probably conscripts. The crowd was otherwise quite mixed, with workers in blue collar clothes and also those 'better dressed,' probably clerks." At about 7:40 p.m. the lights were turned down and two German newsreels with sound were shown, one of which was "pure propaganda," according to Lidblom. Thereafter "a speaker" announced that there was going to be a screening of a "French film" that was "around 50 years old," but that "the subsequent films made in Stockholm were going to be more modern."

> The French film was also very old and badly filmed with blurred images, but showed intimate relationships between both sexes, stripping scenes, etc. The film was equipped with Swedish inter-titles, which like in old movies came before the image. After this film there was a short pause, after which "The Stockholm films" were screened. These were very "nasty" and showed the sexual act between man and woman, different sadistic "treatments," bared sexual organs, artificial penises, which were used by women, among other similar "horrors." "The Stockholm films," which like the French film were silent films, probably consisted of two short films, since it was a short break between them. How the audience reacted during the screening of the latter films, Lidblom could not say since he felt very upset and even nauseated. There were no disturbances from the audience.[41]

After the screening Lidblom called the police and reported what he had seen. He also wrote an article that was on the front page the following day where he considered the screening to be of a "sticky nature" and the porn films to contain "horrors." Lidblom also recalled two things that the following investigation does not mention. First, that the men in the queue suddenly disappeared and came back from the men's room, where they apparently had consumed alcohol—in a venue owned by a temperance movement. The other thing was that the newspaper had been in contact with the superintendent for Blå Salen, a Mr. Bergenblock, who stated that he had been paid the rent in advance without knowing what would take place on the premises.[42]

In the coming days, the four defendants, Söderström, Weidenhayn, Wallin, and Pettersson, together with a fifth witness, Lennart Edlund, who sometimes worked for Söderström as a projectionist, were questioned by the police. Weighed together their testimonies offer further insight about the secretive exchange and illegal screenings of pornographic films.

There was some disagreement between Söderström and Weidenhayn regarding who came up with the idea of the film screenings. Söderström had owned a travelling cinema business since 1940, specializing in screenings for "private parties," and Wiedenhayn worked as a caretaker at Philipson's Bilfirma at Automobilpalatset. Irrespective of who asked whom, they took the opportunity to make some money and the deal was that Weidenhayn would gather a paying audience among the male staff at the workshop, while Söderström would acquire films and a cinema location. Söderström charged 300 crowns for such a screening, covering all expenses, and Weidenhayn would take what was left over as profit. Sometime during the fall of 1942 they had arranged a screening where uncensored "Russian war films, English short films, and German newsreels" were shown, but according to Heidenhayn the workers thought it had been "tedious with only foreign films." Therefore, in February 1943 they decided to arrange another screening and this time the war films would be mixed with "a lighter film of some kind." Söderström asked around and contacted Wallin, who owned a 16mm projector and had access to two porn films made in Stockholm. He agreed to run these films at the Blå Salen on February 8 for a "full house" and then again twice on March 11. When asked about how he in turn had gotten access to the films he stated that he had borrowed them from an acquaintance he did not want to name. However, the police seized the films at his brother's glazing and framing shop a few days later, so we can detect that Wallin and/or his brother were the actual owners. How Söderström found out about Wallin is unknown; both denied that they knew each other. But the projectionist Edlund, who had helped Söderström run the porn films on March 11, says that he "had showed the same films at a stag party, which was completely private, held at a residential flat."[43] This means that the existence of these pornographic films in fact was known, and that they circulated in Stockholm, most probably at private gatherings such as stag parties.

The fourth defendant, Pettersson, was involved in the case because he owned the old "French film" which was shown on March 11 (but apparently not on February 8). In fact, Söderström had gotten notice of Pettersson's film at another stag party, where it had been shown. Söderström knew Pettersson because he used to repair Söderström's cinema equipment. In March, Söderström apparently borrowed the film, but did not say that he was going to screen it for a paying audience. Nonetheless, Pettersson was paid the sum of fifteen crowns "for wear and tear." When asked how he had gotten access to his film Pettersson told the police this story:

> One evening during the winter [of 1937], when he was running a film at the cinema, an unknown man came to the projectionist booth and wanted to borrow 50 crowns on a film that he carried with him. Pettersson examined the film and saw that it was in good condition, and that it was of a pornographic nature. Pettersson then realized that the film was worth more than what the man wanted to borrow on it, and he lent the sum requested. Pettersson asked where the man had gotten hold of the film but could not remember what the man had answered, but probably abroad. He had then not heard from the man, who had not attempted to reclaim his film.[44]

Once again we have a story filled with secretive ingredients, but the testimony also tells us that Pettersson had owned his film for six years, and during that time he claims that he "only had screened it for acquaintances maybe 3 or 4 times." It seems incredible that Pettersson only screened his film on such few occasions, especially since Söderström saw it at a stag party. It is therefore very likely that Pettersson's "French film" also circulated at private gatherings in Stockholm, not least based on Lidblom's report that the film was worn, with blurred images.[45]

The three screenings took place at Blå Salen, another banquet hall which was owned by the Swedish section of the International Federation of the Blue Cross, which was approved for cinema screenings for 160 persons. Lidblom's figure of 250 is therefore exaggerated and the testimonies that mention "a full house" or an audience of 130 to 150 appear to be more accurate. On the screening on February 8, Wallin stated that Söderström screened two German newsreels on a 35mm projector, and that Wallin then was prompted to screen his two pornographic films, which he did, twice in a row with a total screening time of 40 minutes, meaning that each film was approximately 10 minutes. On the next occasion, March 11, Edlund supervised the 35mm projector on which he screened two German propaganda films and Pettersson's "French film," which was 12 minutes in length. According to Edlund, Söderström had borrowed the two uncensored films from the German Legation in Stockholm, and according to the police report Söderström had previously worked as a journalist, significantly at *Den svenske nationalsocialisten* 1936–1938, the Swedish equivalent to the *Völkischer Beobachter* in Nazi Germany.[46]

When Edlund had set up the cinema equipment, Wallin showed up with his 16mm projector. When Edlund saw Wallin's films he thought that they were "more on the 'funny' side" and not as "dirty" as Pettersson's film. However, the audience seemed to like it, "some laughed here and there, and there were no disturbing incidents." As previously, the porn films were screened twice and later the same evening the show was repeated for a smaller audience composed of those who were unable to get to the previous screening due to work.[47] As mentioned, the police seized all three films and this is their description of the content:

> Wallin's films: 1/ Shows a naked man and woman who have sex with each other in different positions on a bed. 2/ Shows two women and a man, who, after having exposed the behinds of the women, hits them, one at a time, with a whip; during the treatment the women twist and turn in different directions.
>
> Pettersson's film: This movie shows both intercourse between a man and a woman in half naked condition and a woman who sucks on a male organ, and two women, who lie head to toe and lick each other on the genitals, and also two women, one of whom has intercourse with the other in different positions by using an "artificial male organ," tied to the woman's waist.[48]

All of the defendants, with the exception of Pettersson who was not present, emphasized that the audience for all three screenings consisted solely of male workers from Philipson's Bilfirma, thereby stressing both the private nature of the screenings and the extenuating circumstance that women had not attended the screening. And although Edlund recalled that "before the lights were turned down, the audience walked around and talked and everybody seemed to know each other pretty well," we also have Lidblom's testimony that mentions thirty men in uniform, who probably did not work at Philipson's Bilfirma.[49]

Despite the efforts to appeal to the principle of private parties, the Stockholm City Court judged the screenings to have "offended decency and morality, so that danger of other's seduction has arisen." Weidenhayn, who temporarily lost his job at Philipson's Bilfirma as a consequence of the unwanted attention surrounding the illegal screenings, was by the court deemed to be the instigator and sentenced to pay 160 crowns in fines. Söderström was sentenced to 120 crowns in fines, and Wallin to 60. Since Petterson did not know that Söderström would show his film "publicly" he was acquitted of all charges, but he also lost his French film.[50]

Conclusion

These three court cases have revealed that there existed secret but semi-public screenings of pornographic films in Sweden long before the legalization of pornography in 1971. In two of the cases the films were homemade, that is, they were made in Stockholm, and at least one of these films seemed to have been made as a "joke," that is, on the spur of the moment. The other films were called French or American, but that does not mean that they can with certainty be placed in terms of production in France or in the U.S. As we have seen, one of the Swedish films was forged with a fake French trademark, and the worn French film screened in 1943 in fact had Swedish subtitles, which could mean that these films were also made in Sweden. According to the detailed description of all films there is no film that stands out as "French," "American," or "Swedish"; on the contrary, the sex acts—male/female intercourse, sucking, "lesbian" love, the use of dildos/strap-ons—could be described as standard fare. The only film that appears to have stood out was the Swedish film with light bondage from 1943.

There have also emerged several implausible stories of how these allegedly foreign films were imported to Sweden. Of more interest is the secretive distribution system for these films within Sweden. Stag films and their viewing context, similar to what has been described by Linda Williams, did exist in Sweden, both in the capital city of Stockholm, but also in provincial towns including Gävle, where an illegal porn film could circulate for four years without being reported to the authorities. In all cases there are testimonies from men who have seen porn films at stag parties and, with the exception of the case from 1932, the films that were screened publicly were the same films that were screened privately at bachelor parties or other private gatherings. Especially the case from 1943 reveals that there existed an informal distribution system for uncensored propaganda films and porn films in Stockholm.

Seen from a class perspective this means that these porn films spilled over from a private sphere, where they probably were viewed by a predominantly middle-class audience of men who could afford to pay for a private screening, to a public sphere where a predominantly working-class and lower middle-class audience of men could afford to see them. Just as Eric Schaefer has pointed out, the fact that these films were primarily viewed by middle-class and wealthier men meant that they drew little attention from the law, mainly because they seldom fell into the hands of children, minorities, and members of the working-class. The legal attention that these public screenings got can therefore be connected to the fact that the audiences were composed of members from the working-class—the main group of the middle-class's concern and fear. And as we have seen, in some instances women had access to these illegal screenings, although it was always promptly denied by those involved. Furthermore, the producers, distributors, and exhibitioners of these films firmly belonged to the lower middle-class, and in some cases the working-class, and while they were protected in the private sphere of the middle-class home they were vulnerable when working in public venues.

In the interwar years and during World War II, a moral ambiguity surrounded these films and their screening. The open secret of screenings of pornographic films in different venues was condemned by society at large. As we have seen, the appeals to the principle of private parties never succeeded and all the defendants, except for Pettersson in 1943, were sentenced according to the penal code. The anger that the writer in *Biografbladet* revealed when he wanted to reintroduce the caning punishment in 1922, and Lidblom's strong emotions of nausea and horror in 1943, are similarly indications of a strong societal rejection. On the other hand, we have an interconnected system of accepted screenings of porn films at stag parties (for middle-class men) and illegal screenings of pornographic films after hours in public where the audiences possibly rejected, got upset, laughed, and were aroused, conceivably all at the same time, by the prohibited images on the screen. And although this essay is based on only three court cases, the sentences with a decade between them indicate that the verdicts for having offended decency and morality became gradually milder between 1921 and 1943, thus foreseeing the sexual revolution in the 1960s.

NOTES

1. Linda Williams, *Hard Core: Power, Pleasure, and the "Frenzy of the Visible"* (Los Angeles and London: University of California Press, 1999), 58–61.

2. Eric Schaefer, "Plain Brown Wrapper: Adult Films for the Home Market, 1930–1969," in *Looking Past the Screen: Case Studies in American Film History and Method*, ed. Jon Lewis and Eric Smoodin (Durham and London: Duke University Press, 2007), 203, 207.

3. Eric Schaefer, "Plain Brown Wrapper," 214; Seth Grahame-Smith, *The Big Book of Porn: A Penetrating Look at the World of Dirty Movies* (Philadelphia: Quirk Books, 2005), 18.
4. Njutafilms, Bonus material on the DVD *Förbjudna filmer från 1920-talets Paris*, released 2005.
5. See, for example, Harry Schein's speech, "What is pornography?," held at Klubb 44, 21 March, 1945. Harry Schein's personarkiv, Volume 2:1. Artiklar och föredrag 1945-1947, Labour Movement Archives and Library.
6. The reviewed trade papers are *Biografbladet* and *Biografägaren* (exhibition), and *Biografrevyn*, *Filmbladet*, and *Svensk Filmtidning* (distribution).
7. SL 18:13, The Swedish Penal Code 1864–1962, replaced by the Swedish Criminal Code in 1965. The three occasions were on 23 September at Österbybruk's Hall, on 24 September at Gimo's Temperance Society, and on 25 September at Temperance Hall in Örbyhus.
8. Verdict and appendix C, Case 267 (1922), Dombokvårtinget 1922, Uppsala läns norra domsaga, The Regional Archives in Uppsala (RAU).
9. Appendix C, Case 267, RAU.
10. Appendix D, Case 267, RAU.
11. See, for example, Mats Björkin, *Amerikanism, bolsjevism och korta kjolar: filmen och dess publik i Sverige under 1920-talet* (Stockholm: Aura förlag, 1998), 103–111.
12. The Trial Protocol, Case 267, RAU.
13. Appendix E, Case 267, RAU.
14. Appendix F and G, Case 267, RAU.
15. See, for example, The Trial protocol and appendix F, Case 267, RAU.
16. The Trial Protocol, Case 267, RAU.
17. The Trial Protocol and appendix F, Case 267, RAU.
18. The Trial protocol and appendix F, Case 267, RAU.
19. The Trial Protocol, Case 267, RAU.
20. Al Di Lauro and Gerald Rabkin, *Dirty movies: an illustrated history of the stag film, 1915–1970* (New York: Chelsea House Publishers, 1976), 25–27; Magnus Ullén, "Pornografi—en mediehistoria," in *Berättande i olika medier*, ed. Leif Dahlberg & Pelle Snickars (Stockholm: Kungliga bibliotektet, 2008), 300.
21. Appendix E, Case 267, RAU.
22. 50 SEK in 1922 corresponded to 8887 SEK in 2015 (roughly $1100), as measured by the wage index for male industrial workers in Sweden.
23. Verdict, Case 267, RAU.
24. "En sedlighetssårande film. Biografägare dömd till fängelse," *Biografbladet*, 8 (1922): 333.
25. *Gävle Dagblad* and *Arbetarbladet*, both 7 April, 1922.
26. "En sedlighetssårande film," 333.
27. Appendix 3, Case 403 (1932), Stockholms rådhusrätt, avd 4, Stockholm City's Archive (SCA).
28. This is a wordplay with the popular Scandinavian nursery rhyme, "Rida, rida, ranka."
29. Appendix 3, Case 403, SCA.
30. Appendix 3, Case 403, SCA.
31. Appendix 3, Case 403, SCA.
32. Appendix 3, Case 403, SCA.
33. Appendix 3, Case 403, SCA.
34. For a further discussion, see Tommy Gustafsson and Klara Arnberg, *Moralpanik och lågkultur: genus- och mediehistoriska analyser 1900–2012* (Stockholm: Atlas akademi, 2013), 28–29; Nikolas Glover and Carl Marklund, "Arabian Nights in the Midnight Sun? Exploring the Temporal Structure of Sexual Geographies," *Historisk tidskrift* 3 (2009), 490–498; Eric Schaefer, "'I'll Take Sweden': The Shifting Discourse of the 'Sexy Nation' in Sexploitation Films," in *Sex Scene: Media and the Sexual Revolution*, ed. Eric Schaefer (Durham and London: Duke University Press, 2014), 207–234.
35. Appendix 4, Case 403, SCA.
36. Appendix 4, Case 403, SCA.
37. Appendix 4, Case 403, SCA.
38. Appendix 7, Case 403, SCA.
39. Verdict, Case 403, SCA.
40. *Nytt juridiskt arkiv. Avd. 1 Tidskriftförlagstiftning* (Stockholm: G B A Holm, 1933), Case 90.
41. Appendix 2, Case 233 (1943), Stockholms rådhusrätt, avd 5, Stockholm City Archive, (SCA). The statement that there were no "disturbances," and that audiences behaved in previous cases, could

mean that the audience was not drunk and disorderly, but it can also be interpreted as a statement assuring that the audience did not masturbate.

42. [Dick Lidblom], "Pornografi lockbete i utlandspropagandan," *Social-Demokraten*, 12 March, 1943.
43. Appendix 2, Case 233, SCA.
44. Appendix 2, Case 233, SCA.
45. Appendix 2, Case 233, SCA.
46. Appendix 2, Case 233, SCA.
47. Appendix 2, Case 233, SCA.
48. Appendix 3, Case 233, SCA.
49. Appendix 2, Case 233, SCA.
50. Verdict, Case 233, SCA.

REFERENCES

Archival Sources

Archive of Harry Schein, Labour Movement Archives and Library, Stockholm

Harry Schein's speech, "What is pornography?," held at Klubb 44, 21 March, 1945. Harry Schein's personarkiv, Volume 2:1. Artiklar och föredrag 1945–1947.

Regional Archives in Uppsala

Appendix C, Case 267 (1922), Dombokvårtinget 1922, Uppsala länsnorradomsaga.
Appendix D, Case 267.
Trial Protocol, Case 267.
Appendix E, Case 267.
Appendix F, Case 267.
Appendix G, Case 267.
Verdict, Case 267.

Stockholm City Archive

Appendix 3, Case 403 (1932), Stockolms rådhusrätt, avd 4.
Appendix 4, Case 403.
Appendix 7, Case 403.
Verdict, Case 403.
Nytt juridiskt arkiv. Avd. 1 Tidskriftförlagstiftning (Stockholm: G B A Holm, 1933), Case 90.
Appendix 2, Case 233 (1943), Stockolms rådhusrätt, avd 5, Stockholm City's Archie.
Appendix 3, Case 233.
Verdict, Case 233.

Non-Archival Sources

Arbetarbladet, 7 April, 1922.
Björkin, Mats. *Amerikanism, bolsjevism och korta kjolar: filmen och dess publik i Sverige under 1920-talet*. Stockholm: Aura förlag, 1998.
Di Lauro, Al, and Gerald Rabkin. *Dirty movies: an illustrated history of the stag film, 1915–1970*. New York: Chelsea House Publishers, 1976.
Gävle Dagblad, 7 April, 1922
Glover, Nikolas, and Carl Marklund. "Arabian Nights in the Midnight Sun? Exploring the Temporal Structure of Sexual Geographies." *Historisk tidskrift* 3 (2009): 490–498.
Grahame-Smith, Seth. *The Big Book of Porn: A Penetrating Look at the World of Dirty Movies*. Philadelphia: Quirk Books, 2005.
Gustafsson, Tommy and Klara Arnberg. *Moralpanik och lågkultur: genus-och mediehistoriska analyser 1900–2012*. Stockholm: Atlas akademi, 2013.
Lidblom, Dick. "Pornografi lockbete i utlandspropagandan." *Social-Demokraten*, March 12, 1943.
Njutafilms. Bonus material on the DVD *Förbjudna filmer från 1920-talets Paris*, released 2005.

Schaefer, Eric. "'I'll Take Sweden': The Shifting Discourse of the 'Sexy Nation' in Sexploitation Films." In *Sex Scene: Media and the Sexual Revolution*, edited by Eric Schaefer. Durham, NC: Duke University Press, 2014.
Schaefer, Eric. "Plain Brown Wrapper: Adult Films for the Home Market, 1930–1969." In *Looking Past the Screen: Case Studies in American Film History and Method*, edited by Jon Lewis and Eric Smoodin. Durham, NC: Duke University Press, 2007.
"En sedlighetssårande film. Biografägaredömd till fängelse." *Biografbladet*, 8 (1922).
Ullén, Magnus. "Pornografi—en mediehistoria." In *Berättande i olika medier*, edited by Leif Dahlberg and Pelle Snickars. Stockholm: Kungliga bibliotektet, 2008.
Williams, Linda. *Hard Core: Power, Pleasure, and the "Frenzy of the Visible."* Los Angeles: University of California Press, 1999.

491 and the Censorship Controversy

Lena Lennerhed

"God gave us *491* to spread the gospel of Jesus Christ," claimed young minister Lars Collmar. "The most upsetting depiction of youth-gone-astray that has ever been made," asserted film critic Mauritz Edström. Critic Kurt Samuelsson was instead of the opinion that *491* was a pretentious and crappy movie, while Lewi Pethrus of the Pentecostal Movement found it to be a sign of the subverted morals of the times.[1]

The year was 1963, the days around Christmas. Director Vilgot Sjöman's film *491* was on its way to the Swedish movie screens, but was stopped by the National Board of Film Censors. *491* was "brutalizing," "harmfully exciting," and obscene, according to the censors. The film was banned for public screening, and this led to one of the most substantial discussions in Swedish history about cinema and censorship. The debate continued well into the following year. Selected groups of social workers, writers on cultural matters, and representatives of Christian organizations were requested to see the film and give their opinions. The press was offered special screenings. Ultimately, the film ended up with the government. On the TV news, serious-looking cabinet ministers in suits were shown on their way to the screening. The government recommended that *491* be released in a cut version, and the film premiered in March 1964. One month later, the political party Christian Democratic Unity (today called the Christian Democrats) was formed. According to Lewi Pethrus, who was one of the initiators, the release of *491* was the straw that broke the camel's back.[2] In the fall of 1964, a public commission of inquiry was appointed with the task of investigating Swedish film censorship.

The situation was, in other words, extraordinary. Opinions were steeply divided on the message of the film and its qualities, its possible influence on the audience, and the "to be or not to be" of film censorship. *491* also had a political aftermath. As noted, the film became a government-issue, resulted in the founding of a political party and the appointment of a public inquiry into national film censorship. What kind of a film could cause so much fuss?

The Film and the Ban

The film *491* was based on the book *491* that had been published in 1962. The author of the book, Lars Görling, became the scriptwriter of the film. The idea to make a film adaptation of the novel was not Sjöman's own, but he was asked to do it for the production company Svensk Filmindustri by Ingmar Bergman, who also introduced him to Görling.[3]

491 is about six criminal young men who have been taken into custody and placed at Saklighetens ungdomspensionat ("the Objectivity Youth Home").[4] The care given to the boys appears like a kind of social experiment. The boys live in a run-down city flat together with the idealistic social worker Krister. Their freedom is relatively unrestricted, but they have to be available for a scientific study every morning. The boys have to talk about themselves and answer a number of questions, but are never told the purpose of the study. An older inspector is responsible for the project.

The young men are angry, critical, and destructive. They challenge and provoke the social care of which they are the center. They steal a tape recorder from a pastor and plan to record how one of the boys is seduced by the homosexual inspector, but the recording fails. They plan to pawn the tape recorder afterwards, but as it is reported stolen, the police get involved. The boys try to become bootleggers, and seek out a German ship in the harbor to buy alcohol. At the ship, they find the girl Steva, who is being raped by the German sailors. The boys take Steva to their home, but feel defied by her, and in one scene they force her to have sex with a German shepherd dog.

Krister has claimed to be a friend of the boys and a person that they can fully trust. But Krister has a secret room in the flat, filled with books and inherited antique furniture. When the boys find the room they feel betrayed, and one of the boys—Nisse—sells Krister's things. Krister is devastated as he cannot afford to buy them back. Nisse persuades Steva to get the money back by prostituting herself and then lending the money to Krister. The film ends with Krister being arrested by the police, accused of being Steva's pimp, and in the following turbulence, one of the boys leaps to his death from a window.

The producer, Svensk Filmindustri, sent *491* to the National Board of Film Censors in December 1963, and the Board referred the film to the Film Review Council (Filmgranskningsrådet) for comments. The Film Review Council had been formed in 1954 and was an advisory body. Its representatives were appointed by the government and selected among people working with culture, children, and youth. The National Board of Film Censors was obliged to consult the council in cases when the total prohibition of a film was considered or, from 1963, when the Board considered banning considerable parts of a film or making cuts in a film that was understood to have artistic value. The duty of the censorship board was not to make aesthetic judgments but to follow the norms for acceptable film content regulated in the Cinema Ordinance (Biografförordningen) regarding mental hygiene, foreign and security policy. However, the new instruction from 1963 meant that art films were clearly treated differently than other films.

The members of the Film Review Council were not in agreement regarding *491*. One wanted to release the film without cuts, one wanted to ban it, while the remaining three argued in favor of an approval after cuts. The censors at the National Board of Film Censors were not in agreement either. Some wanted to release the film with cuts while the majority, including the head of the Board, Erik Skoglund, decided on total prohibition. *491* was judged by the Board be "brutalizing" and "harmfully exciting" (thus violating the norms regarding mental hygiene in the Cinema Ordinance) and partly violating the obscenity clause in the penal code which regulated material that was "offensive to discipline and morality." The ban was motivated by consideration for the young:

As a comment to the decision, the National Board of Film Censors states that the film's depiction of a group of sadistic and destructive young offenders' hatred, twisted or perverted expressions, and brutal, obscene speech is likely to in a shocking way negatively influence above all the scores of young people in puberty who constitute a large segment of the cinema audience. [...] The film's concentrated and intense combination of raw brutality and sexuality in the film (rape, a strange form of bestiality, qualified prostitution and criminal homosexuality) will to a large extent affect human beings who are in a phase of development characterized by emotional instability and hesitant, insecure values.[5]

The National Board of Film Censors found the combination of sex and violence to be particularly problematic. But Ingmar Bergman's *Jungfrukällan/The Virgin Spring* (1960) had premiered at the cinemas in 1960 without being cut, even though it contained a, for the times, very brutal rape scene. Bergman's *Tystnaden/The Silence* from 1963 had not been cut either. That film did not contain sexual violence, but existentially dark sex scenes: a lonely and unhappy woman masturbating, a couple having sex at a variety theater. When *The Silence* premiered in September of 1963, three months before the Board's decision on *491*, it was in the debate understood that Bergman had broken "the sex barrier" and liberalized Swedish film censorship.[6] The head of the National Board of Film Censors, Erik Skoglund, was on vacation when the decision on *The Silence* was taken, and he stated afterwards that he had been informed that the film would be examined later in the fall, and that he in that case would have suggested cuts in the scene from the variety theater. Maybe *The Silence* would have been cut if Skoglund had been present? Maybe Skoglund wanted to create an example when he called for a ban on *491*? Or was *The Silence* allowed to pass because Bergman's name was so well-known and respected? We can only speculate about this. The result was in any case that it is the film *491* that in Sweden has come to be forever associated with conflicts around film censorship.

The scenes in *491* that the censors found especially problematic were the rape of Steva and the scene where she is forced to have sex with the dog. The National Board of Film Censors wrote: "note! the dog's panting in [scene] 97 must not be heard at all."[7] In these scenes sex was not, however, depicted explicitly, but inferred. Still, the Board's decision was to not cut these scenes from the film, but instead ban the film in its entirety.

After this decision by the censors, SIFO, The Swedish Institute of Public Opinion Research, did a study of what the general public thought of the ban. Twenty-two percent were positive to the ban, 26 percent wanted to release the film in a cut version, 13 percent thought that it should be released without cuts, 32 percent were unsure, while 7 percent answered that they had not heard of the film. This means, as film scholar Anders Åberg observes, that 93 percent of a representative sample of the Swedish population knew about *491*, a film that had not yet been shown in cinemas.[8]

The Director Vilgot Sjöman

The man behind the film, Vilgot Sjöman (1924–2006), was born in Stockholm and grew up in a working-class home in the Södermalm area.[9] He graduated from high school in 1945 and was early on interested in literature and film. Sjöman's first novel, *Lektorn/* "The Lecturer" was published in 1948, and he would thereafter publish several novels, as well as books on film. In 1955, a scholarship made a stay at UCLA in the United States possible, which resulted in the book *I Hollywood* (1961). Sjöman debuted as a film director in 1961 with *Älskarinnan/The Mistress*. He was also assistant director to Ingmar Bergman on the film *Nattvardsgästerna/Winter Light* (1963). After *491*, Sjöman made a significant number of films, among them *Lyckliga skitar/Blushing Charlie* (1970), *En handfull kärlek/A Handful of Love* (1974) (for which he was given the Swedish Guldbagge Award for best picture), *Malacca* (1987), and *Alfred/Alfred Nobel*, about the Swedish inventor and founder of the Nobel Prize (1995). Nevertheless, the film that has been given most attention internationally is no doubt *Jag är nyfiken—gul/I Am Curious (Yellow)* (1967), a film critical of class divisions, the weak position of women, and the political indifference in the Swedish welfare state (*folkhem*/"The People's home"). That even with relatively open sex scenes *I Am Curious (Yellow)* was released by the censorship authority without any cuts was seen as a sign that the limits had been pushed considerably regarding depictions of sex on film. In the U.S., the film was seized by customs upon entry and there was a trial. Author Norman Mailer appeared as an expert witness and defended the film that was first judged as obscene but later released for public screenings after an appeal. *I Am Curious (Yellow)* became the, at the time, biggest success for a foreign picture ever in the American market.[10]

It is difficult to say how aware Sjöman was of *491*'s explosive potential. He certainly understood that the film was provocative, but hardly that it would arouse such strong reactions and that it would be banned from public screening. In January of 1964, Sjöman himself commented on the decision of the censors. The novel *491* had not caused as much debate as the film did, and Sjöman found that the indignation about the film disclosed thinking in terms of class; the myth that certain messages harm uneducated people but not educated ones, and a contempt of film; that film was presumed to be sensation-seeking and commercial entertainment. Sjöman:

> Let's not forget this: fiction and images are not attacked everywhere and consistently. You can say whatever you want at the Royal Dramatic Theater and at the Museum of Modern Art—but don't say it in the movies or on TV. It is the way you spread it that causes public outcry. The images of fiction only become offensive when they reach many.[11]

In an interview ten years later, Sjöman emphasized his naïveté and said that it was the author of the novel and the manuscript, Lars Görling, who had supplied the fuel. One thing that had caught Sjöman's attention in the novel was the psychological portrayal of the idealistic and naïve Christ-like character Krister. But he also stressed his own need to take "a radical step," and that step became *491*:

> I had a need for Görling and such aggressive material as 491. I had a need to destroy an image of myself that I had experienced. I had been nice for so many years. There was no room for me in that image.... I sat at home by the TV and heard that the film had been stopped—and felt an enormous satisfaction! I felt that the image of "Nice Vilgot" cracked, in front of all the people....[12]

What the censors at the National Board of Film Censors had put forward as especially aggravating was the depiction of sexuality, and the debate around the film came to a large extent to revolve around this. How central the theme was to Sjöman is hard to determine. Sjöman's depictions of sexuality were provocative because of highlighting dark sides of human sexuality, including sexual violence and assault. At the same time, the representation of sexuality can be seen as quite conventional. Male homosexuality is—through the inspector—only related to assault on young people. This was the kind of cliché image that had been established in particular during the 1950s when rumors were spreading about how men of power took sexual advantage of young boys and ruined their lives.

120 III. Obscenity and Censorship

The issue of boy prostitution can be said to have been one of the great moral panics of the 1950s, and the image of homosexuality of that time stands in stark contrast to the liberal view that was beginning to be heard in the public discussion around the time of *491*'s premiere.

The representation of gender was also quite conventional. The girl Steva's naked body is repeatedly exposed, for example when she is raped. In contrast, the sexual assault on the boy Nisse is narrated through suggestions (although obvious ones): the inspector talks in an oily manner, caresses Nisse's neck, embraces his knees, and shuts the blinds in the room, while Nisse—fully dressed—bends over the desk. The camera then moves away towards the pigeons in the window. In his books and films, Sjöman had since early on been interested in relationships and sexual themes. His first novel, *Lektorn*, dealt with a complicated sexual relationship and an illegal abortion. The manuscript to his film *Syskonbädd 1782/My Sister My Love* (1966) was begun in 1961 and is about a pair of siblings in a sexual relation who have a child. Many of his later films dealt with sexual themes: The aforementioned *I Am Curious (Yellow)* and its second part *Jag är nyfiken—blå/I Am Curious (Blue)* (1968) and *Tabu/Taboo* (1977), a film about sexual minorities and a naïve sexual reformer.

The Times

Sjöman's film and the debate around it need to be put into broader context. The film appeared in the middle of an era characterized by social and cultural debate, criticism

The male gaze. Lena Nyman, Leif Nymark, Bo Andersson in *491* (Vilgot Sjöman, 1964). © 1964 AB Svensk Filmindustri. Still photographer: Jan Halldoff.

of Christianity and, not least, a wave of sex-liberal political demands.[13] During the first half of the 1960s, young liberals and Social Democrats, authors, journalists, and filmmakers struggled for a more open view of sexuality and a more tolerant sexual morality. There was a demand for greater sexual freedom for the young, and school sex education was criticized. A liberalized abortion law was called for, a claim that gave rise to strong reactions, but which eventually resulted in the introduction of abortion on demand in 1975. Moreover, there were demands that discrimination of homosexual people be stopped, and an emphasis on the many expressions and orientations of sexuality. The sex liberals were also strongly critical of the so-called pornography clause in Swedish law, which made what was understood as obscene depictions illegal, as well as extended to the censorship of films aimed at adults.

Christian and conservative people and organizations experienced a backlash during these years. Voices were heard saying that a kind of cultural war was going on in Sweden between Christian and secular forces, in which tradition and order were threatened by decaying norms and immorality. In 1964, 140 physicians put together an official letter against the "over-sexualization" and "increasing promiscuity" among the young. The physicians called for a stronger "fostering of the character" in schools and the replacement of sex education with family life education. The action led to a storm of protests. Another action was a petition to maintain the subject of Christianity in high schools—against the proposal to replace it with the more general subject of Religion—a petition that managed to collect over two million names. But the foremost example of an effort to strengthen the Christian opinion was the founding of the political party Christian Democratic Unity. Preparations had been going on for a while for the possible formation of a Christian party and, as mentioned earlier, Lewi Pethrus, who was one of the founders, claimed that the release of *491* triggered the decision. Christian Democratic Unity was formed in April of 1964. The party was dominated by the Pentecostal Movement, while the second-biggest group consisted of members of the Lutheran Church of Sweden. The leader of the Pentecostal Movement, Pethrus, repeatedly returned to *491* in his articles in the movement's journal *Dagen*. Pethrus thought that the film *491* was made on speculation and for economic profit, that it was a sign of the moral decay of the time, that it was devastating for the morals of the young, and that it was obvious that it should be forbidden.[14]

The Debate

The voices about *491* were many and divided. Partly, the censorship issue was discussed: whether or not it was correct to censor *491* and whether film should be censored at all. Partly, the film was discussed in itself: what its message was and if it was a valuable and successful film or not. In the censorship issue, one can find a—although not consistent—division by which right-wing people and newspapers often advocated censorship, while the group that was opposed to or skeptical of censorship to a large extent consisted of liberals and Social Democrats. The pattern is, however, not unequivocal as some liberals and Social Democrats were also in favor of censorship.

In 1964, the journalist and author Hans Hederberg did a study of how a number of newspapers had positioned themselves during the first four months after the censorship decision, and he could verify that the newspaper *Dagen* had been the most active one, with around thirty editorials and articles on *491* and the censorship issue, all of them negative to the film and in favor of censorship interference. The right-wing press was on the censorship-friendly side, while liberal and Social Democratic newspapers were generally critical.[15] The liberal newspaper *Expressen* regarded the ban of *491* as one of the most serious attacks on freedom of speech since Sweden became a democracy.[16]

Some asked what "brutalizing" and "harmfully exciting"—the norms regarding mental hygiene—really meant. Could a film that depicts reality, a reality that is rough but that actually exists, be brutalizing? Is it rather not this reality that we avoid seeing, and that also the censors avoid, film critic Mauritz Edström asked rhetorically. Edström's conclusion was that the censorship board wanted to prevent people from seeing that some were ruined, also in the *folkhem*, the Swedish welfare state.[17] A similar interpretation was made by author Karl Vennberg, who was very moved by the film and found the decision to ban it to be a way to hinder knowledge about a "world of condemnation in the midst of welfare."[18] Author Erik Hjalmar Linder claimed that censorship was a remnant from an older and undemocratic society, and called attention to the importance of awareness: "We cannot live in well-off welfare states without knowing what the suffering of the world looks like[...]. We cannot live in an idyllic *folkhem* environment, protected from violence and aberrations of sexuality, without knowing how the world looks beyond the borders of the idyll."[19]

These reviewers interpreted *491* as a film about cracks in the welfare state, and as an urgent request to see and take responsibility. Not everyone, however, was as impressed by the film. Film critic Jurgen Schildt placed *491* somewhere in between Luis Buñuel's—according to Schildt—masterpiece *Los Olvidados/The Forgotten Ones* (1950) and Swedish director Gunnar Hellström's—also according to Schildt—commercial and superficial "raggare" film *Chans/Just Once More* from 1962.[20] This view was shared by some other reviewers who characterized the film as pretentious. But in spite of different opinions about the film's qualities, these reviewers still turned against censorship. To other writers, film censorship appeared to be a protection for above all the young from possibly harmful or at least deadening depictions of violence.[21]

In the debate, *491* could be put forward as a speculative sex film or as a film critical of society. But a number of writers instead emphasized the Christian issues raised by the film. To the question about how many times one should forgive a brother, and if seven times seven is enough, Jesus answered: Not seven times, but seventy times seven times (Matt 18: 22). Seventy times seven equals four hundred and ninety, and four hundred and ninety plus one equals four hundred and ninety one—the number that was the title of the film, in which the young men repeatedly committed new violations. One is blind if one cannot see that *491* is a sermon on the Christian theme of forgiveness, theologian Lars Thunberg claimed in a polemic with those Christians who found the film to be the antithesis to Christian values.[22] Minister Lars Collmar wrote in the Christian journal *Vår lösen*/"Our Redemption": "God gave us 491 so that the gospel of Jesus Christ would circulate.[...] He gave us a film which is about our responsibility for these our smallest brother pimps and sister tarts.[...] But we Christians bemoaned it—with a few exceptions—just because the hooligans used such bad language."

Other Christians still interpreted *491* as a film about solidarity, compassion, and—precisely—forgiveness. The Christian camp was, in other words, strongly polarized in its views on *491* and its message.

The "to Be or Not to Be" of Censorship

491 premiered in March of 1964. The rape scene had been shortened and the bestiality scene removed. Moreover, a monologue at the beginning of the film, which had been judged obscene, had been covered by pop music. The producer, Svensk Filmindustri, gave the film an age limit of eighteen years—the adults-only limit was normally fifteen. The great censorship debate was one thing among others that caused the commissioning of a public inquiry into film censorship in the fall of 1964. In the instructions to the inquiry, it was put forward that the recent discussions about film censorship had created an uncertainty concerning whether or not censorship of films aimed at adults was at all motivated, and that a thorough reconsideration of film censorship was necessary. When the film censorship inquiry published its final report in 1969, it was proposed that censorship of films for adults should be abolished. This was, however, not realized at the time, but much later, in 2011.

Parallel to the discussion around film censorship was a discussion of the so-called pornography clause in the Swedish law, according to which texts and images could be convicted of being "offensive to discipline and morality." The law against pornography was challenged in the 1960s, among others by acclaimed Swedish authors who wrote erotic short stories in the book series *Kärlek*/"Love" (1965–). In 1971, the prohibition against pornography in text and images was abandoned (later on, laws against child pornography and depictions of sexual violence would be introduced).[23]

Even though film censorship was maintained, the censorship practice changed considerably. Harry Schein, a key figure in Swedish film history through the film reform and the founding of the Swedish Film Institute, has described the process in an apt way:

> Leading the way towards the liberation were serious filmmakers, Ingmar Bergman (*The Silence*) and Vilgot Sjöman (*491* and *I Am Curious*), not because of any particular moral courage, but for the simple reason that "artistic" films according to the existing law should be treated more liberally than commercial speculation. In this way, the borders were pushed, from female breasts to female genitalia, to a flaccid penis, to an erect one, to sexual intercourse. Every breakthrough was accompanied by an aggressive press campaign, passionate debate articles for or against the freedom of speech. As soon as a respectable filmmaker had conquered new territory, it was occupied by a less respected one. "Why can't I show what Bergman can show," was the eternal question that could never be answered. The only thing that remained was films showing only intercourse, in close-up, in different positions, with different participants.[24]

And there was intercourse. At first in the sex education film *Ur kärlekens språk* (Torgny Wickman, 1969), a big success in the U.S. and Great Britain among other countries under the title *Language of Love*, and then through the great number of pornographic feature-length films that were produced in Sweden during the 1970s, films that underpinned the reputation of sexually liberated Sweden.[25] At the same time, there was a change in the cultural and political debate in Sweden. From parts of the Left and the women's movement came a criticism of what was understood as a commercialization of sexuality and an exploitation of women's bodies in pornography.[26] Censorship thus gained new proponents who used new arguments.

Epilogue

In the 1970s, Vilgot Sjöman asked the National Board of Film Censors to reconsider the decision about *491*, which they did. The original, uncut version of *491* was broadcast on Swedish television in 1979. At this point, not an eyebrow was raised in response to the film that had caused one of the greatest debates on censorship ever in Swedish history.

NOTES

1. Lars Collmar, "491 som skriftermål," *Vår lösen* 55 (1964): 3, Mauritz Edström, "De förlorades ansikten," *Dagens Nyheter*, January 3, 1964, Kurt Samuelsson, "Melodramatiskt pekoral—men varför förbud?," *Aftonbladet*, December 29, 1963, Lewi Pethrus, "En samhällsväckelse," *Dagen*, January 3, 1964. On the debate around *491* and film censorship, see Lena Lennerhed, *Frihet att njuta: Sexualdebatten i Sverige på 1960-talet* (Stockholm: Norstedts, 1994), 170–188.
2. Lewi Pethrus, "491 och regeringen," *Dagen*, March 14, 1964.
3. Anders Åberg, *Tabu: filmaren Vilgot Sjöman* (Lund: Filmhäftet, 2001).
4. Jörn Donner ed., *Svensk filmografi 6: 1960–1969* (Stockholm: Svenska filminstitutet, 1977) contains detailed information about the film's production, content and the press reactions to it.
5. Quoted from film scholar Anders Åberg's dissertation *Tabu*, 121.
6. Donner, *Svensk filmografi* 6, 153–54, Erik Hedling, "Breaking the Swedish Sex Barrier: Painful Lustfulness in Ingmar Bergman's The Silence," *Film International* 6 (2008): 6, 17–26, and Maaret Koskinen, *Ingmar Bergman's The Silence: Pictures in the Typewriter, Writings on the Screen* (Seattle: University of Washington Press, 2010).
7. Donner, *Svensk filmografi* 6, 173.
8. Åberg, *Tabu*, 130
9. For information about Sjöman's life and an analysis of his films, see Åberg, *Tabu*. Sjöman has himself written shortly about his meeting with Görling and the work with *491* in *Mitt personregister. Urval 98* (Stockholm: Natur och kultur, 1998). *491* is also discussed by Klara Arnberg and Mariah Larsson in "Sexualskildringar inför lagen—kommentar till pornografianklagelser," in *Sexualpolitiska nyckeltexter*, eds. Klara Arnberg et al. (Stockholm: Leopard förlag, 2015), 219–227.
10. For further reading on *I Am Curious (Yellow)*, see Anders Wilhelm Åberg's and Ulf Jonas Björk's chapters in this volume.
11. Vilgot Sjöman in *Dagens Nyheter*, January 10, 1964, quoted from Donner, *Svensk filmografi*, 173.
12. Carl Henrik Svenstedt, "Intervju med Vilgot Sjöman om 491" in Donner, *Svensk filmografi*, 178. Åberg's conclusion after having studied interviews with Sjöman over time is that: "The older director wants to deny that 491 ever was the personal expression that the young auteur wanted to suggest that it was," *Tabu*, 119.
13. Vilgot Sjöman participated in 2000 in a seminar at Södertörn University College about the Swedish sexual liberalism during the 1960s, see Lena Lennerhed, ed., *Riv alla murar! Vittnesseminarier om sexliberalism och om Pockettidningen R*, Samtidshistoriska institutet, Samtidshistoriska frågor 3 (Södertörns högskola, 2002). An overview of the sexual liberalism and the debate on *491* is given in Lena Lennerhed, "Sexual Liberalism in Sweden" in *Sexual Revolutions*, ed. Gert Hekma & Alain Giami (London: Palgrave Macmillan, 2014).
14. Lennerhed, *Frihet att njuta*, 183 gives more examples.
15. Hans Hederberg, "7 tidningar, 491 och 140," *BLM* 33 (1964): 6.
16. Editorial "Censurskandalen," *Expressen*, December 29, 1963.
17. Mauritz Edström, "De förlorades ansikten," *Dagens Nyheter*, January 3, 1964.
18. Karl Vennberg, "Den hädiska filmen," *Aftonbladet*, January 13, 1964.
19. Erik Hj. Linder, "Vi kan inte blunda. Om '491' och filmcensuren," *Göteborgs-Posten*, January 2, 1964.
20. Jurgen Schildt, "Full pott," *Aftonbladet*, March 17, 1964. A "raggare" is a member of a Swedish anti-establishment subculture that developed in the 1950s among young working class people in the countryside. Cars and cruising are central to the subculture, which has similarities with the American greaser style. At the time, mainstream society expressed concern about the raggare culture, and it became the topic of several youth problem films.
21. See, e.g., Nils Evander, "Censur och humanitet," *Stockholms-Tidningen*, January 4, 1964.
22. Lars Thunberg, "491 och de kristna," *Svenska Dagbladet*, January 22, 1964.
23. See economic historian Klara Arnberg's dissertation *Motsättningarnas marknad: Den pornografiska pressens kommersiella genombrott och regleringen av pornografi 1950–1980* (Lund: Sekel bokförlag, 2010).

24. Harry Schein, "Det hände på 60-talet," in Donner, *Svensk filmografi*, 29.
25. *Language of Love* is discussed in Elisabet Björklund's dissertation *The Most Delicate Subject: A History of Sex Education Films in Sweden* (PhD diss., Lund University, 2012).
26. See, e.g., Mariah Larsson, "Contested Pleasures," in *Swedish Film—An Introduction and Reader*, eds. Mariah Larsson and Anders Marklund (Lund: Nordic Academic Press, 2010).

REFERENCES

Åberg, Anders. *Tabu: filmaren Vilgot Sjöman*. Lund: Filmhäftet, 2001.
Arnberg, Klara. *Motsättningarnas marknad: Den pornografiska pressens kommersiella genombrott och regleringen av pornografi 1950-1980*. Lund: Sekel bokförlag, 2010.
_____, and Mariah Larsson. "Sexualskildringar inför lagen—kommentar till pornografianklagelser." In *Sexualpolitiska nyckeltexter*, edited by Klara Arnberg, Pia Laskar and Fia Sundevall, 219-227. Stockholm: Leopard förlag, 2015.
Björklund, Elisabet. *The Most Delicate Subject: A History of Sex Education Films in Sweden*. Ph.D. diss., Lund University, 2012.
Collmar, Lars. "491 som skriftermål." *Vår lösen* 55 (1964).
Donner, Jörn, ed. *Svensk filmografi 6: 1960-1969*. Stockholm: Svenska filminstitutet, 1977.
Editorial. "Censurskandalen." *Expressen*, December 29, 1963.
Edström, Mauritz. "De förlorades ansikten." *Dagens Nyheter*, January 3, 1964.
Evander, Nils. "Censur och humanitet." *Stockholms-Tidningen*, January 4, 1964.
Hederberg, Hans. "7 tidningar, 491 och 140." *BLM* 33 (1964).
Hedling, Erik. "Breaking the Swedish Sex Barrier: Painful lustfulness in Ingmar Bergman's *The Silence*." *Film International*, 6: 6 (2008): 17-27.
Koskinen, Maaret. *Ingmar Bergman's The Silence: Pictures in the Typewriter, Writings on the Screen*. Seattle: University of Washington Press, 2010.
Larsson, Mariah. "Contested Pleasures." In *Swedish Film—An Introduction and Reader*, edited by Mariah Larsson and Anders Marklund. Lund: Nordic Academic Press, 2010.
Lennerhed, Lena. *Frihet att njuta: Sexualdebatten i Sverige på 1960-talet*. Stockholm: Norstedts, 1994.
_____, ed. *Riv alla murar! Vittnesseminarier om sexliberalism och om Pockettidningen R*. Samtidshistoriska institutet, Samtidshistoriska frågor 3, Södertörns högskola, 2002.
_____. "Sexual Liberalism in Sweden." In *Sexual Revolutions*, edited by Gert Hekma and Alain Giami. London: Palgrave Macmillan, 2014.
Linder, Erik Hj. "Vi kan inte blunda. Om '491' och filmcensuren." *Göteborgs-Posten*, January 2, 1964.
Pethrus, Lewi. "En samhällsväckelse." *Dagen*, January 3, 1964.
_____. "491 och regeringen." *Dagen*, March 14, 1964.
Samuelsson, Kurt. "Melodramatiskt pekoral—men varför förbud?" *Aftonbladet*, December 29, 1963.
Schein, Harry. "Det hände på 60-talet." In *Svensk filmografi 6: 1960-1969*, edited by Jörn Donner. Stockholm: Svenska filminstitutet, 1977.
Schildt, Jurgen. "Full pott." *Aftonbladet*, March 17, 1964.
Sjöman, Vilgot. *Mitt personregister. Urval 98*. Stockholm: Natur och kultur, 1998.
Svenstedt, Carl Henrik. "Intervju med Vilgot Sjöman om 491." In *Svensk filmografi 6: 1960-1969*, edited by Jörn Donner. Stockholm: Svenska filminstitutet, 1977.
Thunberg, Lars. "491 och de kristna." *Svenska Dagbladet*, January 22, 1964.
Vennberg, Karl. "Den hädiska filmen." *Aftonbladet*, January 13, 1964.

The Limits of Sexual Depictions in the Late 1960s

Elisabet Björklund

Introduction

In the 1960s, Swedish film censorship was liberalized. After the enormous censorship debates in the beginning of the decade, mainly started by Ingmar Bergman's *Tystnaden/ The Silence* (1963), and Vilgot Sjöman's *491*, in 1964 (as discussed in the preceding essay by Lena Lennerhed), a process started in which the censorship authorities gradually became more lenient towards depictions of sexuality.[1] The debates lead to the commissioning of two public inquiries, in 1964 and 1965—the first investigating censorship, the second the limits for freedom of speech—which in 1969 proposed the abolishment of censorship and the removal of the obscenity clause in the penal code, respectively.[2] The result was that while censorship would remain until 2011, pornography was legalized in 1971.[3] This important change in Swedish cinema history has been described by many film historians, and a recurrent metaphor used has been that the Swedish "sex barrier" was broken.[4] Often, however, accounts of the process are characterized by quite sweeping descriptions, which leave an impression that after a few important art films broke through the barrier, nothing could really stop Swedish cinema from evolving into further and further explicitness. In his standard history of Swedish cinema, Leif Furhammar, for example, relates the overall development in the following way, creating an image of collapsing floodgates:

> For the first time in years the Swedish film industry broke new historical ground with these films by violating an international taboo and winning a new freedom for the art form. [---] In only a few years the sluices were opened for a flood of sex films that engulfed the world market, and the pornographic film became a large-scale industry, not least in Sweden.[5]

While this and similar descriptions certainly hold some truth—there is no question that more graphic depictions of sex were permitted in the late 1960s than in the early part of the decade—they do, at the same time, not really explain how this change actually happened. Moreover, what sexuality and sex films mean in these contexts is seldom specified.

In this essay, my aim is to explore these issues through an examination of discussions at the National Board of Film Censors during the latter part of the 1960s, after the crucial censorship debates triggered by *The Silence* and *491*. Two issues are in focus: First, how the borders between what was understood as pornographic and what was not were defined and how these definitions changed. Second: The view of sexuality that one can discern in the discourse around films that were considered problematic in their depictions of sex. The material consists of censorship records for films sent from the National Board of Film Censors to their advisory board, the Film Review Council, between the years 1965 and 1971.[6] This material was chosen as the films referred to this council were ones that existed on the verge of what was allowed—the National Board of Film Censors had to consult the advisory council when they considered banning whole films or considerable parts of them. I have also used other sources, such as the head of the censorship board, Erik Skoglund's, personal history of film censorship in Sweden (published in 1971), official reports, and other relevant documents from the archive of the National Board of Film Censors.

The analysis has been inspired by anthropologist Gayle Rubin's classic article "Thinking Sex" about the hierarchies between good and bad sexuality. In this article, written during the so-called sex wars in the 1980s, Rubin argues that modern Western societies distinguish between approved and unapproved sexual practices according to a system of sexual value. This is famously illustrated by a circle with an inner and an outer area in which practices representing good, normal, and natural sexuality are located in the inner, "charmed," circle, while practices representing bad, abnormal, and unnatural sexuality are located in corresponding areas in the "outer limits" of the circle. In the inner circle, one finds sex within marriage or in a relationship, monogamous sex, heterosexuality, procreative sex, and so forth, while the outer circle includes sex that is promiscuous, casual or "in sin," non-procreative sex, homosexuality, sadomasochism, cross-generational sex, sex for money, pornography and so on.[7] Furthermore, Rubin argues that another aspect of this sexual value system is "the need to draw and maintain an imaginary line between good and bad sex."[8] Here, another image, of three walls, illustrates how there exists a "major area of contest" in between the limits to what is understood as good and bad sex. This area includes sexual behaviors that might be on their way to being accepted. "Unmarried couples living together, masturbation, and some forms of homosexuality are moving in the direction of respectability," Rubin notes.[9]

Rubin's article was written in 1984, and her circle thus captures value hierarchies relevant at that particular historical moment. Nevertheless, her main ideas about discourses of good and bad sexuality and the struggle over where to draw the line between these categories provide a useful way of thinking about the norms for sexual behavior in general. As such, they are clearly of importance when examining material in which the limit between acceptable and unacceptable depictions of sex is the central concern. The essay's main argument is that while the main tendency in the censorship decisions was certainly a growing liberalism when it came to sexual explicitness, it was precisely a "good" form of sexuality that was first and foremost granted this increased freedom.

Censorship and Sexuality

In the history of film censorship in Sweden, sexuality has been controlled through two intertwined regulations: Until 1971, pornography was forbidden through the obscenity law in the penal code, which stated that material that was offensive to "discipline and morality" was illegal. This law did not only apply to films but to all kinds of expressions.

Films, however, were more thoroughly controlled than other media as also the subject of censorship through the National Board of Film Censors—established as early as 1911. Naturally, how depictions of sexuality have been treated has varied. The central paragraph in the law regulating the work of the Board included a number of norms that the Board had to follow when examining films. Originally, it was stated that images that violated general laws (for example, the obscenity law) or "good morals," or that could have an effect that was "brutalizing," "exciting" or "confusing the concepts of justice" were not to be allowed. Furthermore, a fifteen-year age limit was to be imposed when a film was considered harmful to children.[10] These norms changed and were rephrased during the history of the Board. A significant change occurred in the 1950s when the phrase about "good morals" was deleted, and "exciting" was changed to "harmfully exciting." During the last years of the National Board of Film Censors, only the concept of "brutalizing" remained.[11]

The National Board of Film Censors was a small institution. Apart from the manager, who was also a censor, it consisted of three permanent film censors. The power of the Board was, however, not absolute. If a film company did not like a decision taken by the Board, they could make an appeal to the government.[12] Furthermore, from 1954, there was the Film Review Council. This council was an advisory body which was to be consulted in cases when the censorship board considered the total prohibition of a film or when the decision considered by the Board would mean a change of norms. The reasons that the council was established were to counter misuse of power by the Board as well as to create a connection between the Board and individuals who represented the public opinion. The members of the council were therefore selected among individuals "who unite an open mind and experience with documented interest in the educating, generally social and cultural significance of cinema."[13]

The liberalization of film censorship in the 1960s had much to do with a significant turning-point in 1963. From now on, the council also had to be consulted when the censorship board considered cutting significant parts of a film, or cutting films that were considered of artistic value. Moreover, the members of the Film Review Council were replaced, and the new council consisted of people who to a greater extent than before represented so-called cultural radical opinions.[14] These changes had a great impact on the outcome of the censorship decisions in subsequent years, especially regarding depictions of sexuality, for example in the cases of *The Silence* and *491*. As is analyzed in Maaret Koskinen's and Per Vesterlund's essays in this volume, there is convincing evidence that the Swedish Film Institute, through its creator and CEO Harry Schein, had an influence in the appointment of the new council and the creation of the new amendment.

That there was antagonism early on between the National Board of Film Censors and the advisory council is clear. In his history of film censorship in Sweden, Erik Skoglund makes no secret of his opinions about the council and also suggests that it had been deliberately appointed to cause trouble for the Board.[15] Skoglund's description and the statistics he provides reveal that the censorship Board and the advisory council agreed to a greater extent in the period between 1954 and 1963 than in the period between 1963 and 1970, and that the Board was generally stricter than the council. In spite of this, Skoglund characterizes the development as an "anticlimax" in comparison with the development that he had feared.[16] He summarizes the influence of the new advisory council in the period 1963–1970 in three points: Regarding sexuality, the council stimulated a strong liberalization of what Skoglund refers to as an "already before 1963 declining censorship praxis."[17] In the case of violence, however, he notes that the Board has succeeded in maintaining its strict attitude. Finally, the council did have an influence in cases where the possible harm of a film needed to be weighed against its values. In these cases, which Skoglund characterize as "relatively rare, but often given much attention in press debate," the council had favored the films' informational or aesthetic aspects.[18] Skoglund's history is not neutral, but written in a personal style and strongly biased in favor of the work of the National Board of Film Censors, and his interpretation can thus be understood as a way to diminish the importance of the advisory council for the ongoing liberalization. At the same time, he is highly critical of the council, which is obvious as he even ends his entire book with the words: "*The sum of the content:* the Film Review Council can be dismissed. That is my last word about film censorship."[19] The censorship cases that I have chosen to study in this essay thus do not only indicate what kinds of depictions were understood as problematic—they might also testify to conflicting opinions and views about these depictions.

Pornography and Non-Pornography

In their examination of specific films, the National Board of Film Censors had two conflated issues to discuss regarding sexual depictions: whether the depiction was pornographic and thus illegal, and if not, whether it could have a "brutalizing" or "harmfully exciting" effect. Regarding the pornography issue, it is clear that the boundaries between the legal and the illegal were being relaxed in the 1960s. When the erotic book *Kärlek I* was published in 1965, it was not prosecuted; and the late 1960s saw a commercial breakthrough for the pornographic press.[20] Yet, as films were more tightly controlled than other media, pornographic films were generally banned with reference to the obscenity law. In censorship records one can, however, see that ideas about what was pornographic and what was not were seldom unanimous, and furthermore that definitions changed with time.

During the time period studied here, some twenty films were banned with reference to the obscenity clause in the penal code. A majority of them were short pornographic films in the 8 mm format, a type of film that had previously seldom been submitted to the Board.[21] The first one during this period was a film called *Black Power*, depicting a black man and a white woman having sexual intercourse, which was submitted to the Board in 1967 and banned without much discussion of the matter.[22] However, the Film Review Council quite soon changed its attitude towards films of the kind. In 1968, as five pornographic 8 mm films were submitted to the Board by a firm called Stockholm's Nude Centre, the advisory council stated that they did not find the films to be violating any laws and that they could thus be released.[23] And they continued to give the same recommendations when asked to give their opinion on similar films later on: in 1969, when four films were submitted by the company Jet film in Gothenburg, and in 1970, when a total of nine 8 mm pornographic films were submitted by different firms in Gothenburg, Malmö, and Karlstad. The head of the advisory council—Sture Palm—was, however, of a different opinion in the cases during 1968 and 1969, and the National Board of Film Censors banned all the films regardless of the council's recommendations. The National Board of Film Censors was also supported by the government in cases when the decisions for these films were appealed. Judging from the descriptions of the films in the censorship records, the films together represented a variety of sexual practices—intercourse in different positions, fellatio, cunnilingus, anilingus, group sex, a woman urinating in a man's mouth, etc. Most of the films showed heterosexual acts, but there were also films with lesbian scenes.[24]

Apart from eight-millimeter short films, a few feature-length films also triggered discussions regarding the definition of pornography. In 1965, the Swedish film *Tillsammans med Gunilla måndag kväll och tisdag/Guilt* (Lars Görling, 1965) was referred to the advisory council because it contained scenes showing a number of indecent carvings of images and words on a fence (among them the words "cock" and "pussy"). As obscene words in spoken language had previously been banned from *491*, Skoglund thought that the same should apply for written words in this case. The council did not, however, find that the images or words violated any law, and the other censors ultimately voted that the film should be released without cuts.[25] Vilgot Sjöman's *Jag är nyfiken—gul/I Am Curious (Yellow)* (1967) was also referred to the advisory council, partly because there was uncertainty about whether or not some scenes were to be judged as pornographic, but this film was also released uncut.[26] Furthermore, in 1968 Stefan Jarl's and Jan Linqvist's eventually acclaimed documentary *Dom kallar oss mods/They Call us Misfits* became a case for the advisory council as it contained a scene with un-simulated intercourse that the censorship board had cut. Censor Råland Häggbom wrote in a statement that he found the scene problematic due to its authenticity which gave the film a "voyeuristic" character.[27] As the decision was appealed to the government, the advisory council was asked to state their opinion, which differed from the Board's—the council did not find the scene to be violating any law. Ultimately, the film was released without cuts, probably making it the earliest legal film in Sweden to show an un-simulated sex scene.[28]

Soon, more examples of un-simulated sexual acts would be released. In 1969 and 1970, the first two installments of Torgny Wickman's sexually explicit series of sex education films—*Ur kärlekens språk/Language of Love* and *Mera ur kärlekens språk/More about the Language of Love* created substantial censorship discussion. The films contained very explicit depictions of different sexual acts, including un-simulated intercourse, masturbation, and oral sex, and a main issue for the censors was precisely whether or not the films were to be regarded as pornography. While *Language of Love* was released with a fifteen-year age limit without cuts after the Board had received statements from the National Board of Education as well as the National Board of Health and Welfare,[29] *More about the Language of Love* was submitted to the Film Review Council for advice. The most controversial parts of the film were a scene about drugs and sexuality, a long sequence from the shooting of a pornographic film involving group sex, and a visit to a porn club in Copenhagen with a live show.[30] As the scene with drugs was recommended to be cut by both the censorship board and the advisory council, the other two scenes triggered discussion regarding whether or not they could be seen as pornographic in themselves or whether they were motivated by the film's educational aim. As Mariah Larsson has related, the members of the advisory council found that the case was problematic even if the law against pornography was about to change. If the film called itself a sex education film but contained pornographic images it would violate the law even if pornography was allowed, as the proposed new law also stated that the content of pornographic films should be clear to the audiences beforehand. The National Board of Film Censors ultimately made cuts in these scenes, but after appealing the case to the government the film was allowed without these cuts.[31]

As the attitude towards sexuality in words and images was in the late 1960s becoming more liberal, the advisory council thus generally took a more tolerant position than did the National Board of Film Censors. However, the problem did not only have to do with images per se, but with intentions and genre designations, as the case of *More about the Language of Love* illustrates. While films showing a diversity of sexual practices were not considered problematic by the council when occurring in 8 mm films, similar practices became problematic when inserted into a film that did not call itself a pornographic film. Labels were thus important, but one could also surmise that, in the eyes of the Film Review Council, *More about the Language of Love* became a problem because it was a feature-length film directed towards a large audience, while the 8 mm pornographic films were probably aimed at the more limited (male) audience visiting sex clubs and sex shops. However, the government—having the final say—judged the issue in the opposite way by supporting bans on the 8 mm films while freeing *More about the Language of Love*. Releasing this film meant that similar films could also be released with similar arguments, and after 1971 the authenticity or explicitness of a sexual depiction alone could no longer be a reason for banning a film.

Brutalizing Depictions

Can viewing sexual acts in the cinema be harmful? And if so: in what way? These questions were, of course, crucial to the censorship board and in the public debate during the 1960s, but the answers shifted. The norms around mental hygiene that the Board had to follow were general clauses, which means that their meaning was not fixed, but open to interpretation by the censors.[32] During the 1960s, it was the concepts "brutalizing" and "harmfully exciting" that were relevant when discussing films with sexual content, and especially the term "brutalizing." But what, then, was a "brutalizing" depiction? In his history of Swedish film censorship published in 1971, Skoglund writes that when the term was first introduced, it referred to "a type of film whose showing could be considered to be degrading generally accepted humanitarian and ethical core values or contribute to the rise or increase of asocial attitudes and behaviors."[33]

Examining which films were banned and what was generally cut from films, one can conclude that the term was closely connected to violence of different kinds, and sexual violence—meaning, for example, rape, but also different BDSM practices (although this term was not used at the time)—was regularly censored as being "brutalizing." Another thing considered taboo was bestiality—sex between humans and animals.[34] But there were also other interpretations of this concept. If one does not only look at the final decisions of the censorship board, but examines the discussions between the different censors and members of the advisory council before a decision was made, one can note many examples in which norms of what was seen as acceptable sexual behavior and what was not are clearly expressed. Here, a group of sexual acts appears which can be described as existing on the limits of the acceptable, or in the "major area of contest" in Rubin's model. Although attitudes were changing, and different individuals naturally had different opinions, I would argue that throughout the 1960s, acts disconnected from love and outside the norm of heterosexual penetrative intercourse were acts existing within this area of potentially brutalizing depictions.

A person who definitely saw these kinds of acts as brutalizing was Erik Skoglund. A telling document is an internal memo he wrote in 1961, in which he discussed the possible harms of sexual depictions on film. He argued that films can have a great influence on the sexual behavior of the young, and that many contemporary films, in which a "sexual licentiousness" is expressed, probably have the effect of being "vulgarizing and degrading to morals and outlook on life through the devaluation of such things as erotic sublimation and adoration of as well as loyalty to the opposite part in a sexual relationship[…]."[35] Further, he writes about how opposing views about sexuality make things difficult for young people, especially as they are at the same time flooded by depictions of sexuality from films and weekly magazines, in which the physical is given more attention that the psychological: "The young are given a wrongful image of the role of love-making in the life of human beings—it almost becomes their only interest—and their idea of love becomes far too materialistic."[36] Skoglund ends his memo by giving examples of what different experts, according to him, claim that an acceptance of early sexual relationships might lead to: "[…] venereal disease, pregnant teenagers, unsolvable housing-issues, economic catastrophes, tragic and painful family conflicts, and so on in incalculable numbers." In light of this, he claims, sex films might be just as harmful as films containing violence.[37]

Going through the censorship records for films referred to the Film Review Council in the years 1965–1971 further underlines this picture. Apart from violence, one can here discern a number of sexual behaviors understood as problematic. Homosexuality was, for example, for a long time a difficult issue for the censorship board, even though a liberalization can be noticed over time. Towards the end of the 1960s, numerous films appeared that depicted sexuality outside of the heterosexual norm, some of them also explicitly thematizing the issue—including *More about the Language of Love* mentioned earlier. One interesting example here is the film *Kvinnolek/To Ingrid, My Love, Lisa* (Börje Nyberg and Joseph W. Sarno, 1968), a film with a lesbian theme. The film was referred to the advisory council because of its lesbian love story, and it was requested that as many as possible of the council's female members be present during the screening. The council advised cuts in the ending scene with lesbian intercourse as well as in a conversation at the end, which also became the decision of the censorship board. The motivation was that the scenes were offensive to discipline and morality, as well as brutalizing. It is not stated why the dialogue at the end was cut, but in the conversation the two female characters tell each other that their previous experiences with men had been bad, while the one they just had together was good.[38] Three years later, homosexual sex acts could pass without cuts in *More about the Language of Love*. The records reveal, however, that the scenes were understood as problematic by the censors, and as a new version of the film was sent to the Board by the film company, cuts had been made in these scenes, which might have influenced the final decision taken by the Board.[39]

But sexuality outside the heterosexual norm was not the only thing considered problematic. Acts that were not vaginal penetration between two partners in a relationship were also on the border of the unacceptable. For example, in Joe Sarno's *Jag, en oskuld/Inga* (1968), three scenes were cut: The scene from a party in the beginning of the film where a young woman is sentenced at a fictional court trial to lose her virginity with a young man (that is, a scene of sex clearly disconnected from a romantic setting), a masturbation scene, and a scene of intercourse. In the intercourse scene, only a section with the partners face to face was allowed to be shown.[40] Regarding masturbation, the view of this changed, however, as a long scene with female masturbation was allowed uncut in the sex education film *Language of Love* that premiered one year later. Oral and anal sex were also considered problematic. In *More about the Language of Love*, scenes of oral sex were seen as questionable in both the heterosexual and the homosexual acts.[41] And while these scenes were ultimately allowed, anal sex is not depicted in any of the films. When it did appear, anal sex was cut, even after pornography had been legalized in 1971. One example of this is the film *The Sensual Woman* (director unknown, 1971), which was first banned completely, as being "brutalizing," but which was later allowed with cuts in a scene of anal intercourse.[42]

Sexual acts involving objects of different kinds were also generally questioned. If not always cut, scenes of the kind were sometimes noted as "abnormal" in censorship records.[43] In *More about the Language of Love*, a scene with an old heterosexual couple having sex using a vibrator was, for example, allowed to pass, but was understood as problematic. An informally written note appended to the minutes from the meeting with the advisory council in the case illustrates this point. The note made a list of "questionable" scenes in the film and here one can read the following:

> The intercourse scene with the aged couple, she stimulated with a dildo...????? Censorship of taste or brutalizing animalism? The concluding "tender" intercourse with cunnilingus and fellatio and massage of the penis.... Where is LOVE? Does it demand porn images? [---] Where is the intimacy ... the quiet seclusion? Who wants to "make love" with many ... as in the closing scenes from the park.[44]

This quote illustrates how sex with objects, as well as non-penetrative sex acts in general, was understood as mechanized sex and in opposition to sex connected to love. And although this was only an informal opinion expressed by someone at the Board (probably Skoglund), it is reasonable to state that this view was more widespread than that. To just give one other example, a few years earlier, when the Danish film *Uden en trævl/Without a Stitch* (Annelise Meineche, 1968) was submitted to the Board, Skoglund wrote the following comment in a statement about the film:

> Under a shimmering surface of glamour, the film praises a totally uninhibited sexual freedom without dissociating itself from any kind of sexual behavior whatsoever: sadism, masocchism [sic], group sex, homosexuality, autoeroticism, eroticism with prosthesis etc.[45]

It was, however, not only Skoglund who was skeptical to the film. The advisory council stated that the film displayed an "inhuman and mechanized conception of sex and outlook on mankind," and that it therefore was brutalizing and should be banned.[46] In the end, *Without a Stitch* was allowed with a cut in a scene of a whipping (and was thus an example of when the censorship board was actually more liberal than the advisory council).[47] Still, these statements show that disconnecting sex from love was clearly understood as problematic.

Depictions that were understood as potentially unhealthy were also questioned, and sometimes the word "pathological" was used when describing certain sexual behaviors. This was generally found in connection with films in horror genres. For example, a much discussed film among the censors in the 1960s was Roman Polanski's *Repulsion* (1965). This film, with its theme of a young woman sliding into mental illness, was seen as problematic in relation to people with psychiatric problems in general, but was also described by some of the censors as containing "sex-pathology" or as having a "sex-pathological" theme.[48]

Finally, gender equality was also at the heart of the thinking around the right form of sexuality, and depictions considered degrading to women were one thing understood as brutalizing.[49] An interesting case in this context is Mac Ahlberg's film *Jag—en kvinna/I, a Woman* (1965), which is sometimes identified as the first film in the Swedish sex film genre. The advisory council thought that the film could be released, but was not opposed to cuts in a scene with a combination of sex and violence at the end of the film. After the council's recommendation, film censor Leif Furhammar wrote a statement in which he claimed that in spite of the bad quality of the film and its speculative character, the film could be seen as making an argument about gender roles. The film was ultimately released without any cuts.[50] That this film was not regarded as brutalizing—not even in a violent scene—might thus be connected to an evaluation of it as offering an empowering view of women.

Conclusion

This essay has analyzed discussions at the National Board of Film Censors about films considered problematic during the period between 1965 and 1971, a time when a radical liberalization of film censorship occurred in Sweden. The material studied elucidates that this development was perhaps not as straightforward as has sometimes been suggested. Rather, there was substantial discussion and debate at the official level, both between and within the different governmental bodies involved, and many films were met with harsh opposition. Moreover, not all expressions of sexuality were given an increased freedom, but depictions displaying sexuality understood as deviant, disconnected from love, unnatural, unhealthy, or unequal were more closely scrutinized, even when the 1960s turned into the 1970s. A similar point is actually made by the public inquiry on film censorship, published in 1969, which recommended the abolishment of censorship. In the report, it is stated that film censorship in Sweden is generally more liberal in matters concerning sexuality than the censorship authorities in most other countries, "in any case concerning ordinary sexuality."[51] What are usually prohibited, according to the report, are scenes of sexual sadism, coercion, rape, and "perversities."[52] In spite of Sweden's reputation of being a country of sexual liberalism, one can thus conclude that there was still a hierarchy between different sexual acts and behaviors during this era of sexual revolution. And while certain sex acts mentioned in Rubin's circle might not have been considered problematic in Sweden in the 1960s (sex outside of marriage, for example), others were more clearly off-limits, such as BDSM sex.

To put this discourse into broader national perspective, one could connect it to what anthropologist and queer scholar Don Kulick—in an analysis that works well together with Rubin's ideas—has called "good sex in Sweden." Kulick argues that sex in Sweden today is actually conditional: sex should be free, the Swedish attitude says, as long as it is "good sex"—sex connected to love and equality. Kulick claims that laws regulating sexuality in Sweden today are actually among the most restrictive in the Western world, among them the law that criminalizes the purchasing of sexual services and legislation around HIV/AIDS. This, however, is not contradictory to the view on sex during the period when Sweden acquired its reputation of being a country of sexual liberalism, but rather an extension of it. Regarding some of the Swedish films that gave rise to Sweden's reputation as a country of promiscuity, including *Hon dansade en sommar*/*One Summer of Happiness* (Arne Mattsson, 1951) and *I Am Curious (Yellow)*, Kulick writes:

> Films like these were regarded as racy outside Sweden, almost as pornography—yet the "Swedish sin" was never decadent or perverse. On the contrary, such films most commonly represented sex by lingering on clean, fresh, svelte women who without hesitation or guilt had intercourse with their clean, fresh, svelte boyfriends. The "Swedish sin" was healthy, natural, good sex.[53]

Although it could be argued that this statement is a generalization—especially since another prominent feature of many Swedish films during this era is that they represent sexuality as something problematic[54]—I would argue that similar results about which kind of sexuality was officially understood as the right one can be detected in many of the records from the National Board of Film Censors that I have discussed. And although it should be clear that the National Board of Film Censors, especially through its head Erik Skoglund, were one of the more conservative forces in the censorship issue during this time, it is not unreasonable to believe that the discourse accounted for here might still be representative of broader attitudes. The fact that censorship was maintained after pornography became legal in 1971—in spite of the conclusions of the public inquiry—might, for example, be an indication of this as it meant that depictions of sex could still be controlled if they were considered "brutalizing" or "harmfully exciting"—that is, if they were considered to be beyond the limit of the good sexuality.

Notes

1. See, e.g., Lena Lennerhed, *Frihet att njuta—sexualdebatten i Sverige på 1960-talet* (Stockholm: Norstedts, 1994), 170–188, Anders Åberg, *Tabu—filmaren Vilgot Sjöman* (Lund: Filmhäftet, 2001), 117–168, Erik Hedling, "Breaking the Swedish Sex Barrier: Painful Lustfulness in Ingmar Bergman's *The Silence*," *Film International* 6 (2008): 17–27.
2. SOU 1969:14, *Filmen—censur och ansvar. Betänkande avgivet av Filmcensurutredningen* (Stockholm, 1969), SOU 1969:38, *Yttrandefrihetens gränser: sårande av tukt och sedlighet, brott mot trosfrid. Betänkande avgivet av Kommittén för lagstiftningen om yttrande-och tryckfrihet* (Stockholm, 1969).
3. See, e.g., Leif Furhammar, *Filmen i Sverige—en historia i tio kapitel och en fortsättning*, third edition (Stockholm: Dialogos förlag and Svenska filminstitutet, 2003), 288–89, Erik Skoglund, *Filmcensuren* (Stockholm: Bokförlaget PAN/Norstedts, 1971), 226–33, Klara Arnberg, *Motsättningarnas marknad—Den pornografiska pressens kommersiella genombrott och regleringen av pornografi i Sverige 1950–1980* (Lund: Sekel Bokförlag, 2010), 183–89, 229–30.
4. See, e.g., Kerstin Vinterhed, "Genom sexvallen—och sedan? Erotiken i svensk sextiotalsfilm," in *Svensk filmografi 6: 1960–1969*, ed. Jörn Donner (Stockholm: Svenska filminstitutet, 1977) and Hedling, "Breaking."
5. Furhammar, *Filmen i Sverige*, 312–13. All translations of quotes from Swedish sources have been made by me.
6. All archival sources referred to in this chapter are from the archive of the National Board of Film Censors at the National Archives of Sweden in Arninge.
7. Gayle S. Rubin, "Thinking Sex: Notes for a Radical Theory of the Politics of Sexuality," in *Culture, Society & Sexuality*, ed. Richard Parker and Peter Aggleton (London: Routledge 2007 [1984]), 151–53.
8. Rubin, "Thinking Sex," 152.
9. Rubin, "Thinking Sex," 152–54. The quote is on p. 152.
10. Skoglund, *Filmcensuren*, 18.
11. SOU 2009:51 *Avskaffande av filmcensuren för vuxna—med förstärkt skydd för barn och unga mot skadlig mediepåverkan. Betänkande av Utredningen om översyn av filmgranskningslagen m.m.* (Stockholm, 2009), 66.
12. Skoglund, *Filmcensuren*, 94–95, 101–105.
13. Quoted in Skoglund, *Filmcensuren*, 106.
14. Skoglund, *Filmcensuren*, 106, 109–10, Lennerhed, *Frihet att njuta*, 173.
15. Skoglund, *Filmcensuren*, 111.
16. Skoglund, *Filmcensuren*, 107–108, 114–15.
17. Skoglund, *Filmcensuren*, 114.
18. Skoglund, *Filmcensuren*, 114.
19. Skoglund, *Filmcensuren*, 242.
20. Arnberg, *Motsättningarnas marknad*, part 3, 137–223.
21. Skoglund writes that the Board had previously not had to deal with this type of film, see

136   III. Obscenity and Censorship

Skoglund, *Filmcensuren*, 189–90. The Board had, however, banned a number of films of this type already in 1963. See censorship cards 100,447, 100,448, 100,449, 100,450, 100,451, 100,452, 100,453, 100,454, 100, 455, and 101,158, series D1A, vol. 72.

22. Censorship card 106,222, series D1A, vol. 76, and minutes from meeting with the Film Review Council, December 4 1967, series A1B, vol. 2.

23. Censorship cards 107,251–107,255, series D1A, vol. 77, and minutes from meeting with the Film Review Council, August 15 1968 (decision taken September 17), series A1B, vol. 2.

24. Censorship cards 108,195–108,198, series D1A, vol. 77, 109,342–109,348, 109,459, and 109,732, series D1A, vol. 78, and minutes from meeting with the Film Review Council, June 24 1969 (decision taken June 27), August 19 1970, September 15 1970, and December 29 1970, series A1B, vol. 2.

25. Dahmén of the council and Erik Skoglund of the censorship board both raised protests, however. Censorship card 103,661, series D1A, vol. 74, and minutes from meeting with the Film Review Council, September 22 1965, series A1B, vol. 2.

26. Censorship card 105,996, series D1A, vol. 76, and memo appended to the minutes from meeting with the Film Review Council, October 4, 1967, series A1B, vol. 2. See also Skoglund, *Filmcensuren*, 180–87.

27. Råland Häggbom, statement regarding the film *Dom kallar oss mods* dated February 14 1968, series E2, vol. 1048.

28. Censorship card 106,500, series D1A, vol. 76, and minutes from meeting with the Film Review Council, March 7 1968, series A1B, vol. 2.

29. Censorship card 108,409, series D1A, vol. 78.

30. For a detailed account of the censorship of these films, see Björklund, *Most Delicate Subject: A History of Sex Education Films in Sweden* (PhD diss., Lund University, 2012), 181-192.

31. Censorship card 109,427, series D1A, vol. 78, minutes from meeting with the Film Review Council, September 15 1970, series A1B, vol. 2, and Mariah Larsson, "Drawing the Line—Generic Boundaries of the Pornographic Film on Early 1970s Sweden," in Conference Proceedings from NorLit Conference, ed. Magnus Ullén et al (Linköping: Linköping Electronic University Press, 2009–2010).

32. Skoglund, *Filmcensuren*, 115–16.

33. Skoglund, *Filmcensuren*, 132.

34. See, e.g., censorship card 109,970, series D1A, vol. 79, archive of the National Board of Film Censors.

35. Erik Skoglund, "Varför kan filmskildringar av sexuella relationer vara 'skadliga' ur filmcensurens synpunkt?," internal memo dated April 6, 1961, series F 6, vol. 6, 2.

36. Skoglund, "Varför kan filmskildringar," 3.

37. Skoglund, "Varför kan filmskildringar," 4.

38. Censorship card 106,800, series D 1 A, vol. 76, Letter to the Film Review Council from Erik Skoglund dated February 20, 1968, and minutes of a meeting with the Film Review Council March 12, 1968, series A1B, vol. 2.

39. Letter to Erik Skoglund at the National Board of Film Censors from Elit-Film regarding re-editing of *More about the Language of Love*, dated September 28, 1970, and editing report of *More about the Language of Love*, series E2, vol. 1106, no. 819/70.

40. Censorship card 106,674, series D1A, vol. 76.

41. Notes about questionable scenes in *More about the Language of Love* appended to minutes to meeting with the Film Review Council, September 15, 1970, series A1B, vol. 2.

42. Censorship card 110,046 and 110,468, series D1A, vol. 79.

43. See, e.g., censorship card 109,342, series D1A, vol. 78, for the pornographic film *MF 4* where it is noted that the film shows a number of sexual acts "[…] partly outside the borders of the normal, for example the use of a dildo."

44. Notes about questionable scenes in *More about the Language of Love* appended to minutes to meeting with the Film Review Council, September 15, 1970, series A1B, vol. 2, 5.

45. Statement by Erik Skoglund about the film *Without a Stitch*, appended to the minutes from meeting with the Film Review Council, October 18, 1968, series A1B, vol. 2.

46. Minutes from meeting with the Film Review Council, October 18, 1968, series A1B, vol. 2. Two of the council's members, however, registered reservations against the decision.

47. Censorship card 107,388, series D1A, vol. 77.

48. Erik Skoglund, summary of discussion about the film *Repulsion* at the Film Review Council, June 16 1965, series A1B, vol. 2, 2, 9.

49. See, e.g., Skoglund, "Varför kan filmskildringar," 2.
50. Censorship card 103,784, series D1A, vol. 74, minutes from the meeting with the Film Review Council, October 29 1965, and Leif Furhammar, statement regarding *I, a Woman*, November 1 1965, series A1B, vol. 2.
51. SOU 1969: 14, 24.
52. SOU 1969: 14, 24.
53. Don Kulick, "Four Hundred Thousand Swedish Perverts," *GLQ—A Journal of Lesbian and Gay Studies*, 11 (2005): 205–235, 110.
54. See Anu Koivunen's contribution to this volume.

REFERENCES

Archive of the National Board of Film Censors, National Archives of Sweden, Arninge

Censorship cards (series D1A)
Vol. 72: 100,447 (*Garderoben*), 100,448 (*Episod i äktenskap*), 100,449 (*Tjuvgods*), 100,450 (*Kapitalistiska förlustelser*), 100,451 (*Flickan och flaskan*), 100,452 (*Another Soderhamn Exclusive*), 100,453 (*Intermezzo*), 100,454 (*Prelude*), 100,455 (*Beauties Parade*), 101,158 (*Stök i kök*)
Vol. 74: 103,661 (*Guilt*), 103,784 (*I, a Woman*)
Vol. 76: 105,996 (*I Am Curious [Yellow]*), 106,222 (*Black Power*), 106,500 (*They Call Us Misfits*), 106,674 (*Inga*), 106,800 (*To Ingrid, My Love, Lisa*)
Vol. 77: 107,251 (*Pornografi A*), 107,252 (*Pornografi B*), 107,253 (*Sexuality*), 107,254 (*Den erotiska servitrisen/The Erotic Waitress*), 107,255 (*Cowboykärlek/Cowboylove*), 107,388 (*Without a Stitch*), 108,023 (*Vixen!*), 108,195 (*Porrspegel—69*), 108,196 (*Loving Girls*), 108,197 (*Het lek 1*), 108,198 (*Lola som fotomodell*)
Vol. 78: 108,409 (*Language of Love*), 109,342 (*M F 4*), 109,343 (*M F 5*), 109,344 (*M F 6*), 109,345 (*Bed Geisha*), 109,346 (*Whysky*), 109,347 (*Einbrecher*), 109,348 (*He Makes Them Happy*), 109,427 (*More About the Language of Love*), 109,458 (*M F 11/Call Girl*), 109,732 (*Kinky Dreams*)
Vol. 79: 109,970 (*Why?*), 110,046 (*The Sensous Woman*), 110,468 (*The Sensous Woman*)

Correspondence in Censorship Issues

I, a Woman
Furhammar, Leif. Statement regarding *I, a Woman*, dated November 1 1965. Series A1B, vol. 2.
They Call Us Misfits
Häggbom, Råland. Statement regarding the film *They Call Us Misfits*, dated February 14 1968. Series E2, vol. 1048.
I Am Curious (Yellow)
Memo appended to the minutes from meeting with the Film Review Council, October 4, 1967. Series A1B, vol. 2.
To Ingrid, My Love, Lisa
Letter to Statens filmgranskningsråd from Erik Skoglund dated February 20, 1968. Series A1B, vol. 2.
Without a Stitch
Statement by Erik Skoglund appended to the minutes from meeting with the Film Review Council, October 18, 1968. Series A1B, vol. 2.
More About the Language of Love
Letter to Erik Skoglund at the National Board of Film Censors from Elit-Film regarding re-editing of *More About the Language of Love*, dated September 28 1970. Series E2, vol. 1106, no. 819/70.
Editing report of *More About the Language of Love*. Series E2, vol. 1106, no. 819/70.

Minutes from meetings with the Film Review Council

Skoglund, Erik. Summary of discussion about *Repulsion*, June 16 1965. Series A1B, vol. 2.
September 22 1965. Series A1B, vol. 2 (*Guilt*).
October 29 1965. Series A1B, vol. 2 (*I, a Woman*).
December 4 1967. Series A1B, vol. 2 (*Black Power*).
March 7 1968. Series A1B, vol. 2 (*They Call Us Misfits*).

March 12, 1968. Series A1B, vol. 2 (*To Ingrid, My Love, Lisa*).
August 15 1968 (decision taken September 17 1968). Series A1B, vol. 2 (*Pornografi A, Pornografi B, Sexuality, Den erotiska servitrisen/The erotic waitress*, and *Cowboykärlek/Cowboylove*).
October 18, 1968. Series A1B, vol. 2 (*Without a Stitch*).
April 28, 1969. Series A1B, vol. 2 (*Vixen!*).
June 24 1969 (decision taken June 27). Series A1B, vol. 2 (*Porrspegel—69, Loving Girls, Het lek 1, Lola som fotomodell*).
August 19 1970. Series A1B, vol. 2 (*M F 4, M F 5, M F 6, Bed Geisha, Whysky, Einbrecher*, and *He Makes Them Happy*).
September 15 1970. Series A1B, vol. 2 (*M F 11/Call Girl* and *More About the Language of Love*).
December 29 1970. Series A1B, vol. 2 (*Kinky Dreams*).

Other Documents

Skoglund, Erik. "Varför kan filmskildringar av sexuella relationer vara 'skadliga' ur filmcensurens synpunkt?." Internal memo dated April 6, 1961. Series F 6, vol. 6.

Other Sources

Åberg, Anders. *Tabu—filmaren Vilgot Sjöman*. Lund: Filmhäftet, 2001.
Arnberg, Klara. *Motsättningarnas marknad—Den pornografiska pressens kommersiella genombrott och regleringen av pornografi i Sverige 1950-1980*. Lund: Sekel Bokförlag, 2010.
Björklund, Elisabet. *The Most Delicate Subject: A History of Sex Education Films in Sweden*. Ph.D. diss., Lund University, 2012.
Furhammar, Leif. *Filmen i Sverige—en historia i tio kapitel och en fortsättning*, third edition. Stockholm: Dialogos Förlag and Svenska filminstitutet, 2003.
Hedling, Erik. "Breaking the Swedish Sex Barrier: Painful Lustfulness in Ingmar Bergman's *The Silence*." *Film International* 6 (2008): 17–27.
Kulick, Don. "Four Hundred Thousand Swedish Perverts." *GLQ—A Journal of Lesbian and Gay Studies*, 11 (2005): 205–235.
Larsson, Mariah. "Drawing the Line: Generic Boundaries of the Pornographic Film in Early 1970s Sweden." In Conference Proceedings from NorLit Conference, edited by Magnus Ullén et al. Linköping: Linköping University Electronic Press, 2009–2010.
Lennerhed, Lena. *Frihet att njuta—sexualdebatten i Sverige på 1960-talet*. Stockholm: Norstedts, 1994.
Rubin, Gayle S. "Thinking Sex: Notes for a Radical Theory of the Politics of Sexuality." In *Culture, Society & Sexuality*, edited by Richard Parker and Peter Aggleton. London: Routledge 2007 [1984].
Skoglund, Erik. *Filmcensuren*. Stockholm: Bokförlaget PAN/Norstedts, 1971.
SOU 1969:14. *Filmen—censur och ansvar. Betänkande avgivet av Filmcensurutredningen*. Stockholm: 1969.
SOU 1969:38. *Yttrandefrihetens gränser: sårande av tukt och sedlighet, brott mot trosfrid. Betänkande avgivet av Kommittén för lagstiftningen om yttrande- och tryckfrihet*. Stockholm: 1969.
SOU 2009:51. *Avskaffande av filmcensuren för vuxna—med förstärkt skydd för barn och unga mot skadlig mediepåverkan. Betänkande av Utredningen om översyn av filmgranskningslagen m.m.* Stockholm: 2009.
Vinterhed, Kerstin. "Genom sexvallen—och sedan? Erotiken i svensk sextiotalsfilm." In *Svensk filmografi 6: 1960-1969*, edited by Jörn Donner. Stockholm: Svenska filminstitutet, 1977.

IV

The Institutionalization of Sex in Sweden

Institutionalized Sexploitation?
The Swedish Film Institute and Research on the Effects of Cinema in the 1960s

Per Vesterlund

In the archives of the Swedish Film Institute there is a series of letters with an intriguing content. The letters were all written in the spring of 1967 by the managing director of the Institute, Harry Schein. The addressees were a number of film distributors around the world. Schein wrote to small companies in countries such as Denmark and Japan, or to obscure independent distributors in Sweden. The purpose was to request certain kinds of films. Thus, not a very surprising business in a correspondence involving a national film institute?

The surprising matter here is the very detailed descriptions of the films requested. In a memorandum attached to a letter addressed to a managing director by the name Jack Nyman written on March 13, 1967, we can see a concentrate of the very special cinematic requests from Schein and the Film Institute:

> A research project studying the influence of pornographic film on the audiences is contemplated. According to the preliminary plans five programs of each about 30 minutes are requested. At least one program should be composed of films of primarily homosexual contents with men only and lesbian content with women only, while the remaining three programs should be of heterosexual character. One of them with only one woman and one man, while the two others may contain scenes with several people.[1]

This planned project on pornography was one small part of a much bigger project. The Swedish "film reform" of 1963 has generally been associated with changes in the strategies of subsidies to national film production. An oft-neglected aspect of the film reform of 1963 is, however, Harry Schein's explicit ambition to liberalize governmental censorship in Sweden. In 1964, Schein initiated a group of scholars from different academic fields—including sociology, psychology, pedagogy, and political science—with the purpose of studying the effects of the medium of film on audiences. The group worked with individual or collective projects, studying audiences and genres, such as pornography, Westerns, or films containing violence. From Harry Schein's point of view the aim of the research was crystal clear—the purpose was to show that films could not be proven to cause any damage to viewers.

An important area of research that was identified was the impact of the representation of sexuality on film audiences. One problem was, however, gaining legal access to appropriate films usable for the project. The Film Institute, through Harry Schein, tried to solve the problem by attempting to buy porn films from abroad (i.e. Denmark or Japan) or by asking the Swedish army (where pornographic films were shown to soldiers in different psychological experiments) to cooperate. There were even plans for the Film Institute to produce its own films with sexual content. Apparently this topic was an essential one to study.

This essay is not primarily a study of pornography, liberalization, or moralism—even if these three topics are in focus throughout. The aim is rather to highlight tensions between political power, scholarship, and public debate in Swedish society of the 1960s. The research on cinema financed by the Swedish Film Institute is a case that provides both symptomatic and extraordinary views of its time. The way liberalization and governmentality interacted when the effects of film were handled by politicians, by filmmakers, or by scholars and intellectuals in the Swedish welfare state is paradoxical. On the one hand, there seems to have existed an apparent belief in freedom of speech and thought, with a liberal and anti-authoritarian pathos that found one of its expressions in the debate on film censorship. On the other hand, the way Harry Schein—and the Film Institute—handled this urgent question is at the same time an example of research governed and controlled by the financiers in a manner that not only can be seen as dubious, but which is also an example of social engineering that might be regarded as patronizing in its use of the social sciences.

Another purpose of this essay is to highlight the hitherto neglected work of the SFI Film Research Group. This scholarly group, partly situated outside academia, can first be assumed to have had at least some impact on the forthcoming academic field of media studies, as well as on cinema studies of the Swedish future (i.e., from 1970 and onwards). Second, and more interestingly, the group appears to have been an important impetus in both public debate and actual political action regarding national film censorship in Sweden in the 1960s. Third, documents from the work of this group of scholars seem to express a kind of zeitgeist. They are historical traces from a time of radical changes. In the 1960s, media use changed rapidly, cinema became an art form in the public mind, and the content in even mainstream films—for the same public mind—became more challenging, not least regarding representations of sexuality.

Below I will discuss documents from the Film Research Group. To some extent the material consists of official reports, but mostly I will base the discussion on memoranda and correspondence of a more unofficial kind from the archives of Harry Schein and of the Swedish Film Institute; not with the expectation of finding a very representative or reliable picture of the general discourse on media (or film) effects, or even sexuality, of the time, but rather with an aim to study a more rare case of political power, liberalization, and commerce in flux. In the case of Sweden, a moral discourse on media content seems to have been at stake.[2] Not least the discourse on sexual matters and cinema, in this case more precisely pornography, was as we shall see a crucial matter in the discussions on these questions. The institutional setting of the work of the group was complex, with representatives from the academy, the film industry and governmental authorities involved.

The Establishment of the Film Research Group

In the beginning of 1964, Harry Schein and The Swedish Film Institute initiated a group of scholars named the Film Research Group to be financed by the Institute. The aim of institutionalizing scholarly studies of cinema was in itself not surprising. One of the intentions of the Swedish film reform of 1963 was to account for finance and organize film cultural activities such as film archives and the knowledge of cinema in society as a whole. But these scholars were not experts in the field of cinema, a field which for that matter was in Sweden not yet really subject to any serious academic interest. Rather, the academic skills of the researchers chosen were of the kind that was most trusted in the expert society of its time. Hence the group consisted mainly of senior scholars from the fields of psychology, pedagogy, and sociology, and the purpose was solely to study the effects of films on viewers and audiences.

Harry Schein himself was no scholar at all. This is an important fact to bear in mind. He was an engineer, a businessman, and a public intellectual with widespread contacts in the national political elite. His position in the film research group was foremost administrative, but he nevertheless seems to have been able to exert a vast influence on the content and direction of the research. The very idea of the Film Institute funding film research was in fact his idea.

Apart from being a neglected part in the history of the Swedish film reform, the work of the Film Research Group is a both overlooked and important chapter in the history of Swedish film and media studies.[3] The research questions that the Film Research Group posed were not primarily based in any pure scholarly curiosity of the representatives of SFI (i.e. Harry Schein), nor of the researchers themselves. And the intention behind this large research project on the effects of film cannot be identified as an example of moral panic. Neither were the researchers—or the Institute—interested in efficient ways to conduct film propaganda. Instead the ambition was to challenge the national institution of governmental film censorship and provide an intellectual and scientific ground for its future abolishment.

Harry Schein had for a long time been a devoted enemy of censorship. Already a couple of weeks after the very founding of the SFI in the summer of 1963, he had told the managing director of the National Board of Film Censors, Erik Skoglund, that he (i.e. Skoglund) would be going through a hard time in the near future.[4] And hard times were going to come.

These "hard times" for Swedish censorship were of course due not only to the workings of Harry Schein and of the Film Research Group. This was the early sixties. It was a time of youth revolution, political awakenings, liberalization of sexuality, etcetera. But it is nevertheless interesting to note this very explicit initiative from the managing director of the SFI, not least when it comes to the use of research.

The core of the research group consisted of four distinguished professors: Sven Ahnsjö (child psychiatry), Torgny Segerstedt (sociology), Gudmund Smith (psychology) and Arne Trankell (pedagogy). Harry Schein functioned as chairman of the group, and the secretary was Leif Furhammar, Ph.Lic. in pedagogy (later to become professor in cinema studies at Stockholm University in the 1980s). The group worked on individual or collective projects, studying audiences and genres. If the aim from Schein's point of view was to advocate a political position vis-à-vis censorship—that films cannot be proven to cause damage or to have severe effects on its audiences and on the society—for the researchers, on the other hand, the initiative from SFI provided an opportunity to institute clusters of scholars oriented towards identifying new research on media effects.

In a memorandum signed by Harry Schein in October 1964—thus barely a year since the group first was initiated—no fewer than fifteen different topics were listed as projects to be financed by the film institute. Some of them were aimed at more general questions on the effects of film—such as a research overview of the whole field of film and psychology, or Leif Furhammar's dissertation in pedagogy on the effects of film on spectators. Others were more narrow surveys, such as one on audiences' experiences of Western films or a reception study on Ingmar Bergman's *Tystnaden/The Silence* (1963). A couple of projects focused on youth and children, through topics such as juvenile delinquency or the ways film viewing might influence school work.[5]

During the first years the tensions between Schein's intentions for the group on the one hand, and the scholarly practice of the group on the other hand, became apparent in the correspondence around the projects. According to later comments by Schein, the freedom of research would of course be guaranteed. But he also said that with respect to the "primary aim of our investment in research, it would be good if the members of the film research group were radicals."[6]

Not all the researchers seem to have been comfortable with the expectations regarding their research or, more precisely, with the fact that the institution that paid for the research had also decided which results were desirable. One member of the very core of the group, sociologist Torgny Segerstedt (also vice-chancellor of Uppsala University), was, for example an eager advocate for the maintenance of film censorship.

These tensions were perhaps not only due to political, scientific, or scholarly ideals. An obvious fact was, of course, that if research on media effects should be able to prove that the medium under study—in this case film—had no evident effects on audiences, it would at the same time be a way to say that any further research on the subject of film effects would probably be in vain. It might even—in an exaggerated scenario—make the researchers themselves redundant, as their own research would become unnecessary.

The different projects were mainly conducted at the respective university of each individual researcher. But the Film Institute paid for the projects and provided a common platform for interdisciplinary discussions. In the autumn of 1964, however, the Institute created another function for the group. An official inquiry was set up by the Department of Culture and Education to investigate governmental film censorship and to propose new instructions for the future. Close cooperation between the Film Research Group and this public inquiry was immediately initiated. Schein had an extensive network of connections in the political sphere. So, even if the Film Research Group had no actual authority from the government, the group (under the command from Schein) took the initiative to publish conclusive parts of their results as a separate public official report—independently of the report that the main governmental inquiry was going to produce.

So which were the possible reasons for the Film Institute to interfere in the public inquiry of film censorship? The answer must be divided into personal, institutional, and historical explanations. The regulation of public film exhibition can of course be proposed to be a topic of vast interest for the film industry for commercial reasons, with the major companies represented on the board of the Institute; and the general liberalization and secularization of society may be seen as a force in itself, not least in the realm of filmmaking. The freedom of art for filmmakers in the 1960s was to a huge extent a matter of being at the cutting edge—politically, morally, and aesthetically. And then there was Harry Schein himself.

Harry Schein Fighting Moralism

Swedish film was in the 1960s a huge success abroad. But was that success not founded on pure speculation? Domestic enthusiasm about overseas success was not always overwhelming.[7] Harry Schein defended the erotica of the much talked about Swedish films—it was, according to him, foremost a reflection of a society where the attitude towards sexuality was liberal and free. This was the case in Sweden more than in other countries, when it came to acceptance by the press, churches, audiences, and public opinion. Swedes were perhaps not ahead of their time, but at least they tried to keep up with it, and that was not a matter that should be apologized for. But the accusations of exploitation were a matter to be challenged. Schein used irony in his defense:

> For sure, Swedish film producers speculate in sex. In contrast to foreign producers, they want to make money, and they imagine that you do that by speculating in the kinds of films that people want to see. But the producers are not our only sex speculators. Our film directors also speculate in sex. Not only in sex. Every shot, every cut is a speculation—in sex, in suspense, in lyrical, epic, and dramatic effects. Sometimes speculation fails; then the film turns out bad. Sometimes it succeeds; then the film turns out to be good.
>
> Thus speculation is the big problem of Swedish film. Not until we have eliminated speculation from Swedish film can we meet the foreign press in good conscience, as open-minded equals. For no one has ever met a newspaper owner who speculates with his paper, or a film critic who speculates when he writes.[8]

A society free from speculation is a utopia, according to Harry Schein. For more than twenty years he had been a part of Swedish public life, and throughout all those years he had been an enemy of moralism. But he was also an advocate of what could be described as a pessimistic pragmatism, in his early years with a slight touch of anarchy. The rejection of moralism was for the young Harry Schein paralleled with an outspoken resistance towards all kinds of authorities, a somewhat ironic fact considering his later connections in the national field of political power. Already in his very first public speech—at the modernist literary society Klubb 44 in 1945—he had been discussing pornography, eager to display no moral prejudices towards the subject. Also in the Film Research Group, Schein pleaded that studies of pornography—if included in the work of the scholars—should be handled without any moral presumptions.

The theme of pornography was proposed by Schein as a convenient subject for the group to study.[9] In a memorandum from a meeting in December 1966, where the official governmental inquiry on film censorship and the Film Research Group together discussed the future direction of their joint work, the question was raised whether the group should focus not only on sex and violence in mainstream cinema but also make pornography a part of the investigation. Besides being head of the SFI, Schein was also at this time a member of the board of the RFSU—The Swedish Association for Sexuality Education—and shared an interest in questions of attitudes towards representations of sexuality in general. The proposed investigation would include both surveys on the use of pornography by Swedish citizens, as well as psychological tests with pornographic films shown to a test audience.

An initial difficulty of this task was to find proper objects to study. Just as concerned as Harry Schein was to accomplish the studies on pornography, just as eager was he to make this part of the work of the Film Research Group be carried out with relative discretion. An investigation based on showings of pornographic films—still illegal in Sweden at this time—to average Swedish citizens, some of them even teenagers according to the design of the experiments, would be highly controversial, despite the so much talked about liberal Swedish attitudes towards sexuality. Schein tried to persuade established directors including Vilgot Sjöman to produce pornographic films to use in the investigations.[10] He wrote to distributors around the world. He even tried to borrow pornographic films that he knew had been used at Karolinska university hospital for psychological tests, but none of these films were available at this time due to a big ongoing investigation on stress for the Swedish army.[11]

The Question of Pornography

The concept of pornography seems to have been a recurrent issue in the meetings of the Film Research Group since the beginning of 1964. But it was not until the autumn of 1966 that the members of the group seem to have seriously considered turning the question of pornography into a project of its own.

So what was the question? As (for instance) Klara Arnberg has stated in her research on the pornographic press in Sweden during the same years, the 1960s was a decade when liberal and radical voices around the issue of sexuality and pornography were strengthened at the same time as conservative groups tended to use more radical methods in debating this phenomenon.[12] In the midst of this force field, one urgent question for the Film Research Group seems to have been to define the very concept of pornography. A film such as Bergman's *The Silence* was for many Swedes, not least from the perspective of the more conservative groups in national public life, considered to be sheer pornography. For others in Swedish society—not least the growing group of so-called cultural radicals in political life, media, and the film industry—this film was for sure art. The interest of the film industry seems to have been to define boundaries towards real pornography. For the Swedish Film Institute the task was to be able to motivate a publicly supported subsidy on films that for a vast part of the audience were regarded as indecent. At the same time, they needed to discuss these matters in a way that would not seem too defensive in the eyes of the cultural radicals, who by the mid–1960s dominated the parts of the intelligentsia who were interested in film as an art form. The interpretation of the very concept of pornography seems to have been surrounded by uncertainty, at least when it came to pornographic films which, unlike pornographic books and magazines, were censored. Because of this, the common knowledge of these kinds of films was low.

It could be tempting to look for expressions of the two extreme positions in the documents—to capture a contest between on the one hand moralism and on the other liberalism or cultural radicalism. Maybe disappointedly, but interestingly, this battle seems not to have been fought in the discussions held in the Film Research Group or at the film researchers' frequent meetings with the official film censorship inquiry. Neither is the discussion dominated by either of the two extreme sides. Rather, the participants seem to have been more eager to speculate about the possible outcome of a situation with no more censorship of films for an adult audience. Would pornography increase? Would the behavior of the audience change? Would the major companies turn their production to pornography proper, or would new minor film companies appear, companies that mainly produced porno, i.e., a situation already prevalent for the press? And what would be the effects on audiences in that case?

The researchers' and censorship investigation members' familiarity with the pornographic press (and books) seems to have been much deeper than their knowledge about pornographic films. This is not surprising as printed pornography had been available for a long time, and in the mid–1960s increased rapidly due to liberal opinion on these matters.[13] One example is the protocol from the meeting on December 16, 1966, where thirty-one of the fifty-seven pages are about the question of pornography. Most of this space is devoted to questions like the ones above. And on an explicit level, the questions and the tentative answers seem to have been focused on knowledge rather than on morals. And this knowledge concerned the press, not moving pictures. The opinions and experiences of the printed media were thus transferred to the yet unknown field of pornographic film of the future.

But behind the seemingly neutral way of talking about things that no one seemed to know anything about, a more biased discourse is apparent. For example, psychologist Claes Janssen describes pornography as—besides of course being hypothetically damaging for people—having three hypothetical effects of an important kind: It could be arousing, it could be a surrogate (i.e. for prisoners or for people with "such perversions that could be hard to satisfy otherwise"), and it could have a learning outcome.[14] People could, according to Janssen, learn incredibly much about the relationship between the two sexes from pornography. It could make prejudices disappear and make people less suppressed and more relaxed. Janssen's friendly attitude towards pornography is obvious, but it is hidden behind a hypothetical scientific discussion that foregrounds the effects of pornography. His arguments are mainly derived from observations of pornographic novels and short stories. Janssen stated that he actually did not know anything about pornographic films, though a member of the Film Research Group since almost three years.

Harry Schein finished the meeting on December 16 by stating that more knowledge was needed; and as a summary of a long discussion he proposed two kinds of studies. The first would focus on getting an overview of the consumption of pornography. With more knowledge on recent pornographic consumption a more experimental investigation on the effects of pornography on real people—maybe frequent consumers—could be done later.

On February 3, 1967, the next meeting in the same institutional context was held. The first sociological survey of consumption would now be done (in cooperation with the press distribution company Svenska Pressbyrån) to gather information about the consumers of actual pornographic magazines. This is somewhat ironic, since the producers of pornographic press in these years (1966–1969) used other distributors than Svenska Pressbyrån.[15] In the meeting, Professor Olaf Elthammar, a psychiatrist, proposed an investigation where two groups of youths aged thirteen and sixteen years respectively would be shown pornographic pictures—stills and movies—to compare their reactions. The intensity of the reactions of the individuals involved would be measured, and interviews conducted. Also Maj-Briht Bergström-Walan, established public sexologist and psychologist, who participated in the meeting as a member of the USSU (the governmental investigation on sex education), stressed the question of sex education. The discussion turned out to focus on the age groups of the surveys to be made. The youth was important, but would it be ethical to ask thirteen- or fifteen year olds about their consumption of pornography? Bergström-Walan objected that opposition from parents would be expected if school children were asked about such private matters. Besides, children in their early teens would be too shy to give valuable answers to such questions. Child psychiatrist Sven Ahnsjö responded that the most important thing was to find out how youths—twelve to eighteen years old—experienced these problems, whatever their parents said.¹⁶ Professor Elthammar told the group about a current experiment on the effects of "highly provocative films" on eleven, thirteen, fifteen, and eighteen year-olds.

By the end of the month, in February 1967, yet another meeting was held. Unfortunately, no protocol from this occasion is preserved in the archives of the Swedish Film Institute. By this time the projects on pornography seem to have been initiated, at least Harry Schein's efforts to find appropriate films for the projects. Some project abstracts (undated) exist in the archive, among others one by a Ragnar Montelius at the Department of Pedagogy at Stockholm University who was going to examine the "Effects of representations of intercourse." A project that was motivated by the present political situation of national film censorship.

The Influence of Film on Its Audience—An Official Report from the Swedish Film Institute

As things turned out, the investigations into the effects of pornography were never conducted. Maybe the proper film material was not to be found on the tight time schedule that the research group now faced.¹⁷ All the other results of the research group were nevertheless sufficient. The results could now be sampled in the Research Group's own *public* investigation: *Filmens inflytande på sin publik: rapport från Svenska filminstitutets filmforskningsgrupp*/"The Influence of Film on Its Audience: Report from the Film Research Group of the Swedish Film Institute."

The report preceded the major public inquiry on film censorship by two years when it was published in June 1967, as a part of the main report to come. The results were unambiguous. No effects whatsoever of films on audiences could be proven to exist. It was indeed impossible to measure or verify the possibility or power of films to influence people. The researchers were unanimous. Even Vice Chancellor Segerstedt, the sociologist from Uppsala, who had entered the research group with a very supportive attitude towards film censorship, had now agreed to sign the conclusion of the investigation. According to the secretary of the group, Leif Furhammar, Harry Schein had prepared Segerstedt with flattering remarks on his integrity, how he had stuck to his conviction all the way until the end. Despite the compelling research by his colleagues from the group on the opposite position, he did not abandon the thought of film censorship as having an important function in society.¹⁸ But Schein was also very pleased that Segerstedt had changed his opinion, a pleasure Schein without doubts shared with the chair of the main censorship inquiry, Gunnar Ekbladh:

> Brother,
> The Film Research group had a meeting yesterday where we agreed on the design of our final report. Its conclusions will give an unambiguous picture and I am very pleased that consensus has been reached on this matter, not least since Segerstedt earlier declared himself supportive of censorship.¹⁹

The point of view regarding censorship from the chair of the Film Research Group was indeed no secret. Not even to the chair of the public inquiry proper that was about to make recommendations about the future of the National Board of Film Censors.

So by the end of June 1967 the Film Research Group presented their collected results so far. The report also achieved official status as a public governmental inquiry, which is perhaps one of the most surprising things in the whole case of the Film Research Group. The report, which was written mainly by Furhammar, consisted of eleven chapters, each one dealing with different aspects of the subject: "The concept of damage," "Film as a pedagogical tool," "Influence on attitudes," "Frequency of cinema going," "Age and effects of film," "Psychiatric disturbances," "Film and criminality" (two chapters), "Film experience and defense mechanisms," "Effects of censorship," and "The will to censor and the image of reality."

The concept of damage was deconstructed. According to the report, it was almost impossible to define. And the value of film as a pedagogic tool was also impossible to specify. Further, the report stated that the "ways the film inflects the attitudes of the audience cannot be isolated from the constant co-operation with other sources of influence," but education on the language of film could counteract "effects of displaced attitude from tendentious films."[20]

Cinema audiences consist mainly of young people (seventeen-year olds are top rated) and connections exist between bad results in school, reading of comic books instead of good literature, and a "negative correlation with intelligence." According to the report, the cause and effect are not obvious, however. The most voluminous chapter discusses age and influence from films, concluding that it is not possible to extract any general pattern when it comes to influences on children, regarding age, content, or effects. Films can cause anguish and fear, but an investigation made of watching films on television had shown that 35 per cent of a group of nine and eleven year old children had actually seen films with a 15-year age limit on television, and "nearly all of them approved of it."

The connection between films and criminality is also, not surprisingly, according to the report almost impossible to prove, with one expectation: films that function as instructions on certain criminal techniques. But such information ought to be easier to get from other sources than films. Experiments with showing films containing violence have actually been seen to have effects for certain groups of viewers. The hypothesis of the report is that individuals in these groups have special dispositions to perceive violent scenes in certain manners.

What really had effects, according to the report, was censorship. The report suggested in the tenth chapter that censoring film, cutting away scenes etcetera, would produce in the audiences an expectation of sensational and controversial content. As a result, censorship counteracts the intentions of its own measures. The last chapter, finally, contains a discussion on how people who support censorship in general build their opinion on emotional rather than rational grounds.

Cinema was thus not a dangerous medium, and the Film Research Group was unambiguous when reporting its results. It was, in fact, hard to prove any general sort of effects of moving images on audiences. Apart from being a result that pleased Harry Schein, it probably also pleased the Swedish film industry, which through the deal from 1963 financed the SFI, and thereby the Film Research Group.

But what was the point of view of Harry Schein regarding scientific matters? Had he been willing to consider a different conclusion than the one proposed by the Film Research Group to be reliable? Was it, in the eyes of Harry Schein, possible, based on scholarly work on the effects of film, to suggest the existence of such effects at all?

And how honest was he in his belief in the methods of the research group? Was it actually possible, from Schein's point of view, to prove whether any general idea of films affecting their audiences was reliable or not? Was the measurability such a reliable method in the eyes of Schein that it would have made him leave all his ideals, just like Segerstedt had done? Since his late teens Schein had in public repeatedly argued as a matter of principle against any kind of interference in films and other cultural products. Perhaps the work of the Film Research Group can as such also be seen as speculation—but not in sex, suspense, in lyrical or epic and dramatic effects, but on measurability. If Schein could convince a group of scholars to participate in a big project on film effects, and if that big project could convince them all to question the possibility to prove the effects of film, then a convincing argument against Skoglund and the institution of censorship would be made.

And what would be the function of the pornography studies of which he was such an eager advocate? They all presupposed the possibility to measure effects—good or bad—of pornography. What was the use of such studies, if effects of films on audiences were not at all possible to study? On March 13, Schein asks for porn films to study, on March 21, the last hand is laid on an investigation that states that film effects is a concept with no real meaning.

The Political Result of the Film Research Group

The main public inquiry on film censorship followed the conclusions of the Film Research Group from 1967. In their final report *Filmen—censur och ansvar*/"Film—Censorship and Responsibility" censorship for adults was as heavily questioned as in the earlier research report.[21] Six years after Schein's meeting with Erik Skoglund, the existence of the National Board of Film Censors was actually in danger. But nothing happened. The institution of censorship survived until 2011, when it finally was abandoned.

This might come as a surprise. Why was the national film censorship not abandoned, when two different official governmental investigations both stated that no effects of film were ever possible to prove? This was due to several reasons. One was that the interest of the film industry in abolishing censorship was perhaps less consistent than might be expected. Governmental control stopped certain films, but it also served to keep an appropriate level in the content of films produced regarding sex, violence or other controversial topics, especially in the very late 1960s and early 1970s, when the earlier dominance of cultural radicals in the national public sphere was hastily waning. In an interview in 1969, Harry Schein made a harsh statement about the young left-wing intellectuals who made up the new national "in-crowd." According to him, they were "like Pentecostals in a night club."[22] In the year of the film reform, 1963, the most radical position had been to argue for a liberalization of sexual representations in all media. The radical left-wing stance of 1969 was, to the contrary, to see pornography as well as graphic violence as capitalistic exploitations of bodies and minds. Schein was now heavily criticized for the work of the Film Research Group.[23]

But the cultural radical movement in Sweden actually won one victory in this last year of the 1960s when another public investigation—Yttrandefrihetsutredningen (The inquiry on free speech)—released its report on the limits of freedom of speech in 1969.[24] The report proposed the liberation of pornography, and in 1971 the law was changed. Thus the control of film was maintained, but pornography was free.[25]

Notes

1. Letter from Harry Schein to Jack Nyman, March 13, 1967. Forskningsgruppen [the Film Research Group]. VD-korrespondens [CEO correspondence]. Process 1-3. The Archive of the Swedish Film Institute. (SFI).
2. Films of Ingmar Bergman (*Tystnaden/The Silence*, 1963) and Vilgot Sjöman (*491*, 1963) had led to extensive debates regarding moral and film censorship, that even saw the introduction of a new political party, Kristen demokratisk samling. See Per Vesterlund, "En ohelig allians," in *Bogart och Betel*, ed. Lena Roos and Per Vesterlund (Gävle: Swedish Science Press, 2008). See also Lena Lennerhed's contribution to this volume.
3. A recent exception is found in Olof Hedling and Pelle Snickars "Film studies anno 2013: A bird's eye view," *Journal of Scandinavian Cinema*, 4:3 (2014): 35–41, 36.
4. Erik Skoglund, *Filmcensuren* (Stockholm: PAN Norstedts, 1971), 111.
5. Memorandum, Film Research Group, Projects. October, 1964. The Archive of the Swedish Film Institute.
6. Harry Schein, *I själva verket* (Stockholm: Norstedts, 1970), 75.
7. See Lars Diurlin's contribution to this volume.
8. Script for speech, February 22, 1966. Archive of Harry Schein, Labour Movement Archives and Library, Stockholm. Volume 2:4.
9. Memorandum from a meeting December 16 1966. Forskningsgruppen [the Film Research Group]. VD-korrespondens [CEO correspondence]. Process 1-3. The Archive of the Swedish Film Institute.
10. Vilgot Sjöman, *Äntligen rebell. Mitt personregister, Urval 01* (Stockholm: Natur och kultur, 2001), 200.
11. Letter from Dr. Lennart Levi, Karolinska sjukhuset, to Harry Schein, April 7, 1967. Forskningsgruppen [the Film Research Group]. VD-korrespondens [CEO correspondence]. Process 1-3. The Archive of the Swedish Film Institute.
12. Klara Arnberg, *Motsättningarnas marknad. Den pornografiska pressens genombrott och regleringen av pornografi i Sverige 1950–1980* (Lund: Sekel förlag, 2010) 149–50; Lena Lennerhed, *Frihet att njuta: Sexualdebatten i Sverige på 1960-talet* (Stockholm: Norstedts, 1994).
13. Arnberg, *Motsättningarnas marknad*, 192–95
14. Appendix to protocol from Filmcensurutredningen, questions on film research, December 16, 1966. Forskningsgruppen [the Film Research Group]. VD-korrespondens [CEO correspondence]. Process 1-3. The Archive of the Swedish Film Institute, 88.
15. Arnberg, *Motsättningarnas marknad*, 202–203.
16. Appendix to protocol from Filmcensurutredningen, February 3, 1967. Forskningsgruppen [the Film Research Group]. VD-korrespondens [CEO correspondence]. Process 1-3. The Archive of the Swedish Film Institute, 88.
17. Interestingly, there are witnesses of how Schein himself was in possession of pornographic films in the spring of 1967. In his diary Olof Lagercrantz, editor-in-chief of daily newspaper *Dagens Nyheter* and close friend of Schein's, described a dinner party on March 28, 1967, where Schein showed two pornographic films—according to Lagercrantz one Japanese and one Norwegian—to a small group of friends. Lagercrantz, who can also be included in the public sphere of cultural radicals, found it "deliberating that even this part of life which plays such a crucial role in the doings and thinking of all human beings [could] be so openly depicted." Quoted in Lagercrantz published diaries *Vid sidan av: Olof Lagercrantz/möten med författare från fyrtital till sjuttiotal*, eds. Richard Lagercrantz and Stina Otterberg (Stockholm: Wahlström & Widstrand, 2012), 50.
18. Leif Furhammar in an interview with the author, September 5, 2014.
19. Letter from Harry Schein to Gunnar Ekbladh, Chair of the Governmental Inquiry on Film Censorship, March 21, 1967 Archive of the Swedish Film Institute. Correspondence 1967.
20. SOU 1967:31, *Filmens inflytande på sin publik: rapport från Svenska filminstitutets filmforskningsgrupp* (Stockholm: Ecklesiastikdepartementet, 1967), 14.
21. SOU 1969:14, *Filmen—censur och ansvar* (Stockholm: Allmänna förlaget, 1969).
22. Nordal Åkerman, *Apparaten Sverige: Samtal med beslutsfattare i politik, ämbetsverk, företag* (Stockholm: Wahlströms & Widstrand, 1969), 322.
23. One example is the first number of the journal *Filmfront* in 1970, which was solely dedicated to a critique on the doings of Harry Schein.

24. SOU 1969:38, *Yttrandefrihetens gränser: Sårande av tukt och sedlighet. Brott mot trosfrid.* (Stockholm: Allmänna förlaget, 1969).

25. See Mariah Larsson, "Drömmen om den goda pornografin," *Tidskrift för genusvetenskap,* 1–2 (2007): 93–111.

REFERENCES

Material from the Archive of the Swedish Film Institute

Appendix to protocol from Filmcensurutredningen, questions on film research, December 16, 1966. Forskningsgruppen [the Film Research Group]. VD-korrespondens [CEO correspondence]. Process 1–3.
Appendix to protocol from Filmcensurutredningen, February 3, 1967. Forskningsgruppen [the Film Research Group]. VD-korrespondens [CEO correspondence]. Process 1–3.
Letter from Harry Schein to Gunnar Ekbladh, Chair of the Governmental Inquiry on Film Censorship, March 21, 1967. Correspondence 1967.
Letter from Harry Schein to Jack Nyman, March 13, 1967. Forskningsgruppen [the Film Research Group]. VD-korrespondens [CEO correspondence]. Process 1–3.
Letter from Dr. Lennart Levi, Karolinska sjukhuset, to Harry Schein, April 7, 1967. Forskningsgruppen [the Film Research Group]. VD-korrespondens [CEO correspondence]. Process 1–3.
Memorandum, Film Research Group, Projects. October, 1964.
Memorandum from a meeting December 16 1966. Forskningsgruppen [the Film Research Group]. VD-korrespondens [CEO correspondence]. Process 1–3.

Other Sources

Åkerman, Nordal. *Apparaten Sverige: Samtal med beslutsfattare i politik, ämbetsverk, företag.* Stockholm: Wahlströms & Widstrand, 1969.
Arnberg, Klara. *Motsättningarnas marknad. Den pornografiska pressens genombrott och regleringen av pornografi i Sverige 1950–1980.* Lund: Sekel förlag, 2010.
Furhammar, Leif. Interview by Per Vesterlund, September 5, 2014.
Hedling, Olof, and Pelle Snickars. "Film studies anno 2013: A bird's eye view." *Journal of Scandinavian Cinema,* 4:3 (2014): 35–41.
Lagercrantz, Olof. *Vid sidan av: Olof Lagercrantz/möten med författare från fyrtital till sjuttiotal.* edited by Richard Lagercrantz and Stina Otterberg. Stockholm: Wahlström & Widstrand, 2012.
Larsson, Mariah. "Drömmen om den goda pornografin." *Tidskrift för genusvetenskap* 1–2 (2007): 93–111.
Lennerhed, Lena. *Frihet att njuta: Sexualdebatten i Sverige på 1960-talet.* Stockholm: Norstedts, 1994.
Schein, Harry. *I själva verket.* Stockholm: Norstedts, 1970.
———. Script for speech, February 22, 1966. Volume 2:4. Archive of Harry Schein, Labour Movement Archives and Library, Stockholm.
Sjöman, Vilgot. *Äntligen rebell. Mitt personregister, Urval 01.* Stockholm: Natur och kultur, 2001.
Skoglund, Erik. *Filmcensuren.* Stockholm: PAN Norstedts, 1971.
SOU 1967:31. *Filmens inflytande på sin publik: rapport från Svenska filminstitutets filmforskningsgrupp.* Stockholm: Ecklesiastikdepartementet, 1967.
SOU 1969:14. *Filmen—censur och ansvar.* Stockholm: Allmänna förlaget, 1969.
SOU 1969:38. *Yttrandefrihetens gränser: Sårande av tukt och sedlighet. Brott mot trosfrid.* Stockholm: Allmänna förlaget, 1969.
Vesterlund, Per. "En ohelig allians." In *Bogart och Betel,* edited by Lena Roos and Per Vesterlund. Gävle: Swedish Science Press, 2008.

P(owe)R, Sex and *Mad Men* Swedish Style—Or How the Personal Can Become the Political

MAARET KOSKINEN

Let us start with a short letter written mid-summer, 1967. Its subject is a simple inquiry about a social get-together on the small Baltic island of Fårö off the east coast of Sweden:

Cabinet Minister Olof Palme
c/o Norman
Ava, Fårö
                                    Stockholm, August 2 1967
Dear Olof,
 I will be coming to Fårö on Friday evening and staying at Ingmar's until Sunday. Then later I'd like to visit Krister, and return [to Stockholm] on Monday afternoon.
 Do you want to meet on Saturday or Sunday? In that case please call me either at home [...] or at Ingmar's Friday evening.
                    Hej!
                    Harry[1]

This inquiry is innocuous enough, to be sure. But at the same time, these few lines represent a condensed axis of power in the cultural and political life in Sweden at the time. For "Harry," the author of the letter, is Harry Schein (mentioned several times in this volume), the flamboyant founder of the Swedish Film Institute and creator of the so-called film reform in 1963, that is the agreement between commerce and state aimed at guaranteeing an ongoing production of Swedish film (for the next fifty years the prevalent film policy in Sweden). "Olof" is Olof Palme, at the time Minister of Education and Culture in the Swedish Parliament, and only two years later elected Prime Minister. "Ingmar" is Ingmar Bergman, world-famous art film director who, particularly during the 1960s, put the island of Fårö on both the cinematic and mental maps, virtually conflating its rocky shores with something putatively "Swedish," at least as interpreted abroad. And as a special treat there is a "Krister"—Krister Wickman, representing the up and coming, modernistically-minded young men of the Social Democratic Party, to which we will have reason to return.

 But besides these *dramatis personae*, there is the location and general milieu to consider; for, particularly in the summer months, the island of Fårö was (and arguably still is), a location of condensed political power—in fact nothing less than the Swedish counterpart to Martha's Vineyard of the Washington elite.² If nothing else Fårö, in its very smallness, is a reminder of the fact that no man is an island, but on the contrary always enmeshed in relations, small and large, private and public, personal and political. Or, as George Orwell would have it, some are more entangled than others—and the physically closer such entanglements, the more tight-knit and intimate they are likely to be. It is on such entanglements that this essay will focus, with the aim of delineating some of the close to incestuous cultural and political liaisons in Swedish cultural and political life in the 1960s, all with a bearing on the question of sexual mores on film and film censorship in Sweden at this time.

It goes without saying that such a project in part entails delving into what might be defined as gossip, speculation, and conjecture. This obviously poses a methodological challenge, particularly in a field such as cinema studies, in which even the notion of the auteur has been accused of being mere gossip dressed as scholarship.³ However, the usual suspects should be kept in check with the help of at least two factors. First the fact that both observations and conclusions drawn from this venture will be grounded in the empirical material of the archives of (mainly) Harry Schein, Olof Palme, and Ingmar Bergman, and secondly that any "gossip" discerned in the halls of power may be framed by the meta-critical power inquiry of Pierre Bourdieu. For even if Bourdieu's notions can (rightly) be criticized for being too bound up with the particular circumstances of the elitist French (cultural/political) system, still his basic notions are useful in considering the power structures of any given society, including Sweden at this time.

One such notion is of course the overarching one of "culture," defined as that which is intimately linked to the perception of the existing powers that be as the legitimate or dominating one. This is certainly relevant in a country such as Sweden, in which by the early 1960s one and the same political party, the Social Democrats, had remained in power for a record long time as far as European democracies are concerned. Equally applicable is the notion of "cultural field," one that presupposes specialists, institutions and acknowledged hierarchies of value.⁴ This is, as we will see, certainly relevant in the context of Swedish state supported art or cinema, which was essentially Harry Schein's invention, but that would not have come to fruition without support by, amongst others Olof Palme—and of which Ingmar Bergman was perhaps the foremost exponent.

But as mentioned, equally important in this context is that Bourdieu's notions not only deal with official power structures but also encompass informal power. It goes without saying, then, that more recent theoretical approaches could equally well frame or be applied to any empirical results presented below, for instance sociological and/or feminist thinking dealing with concepts such as networking and homosociality.⁵

* * *

It is hard to find a more rewarding case study for a Bourdieu-inspired analysis than Harry Schein. After all, Schein was a Jewish immigrant who came from Austria to Sweden at age fourteen, and whose entire family except for his sister was wiped out in the Holocaust. Even so, he became an entrepreneur and independently wealthy in his 20s, and went on to become a highly influential factor for thirty more years in not only Swedish film culture and culture at large, but also in business life as well as hard-core politics. For instance, later in life he was appointed head of the so-called Investmentbank, and was also recruited as an independent columnist for *Dagens Nyheter*, the (then) largest morning broadsheet in Sweden, while remaining in demand as a voice on television and in the media at large, up until the new millennium. To cite the introduction of a Swedish book with the telling title *Citizen Schein*, "to take Schein seriously entails regarding him as a kind of media-modern phenomenon," in that he exemplifies "tendencies and structures in Swedish views of culture, media, and political communication."[6] And, indeed, as the book's title suggests, Schein is nothing less than comparable to Randolph Hearst, as portrayed in Orson Welles' film *Citizen Kane* (1941). But in an international perspective he can also be compared to the controversial position occupied in public discourse by his contemporary, American writer Gore Vidal. For just like Vidal, Schein was often invited to talk shows on television, in order to give his acidly humorous views on various phenomena in contemporary culture, while at the same time, just like Vidal, being considered somewhat of a playboy—yet improbably also highly respected as writer and intellectual.

As mentioned, the focus here will remain mainly on the 1960s and 70s, as this is a time-frame in which Harry Schein's role was particularly important, on two fronts. The first one was cultural policymaking in the area of film, the other area political life at large, which at least in his particular case, were inextricably intertwined. For, as is well known to Swedes of an older generation, Schein was a fiercely political ally of the Social Democratic party, which at times gave him a position of formal power (he was for instance appointed special advisor in the Department of Culture and Education during a few years in the early 1970s). But more importantly it also seems to have given him informal access to the corridors of power, particularly in the 1960s. It is this informal power that will be the focus here, and the opportunities for what today probably would be called networking and professional lobbying. If nothing else the material in the Schein archive shows ample proof of his fierce loyalty to the Social Democratic government, to a degree that it at times seems to have transgressed the boundaries of both decorum and corruption.

What is particularly astounding is the degree to which certain personal liaisons at this time seem to have played a role in political matters and policymaking, and also the degree to which such relations seem to have been taken for granted. To my knowledge, however, it has never really been substantiated or analyzed (at least in cinema studies) what such liaisons and informal power relations ultimately meant with respect to actual results.

As already intimated by the letter cited above, one such crucial liaison lies in the fact that Schein, the CEO of the Swedish Film Institute, was a close friend of Ingmar Bergman's, and on top of it was married to prominent Bergman actress Ingrid Thulin, all during a highly lucrative period in Swedish film production. Another crucial liaison is Schein's friendship with the addressee of that letter, the future Prime Minister Olof Palme with whom he played tennis weekly for two decades. In light of this, it is relevant to ask to what degree there is substance to Harry Schein's reputation (so far largely mythologized) as some kind of *l'éminence gris* ("grey eminence"), acting invisibly from behind the scenes, regarding for instance policymaking in the area of sex on film?

Or, put in the parlance of the time—to what degree did the personal blur into the political, and vice versa?

"Palme Boys"—Or "Mad Men"?

Before venturing deeper into such liaisons, however, let us first make a few additional contextual notes. The first factor to consider is the (seemingly) simple one that political culture in Sweden at this time was different compared to the present situation. For instance, there is no doubt that the Social Democratic government, which already by the early 1960s had been in power for three decades, ran the risk of a higher degree of corruption.

In this context there is good reason to return to the aforementioned factors—geography, scale, and vicinity. For this issue, so obvious in the case of the summer island of Fårö, is equally important, if not more so, in regards to another "island" of sorts—that of the country's capital. Stockholm of the 1960s was a small city in an affluent, highly organized, and politically homogenous country, where most of the national, cultural, and political capital was gathered. Hence Stockholm was likely at high risk for various blurred boundaries between personal and political power. This seems to have been the case particularly amongst the up and coming, politically radical young men, referred to as "broilers" due to their lack of experience outside of politics, and whose main wish was to partake in the development of a country considered the most modern in the western world. Thus have, for instance, social and political historians shown the degree to which the Social Democratic party was considered hot as a career route and, for being a labor party it certainly attracted an inordinate number of academics—an entourage who significantly became labeled the "Palme boys."[7]

Perhaps not surprisingly, one of the culturally and politically sexiest areas up for grabs among the various modernity-projects in Sweden at this time was film. Of course art film in Sweden after the Second World War, just as in other European countries, had been targeted as a major project for modernity, and in that sense was not unique. But it seems to have been the object of political support earlier than in other comparable nations. As Mikael Timm puts it in his historical study of the Swedish Film Institute, that "film was no longer considered a marginal art-form is clear from the fact that it was integrated by the Social Democratic party into the national plan for primary school in 1962."[8] The next step in supporting film as a modern art medium was, not surprisingly, freeing it from its other shackles, not least those of censorship. Significantly, recent research into the various cultural debates of the time clearly shows that anyone who regarded himself (it was usually a "he") as progressive and socially rational had to be not only pro-equality but "pro-sex" as well.[9] What, then, could have been more attractive to a rising political and cultural elite of men such as Schein, Palme, and Bergman, harboring culturally radical values, than the liberalization of sexual mores in and through the medium of film?[10]

All in all, then, certain factors at hand—individuals, locations, political and cultural modernity, liberal views on equality and sex—seem to have coalesced into a perfect storm, while art film and issues concerning its freedoms became virgin territory of sorts, characterized by a kind of frontier mentality. This, I imagine, is not entirely dissimilar to the bourgeoning PR/advertising industry on Manhattan in the early 60s, at least as portrayed in the TV series *Mad Men*. Naturally, there are major differences involved, an obvious one being nation, and another the ontological line that has to be drawn between fiction and historical reality. But it may be of interest to consider the following striking similarities. First that the goings-on in both the television series and in the Swedish cultural and political life are played out during approximately the same period—from the late 1950s, through the 1960s, with certain forays into the early 1970s. Second, that both are playing themselves out on "islands," so to speak—the delimited geographical space of Stockholm and Manhattan, respectively, with a certain inbuilt critical and lucrative competition. Third, that there are in both the exhilarating opportunities that virgin territories offer those who want to conquer them. In the television series it is the advertising and business world, while Swedish film production is partaking of both business and state (through the subsidies of the film reform)—yet in both the products are referred to as "art."

Indeed, even certain themes tend to conflate, among them women's equality, as exemplified by Peggy's career rise in *Mad Men,* while in contemporary Swedish film the counterpart was for instance the portrayal of women's sexuality, as in Bergman's *Tystnaden/The Silence* from 1963 (which, as we will see below was virtually designed as an attack on the institution of censorship). Interestingly, too, in both the television series and in Swedish film culture (as elsewhere in Swedish academia of the time), the notion of "stimulus-response" in relation to the targeted audiences played a major part. In *Mad Men* it obviously comes with the territory, but it also played an important role on the intellectual horizon in Swedish film at this time, particularly with regard to the audience's expected reactions to sex on film (see Per Vesterlund's article in this book).

Indeed, when comparing *Mad Men* with the "mad men" of political and cultural life in Stockholm, one cannot ignore another fact—that they even look good! This is certainly so in *Mad Men,* in which the importance of the main character Don Draper's good looks and attractiveness as a man is quite on par with and arguably even more important than those of the female characters in the series, and in which the role of 1960s fashion plays such an integral part. But fashion and the importance of good looks was no less important for the men in politics and culture in Stockholm at this time. A corroboration can be found in contemporary print media, and the fact that their attention was hardly limited to hard-core issues related to the influence and power that these three individual men—Schein, Bergman and Palme—swayed in their respective spheres. On the contrary, just as in the case of *Mad Men,* the focus of media interest rested just as much on the looks, style and, not least, the perceived sex appeal of all three men—and accordingly, their relationships with women.

Elegance and style. Ingrid Thulin and Harry Schein on the cover of Idun-Veckojournalen.

Let us focus on our first mad man, Harry Schein. As

fashion scholar Louise Wallenberg has noted, it is significant that, at the time, Schein's masculinity was considered by many, particularly in the traditionally minded blue-collar camp of Social Democrats, as vaguely effeminate and "European." Indeed, his was a new ideal of manhood, the modern, middle/upper class, white-collar look of meritocracy of the up and coming young men in culture and politics.[11] Most importantly, Schein was hardly an unwilling victim of circumstances in relation to the print media, which is obvious from the fact that he took the opportunity to flaunt himself on the cover of a women's magazine with his wife, Bergman-actress Ingrid Thulin.

But Schein was certainly not alone in such media savviness, for around the same time other prominent men in culture and politics had begun to see the (media) light, among them Schein's friends Ingmar Bergman and Olof Palme. Bergman was, up until the early 1960s, known not only as a womanizer but also somewhat of a bohemian, always dressed in the same garb of beret and worn jackets. But when he became Head of the Royal Dramatic Theatre in 1963, and so moved up the ranks from mere film into what was (at least at the time) defined as high culture, he suddenly, for the first time ever, decided to promote himself, in intimate at-home reportages, as a devoted, properly dressed family man and father.

Interestingly, only two years later Olof Palme followed suit when he flaunted his growing family in at-home features, for example in *Dagens Nyheter* as an ideal among modern men in his role as one of the nation's "diaper-changing," "fairy-tale-reading," and "nurturing fathers."[12] It is hardly mere coincidence that such a sudden interest in the family-life of men in power was preceded by photos of President Kennedy and his growing, handsome family—images that now of course are iconic, but in the early 1960s were groundbreaking in their (seeming) intimacy.

However, Olof Palme went quite a bit further when participating, with his family, in Vilgot Sjöman's highly controversial feature *Jag är nyfiken—gul/I Am Curious (Yellow)* from 1967. For at this point in time Palme was of course perfectly aware of Sjöman's controversial status as the director who had gotten into difficulties with the Swedish National Board of Film Censors several years earlier with *491* (1964), but he still took the risk of being interviewed on the lawn of his suburban house, with his wife and children in the background. Why such a move, potentially compromising his political career? One obvious answer is crass media-savviness, coupled perhaps with a touch of arrogance. Another is the one intimated at already—that an important part of the agenda of the up and coming men in politics at this time (Palme was still not PM), in this most progressive of countries, harbored a modern, rational view on sexuality. Thus, by participating in a film by a director who had made his name specifically in this area, Palme arguably showed his allegiance to those new, liberal, and rational forces in matters, political and sexual, that were also on his own political agenda.[13]

What we see here, then, are men in power, all in their prime so to speak, who very consciously encouraged media exposure of their intimate family spheres, a domain that previously had almost exclusively been identified with femininity. In doing so, they also ended up cultivating certain fashions and styles (quite literally those that by now have been iconized through *Mad Men*), and not least importantly their "styles" or "performances" as progressive and attractive *men*—even though they themselves most likely would not have conceived of the abovementioned images either in performative or gender terms. Thus what the media savviness of these "mad men," Swedish style, points at is not only the growing importance at that time of media in the western world at large (not least in the wake of the Vietnam war), but also the increasingly blurred boundaries between what previously had been perceived as either feminine or masculine, private or public—personal or political.

Censorship Versus Schein and Bergman

In the more explicitly political sphere, and policymaking in the field of film, it was not only the film agreement between business and state that arguably belonged to new and virgin territory. There was also another frontier to strive toward, namely new sexual mores on film, which meant taking on the issue of censorship. In fact, toppling the entire censorship as an institution was, as Leif Furhammar has noted, on the very top of Schein's agenda when he became the CEO of the Swedish Film Institute.[14]

In this area, Ingmar Bergman and Harry Schein constituted a formidable pact in film culture at this time, both on an informal basis (into which we will delve further below) and in a more formal one. In the latter case it was mainly through the institution of art film or, in Schein's own (in)famous parlance, "quality film," which of course was the very *raison d'être* for the foundation of the SFI. This, in fact, proved the perfect platform from which to launch a joint attack at the bastion of censorship. Thus, as mentioned, Bergman's film *The Silence* seemed virtually designed to test the existing censorship regulations for sex on film, for when the film premiered on September 23 in 1963, it led to an unusually (even for Bergman) extensive debate in the papers. True enough, it became a test case not only for the National Board of Film Censors but also, among others, its (formerly West) German counterpart, and was also discussed in the Bundestag, the German Parliament.[15]

However, in this context one should not forget the importance of the amendment that was added to the instructions regulating the National Board of Film Censors. In fact, it was only three days before *The Silence* reached the Board that a new paragraph had been added, stipulating that it could not as a matter of course censor portions of a film which had "won recognition as a valuable work of art, or that apparently can be deemed to win such recognition." It comes as no surprise that *The Silence* was eventually released uncut, based on this new paragraph. Significantly, even the Minister of Culture at the time pointed out that, in view of Bergman's great international reputation and the fact that he had recently been appointed CEO (Head) of the Royal Dramatic Theatre, "there could be no doubts as to his artistic intentions."[16] Finally, when in January 1964 *The Silence* was nominated as the Swedish candidate for the Oscars, the film had struck a virtual homerun.

Thus there is much truth to the fact that mere cultural capital, which Bergman had accrued by this time, with no less than two recent Oscars for best foreign film (*Jungfrukällan/The Virgin Spring* in 1960 and *Såsom i en spegel/Through a Glass Darkly* in 1961), had worked in his favor. Yet it is arguably also so that this was no guarantee that *The Silence* would weather objections of the censorship board, and that the whole venture was a calculated risk.[17] On the other hand, Bergman worked in other ways against censorship, given that it was he, in his function as "artistic director" for Svensk Filmindustri, the largest production company in Sweden, who initiated the production of Vilgot Sjöman's aforementioned controversial *491*, which also got into trouble with the censorship board—most likely, as planned.[18]

At the same time, the question is to what degree Bergman can be regarded as the "lone artist as hero" against the system and would have taken on such a challenge entirely by himself, had he not had his close friend and creative power mogul Harry Schein to cover his back. But what role, if any, did Schein play when the 1963 amendment to the instructions of the National Board of Film Censors was made? When reading his own piece on the 1960s in *Svensk filmografi*, he does not mention himself at all in this context, and credits only the filmmakers in pushing the envelope.[19] But as Swedish film historian Leif Furhammar (who at the time was working for the National Board of Film Censors) notes in an unpublished paper, it was most likely none other than Schein who managed to launch this very important amendment. As Furhammar puts it (in my translation), "with his connections in governmental quarters, the cultural lobbyist Harry Schein in any case fairly soon managed to launch the first major assault against the authority of film censorship."[20]

The most important connection in the governmental corridors was no doubt Olof Palme, at the time member of the Cabinet (minister without a portfolio) and thus a close advisor to the Prime Minister. And to the extent that Schein could not count on Palme directly, he certainly knew how to use his friendship. As noted by Bengt Göransson, later Minister of Culture but at this time a lowly officer in the department, whenever it was time to renegotiate the film agreement between the state and the film production companies, Schein "always used Olof Palme [...] as blackmail"—that he supposedly had "received directives from Palme" regarding certain points. But that, Göransson continues, "was just something he made up. The industry was scared to death, thinking that the parliament was ready to throw them out of the Film Institute" which was powerful at the time.[21] Equally important in this context, however, was Palme's associate and Schein's good friend Krister Wickman, who at the time was not only minister without portfolio in the Department of Finance (which included industry, to which film production belonged besides being under the jurisdiction of the Department of Culture and Education), but on top of it also Chairman for the Film Institute's Board between 1963–67, whose director was none other than Schein. Quite a formidable constellation, then—Schein, Palme, and/or Wickman, all working for an amendment in the Cinema Ordinance, for the benefit of a film made by—Bergman.

In sum, even if the institution of censorship was not done away with entirely at this time, Schein did manage to weaken its power and influence. For, as Furhammar writes, in this context one should not forget that what the abovementioned amendment meant was more power for the so-called Film Review Council, that is, the political control organ instituted in 1954, the role of which was to supervise censorship on behalf of the public. While this council previously had acted in solidarity with the censorship board's decisions, from now on it was clear that the Board would have to actively seek support from the Film Review Council, at least in cases in which the censors considered banning or in part censoring films that were likely to win recognition as valuable works of art—which, of course, is exactly what happened in the case of *The Silence*. Important in this context was not least that at this time the individual members of the Film Council increasingly were of the politically and culturally radical persuasion. To cite Furhammar's laconic conclusion, "it seemed fairly clear that Harry Schein, also in that context, had pulled some strings in the corridors of the Department of Culture and Education."[22]

Schein, Bergman, Palme—Some More Informal Business

Clearly, then, when film policy and the exercise of power within an existing infrastructural frame was teamed with Ingmar Bergman's artistic power, it produced concrete results. But as mentioned, there were also goings-on of a more informal, clandestine sort between these men, not least due to Harry Schein's mastery of unorthodox working methods.

When one peruses the correspondence in the Schein archive and also the Bergman Foundation archive, it soon becomes clear the inordinate degree to which Schein took upon himself to act not only as Bergman's Swedish producer, but also his agent, deal-fixer, and glorified secretary, writing scores of letters on his behalf, not least to Bergman's American agent Paul Kohner—while also arranging acting deals for his wife Ingrid Thulin, while he was at it. However, when other Swedish directors sought his assistance, Schein seemed rather cool, even towards an internationally noted director such as Bo Widerberg. As he wrote to Kohner: "he [Widerberg] signed the contract with you and I don't feel that I in my position should take any initiative"—a marked contrast to his activities in Bergman's case.[23] Not least interesting in this context is that many of these letters are signed "HS/AB," which means that they were typed by Schein's secretary at the Film Institute, Aina Bellis, and on letter paper with the SFI-logo—even though the borders between official letters of the institute and those regarding private matters are highly questionable. Here, certainly, the personal had become the political—and vice versa.

Examples can be multiplied, but for the sake of space, suffice it to cite from two letters. The first one is from Schein to Bergman, written it seems at a point when Schein was considering leaving the Film Institute in 1964. "I just want to tell you that I've decided to stay [at the institute]," he begins. One reason for doing so, he continues, is based on conversations he has had with Bergman, which have culminated in a realization that there is "a challenge" to take on (unclear of what kind). And, he concludes, "when I finally do so, I ask that you help me—with the self-evident influence you possess and always will possess in Swedish film."[24]

Clearly this letter reveals an intimacy both on a private and professional level. More than that, it is an outright plea ("I ask that you help me"), while the letter also, with reference to Bergman's brilliance and influence as an artist—implies a promise that he, Schein, in return will act as future trailblazer in order for Bergman to keep making his films. Not surprisingly, just one year later Schein was busy acting on Bergman's behalf. Let us take a look at the other letter, this time written (in English) to the above mentioned Kohner, Bergman's American agent. Here Schein sets down, in no uncertain terms, instructions of how to go about releasing actor Max von Sydow from a film that supposedly was to be made by Bergman, but which now has clashed with an American production. Interestingly, in this case, Schein saw it fit to not write on SFI-paper, but rather using his own company paper ("Conseil aktiebolag," which dealt with water purification!)—and, having read the contents of the letter, one understands why. Of interest in this context is not least the handwritten note attached to the letter: "Ingmar—for your information, but no one else's. Your Harry."

January 17, 1965

Mr Paul Kohner
9169 Sunset Boulevard
Hollywood 69
California, U.S.A.

Dear Paul,

    I confirm the following cable, sent today: SF WILL CABLE ACCEPTING 50.000 DOLLAR [sic] TO RELEASE MAX STOP INGMARS [sic] ADDITIONAL CONDITIONS ARE 100.000

162   IV. The Institutionalization of Sex in Sweden

DOLLAR [sic] AND SIMULTANEOUS PRESS RELEASE STOP NEITHER SF NOR ANYBODY ELSE IS TO BE INFORMED ABOUT LATTER DEAL STOP LETTER FOLLOWS […]

The compensation due to Ingmar should be deposited in your office or his account. You will then receive further informations [sic] about this amount *by me*. Max will be able to vouch for my authority to instruct you in this respect.

By this somewhat complicated method the deal with Ingmar will therefore remain a matter between you, Max, Ingmar and myself—*which is the major condition to get Max released*. [---]

I should also like to add that the sice [sic] of the compensation to Ingmar as well as the unconventional form of the deal and the suggested method of payment should, if possible, not be subject to further discussion. Ingmar is not a businessman and certainly not prepared to prolongued [sic] negotiations. If the deal comes through in this form, Ingmar will be quite satisfied. If it does not come through, Ingmar will simply inform SF that he cannot release Max. I have no idea what SF will do in such a situation. I am not convinced that they will start a legal action. But even if they dont [sic] one will have to consider the dominating position of SF in the Swedish film business, the possible future relations of the Mirsich Company and your self [sic] with SF and Ingmar and last but not least Max' reputation in Sweden in general and with Ingmar in particular. [---]

> With kindest personal regards,
> Sincerely yours,
> Harry Schein[25]

Even an idiot in legalese can smell something fishy here. Why was SF, that is, Sweden's largest film producer, which is expected to provide the compensatory cash, not to be informed of this deal, which *nota bene* Schein himself admits is "unconventional"? And why is the money to be stored with Bergman's American agent? Note also the implied threat as to what legal measures SF might take, not to mention Kohner's own future standing with Bergman—and so on and so forth.

From the wording it seems as if Schein wrote the letter so to speak behind Bergman's back, yet the fact that it is stored in the Ingmar Bergman Foundation archive shows that it is reasonable to assume that he must have partaken of its contents. Regardless, what these two letters clearly reveal is the informal power that these two men wielded not only in Swedish film culture at the time, but also regarding its various international relations.

* * *

But where does Olof Palme come into the equation in this context? While the main object of this work is not Harry Schein's relations to Olof Palme, it may still prove illustrative to present some circumstantial evidence in support of the general argument. Because if one peruses the Palme archive it becomes clear that in relation to Palme as well, Schein was an ever-willing errand boy, in a way that far exceeded his duties as both CEO of the Film Institute, and when he, as mentioned, for a brief period was appointed political advisor in the Department of Culture and Education. Thus Schein sends suggestions for books that Palme should read, offers financial advice, writes political analyses on the state budget, environmental policy, election results, the style of the Social Democratic Party Program, and even, at every New Year, sends charts detailing the statistics of his and Palme's weekly tennis games—the latter, *nota bene*, oftentimes written while performing his duties at the Film Institute, as these private notes are typed by his secretary, Aina Bellis.

Schein even sought control over the sayings and doings of Swedish actors in the press, at least to the extent these could be related to Palme and/or Swedish Social Democracy. For instance, when Bergman actress Liv Ullmann made a comment in a newspaper interview in relation to the Vietnam War, Schein was prompted to write her, demanding to know more of what she had said, while also asking her for information as to Henry Kissinger's view of Palme. With some misgivings ("I don't know why you want to know—in any case please don't cite me publically") she answered with a handwritten, three-page letter. "What I say in *Expressen* [a daily tabloid] is true. Henry Kissinger was very hurt and upset that Olof Palme had accused him of acting like a Nazi. When and where Palme did this I don't know, but it must have been at some official occasion, as Kissinger apparently doesn't want to meet Palme—until the accusation is taken back. [...] Now I personally don't want to have anything more to do with this [...]." In his answer, Schein saw it fit to admonish her: "For your information, Palme has in no shape or form talked about Kissinger and Nazism. What he has said was that the Christmas bombings over Hanoi will in their cruel meaninglessness go down in history in the same way as other atrocities in history. He listed some of these, among them also some committed by the Germans during the war...."[26]

It goes without saying that such an exchange of letters is fascinating in and of itself, as a kind of time capsule containing some of the most burning political issues of the day, dealing with the complicated Swedish-U.S. relations due to the Vietnam war. But who would have thought that the views of an actress were considered important enough for a civil Servant, albeit with ties in the corridors of power, to take the time to correct her, almost as if expecting her to stick to official doctrines as if she were some kind of ambassador. Perhaps even more revealing in this context is that Schein, like a dutiful errand boy, sent a copy of Ullmann's hand-written letter to Palme, as this is where the letter is archived.

A few years later, in 1976 when Ingmar Bergman got into dire straits with the Swedish tax authorities and under much national and international media glare left Sweden for "exile" in West Germany, Schein was immediately there to console—no, not Bergman but Palme. For in a letter to him he writes: "I spoke to Ingmar last Sunday. He was interviewed twice by German television in München. Both times there were attempts at provoking him. He clearly said that his leaving Sweden should not be interpreted as criticism of Swedish Social Democracy. This statement was cut before it was broadcast. We live in a beautiful world."[27]

No doubt Palme, just like Bergman, must have had much use of his energetic friend, although it is hard to find any transgressions on his behalf in the Olof Palme archives. However, Palme did actively appear in a short celebratory film made by Swedish Film Institute personnel on the occasion of Harry Schein's birthday, acting as tennis umpire, no less, together with the artistic elite of the day, amongst them Bergman actress Bibi Andersson, and with Ingmar Bergman also in the credits of the film. At the very least, the production of this film was questionable already for the fact that it must have been made with state funds, earmarked for Swedish "quality" film. Palme also appeared as a guest on the popular television-talk show *Här har du ditt liv/Here Is Your Life*, in which some well-known person, in this case Schein, was "kidnapped" by the host, and then, in the television studio, met a number of people that had been influential in his or her life. Here, the host actually has the wherewithal to ask Palme about the risk of friendship corruption, but Palme elegantly avoids the issue by quipping that he has "never offered Schein a job"[28] In a strictly formal sense this might be true, but should be qualified by the evidence in the Schein archive. For here there are no less than four letters from Schein to Palme, amounting to several densely typed pages, in which Schein in great detail outlines his wishes for the future, the position of Minister of Culture being one of them. In one letter, moreover, the so-called Investment Bank was mentioned, as well—a job that Schein did get.[29]

The Grey Eminence?

In hindsight there is certainly cause to wonder about such intricate personal and political power liaisons. As Mikael Timm writes, "in other countries Schein's ways of governing would perhaps not have caused any debate, but it was foreign to Swedish tradition."[30] True—and then again, perhaps not. For obviously one has to ask whether his way of governing was so "un–Swedish" and controversial after all, given that he stayed in power for so long. Perhaps it was, indeed, only too "Swedish," according to the general standards and political culture of the time? One should keep in mind that while Schein may have started as Chairman of the Film Institute Board of Directors, he soon became its CEO and remained so until 1970. Also, when he stepped down that same year during his two year hiatus as special advisor to the government, one should not forget as Mikael Timm notes, that since Schein stayed on as working chairman during this time he in effect remained as managing director, even after formally having left the position.[31] Sure enough, in 1972, he formally regained his position as CEO, staying until 1978. But most importantly, if Schein acted a bit like a dictator (albeit benevolent) he could not have remained so—without the right kind of backing.

While it is true, then, that Schein was in many ways an exception, and exceptionally talented as an individual, and that he—fortunately—did many good things for Swedish film culture, at the same time he must be considered quite representative of the political culture and those other "mad men" of his day.[32]

Harry Schein, then, a "grey eminence"? Hardly. Or to be more specific: yes, certainly, as an ideal; but in terms of crass *Real Politik*, those several shades of grey also managed to hide clandestine doings. But let it be said that as far as Swedish film culture is concerned, it seems that Schein's inordinate busy-bodying for the most part acted for the good. Regardless, it is difficult to deny that, given the circumstances, and in a time in which the personal was the political, and the political the personal—Harry Schein not only personified but played that system magnificently.

Notes

1. Letter from Harry Schein to Olof Palme dated August 2, 1967. The Harry Schein archive, the Labour Movement Archives and Library, Stockholm. Translation by me.
2. The origin of the so-called "Almedalen-week" in July each year, located on the larger island adjacent to Fårö, was in fact the speeches held there by Olof Palme in the 1960s, an event which has now grown into a highly influential as well as internationally noted get-together between all political parties, lobbyists, and, not least, media. See e.g. "Almedalen Week: At Sweden's One-of-a-Kind Festival, All Political Parties Gather in One Place." http://www.democracynow.org/2014/7/2/dn_at_almedalen_week_at_swedens, and "Almedalen Week," http://en.wikipedia.org/wiki/Almedalen_Week.
3. See for instance Janet Staiger, "The Politics of Film Canons," *Cinema Journal* 24:3 (1985): 4–23, and *Perverse Spectators The Practices of Film Reception* (New York and London: New York University Press, 2000).
4. Pierre Bourdieu, *The Field of Cultural Production* (Cambridge, UK: Polity Press, 1993 [1972]).
5. See for instance Sharon R. Bird, "Welcome to the Men's Club: Homosociality and the Maintenance of Hegemonic Masculinity," *Gender and Society* 10:2 (April 1996): 120-132.

6. Lars Ilshammar, Pelle Snickars and Per Vesterlund, "Citizen Schein—En introduktion," in *Citizen Schein* ed. Lars Ilshammar, et al (Stockholm: KB/Mediehistoriskt Arkiv 14, 2010), 10–11. My translation.
7. See for instance the memoirs of former PM of the Social Democratic party Ingvar Carlsson, *Lärdomar, personliga och politiska* (Stockholm: Natur och Kultur, 2014).
8. Mikael Timm, *Dröm och förbannad verklighet. Spelet kring svensk film under 40 år* (Stockholm: Brombergs, 2003), 24. My translation.
9. See for instance Mariah Larsson, "Drömmen om den goda pornografin," *Tidskrift för genusvetenskap* 1–2 (2007): 93–111.
10. Although Bergman was hardly politically radical, there is a stronger correspondence than is usually thought between his work and society. For instance *Scenes from a Marriage* would hardly have been made without the rise of 1970s feminism, and note too that in the theatre Bergman also staged Peter Weiss' overtly political play *Rannsakningen* in 1966, as well as *Woyzeck* in 1969, and a political cabaret by Lars Forsell, *Show* in 1971. See also Maria Bergom Larsson, *Ingmar Bergman and Society* (London: The Tantativity Press, 1978), and Erik Hedling, "The Welfare State Depicted: Post-Utopian Landscapes in Ingmar Bergman's Films," in *Ingmar Bergman Revisited. Performance, Cinema and the Arts* ed. Maaret Koskinen (London: Wallflower Press, 2008).
11. Louise Wallenberg, "Eleganten: om manlig elegans, behörighet och utanförskap," in *Citizen Schein*, ed. Lars Ilshammar, *et al.* (Stockholm: KB/Mediehistoriskt Arkiv 14, 2010).
12. Cited in (former) broadsheet daily *Dagens Nyheter,* Familjesidan [Family page, no author], March 25, 2013, with reference to an article published in the same paper 31 October 1965.
13. As a kind of anecdotal evidence it could be mentioned that Olof Palme's son Mårten Palme, professor of Political Economy at Stockholm University, told me a few years ago that he had never dared see the film with himself as a small boy, since it had "a reputation for being a porn-flick"!
14. Leif Furhammar, "Harry Schein vs State Censorship." Unpublished manuscript, 2011.
15. Maaret Koskinen, *Ingmar Bergman's* The Silence. *Pictures in the Typewriter, Writings on the Screen* (Seattle: University of Washington Press, 2010), see especially 44–54.
16. Jörn Donner, ed., *Svensk filmografi 6: 1960–1969* (Stockholm: Svenska filminstitutet, 1977), 154.
17. Koskinen, *Ingmar Bergman's* The Silence, 47.
18. As for instance claimed in Anders Åberg's dissertation on Sjöman, *Tabu: Filmaren Vilgot Sjöman* (Lund: Filmhäftet, 2001). See also Erik Hedling, "Breaking the Swedish Sex Barrier: Painful Lustfulness in Ingmar Bergman's *The Silence*," *Film International* 6:6 (2008): 17–27.
19. Harry Schein, "Det hände på 60-talet," in *Svensk filmografi 6: 1960–1969* ed. Jörn Donner (Stockholm: SFI, 1977), 19.
20. Furhammar, "Harry Schein vs State Censorship."
21. Timm, *Dröm och förbannad verklighet*, 55.
22. Furhammar, "Harry Schein vs State Censorship."
23. Letter from Harry Schein to Paul Kohner dated December 11, 1967. The Harry Schein archive, the Labour Movement Archives and Library, Stockholm.
24. Letter from Harry Schein to Ingmar Bergman, dated November 24, 1964. Bergman Foundation Archive/Letters K:1049. My translation.
25. Letter from Harry Schein to Paul Kohner, dated January 17, 1965. Bergman Foundation Archive/Letters K:1049:1. Emphases in the original.
26. Correspondence between Harry Schein and Liv Ullmann, dated May 1973. Letters/Schein, the Olof Palme Archive, the Labour Movement Archives and Library, Stockholm. My translation.
27. Letter from Harry Schein to Olof Palme, dated May 31, 1976. Letters/Schein, the Olof Palme Archive, the Labour Movement Archives and Library.
28. DVD number 1, track 2: "Här är ditt liv," included in *Citizen Schein*, ed. Lars Ilshammar, Pelle Snickars and Per Vesterluud (Stockholm: KB/Mediehistoriskt Arkiv 14, 2010).
29. Letter from Harry Schein to Olof Palme, dated October 25, 1982. The Harry Schein archive, the Labour Movement Archives and Library, Stockholm.
30. Timm, *Dröm och förbannad verklighet*, 43. My translation.
31. Timm, *Dröm och förbannad verklighet*, 51. It was likely no coincidence that it was exactly during this hiatus that Schein received an honorary "Guldbagge" (Golden Beetle), the Swedish counterpart to the Oscars, for his services for Swedish film in 1970. See the Swedish Film Database, entry "Harry Schein." http://www.sfi.se/sv/svensk-filmdatabas/Item/?type=PERSON&itemid=65964&iv=Awards.

32. As such Schein may be relevant as regards certain remaining problematic phenomena in Swedish politics today, for instance the fact that in Sweden there are still no rules (as in other countries) regulating how soon a politician can take a paid position in the private sector, sometimes even transferring directly from Minister to working as consultant with organizations that previously was his or her job to regulate. Peter Wolodarski, the Editor in Chief of *Dagens Nyheter*, writes that while there is no reason to suspect lobbying or political consultants per se, as "they are part of democracy," this odd *laissez faire* represents a naïve attitude regarding Swedish incorruptibility, including that which is defined narrowly as involving favoring friends and family. "Sverige förenar naivitet med självgodhet," *Dagens Nyheter* May 5, 2013.

REFERENCES

Swedish Archival Material

The Harry Schein Archive, the Labour Movement Archives and Library, Stockholm

Letter from Harry Schein to Olof Palme, August 2, 1967.
Letter from Harry Schein to Paul Kohner, December 11, 1967.
Letter from Harry Schein to Olof Palme, October 25, 1982.

The Olof Palme Archive, the Labour Movement Archives and Library, Stockholm

Correspondence between Harry Schein and Liv Ullmann, May 1973.
Letter from Harry Schein to Olof Palme, May 31, 1976.

The Bergman Foundation Archive, Stockholm

Letter from Harry Schein to Ingmar Bergman, dated November 24, 1964. Letters K:1049
Letter from Harry Schein to Paul Kohner, dated January 17, 1965. Letters K:1049:1
Citizen Schein. DVD number 1, track 2: "Här är ditt liv." Edited by Lars Ilshammar, Pelle Snickars and Per Versterlund. Stockholm: KB/Mediehistoriskt Arkiv 14, 2010.

Other Sources

Åberg, Anders. *Tabu: Filmaren Vilgot Sjöman*. Lund: Filmhäftet, 2001.
"Almedalen Week." Wikipedia. http://en.wikipedia.org/wiki/Almedalen_Week.
"Almedalen Week: At Sweden's One-of-a-Kind Festival, All Political Parties Gather in One Place." Democracy Now!
http://www.democracynow.org/2014/7/2/dn_at_almedalen_week_at_swedens
Bergom Larsson, Maria. *Ingmar Bergman and Society*. London: The Tantativity Press, 1978.
Bird, Sharon R. "Welcome to the Men's Club: Homosociality and the Maintenance of Hegemonic Masculinity." *Gender and Society* 10:2 (April 1996): 120–132.
Bourdieu, Pierre. *The Field of Cultural Production*. Cambridge, UK: Polity Press, 1993 [1972].
Carlsson, Ingvar. *Lärdomar, personliga och politiska*. Stockholm: Natur och Kultur, 2014.
Dagens Nyheter, Familjesidan [Family page, no author], March 25, 2013.
Donner, Jörn, ed. *Svensk filmografi 6: 1960–1969*. Stockholm: Svenska filminstitutet, 1977.
Furhammar, Leif. "Harry Schein vs. State Censorship." Unpublished manuscript, 2011.
Hedling, Erik. "Breaking the Swedish Sex Barrier: Painful Lustfulness in Ingmar Bergman's *The Silence*." *Film International* 6:6 (2008): 17–27.
_____. "The Welfare State Depicted: Post-Utopian Landscapes in Ingmar Bergman's Films." In *Ingmar Bergman Revisited. Performance, Cinema and the Arts*, edited by Maaret Koskinen. London: Wallflower Press, 2008.
Ilshammar, Lars, Pelle Snickars, and Per Vesterlund. "Citizen Schein—En introduktion." In *Citizen Schein*, edited by Lars Ilshammar, Pelle Snickars and Per Vesterlund. Stockholm: KB/Mediehistoriskt Arkiv 14, 2010.
Koskinen, Maaret. *Ingmar Bergman's* The Silence. *Pictures in the Typewriter, Writings on the Screen*. Seattle: University of Washington Press, 2010.
Larsson, Mariah. "Drömmen om den goda pornografin." *Tidskrift för genusvetenskap* 1–2 (2007): 93–111.

Schein, Harry. "Det hände på 60-talet." In *Svensk filmografi 6: 1960–1969*, edited by Jörn Donner. Stockholm: SFI, 1977.
Staiger, Janet. "The Politics of Film Canons." *Cinema Journal* 24:3 (1985): 4–23.
_____. *Perverse Spectators: The Practices of Film Reception*. New York: New York University Press, 2000.
The Swedish Film Database. "Harry Schein." http://www.sfi.se/sv/svensk-filmdatabas/Item/?type=PERSON&itemid=65964&iv=Awards.
Timm, Mikael. *Dröm och förbannad verklighet. Spelet kring svensk film under 40 år*. Stockholm: Brombergs, 2003.
Wallenberg, Louise. "Eleganten: om manlig elegans, behörighet och utanförskap." In *Citizen* Schein, edited by Lars Ilshammar, Pelle Snickars and Per Vesterlund. Stockholm: KB/Mediehistoriskt Arkiv 14, 2010.
Wolodarski, Peter. "Sverige förenar naivitet med självgodhet." *Dagens Nyheter*, May 5, 2013.

Egrets in the Porno Swamp
The Swedish Film Institute and Swedish Sin

LARS DIURLIN

1963 saw the establishment of the Swedish Film Institute. It was the brainchild of the engineer turned film critic and writer Harry Schein, who also took on the role as the new foundation's CEO and soon became one of Sweden's most visible as well as prolific cultural personalities.

Prior to 1963, Sweden had a special entertainment tax amounting to 25 percent of theatrical box-office receipts. Schein's idea was to come to an agreement between the film industry and the state to abolish the tax and replace it with a 10 percent fee on mentioned receipts, which would in turn finance the Swedish Film Institute (from now on referred to as the SFI). Sixty-five percent of the gross revenue was then to be redistributed back to the film industry in the form of financial support, both to artistic so called "quality films" as well as to more commercial titles. Thirty percent was to cover administrative costs, archival services, as well as a new film school.[1] This article will focus on the remaining 5 percent, a portion that was reserved for "[...] certain mutual public relations purposes."[2] In this essay, I will uncover some of the strategies behind these public relation activities, putting focus on two hitherto unstudied phenomena during the first decade of the SFI's existence—the official international publication *Film in Sweden*, renamed *Swedish Films* in 1973, as well as a specific promotional fortnight-long event, the Scandinavia Now fair, arranged in 1971 by the department store chain Gimbels in New York. This happening was to be, according to Gimbels: "[...] a two week salute highlighting the products, travel, tourist attractions, cultural contributions, historic background, panoramic vistas of Sweden in the greatest fair ever presented by a department store."[3] Its large scale aside, the fair is of particular film historical interest as it was the first (and perhaps only) publicity event to result in promotional moving images to be produced by the SFI for the specific purpose of selling Swedish film culture. Likewise, the publication *Film in Sweden/Swedish Films* was the first nationally coordinated publicity material specifically designed to promote Swedish films in the international market. Here, I will connect these two marketing schemes to the internationally widespread notion of Swedish sin and how the SFI in various ways decided to relate its promotion to this very notion.

The two cases examined in this text represent telling examples of how the marketers at the SFI suddenly found themselves sandwiched in an intricate position between art and commerce. What started as a naïve effort to adapt to a modern commercial film export market soon snowballed into a seemingly uncontrollable as well as highly paradoxical situation, in which the SFI ended up encouraging the sexualized image of Sweden. In the case of *Film in Sweden/Swedish Films*, the SFI went so far as to actively promote hardcore pornographic material, while at the same time trying desperately to save face and uphold the idea of Swedish films preferably being synonymous with "quality films"—the essential but difficult to define concept which the film reform of 1963 was somewhat unstably buttressed upon.[4] When it came to the Gimbels-affair, the SFI again tried to mix a promotional cocktail containing both allusions to Swedish sexual progressiveness as well as emphasizing the serious caliber and earnest quality of Swedish films. Here the SFI eventually came out cheated by the powers of prejudice regarding what representation of "Sweden" the American store-chain really wanted to see and sell, as Gimbels deliberately modified the ingredients of the mix to instead highlight that particular image of sinfulness for which Sweden, and particularly Swedish films, had become known abroad.

Sweden Unifies Towards a World Market

The SFI was constituted as an independent foundation without direct financial contributions from the state and thus it was not a public authority or public body per se. Still, it can be emphasized that half of the SFI's board members were chosen by the government, which makes the issue of governmental influence quite debatable. Despite its alleged independence from the state, the SFI soon gained influence abroad as a national film authority, much due to the fact that the bulk of the 5 percent-PR-portfolio was aimed at various international film festivals. The SFI shortly became a respected natural intermediary not just when it came to films but regarding various cultural representations of Sweden abroad, used among others by embassies around the world as well as the national Department for Foreign Affairs. Until the mid-sixties, each production company decided if and how to promote their films internationally, something often neglected due to the significant costs and risks involved.[5] Consequently, Sweden was to have its first nationally coordinated festival delegation as well as official publicity material specifically designed to promote Swedish films in an international market of buyers, critics, festivals, and future co-producers. The primary physical product that followed was the tri-lingual quarterly publication *Film in Sweden*. It was a richly illustrated magazine initiated in 1965 by Schein, who also contributed with various editorials and articles until he left the helm of the organization in 1978.

Mainly due to the introduction of television, theatrical attendance in Sweden was in steady decline during the 1960s and 1970s. Still, the film reform of 1963 stimulated film production. The five years that followed the reform saw an almost doubled number of films as compared to the five years before.[6] Corresponding with the wave of younger filmmakers in Europe, the number of first-time directors was boosted in Sweden as well, much in line with the SFI's aim of renewing the artistic aspirations of Swedish film.[7] All these films needed an audience, and 7.5 million Swedes was not enough. Thus, it was imperative to "Export or Die," according to an article in the Swedish special edition of the renowned U.S. magazine *Film Comment*, an edition interestingly enough jointly funded by the SFI and the Swedish Institute for Cultural Relations with Foreign Countries (from now on referred to as the SI), with a rather hefty donation of 2,000 USD.[8] It was apparently not just imperative to export the products in themselves but to create and uphold an *image* of a prosperous exporting film industry. In line with this assumption the article stated that the export share grew considerably during the sixties and that in 1970 it constituted up to 50 percent of the total income of the major Swedish production companies.[9] Three years later, in *Swedish Films*, Schein in a similar vein claimed that the export share of total receipts was greater in the case of Swedish films than for those of any other country but the United States.[10] Although the correctness of these numbers may be questioned, they undeniably point to the significance of the international promotional activities of the SFI.

Fighting Prejudice with Prejudice—The Paradox Ensues

The official statements and promotional strategies employed by the SFI illustrate an ambiguous approach to how the organization chose to officially handle the image of Sweden on the international market, specifically connected to the image of Sweden's alleged sinfulness. In his article "*Time* for Sex in Sweden," Frederick Hale dates the breakthrough of the sexually oriented image of Sweden to the early 1950s, due to the wide circulation of a number of Swedish films depicting nudity as well as displaying a rather relaxed approach to premarital sex, but also Joe David Brown's 1955 *Time*-article "Sin & Sweden."[11] The further international success of early sixties films including Lars-Magnus Lindgren's *Käre John/Dear John* (1964) and Bergman's *Tystnaden/The Silence* (1963) helped to cultivate this image, which became even more consolidated with Vilgot Sjöman's *Jag är nyfiken—gul/I Am Curious (Yellow)* (1967).[12] Consequently, it was into this discourse that the staff of the SFI launched its promotional travels and thus wherever they went they had to relate to, and many times felt obligated to contradict, the image of sex-crazed Sweden. One example can be taken from the San Francisco Film Festival, when Schein in 1966, while promoting the Mai Zetterling-film *Nattlek/Night Games* (1966), pointed out that the institute was "[…] not too enthusiastic about that image" as well as claiming that "Sex isn't much different in Sweden than other countries."[13] A few years later Schein wrote the following statement, which can summarize his view on the matter:

> There is an underbrush of Swedish films that have been successful on the world market. The term "Schwedenfilm" signifies in Germany not Swedish films but soft-core pornography. Certainly, when travelling abroad to promote Swedish films, one feels ashamed of one's role, ashamed of the utter trash that Swedish producers scatter across the globe. [---] One of the main objectives of our intense international activities is precisely to counteract this distorted one-dimensional image of Swedish film.[14]

This objective could not have been an easy task for the SFI, given the fact that during the sixties the boundaries of on-screen nudity were pushed further back by domestic filmmakers, who on a wide scale adopted a socially committed style where sexuality was considered an important part of their freedom of expression as well as tying in with a desired realistic depiction of the world.[15] Due to the commercial success of taboo-breaking and sexually controversial art films the subject of sex was more often than not cheered on by the Swedish production companies. In the afore-mentioned article "Export or Die" top executive Göran Lindgren at Sandrews, one of Sweden's major producers at the time, summed it up simply; "We are lucky that our directors are so interested in sex."[16]

The Swedish Knack—Sex as Good Taste

The publication *Film in Sweden* was initially designed as a regular film magazine with news articles, interviews, and promotional images of upcoming titles. According to in-house correspondence at the SFI the publication had 3,333 international industry subscribers in 1970 and was printed in a total circulation of 6,000.[17] The publication could be received by mail free of charge anywhere in the world as long as the receiver had any presumable connection to the film industry.[18] After a substantial make-over and name switch to *Swedish Films* in 1973 it changed format into an annual catalogue, listing new films but also incorporating a few selected essays reporting on the current state of Swedish film. When examining the issues from the sixties and seventies one can discern a constant editorial awareness of the image of Swedish sin, beginning already in *Film in Sweden*'s third issue in an article signed by no other than Schein and titled "The Swedish Knack." The use of the word "Knack" was not only a nod at the recent Palme d'Or–winning film *The Knack ... and How to Get It* (1965) by director Richard Lester, but it also signaled that the SFI wanted to turn the notion of Swedish sin into something favorable, a quality or an ability that other countries lacked, similar to the tagline of the aforementioned film: "Some have it, some don't."[19] Schein's article concluded that:

> Swedish love is not freer, more immoral, more healthy, more perverse than love in other nations. But the attitude of Swedish society towards sex is more liberal and more relaxed. This is reflected in Swedish films—not only through what is allowed or prohibited by the film censors but by what is accepted by the press, the churches, the audiences and the opinion-makers—what our establishment considers to be good taste. [---] Love in Swedish films is certainly not ahead of its time. But it at least tries to keep pace, and this is not something for us to bemoan.[20]

The same exploitative urge that once led *Time*'s Joe David Brown to Stockholm in search of an alluring scoop resulted in many foreign journalists visiting Stockholm to get a piece of sinful Sweden to send home to their hopefully shocked readers. One such journalist was the *Omaha World-Herald*'s Darwin Olofsson, who in 1967 wrote the article "No Imagination Needed on Swedish Sex Films." Here, the statement of Information Director of the SFI, and later-to-be editor of *Film in Sweden*, Gun Hyltén-Cavallius echoed the earlier official declaration made by Schein. She was quoted as having said: "The attitude in Sweden is very free [...]. We have a more open attitude towards sex and can discuss it with friends. [---] So why should not our (film) directors follow this attitude? [---] People just got used to the idea that Swedish movies are sexy—that's what they want to buy, that's where the money is." The article continued: "The trend towards frankness in films, while in keeping with the attitudes of a people 'outspoken about sex,' does have certain risks according to Mrs. Hylten-Cavallius." And she concluded: "There is the possibility that you go so far that you don't see that little light in people's eyes any more."[21] In hindsight, knowing of the coming development of an increasing Swedish production of more or less explicit pornography, it is fair to say that the premonition felt by Hyltén-Cavallius was indeed to develop into certain complexities for the SFI. How relaxed an attitude could they keep towards sex and still consider it "good taste" and in line with the quality directives of the film reform?

The Swedish Model—Turning Faults into Traits

The tactics of turning ones alleged faults into knacks or positive traits is actually analogous with the strategy of the aforementioned SI, particularly in how that organization dodged accusations of immorality and promiscuity from foreign media in the wake of the *Time* article. The director of the SI, Tore Tallroth, had already elucidated the matter in 1962: "One's work will be handicapped if one does not use existing interests and environments abroad, allowing the recipient country to dictate the direction of what it wants to know, see, and hear."[22] As scholars Nikolas Glover and Carl Marklund have demonstrated, the scheme of the SI was expressed in a shift of attention, from promiscuity to progressiveness and equality of the sexes, as a supposed effect of Swedes' rational, democratic, and modern view on sex and sex-roles. The connection between Sweden and sex was consequently not only confirmed by the SI, but also nurtured as an intentional marketing strategy for the whole nation.[23] One example can be taken from how the Swedish Chamber of Commerce of the United States of America approached the same issues in their promotional magazine *The American Swedish Monthly* published between 1934 and 1967. In an obvious effort to make favorable and thus in a way normalize the image of sexually liberal Sweden, often frowned upon by Americans, the publication rather frequently featured comprehensive entries on these matters, clearly not connected to topics of industrial export, which was its official purpose. Articles with titles such as: "Scandinavia's Approach to Sex Education," "Women's Rights in Sweden: What Is There to Discuss?" and "A Woman's Lot Is Quite a Happy One—And Successful Too," all bear witness of a greater agenda in which ideas and images of "Swedes" were to be sold, along the line of Swedish commercial products.[24] Where the Swedish Chamber of Commerce and the SI favored a rather modest, virtuous, and well-behaved tone in their approach, often focusing on equality and rationality, the SFI on the other hand went a bit further.

Selling Sweden Wholesale at Gimbels, New York

Early in 1971 the legendary American department store chain Gimbels, once the world's largest of its kind, contacted the SI to suggest a grand two-week showcase devoting the entirety of their ten stores in the state of New York to the crafts, products, arts, and cultural contributions of Scandinavia. Gimbels could at the time, they claimed, boast two million visitors in two business weeks.[25] The SI sent the proposition on to Bo Jonsson, who welcomed the Gimbels representatives to Stockholm. The young Jonsson had just been elected CEO of the SFI. The appointment was a construction designed entirely by Schein, due in part to years of criticism from journalists and film-makers regarding Schein's alleged authoritarian ways of managing the institute, as well as part of Schein's own scheme to rearrange the board of directors.[26] In a game of titles, Schein switched to Chairman of the Board and saw Jonsson as his mere "assistant."[27] Jonsson, who disliked the puppet-like position, left the SFI after only two years and the manifestation at Gimbels was to be one of few imprints during his short sojourn as CEO.[28]

Although the event focused on all the Scandinavian countries, Sweden was the preferred choice by the Americans when it came to representations of cinematic importance. Gimbels even proposed to pay for a couple of promotional films to be produced by the SFI specifically for the event, namely two films Gimbels suggested be called "The Filminstitutet Story" and "The History of Swedish Films." Furthermore, the SFI was to provide Gimbels with an exhibition of glossy photos and film posters along with actual Swedish film stars to show up at the event, all paid for by Gimbels.[29] It was naturally an offer Jonsson could not refuse. Luckily enough, Jonsson and the SFI, together with the documentary filmmaker and scriptwriter Gardar Sahlberg, had just produced a 33-minute collage film covering 60 years and 23 movie clips of Swedish films, called *Från spex till sex* (1971), which would translate into "From Farce to Sex."[30] Among the clips were films that had all in one way or another helped sustain the image of sinful Sweden: *Hon dansade en sommar/One Summer of Happiness* (Arne Mattsson, 1951), *Sommaren med Monika/Summer with Monika* (Ingmar Bergman, 1953), *491* (Vilgot Sjöman, 1964), and *The Silence*. The choice of this particular film fitted right into the overall strategy of turning promiscuity into progressiveness and, like Schein, not bemoaning the natural side of sex and love. After leafing through a number of Swedish classics, ending with scenes from the sex-education film *Ur kärlekens språk/Language of Love* (Torgny Wickman, 1969), Sahlberg's narration rationally sums up that by the end of the sixties the Swedish film directors preferred to speak the kind of language that knows no borders and is understood by all people in all countries, underscoring the Swedish trope that sex equals democracy and understanding between people.

The second film, suggested by Gimbels to be called "The Filminstitutet Story," was to be produced by Jonsson in its entirety for the occasion of the Scandinavia Now fair and was the first and perhaps only promotion film ever produced by the SFI on behalf of a commercial company.[31] Domestically well-known feature filmmaker Jonas Cornell was assigned director and the narration was written by Lars-Magnus Lindgren, the director of such Swedish summer-love classics as *Änglar, finns dom?/Love Mates* (1961) and *Dear John*, the latter being one of the biggest grossing foreign films in North America until 1968, as well as nominated for an Oscar.[32] The promotion film was given the apt but dry name *A Brief Survey of Film in Sweden, Presented to Gimbels' Visitors by Gimbels and SFI* and focused mainly on a backstage view of the on-going children's film production *Niklas och figuren/Niklas and the Figure* (Ulf Andrée, 1971). The film's initial scenes, however, use the strategy of employing the stereotype of Swedish sinfulness as an attention grabber and entry into the film. It begins with the sound of typical traditional Swedish folk music accompanying an image of an open grassy field with a backdrop composed of modern functional architecture (actually the then newly constructed Film House, the office of the SFI). This audiovisual mix comprises a perfect "Swedish" example of modernity and tradition in harmony. Lindgren's narration then explicitly alludes to Swedish sinfulness and other stereotypical traits well-known abroad, using the stereotype as a catch to gain attention from the viewer and then turning attention towards something else.

The Swedish Film Institute Misses the (Selling) Point

In both film cases we find perfect examples of how the SFI decided to go with Tallroth's afore-mentioned strategy and that meant not just using the stereotypes as marketing tools, but also defending and thus reproducing and amplifying them. These two films were subsequently shown in a package called "Swedish Film Celebration" on the 6th floor of the flagship store on Broadway in New York City. On the same floor visitors could delve into everything from authentic Danish *smörrebröd* to Swedish crystal, Finnish candle dipping, and the possibility of winning a new Saab Sonett III sports car. On other floors there were exhibits covering the famous Swedish 400-year old Wasa ship, as well as a miniature Norwegian Vigeland Sculpture Garden, a Danish Legoland Village for the kids, and a Finnish Sauna bar for the adults. It was indeed a commercial storewide celebration—American style. And it had its price, of which Jonsson soon became aware. He had according to his correspondence with Gimbels booked the established international authority on Scandinavian film at the time, British writer and film historian Peter Cowie, to introduce every daily screening of the "Swedish Film Celebration" for 14 days, and Gimbels was to pay his expenses.[33] At least up until a couple of weeks before the event, this was agreed upon. What Jonsson did not foresee was the total disinterest of any Swedish actors or directors in joining Cowie in such an utterly commercial endeavor. Considering the strong anti-capitalist winds blowing at the time, Jonsson should indeed have been prepared for this. The only director who volunteered to participate at the Scandinavia Now fair was Jan Troell and, considering the American interest in his new film *Utvandrarna/The Emigrants* (1971), that choice could easily be understood from a marketing perspective.[34] When Jonsson and the SFI failed to provide the Americans with any attractive faces and the desirable Swedish beauty connected with their image of Swedish films, only a serious male historian (and British to boot!), they suddenly altered the deal. Without explanation they changed the setup completely, excluding Cowie and replacing him with recent *Life Magazine* cover girl and 1961 Miss Sweden and Miss Universe semifinalist, blonde bombshell Gunilla Knutsson. Billed only as "Sweden's famous beauty" she had actually never acted in any Swedish films, and her experience with moving images was principally related to urging American men to "take it off, take it all off!," in Noxzema's shaving cream commercials.

This apparent anti-climax could be considered an expected backfire in the strategy of the SFI. When the fully commercial company Gimbels did not achieve the appealing selling point that they wanted, they simply decided to form their own image of Sweden to suit the preconception that they, and the visitors of Gimbels, probably already nurtured and wanted to have confirmed. In many ways what happened at Gimbels was part of the same fate that befell several of the classic Swedish summer-love films sold to North America, where titles would change into more smutty ones and wordy dialogue scenes, much like Cowie, were cut and instead replaced with new images of locally filmed skin—all because the original product failed to live up to its reputation.[35] In a letter to Cowie, Jonsson expressed his anger and disappointment with Gimbels in a way much tied in with the specific time and place, as it hints at the apparent doubtfulness towards American commercialism: "This has, however, taught us not to enter the commercial side of the business [---]. Please excuse us for cooperating with the department store."[36] The irony in this remark is that, one year later, the SFI for the first time entered the scene as a producer of commercial feature films in its own right, but by then Jonsson was already again replaced by Schein as CEO.[37]

Selling "Quality" with Nudity

The editors of *Film in Sweden* seemed to have made a conscious decision to deliberately uphold, for effect, the stereotypical connection between sex and Sweden. Overall, from the first issue in 1965 up until the mid-seventies, the focus is often on films with sexual subjects and imagery, something often emphasized in accompanying advertisements as well as editorially chosen film stills. A few textual excerpts can be quoted. In a 1966 article called "What the world should know about *Att angöra en brygga (To Go Ashore)*" the following was humorously affirmed: "N.B.!!!!!! No nude bathing, no Polar bears—but a hell of a lot of mosquitoes."[38] The first issue of 1971 had the front page covered with the following statement: "This is Film in Sweden in new clothes; we hope, indeed, they are not the Emperor's new clothes. Although many in the world still believe that we in Sweden hop delightedly out of our underwear as soon as a movie camera starts to grind."[39] If the aim of the SI was to direct international attention towards sexual democracy, this was far from the result regarding the marketing strategies of *Film in Sweden*. When browsing through the aforementioned issue of 1971, we find that only three out of thirteen females, all of them actresses, have their clothes on, while all males, most of them directors, are fully dressed.

The stereotypical role of Swedish women as objects of lust—willing, blond, beautiful, and remarkably often undressed—was thus constantly reproduced by the SFI. It can be viewed as merely a conventional, albeit crude, marketing strategy but, as scholars Mariah Larsson and Lena Lennerhed have pointed out, there was a prevalent view during the late sixties among Swedish filmmakers and critics that sex and eroticism were topics that should be embraced, and if done in an artistic way, a good quality pornographic film could be the result.[40] The idea of good pornography had little, or anything, to do with latter day feminist anti-porn notions that pornography is offensive because it is misogynist and oppressive to women. The essential question of female objectification in moving images was yet to be addressed by the likes of Laura Mulvey and other feminist theorists a couple of years later. In the Swedish 1960s, the to-be-looked-at-ness of a female body was unquestioned, and the idea of good pornography was simply a desire for higher aesthetic quality. This opinion culminated in the legalization of pornography in 1971, which in turn very soon led to a fair number of more or less pornographic feature films being produced in Sweden.

Pornography—The Uncomfortable Bed Partner

The years following the legalization are perhaps the most interesting when it comes to the SFI's marketing publications. The previously cited confident statement from Schein about not bemoaning the sex-centered image of Sweden did suddenly turn to lament in essays such as "The Sex Trauma in Swedish Films," featured in 1973, in which film critic Torsten Manns deplores Sweden's hypocritical attitude towards sex, and proposes: "To claim that *The Language of Love* is the voice of Swedish movies abroad would be equally unjust as to claim that Louis de Funès was the voice of French movies."[41] It's interesting to note that only two years earlier Sahlberg's narration in the official SFI-produced product *From Farce to Sex* had insisted that indeed each and every Swedish film spoke the language of love. Even more distressed about the meager outcome of his years of battling censorship laws was director Vilgot Sjöman, who in 1976 contributed an essay where he portrayed himself as "[…] an egret, standing on one leg, in the middle of the porno swamp!"[42] Sjöman concluded: "The gates of censorship were flung open; and the rats of commercialism swarmed over the movie screens," and continuing just as ferociously:

> […] nothing new is going to happen until first-rate directors and first-rate actors and actresses start making use of the new freedom of censorship. [---] Until that happens, we shall remain stuck in the porno swamp as though in mud. We shall have to put up with these amateurs with lifeless faces who have spread all over our movie screens in everything from *The Language of Love* to the latest American pornographic films.[43]

Now let us not forget that these unrelenting statements regarding amateurs, rats, and hypocrisy were to be found in the official Swedish promotion materials, the face of Swedish films towards the world market. While browsing through the collected issues one can find an additional twist to this poorly executed marketing strategy. In the illustrated list of upcoming Swedish titles we find the very same hard-core and soft-core pornography that was scorned by the institute just a few pages earlier. Featured titles include: *Porr i skandalskolan/The Scandal School* (Mac Ahlberg, 1974), *Kär lek—Så gör vi/Love Play—This is our Way* (Torgny Wickman, 1972), *Bäddat för lusta/Bed of Lust* (Rune Ljungberg, 1972), *Rapport från Stockholms sexträsk/Report from the Stockholm Sex Jungle* (Arne Brandhild, 1974), *Thriller—en grym film/Thriller—a Cruel Picture* (Bo Arne Vibenius, 1974) and *Sams/Swedish Family Games* (Calvin Floyd, 1974). The two juxtaposed pages featuring *Hallo Baby* (Johan Bergenstråhle, 1976) and *Inkräktarna/The Intruders* (Torgny Wickman, 1974) are especially telling as to how art films and sexploitation films walked hand in hand with the same evocative selling points, with limited possibility for an outside reader to determine which was which.[44] How utterly confusing and paradoxical it must have seemed for the buyers and critics of the Promenade de la Croisette at the Cannes Film Festival Market, when the core of the SFI's selling point could be summed up into something close to: We think it's hogwash, but we would like for you to buy it!

The liberal and relaxed view on sex, which Schein and Hyltén-Cavallius in 1966–67 had described as representing the "good taste" of the Swedish establishment, had in ten years time been transformed into a seemingly uncontrollable and contradictory approach to marketing. The two juxtaposed pages, due to the pragmatic decision to present the films in alphabetical order, featuring the hard-core film *Breaking Point* (Bo A. Vibenius, 1975) next to the animated children's film *Agaton Sax och Byköpings gästabud/Agaton Sax and the Byköping Feast* (Stig Lasseby, 1976) is certainly an example of this.

Conclusion

A possible explanation for these confusing double standards could be, simply put, that the SFI was trying to find a way to adapt itself to a modern, progressive, and versatile commercial film export market. This new market saw its formative years during the early seventies, when strictly commercial private sales companies started to replace national institutes.[45] When studying the correspondence in 1970 between the editor of *Film in Sweden*, Lars-Olof Löthwall, and Jonsson and Schein it is apparent that they found it challenging but important to adapt to the new order of things. Schein even initiated Löthwall to carry out a survey among Swedish and international film professionals regarding the actual marketing value of the magazine.[46]

The SFI probably realized some domestic financial importance in backing up all Swedish film producers, including the more dubious ones, but at the same time they tried to keep their dignity and cultural capital intact towards the key concept of "quality." The result was not unlike trying to send intellectual Cowie to New York but unwillingly ending up with bombshell beauty Knutsson. These were inevitable growing pains the SFI experienced when having to adapt to an increasingly commodified and elaborate film-sales culture where the exploitative film producers, perhaps reluctantly, had to be seen as important as the ones with more artistic ambitions. It called for a more relaxed attitude towards the cardinal quality formula—a compromise that in turn made it possible for hard-core pornographic films to enter into the sales materials of the SFI. This concession certainly becomes peculiar when juxtaposed to one of the most impetuous domestic film debates during the sixties, namely the one related to the Filmcentrum catalogue.

Much in line with Jonas Mekas' Film-Makers' Cooperative, although agitating a more overt left-wing objective, Filmcentrum was created in 1968 as an independent distributor of documentaries, shorts, and experimental films, all with the common denominator of being more or less non-commercial. The main principle was that of a free cinema not guided by any authoritarian quality directive.[47] Filmcentrum applied for a grant from the SFI to print their distribution catalogue. They were handed an ultimatum: to obtain financial support they would have to—quoting Schein—formulate a system to "[…] weed out the worst filth […]" in their selection.[48] Schein even went so far as using the words "crappy films" when categorizing what would end up in the catalogue if there were no quality assuring filtering process.[49] The question certainly arises why Schein and thereby the SFI were so eager to discriminate and judge when it came to free non-commercial cinema and yet decided to include what Schein called "utter trash that Swedish producers scatter across the globe," into its own promotion material.[50] Noteworthy is that the range of moving images that an organization such as Filmcentrum represented generally was excluded from the promotional undertakings of the SFI, thus rendering only commercial feature length products intended for theatrical release visible for an international market. In that very observation lies, perhaps, the heart of the matter. The reason why the SFI advertised hard-core pornographic features in international markets—instead of short, experimental, films or political essays—was that they had locked themselves into a purely commercial and technical matrix, which created a close-to ontological definition of the intrinsic nature of "cinema," determining, as an official national body, what it *could* and *could not be*. Thus, the revered quality-directive of the SFI was simply forced to yield to the fact that the "utter trash," at the end of the day, was a better-suited cinema than anything non-theatrical or non-commercial. In their study of Swedish free cinema, scholars Lars Gustaf Andersson and John Sundholm point out that the freer definition of cinema advocated by the likes of Filmcentrum, if implemented, would have shaken the very foundation that the SFI was built upon.[51]

To sum up, one can conclude that Schein's previously mentioned main objective of the SFI's international activities—to counteract the distorted one-dimensional sexualized image of Swedish film—was a case lost. In the case of the Gimbels fair, Swedish culture was deliberately hi-jacked and lusciously re-packaged by American commercial interests, and in the case of *Film in Sweden/Swedish Films* the institute actively broadcast wooden stereotypes of naked actresses and male directors. It is safe to presume that these images did everything but counteract the image of Swedish sin. When eventually some of their advertised products were hard-core pornography, the marketers of the SFI were forced to both promote and condemn at the same time, due to the institute's own limited principles on what cinema could be. To paraphrase Sjöman, they turned themselves into nothing but frustrated egrets in a porno swamp, with mud up to their ankles.

NOTES

1. Harry Schein, *I själva verket* (Stockholm: Nordstedts, 1970), 234.
2. Schein, *I själva verket*, 234, my translation.
3. Letter to Bo Jonsson (CEO of the SFI in 1971) signed by Peter Shyne, Director Special Promotions and Events at Gimbles New York. Date: February 24, 1971. Swedish Film Institute Archive.
4. For a discussion on the term "quality-film" (kvalitetsfilm), made famous by Harry Schein in

conjunction with the film reform of 1963, see Pelle Snickars "Vad är kvalitet?" in *Citizen Schein*, ed. Lars Ilshammar et al, (Stockholm: Kungliga biblioteket, 2010), 158–173.

5. Schein, *I själva verket*, 85.

6. For a complete survey of Swedish feature films produced between 1950 and 1969 see *Svensk filmografi 5: 1950–1959*, ed. Lars Åhlander, (Stockholm: Svenska filminstitutet, 1984) and *Svensk filmografi 6: 1960–1969*, ed. Jörn Donner, (Stockholm: Svenska filminstitutet, 1977).

7. Harry Schein, "Det hände på sextiotalet" in *Svensk filmografi 6: 1960–1969*, ed. Jörn Donner (Stockholm: Svenska filminstitutet, 1977), 9–31, 12.

8. Letter from the Vice President of the Swedish Institute for Cultural Relations with Foreign Countries Lars Björkbom to the Managing Director of Film Comment Austin F. Lamont, dated August 4, 1969. Swedish Film Institute Archive.

9. Frederic Fleisher, "Export or Die," *Film Comment*, Vol. 6 No. 2 Summer (1970): 36–37.

10. Harry Schein, "Swedish Film Policy," *Swedish Films* (1973): 8.

11. Frederick Hale, "*Time* for Sex in Sweden—Enhancing the Myth of the 'Swedish Sin' during the 1950s," *Scandinavian Studies*, vol. 75, no. 3, (2003): 353. See also Klara Arnberg and Carl Marklund's chapter in this volume. Joe David Brown, "Sin & Sweden," *Time*, April 25, 1955. See also Lena Lennerhed, *Frihet att njuta—sexualdebatten i Sverige på 1960-talet* (Stockholm: Nordstedts, 1994), 90.

12. Anders Åberg, *Tabu: filmaren Vilgot Sjöman* (Lund: Filmhäftet, 2001), 201.

13. Norman K. Dorn, "Sex isn't much different in Sweden than other countries," *S.F. Sunday Examiner & Chronicle*, October 30, 1966.

14. Schein, *I själva verket*, 96. My translation.

15. Åberg, *Tabu: filmaren Vilgot Sjöman*, 201.

16. Fleisher, "Export or Die," 37.

17. According to a letter from editor Lars-Olof Löthwall to Harry Schein dated May 11 1970 as well as a quote from Tryckeri AB Björkmans Eftr. dated August 11 1970. Both found in the archive of the Swedish Film Institute. In his 1970 book *I själva verket* Schein states that the publication had over 5000 international subscribers. 97.

18. See for example a letter to Leo Bottenweiser at Imexport in Uruguay from the Information Director at the Swedish Film Institute Gun Hyltén-Cavallius, dated October 9, 1969. Swedish Film Institute Archive.

19. "The Knack ... and How to Get It," IMDb, accessed May 5 2015, http://www.imdb.com/title/tt0059362/?ref_=fn_al_tt_2

20. Harry Schein, "The Swedish Knack," *Film in Sweden* 1 (1966): 3–4.

21. Darwin Olofsson, "No Imagination Needed on Swedish Sex Films," *Omaha World-Herald*, December 13, 1967.

22. Cited in Nikolas Glover and Carl Marklund, "Arabian Nights in the Midnight Sun? Exploring the Temporal Structure of Sexual Geographics," *Historisk Tidskrift* 129 no. 3 (2009): 494.

23. Glover and Marklund, "Arabian Nights in the Midnight Sun?," 495.

24. Heather L. Barbash, "Scandinavia's Approach to Sex Education," September 1966, 22–23. Edward Maze, "Women's Rights in Sweden: What is There to Discuss?," December 1966, 21–22. Mary R. Johnson "A Woman's Lot is quite a happy one—and successful too," July 1964, 14–17. All from *The American Swedish Monthly*.

25. Proposition of collaboration from Gimbles New York called "Gimbels presents Scandinavia '71." Not dated. Swedish Film Institute Archive.

26. The critique of Schein as a seemingly corrupt "film-dictator" was a recurring subject in Swedish news media from 1965 until he left the Institute in 1978. See for example the articles "Konstnärligt onödig" *Aftonbladet*, January 18, 1965 and "Filmdiktatur" *Dagens Nyheter*, September 20, 1965. See also Bengt Forslund, "Filmentreprenören" and Jonas Sima, "Konflikternas mästare: Berättelse om en filmfurstes uppgång och fall" in *Citizen Schein*, ed. Lars Ilshammar et al. (Stockholm: Kungliga biblioteket, 2010), 208 and 88 respectively.

27. Schein himself acknowledged the reasons for this peculiar episode in Harry Schein, *Schein* (Stockholm: Bonniers, 1980), 356–358.

28. Jonsson went on to become one of Sweden's most successful independent film producers.

29. May 12, 1971, draft of contract between Peter Shyne, Director Special Promotions and Events at Gimbles and the Swedish Film Institute. Swedish Film Institute Archive.

30. Although the film was already finished and had had its Swedish theatrical premiere in January that year, Jonsson charged Gimbels USD 2000 for it (almost USD 12.000 today). The film pre-

miered at the Film House in Stockholm on January 18, 1971. "Från spex till sex," Svensk Filmdatabas, accessed May 5, 2015, http://www.sfi.se/sv/svensk-filmdatabas. Jonsson at least gave Gimbels the chance to change the salacious name of the film, an opportunity they took twice and programed the film as *Celebration of the Art of Swedish Film-Making*—via the more generic suggestion *Swedish Film—All The Way*. According to a letter from Bo Jonsson to Peter Shyne dated June 17 1971, the final floor-by-floor guide of the event and an invoice regarding the two film productions dated September 29 1971. All three from the Swedish Film Institute Archive.

31. According to an invoice regarding the two film productions dated September 29 1971, Gimbels paid USD 5000 for the film. Swedish Film Institute Archive.

32. Donner, *Svensk filmografi 6: 1960–1969*, 198. The fact that Lindgren was assigned writing the narration is confirmed by a letter from Bo Jonsson to Lindgren dated June 24 1971. Lindgren was given 500 SEK for the job. Swedish Film Institute Archive.

33. See for example Bo Jonsson's letter to Peter Shyne at Gimbles, dated August 23 1971. Swedish Film Institute Archive.

34. Bo Jonsson's letter to Peter Shyne at Gimbles, dated August 23 1971. Swedish Film Institute Archive.

35. See for example Arne Lunde's contribution to this volume.

36. Letter from Bo Jonsson to Peter Cowie dated September 2 1971. Swedish Film Institute Archive.

37. Leif Furhammar, *Filmen i Sverige—en historia i tio kapitel och en fortsättning* (Stockholm: Dialogos förlag och Svenska filminstitutet, 2003), 318. The Institute had co-produced commercial features since 1965.

38. Hans Alfredson and Tage Danielsson, "What the world should know about Att angöra en brygga (To Go Ashore)," *Film in Sweden* 1 (1966): 11.

39. Lars-Olof Löthwall, "Editorial," *Film in Sweden* 1 (1971): 1–2

40. Mariah Larsson, "Drömmen om den goda pornografin—om sextio-och sjuttiotalsfilmen och gränsen mellan konst och pornografi," *Tidsskrift för genusvetenskap* 1–2 (2007): 93–111, 94 and Lennerhed, *Frihet att njuta—sexualdebatten i Sverige på 1960-talet*, 189.

41. Torsten Manns, "The Sex Trauma in Swedish Films," *Swedish Films* (1973): 24.

42. Vilgot Sjöman, "An Egret in the Porno Swamp," *Swedish Films* (1976): 29.

43. Sjöman, "An Egret in the Porno Swamp," 32–33.

44. *Swedish Films* (1975), 70–71.

45. See Mark Peranson, "First You Get the Power, Then You Get the Money: Two Models of Film Festivals" in *Dekalog³: On Film Festivals*, ed. Richard Porton (London: Wallflower, 2009), 23–30.

46. Letter from Lars-Olof Löthwall to Harry Schein. The letter is dated "Grand Joke Day Although It's Serious" so it's obvious that Löthwall refers to April 1. The year is most certainly 1970 since it is part of a longer correspondence taking place that year. Swedish Film Institute Archive.

47. Sven Frostenson, "Fri Film i Sverige: Filmcentrum," *Chaplin* 84 (1968): 256.

48. Schein, *I själva verket*, 124. My translation.

49. Schein, *I själva verket*, 124. My translation.

50. Schein, *I själva verket*, 96.

51. Lars Gustaf Andersson and John Sundholm, *"Hellre fri än filmare": Filmverkstan och den fria filmen* (Lund: Nordic Academic Press, 2014), 68.

REFERENCES

Archive of the Swedish Film Institute

Bo Jonsson's letter to Peter Shyne at Gimbles, dated August 23, 1971.
Invoice regarding SFI's two films productions for Gimbels, dated September 29, 1971.
Letter from Bo Jonsson to Lars-Magnus Lindgren dated June 24, 1971.
Letter from Bo Jonsson to Peter Cowie dated September 2, 1971.
Letter from Bo Jonsson to Peter Shyne dated June 17, 1971.
Letter from editor Lars-Olof Löthwall to Harry Schein dated May 11, 1970.
Letter from Lars-Olof Löthwall to Harry Schein, April 1, 1970.
Letter from the Vice President of the Swedish Institute for Cultural Relations with Foreign Countries Lars Björkbom to the Managing Director of Film Comment Austin F Lamont, dated August 4, 1969.

Letter to Bo Jonsson (CEO of the SFI in 1971) signed by Peter Shyne, Director Special Promotions and Events at Gimbles New York, dated February 24, 1971.
Letter to Leo Bottenweiser at Imexport in Uruguay from the Information Director at the Swedish Film Institute Gun Hyltén-Cavallius, dated October 9, 1969.
Draft of contract between Peter Shyne, Director Special Promotions and Events at Gimbles and the Swedish Film Institute, dated May 12, 1971.
Proposition of collaboration from Gimbles New York called "Gimbels presents Scandinavia '71." Not dated.
Quote from Tryckeri AB Björkmans Eftr., dated August 11 1970.

Other Sources

Åberg, Anders. *Tabu: filmaren Vilgot Sjöman*. Lund: Filmhäftet, 2001.
Åhlander, Lars, ed. *Svensk filmografi 5: 1950–1959*. Stockholm: Svenska filminstitutet, 1984.
Alfredson, Hans, and Tage Danielsson. "What the world should know about Att angöra en brygga (To Go Ashore)." *Film in Sweden* 1 (1966).
Andersson, Lars Gustaf, and John Sundholm. *"Hellre fri än filmare": Filmverkstan och den fria filmen*. Lund: Nordic Academic Press, 2014.
Barbash, Heather L. "Scandinavia's Approach to Sex Education." *The American Swedish Monthly*, September 1966: 22–23.
Brown, Joe David. "Sin & Sweden." *Time*, April 25, 1955.
Donner, Jörn, ed. *Svensk filmografi 6: 1960–1969*. Stockholm: Svenska filminstitutet, 1977.
Dorn, Norman K. "Sex isn't much different in Sweden than other countries." *San Francisco Sunday Examiner & Chronicle*, October 30, 1966.
"Filmdiktatur." *Dagens Nyheter*, September 20, 1965.
Fleisher, Frederic. "Export or Die." *Film Comment*, 6:2 (1970): 36–37.
Forslund, Bengt. "Filmentreprenören." In *Citizen Schein*, edited by Lars Ilshammar, Pelle Snickars and Per Vesterlund. Stockholm: Kungliga biblioteket, 2010.
Frostenson, Sven. "Fri Film i Sverige: Filmcentrum." *Chaplin* 84 (1968): 256.
Furhammar, Leif. *Filmen i Sverige—en historia i tio kapitel och en fortsättning*, third edition. Stockholm: Dialogos Förlag and Svenska filminstitutet, 2003.
Glover, Nikolas, and Carl Marklund. "Arabian Nights in the Midnight Sun? Exploring the Temporal Structure of Sexual Geographics." *Historisk Tidskrift*, 129:3 (2009): 487–510.
Hale, Frederick. "*Time* for Sex in Sweden—Enhancing the Myth of the 'Swedish Sin' during the 1950s." *Scandinavian Studies*, 75: 3 (2003): 351–374.
Johnson, Mary R. "A Woman's Lot is Quite a Happy One—and Successful Too." *The American Swedish Monthly*, July (1964): 14–17.
"The Knack ... and How to Get It." The Internet Movie Database. Accessed May 5 2015, http://www.imdb.com/title/tt0059362/?ref_=fn_al_tt_2.
"Konstnärligt onödig." *Aftonbladet*, January 18, 1965.
Larsson, Mariah. "Drömmen om den goda pornografin—om sextio-och sjuttiotalsfilmen och gränsen mellan konst och pornografi." *Tidsskrift för genusvetenskap*, 1–2 (2007): 93–111.
Lennerhed, Lena. *Frihet att njuta—sexualdebatten i Sverige på 1960-talet*. Stockholm: Nordstedts, 1994.
Löthwall, Lars-Olof. "Editorial." *Film in Sweden* 1 (1971).
Manns, Torsten. "The Sex Trauma in Swedish Films." *Swedish Films* (1973).
Maze, Edward. "Women's Rights in Sweden: What Is There to Discuss?" *The American Swedish Monthly*. December (1966): 21–22.
Olofsson, Darwin. "No Imagination Needed on Swedish Sex Films." *Omaha World-Herald*, December 13, 1967.
Peranson, Mark. "First You Get the Power, Then You Get the Money: Two Models of Film Festivals." In *Dekalog³: On Film Festivals*, edited by Richard Porton, 23–30. London: Wallflower, 2009.
Schein, Harry. "Det hände på sextiotalet." *Svensk filmografi 6: 1960–1969*, edited by Jörn Donner, 9–31. Stockholm: Svenska filminstitutet, 1977.
_____. *Schein*. Stockholm: Bonniers, 1980.
_____. *I själva verket*. Stockholm: Nordstedts, 1970.
_____. "Swedish Film Policy" *Swedish Films* (1973).

———. "The Swedish Knack." *Film in Sweden* 1 (1966).
Sima, Jonas. "Konflikternas mästare: Berättelse om en filmfurstes uppgång och fall." In *Citizen Schein*, edited by Lars Ilshammar, Pelle Snickars and Per Vesterlund. Stockholm: Kungliga biblioteket, 2010.
Sjöman, Vilgot. "An Egret in the Porno Swamp." *Swedish Films* (1976).
Snickars, Pelle. "Vad är kvalitet?" In *Citizen Schein*, edited by Lars Ilshammar, Pelle Snickars and Per Vesterlund, 158–173. Stockholm: Kungliga biblioteket, 2010.

V

The American Reception of Swedish Sin

Illegally Blonde
Swedish Sin and Pornography in U.S. and Swedish Imaginations 1955–1971

KLARA ARNBERG *and* CARL MARKLUND

> There was a young lady in Sweden
> Who dreamed she was sinning in Eden
> She awoke from the dream
> with a terrible scream
> For there was no sinning
> Or Eden, just Sweden.[1]

This essay focuses on the development of the notion of "Swedish sin" and its connection to the pornography issue from the late 1950s to the early 1970s, both in film and in print. The chapter also follows how Swedish politicians handled this imagination of Sweden as a sexual paradise (or possibly Gomorrah) and how these circulating images touched upon anxieties in both Sweden and the U.S. about gender and sexuality.[2] Additionally, a closer study of one of the Swedish pornographic magazines produced for an international audience—*Private*—in order to see how Swedish sin was used and interpreted in pornographic production, is offered here. We have chosen to focus on the period beginning with the influential article "Sin & Sweden" in *Time* 1955 and ending with the legalization of pornography in Sweden in 1971. During this period, the idea of Swedish sin was widespread internationally, not the least in the U.S. With the legal amendment, the perceived problems with pornography—proliferation to foreigners by mail and "pornography tourists" window-shopping in Swedish towns—were legally solved by combining the prohibition of pornographic display and mail-proliferation with the legalization of the production, thus serving as a natural ending point for this text.

The essay is divided into two empirical sections, where the first is built on parliamentary documents, official reports and press material from the debates in the U.S. and in Sweden.[3] The second section follows more closely the development of the 10 first issues of *Private* (1965–1968) and how this publication used notions of "promiscuous" female Swedishness commercially.[4]

Gender, Nationality and Pornography

Inspired by Benedict Anderson's suggestion to see nations as "imagined communities," we will analyze how the Swedish community has been imagined in terms of gender and sexuality both domestically and from abroad, here focusing on the U.S.[5] Being an industrialized and small country, Sweden has been heavily dependent on export trade, and its public opinion has been very sensitive to other countries' perceptions of it.[6] In the Cold War tensions between East and West, the U.S. became the most important nation to (often critically) relate to culturally and politically.[7] During the 1930s, Sweden was looked upon favorably by many in the U.S. as a "middle way" between capitalism and socialism.[8] During the 1950s and 1960s, however, this view changed and Sweden's "socialistic" welfare state was increasingly used as a warning example by U.S. conservatives.[9] Moreover, in the U.S., Sweden was also looked upon as a small but outspoken country when for example Prime Minister Olof Palme criticized U.S. aerial bombing of Hanoi in 1972. If the U.S. often was disparagingly viewed as a kind of "world police" in the 1970s, Sweden was sometimes depicted as the "world's conscience."[10]

The Swedish sense of national identity is tightly connected to the social security and gender equality of the welfare state.[11] As the Social Democrats gained power in the early 1930s (which they retained until the mid–1970s), the usage of the term *folkhemmet*, "the people's home," would in the post-war era evolve into a concrete manifestation of community. The Social Democratic welfare state should resemble the proverbial good home, where everyone got what they needed and no one was left behind.[12] The notion of a people's home was, however, clearly based on gendered norms and implicit heterosexuality.[13]

Women's relation to the nation has historically been of a complex nature—in Sweden and elsewhere. Women have been seen as both biological and cultural reproducers of the ethnic and national collective. In this kind of motherhood, women have often become symbols of nations. Women's sexual behavior has thus symbolically become central for the "honor" of the people and the narrative of the nation.[14]

In pornography, nationality and ethnicities have often been represented in stereotypical and exaggerated ways. In many of the examples discussed here, pornography becomes a kind of distorting mirror of the national narrative.[15] In relation to the close association between the control of women's decency and the reproduction of the nation, pornographers can either be seen as national betrayers when sexualizing the nation's "own" women for export, or as symbolic attackers when sexualizing for consumption women of foreign nationality.[16]

Swedish Sin in the U.S. Press

The modern critique of Sweden as a somehow inherently sinful country began with an article in *Time* in 1955 by journalist Joe David Brown.[17] Brown claimed that in modern Sweden "sociology has become a religion in itself, and birth control, abortion and promiscuity—especially among the young—are recognized as inalienable rights." The church was said to be more or less under the control of the state, and unwed mothers were "practically heroines" in secular Sweden. Educators supposedly encouraged sex before marriage as long as love was involved and the article ended with a quote by a young boy claiming that he would never give up his freedom by marrying a girl just because he had made her pregnant.[18] In a reply published in *Time*, The Swedish Ambassador to the U.S., Erik Boheman, regretted that a respectable magazine published such a "vicious" article. He rejected most of Brown's statements as exaggerated, misleading, or outright false.[19] Brown's article nevertheless caused Western press to describe Sweden as a land of sexual liberties and lax moral standards.

The article in *Time* was published at a turning point when the admiration for the pragmatic "middle way" changed and the "Swedish model" was increasingly seen (especially in the U.S.) as built upon a socialistic and overly rationalistic view of human beings.[20] To escape the monotonous life in a state that allegedly took care of everything, the only release was through alcohol, sex, or ultimately suicide, several foreign journalists argued. This view sometimes led to tensions, when for example U.S. president Dwight D. Eisenhower in 1960 described Sweden as a "fairly friendly Socialist governed country in Europe where suicides and drunkenness reigns."[21]

Later in that fall, the *New York Times*' correspondent in Stockholm, Werner Wiskari, wrote a "Rejoinder to Sweden's Critics" where he rejected most statements of Sweden as a country of "sin, suicides, socialism, and smorgasbord." Swedes talked frankly about sexuality without embarrassment, something that might appear shocking to Americans, Wiskari wrote. Premarital sex was accepted if love was involved and if the couple could take responsibility for the possible outcome. According to Wiskari, Sweden was culturally Western but also proud of its position in-between East and West.[22]

A few years later, in 1966, Swedish economist and government advisor Gunnar Myrdal also wrote in defense of the Swedish welfare state in *New York Times*:

> There is a popular theory that the Swedes have been mentally and morally damaged by having too much welfare and security. In a society organized to eliminate the risks in life there must be such a lack of adventure and drama that people become frustrated and unhappy. So runs the theory of the malaise in the welfare state. Frankly, I believe it is bunk.[23]

Myrdal claimed that the external critique of Sweden often built on envy of it being the richest country in Europe at the time. Due to the system of wealth distribution, the average Swede was probably better off than the average American, he argued: "Sweden's opulence gives an emotional motive to fault-finding." Myrdal described a consensus in Sweden about welfare; political parties of all colors competed in proposing reforms to make it even more perfect.[24] With lesser social problems, the causes for political struggle and rebellious radicalism diminished according to Myrdal, apparently unaware of the criticism that was growing among the New Left.[25]

From the start, the focus on Sweden in the U.S. press was mainly on sexual behavior, divorce rates, children born out of wedlock, alcohol problems, and suicide rates. In the latter half of the 1960s, however, the focus shifted to legal matters in the field of sexuality, such as legislations concerning abortions, divorces, and—most importantly— pornography. This shift was also followed by an increasing fascination with Denmark, where pornography was decriminalized in 1969.[26] Denmark also became an important country of reference in U.S. policy-making, since Danish Professor of Criminology Berl Kutchinsky did a (later contested) study there for the President's Commission on Pornography and Obscenity regarding the effect of decriminalization on, for example, sex crimes.[27]

Swedish Sin and Swedish Films

The international press debates paralleled Swedish film productions from the early 1950s onwards, placing "Swedish" sexuality in summer landscapes with nude swimming and premarital love and sex. When Ingmar Bergman's The Silence had its U.S. premiere in 1964, the promotion emphasized the sexually explicit and titillating qualities of the film. One ad, for example, read "The Silence—pornography or masterpiece?" with an additional statement from the Swedish board of censors arguing that some of the scenes could be considered pornographic if put together as a short film. Taken as a whole, however, one must see the film's artistic value, the ad noted, thus cleverly fusing artistic and pornographic selling points.[28]

In a similar advertising move, the trailer for the film Sweden: Heaven and Hell (Luigi Scattini, 1968), released in the U.S. in 1969, sought to concoct a powerful mix of Nordic exoticism, libertine radicalism, and traditional voyeurism, as expressed by a voice-over in the trailer of the film:

> This is Sweden: land of enchantment, land of freedom, where you are about to see things, which you just don't see at home. In America, you don't see beautiful girls bouncing boldly out of the sauna into the snow. In America, you don't see public pornography shops where erotic books are displayed—for both sexes ... with government approval.[29]

The admixture of diverse elements of life provided a kind of sexualized kaleidoscope, where "everything, and anything, goes," if we are to trust the marketing of the film:

> See the sex capital of the world, where topless bands beat out the throbbing rhythms of a turned on generation. See the swap-shop, where married couples get a one-night trade-in on the turn of a card, and get to know each other by the flicker-

Sweden—Heaven and Hell movie poster. Courtesy of Klubb Super 8.

ing light of films ... whose titles we dare not mention. See the floating sex lab, a moon-lit cruise where 15 year-old girls learn the practical side of sex. [---] This is Sweden—where everything, and anything, goes. An inside look at Sweden's inside, where the New Morality is Old Hat. You owe it to all your senses to see: *Sweden: Heaven and Hell*.[30]

The film was made by an Italian, Luigi Scattini, in the sensationalist pseudo-documentary style of the so-called *mondo* films. The film was originally in Italian but was also released with English voice-over for the American market. The film is a good example of the myth of Swedish sin and how it was conceptualized in the 1960s Western European and U.S. discourse. When seeing the actual film, it is also clear that the freedom of sex in Sweden was imagined as a threat to traditional gender roles possibly blurred by the secular welfare state.[31]

The films from the 1950s were certainly quite daring for their time, but with Vilgot Sjöman's *I Am Curious (Yellow)* (1967) and *I Am Curious (Blue)* (1968), the mixing of artistic and political expressions with sexual content clearly became a part of the counter-culture of the late 1960s.[32] This could be seen also in other artistic works, such as in Carl Johan De Geer's poster "Skända flaggan" (Desecrate the flag), where a burning Swedish flag was pictured with the word "cock" written on it along with a call to "desecrate the flag, refuse weapons, betray the motherland, be unpatriotic." In both Sjöman's and De Geer's work, the questioning of the nation was central. The critique from intellectuals and the New Left provided a pervasive problem for the ruling Social Democratic party, which had previously largely managed to ally itself with such groups. But when radical left-wing artists increasingly made use of sexual images in their artistic works, it also became more difficult to maintain the obscenity legislation directed towards explicitly commercial pornography.[33]

The Swedish films further promoted the imagination of Swedish sin to the U.S. and sometimes challenged American obscenity legislation.[34] *I Am Curious (Yellow)*, for example, turned out to be one of the best-selling Swedish films ever, although it was banned in eighteen U.S. states. The 1969 Swedish sex education film, *Language of Love*, was not considered obscene in the U.S. even though it included explicit sex scenes, since it also contained material considered of social value to married couples.[35] These films were explicitly marketed as being Swedish, thereby implicitly promising sexual content. In the U.S. press, for example, *Language of Love* was advertised with the slogan: "Everything you've always wanted to learn about the 'language of love' (but couldn't afford a trip to Sweden to find out)."[36]

Turning Swedish Sin into Gender Equality

Instead of defending the welfare state by stressing the exaggerations and the contrived connections between social policies and sexual morals—as for example Gunnar Myrdal had done in 1966—Swedish politicians, public intellectuals, and health professionals soon began to reframe Swedish sin as a matter of gender equality and of Swedish frankness in sexual matters in contrast to the U.S. alleged "double standard."[37] In an interview with the *New York Times,* Swedish Minister of Justice, Herman Kling, related that both he and the Swedish King had received protest letters from worried parents in the U.S. about the sale of Swedish pornography there. Kling responded that the average Swede was more tolerant towards pornography than Americans: "If people want to buy pornography—why should they not have the possibility? Why should I be the one to decide what they are permitted to have?" Kling also expressed that "with the liberty existing between boys and girls in Sweden, they have no need for pornography. They look upon sex as a natural thing." Consequently, Kling stressed, pornography was in Sweden mostly sold to older people.[38]

When British journalist David Frost interviewed Olof Palme in 1969—just before Palme was elected new Social Democratic leader and Prime Minister—Palme presented similar arguments. In a long segment of the interview, Frost asked him about the connections between sex, eroticism, and Sweden. Palme answered that it had to do with certain films and images that could be produced and spread abroad because of Sweden's less strict censorship regulations. Palme explained that he did not believe in trying to keep high morals by prohibiting things. Just like Kling, Palme stressed that Swedish youth had a very "natural and normal" attitude towards sex. Accusations of a sexualized Sweden were primarily used as a tool to criticize Swedish politics, he argued.[39]

U.S. criticism of Swedish loose morals and lack of censorship could be used to turn the tables back on the Americans.[40] In the interview, Palme took the opportunity to stress that Swedish censorship primarily turned against violence and sadistic elements, prevalent even in Disney films.[41] Thereby, Palme contrasted the Swedish relaxed view on sexuality with the acceptance of violence in U.S. cultural productions. Yet, Palme admitted that there was a vulgar element in modern pornography that he personally strongly disliked and which he surmised would probably generate a backlash. But if pornography was made with good taste, Palme saw no reason to stop it, adding that there were probably people who needed it.[42]

If pornography was made with good taste, Palme saw no reason to stop it. David Frost and Olof Palme, on BBC, 1969. Jan Collsiöö / TT.

This kind of cautious semi-official endorsement by Palme and Kling indicate the extent to which sexual liberalism had at that point become both accepted and influential in Swedish politics and society. More importantly, however, sexual liberalism did not only result in profound changes in sexual ethics in the 1960s and 1970s, but also led to several radical legal amendments. These changes were not, however, put into practice without resistance. There was a strong conservative and mainly religious resistance against what was seen as moral decay and commercialization around sexuality in Sweden. The Pentecostal Maranata movement, for example, enacted direct actions against pornography shops and movie theatres.[43] These dramatic actions were well covered by mass media, and U.S. television and Italian film teams were said to have come to record the attacks, further cementing the international view of Sweden as a sexually charged place.[44] However, this resistance was not only isolated to a media-friendly fringe movement. It also found relatively strong support in the parliament. Here, the anxieties of tourists having their prejudices confirmed in Swedish pornography shops were certainly taken seriously.

This dual concern with both conservatives championing domestic morality and progressives concerned with Sweden's reputation abroad fused in the preparatory work undertaken by a government commission appointed in 1965 to investigate whether the regulation on pornography should be relaxed or even abolished altogether.[45] In its proposals, the commission addressed the problems with tourists gathering outside pornography shops and the mail advertising of Swedish pornography abroad by suggesting a ban on pornographic displays and unsolicited dissemination. The commission also suggested a legal possibility for authorities to intervene in case decriminalization would result in the proliferation of violent content or child pornography. In the final bill, however, this possibility was removed and pornography became completely legalized (albeit with restrictions on display and dissemination) in 1971.[46]

Private *and the "Swedification" of Pornography*

Swedish, as well as Danish, pornography was being illegally imported to the U.S. through various means of smuggling in the 1960s. Here, Swedish producers of pornography were likely at a certain advantage, since Denmark was a signatory of the 1910 Agreement for the Suppression of the Circulation of Obscene Publications, amended in 1949, while Sweden was not.[47]

The above-mentioned American Report of the Commission on Obscenity and Pornography stated in 1970 that the under-the-counter pornographic magazines on the U.S. market primarily came from Scandinavia or were domestic copies of such publications. Imports from Scandinavia were increasing, according to the Commission, but retail sales were still less than five million dollars per year. This import was described as a "flooding" of raw pornography by the U.S. press where it was claimed to be a multi-billion-dollar industry, the Commission stated.[48]

Regardless of the actual size of U.S. imports of Scandinavian pornography, the growing American interest undoubtedly followed from the emergence of a new genre of sexually explicit picture magazines that began to appear in both Denmark and Sweden during the latter half of the 1960s. This new genre was mainly directed at an international (heterosexual and male) audience, with additional texts in English and German. The new magazines profited on the image of a sexually liberated Scandinavia.[49]

The change in terms of representation of nationality and ethnicity and the connections between these identities and sexuality is striking: During the 1950s the Swedish magazines were often referring to a foreign mystique picturing oriental settings or constructing the sexual as French.[50] In the 1960s, however, pornography publishers began to use the concept of Swedish sin as a marketing strategy for foreign audiences. During the late 1960s and 1970s, the magazines also became more clearly defined in relation to target groups, as the male nudes disappeared from straight publications and reappeared in gay magazines.[51]

One of these heterosexually oriented magazines was *Private*, which has been described as setting the standard for the international pornographic print genre.[52] The first issue was published in 1965 with the slogan "Svenska modeller i färg—Swedish models in color—Schwedische Modelle in Farben." One of the spreads pictured a woman named Britt, with the caption, "Britt, 18. A blonde incarnation of all that is typical for the Swedish woman. Emancipated—honest yet sweet like no other women-type wherever you search the globe."[53]

Like Britt, the Swedish women in *Private* were often blonde, described as emancipated and having a frank view of their own sexuality. The texts spoke directly to the reader, as if he were a foreigner visiting Sweden. The girls were presented with their names and their age: "Ulla, 19," "Ingrid, 23." Most of them were described as ordinary Swedish girls, crazy for sex and in search of a *real* man. The sexualization of Swedish women was paralleled by the sexualization of Sweden as a location, as emphasized by photos taken outdoors, on the streets of Stockholm, outside the royal castle, or in the countryside, where nature served as a prop to underline the supposed "Swedishness" of the sexuality on display.[54]

One of the girls, Anita, was pictured naked in the water and the description of her stated that she was a typical Swedish woman, not only because of her appearance (blonde and pale) but also because of her "openness, frankness and earnestness," implying the construction of a specifically natural, Nordic and exotic sexuality which rejects the connection between sexuality and sin.[55] In another story entitled "The Mona-Lisa of the North," blondness was constructed alongside other signifiers such as cleanliness and freshness, sexual eagerness and youth. Waking up from the ecstasy of sex, the "goddess of the North" in this story asked her lover casually "by the way, what is your name?" as her thighs were "catching the rays of the North's never sleeping sun."[56]

When the Swedish obscenity legislation was first more liberally practiced and then finally abolished in 1971, Swedish pornographers such as Berth Milton (Senior), owner of *Private*, held an advantage on the international market. When other countries relaxed their legislations in the 1970s, Swedish pornographers could naturally expand their markets. But they also experienced increased international competition from foreign publishers copying Milton's pornographic concept.[57]

Nevertheless, *Private* does in fact seem to have maintained its leading position at least in Europe, with a circulation of over 100,000 copies per issue in the late 1980s.[58] Although legally and economically a Swedish publication, *Private* was one of the first international pornographic magazines providing parallel editorial material in several languages. The descriptions of the (Swedish) girls in the magazines manifested a kind of sexual radicalism. An English-language ad for the magazine read:

> In PRIVATE you will find a sincere presentation of the Swedish freed moral-comprehension, which has been spoken of and discussed all over the world. The unique picture-material, articles and reports declare

in an absolutely extraordinary way the emancipation and honesty towards her sex, which the Swedish woman represents.[59]

The "Morals by Milton" editorials often stressed that there were no "right," "wrong," or "normal" sexuality, and that all sexual behaviors were permissible if no one was hurt. Milton advocated sex education in schools and took a stand against the Catholic Church on the issue of birth control.[60] In Sweden, Milton emphasized, all women over fourteen years of age had the right to contraceptives such as the pill: "We don't feel that this way of thinking as regards the respect for a woman, her integrity or capacity to bear children, will do any harm. On the contrary."[61] Here, Milton's views paralleled those of earlier Swedish sexual liberals who had exercised some influence over the reforms in sexual policy during the 1960s.[62]

This discursive reframing of pornography—from something sinful and dangerous to something liberating and radical—was actively promoted by the producers of pornography, both through their own magazines and by their direct participation in mass media debates. The relative acceptance extended to pornographers by the regular media had as a result that they were held openly accountable for their products, but also that they could share publicly their own opinions on sexuality and pornography. For example, the most influential Milton editorial from *Private* was a spread with four photos: two bloody pictures from the Vietnam War, one of bank robber Clyde Barrow's dead body, and one explicit picture of a man and a woman having sexual intercourse. The caption read:

> Murders and throat-cuttings are obviously matters within the limits of decency. Why is it then, that [in] so many parts of the world realism in love-making and sexual intercourse between human beings are not allowed to be shown? There is only one picture in this spread showing normal human behavior. Without violence, without bestiality, without hatred, without revenge. Is it not a proof of the Swedish "sin," just normal good sense and honesty?[63]

By contrasting love and sexuality to murder and bestiality, Milton criticized regulations of pornography, both in Sweden and elsewhere, akin to what Palme argued when interviewed by Frost the same year. When explicitly using the notion of Swedish sin, Milton connected it to both pornography and his own morality, arguing that feelings of shame surrounding sexuality should be eliminated.[64] The example with the four pictures was used as an important argument for the deregulation of pornography.[65] In 1969, for example, lawyer Leif Silbersky used this particular example in his argumentation for abolishing the censorship of pornographic pictures.[66]

However, this notion of sexual liberty and emancipated women clearly did not deconstruct gender divisions. As Carrie Pitzulo has observed, radicalism in pornography and men's magazines in the 1960s and 1970s halted when it came to gender diversity, even if the depicted women were typically presented as emancipated, as in the examples above.[67] In spite of their radical and sexual agency, women were still presented as sexual objects for the readers of *Private*. "Eva, 18" was, for example, described as requesting the same rights as men. "Yet," the magazine noted, she was modest and respectable: "A wonderful mixture of innocence and playful nymphomania."[68]

Conclusion

The imaginations of Swedish sin and pornography were, in Sweden as well as in the U.S. and in both official documents and in pornographic production, constructed along gendered and sexualized understandings of nationality. The imagination of a Swedish community was built upon a notion of young women's role in a modern secular society where the traditional connection between reproduction and femininity was partially decoupled.

The imagination of Swedish sin was from the start constructed mainly from the outside in the context of the Cold War. The Cold War was not only a contestation between different political economical systems. It also embodied a conflict with regard to freedom of thought and freedom of religion, as well as tensions between rational modernism and traditional values. Notions of religiosity and morality were more important in this global contestation than is often recognized in contemporary scholarly literature. The logic of connecting Sweden with sin and sexuality here followed from what Melvin Tumin at the time called the "Eisenhower-hypothesis" on the welfare state, e.g., that Social Democratic policies would not only lead to social security but also to secularism and thus moral decline, eventually turning people onto alcohol, drugs, sex, and ultimately suicide as a way out of boredom.[69]

From the start, Swedish officials tried to confront these misrepresentations and protect the image of Sweden as a "decent" country. Nevertheless, the image of a sinful Sweden was hard to get rid of and Swedish politicians tried to turn it into something positive, linking free sexual morals to women-friendly legislation, progressiveness in social matters, and a free view of culture and pornography.[70] This was also put in contrast to an imagined U.S. double standard and moral acceptance of violence, another sin according to Christian beliefs, not only by official Swedish representatives but also, as we have seen, by Swedish pornographers.

The shift from a discussion of the welfare state to a more clear focus on pornography itself can partly be seen as a reaction to changes in the pornography market where Swedish production could expand due to a lax application of the law—and a certain element of ingenuity by some producers in evading it—resulting both in exports of magazines and in growing pornography tourism. New pornographic publishers such as Milton took advantage of the image of the Swedish girl as sexually liberated and made it a part of their marketing strategy. Sexual liberal discourse also opened an understanding of pornography as a substitute of real love, as when for example Kling claimed that young gender-equal Swedes involved in real-life amorous relations did not need pornography. However, there was a prevailing anxiety over the pornographic dissemination connected to the image of the nation, resulting in the prohibition of pornographic display and mail proliferation when pornography was otherwise decriminalized in 1971.

As religious rationales lost influence in public discourse during the radical 1960s and 1970s, and while the feminist movement primarily focused until the 1970s on economic and social justice, this possibly unlikely window of opportunity provided for a temporary mutual affinity between the commercial pornographic industry and the sexual liberals and radicals. Later, however, it became more difficult to claim that the resistance against pornography was a generational issue that would soon dissipate, as a more vocal opposition within the young feminist movement began to protest commercialized appropriation and sexual objectification of women. This widening rift probably made it more difficult for Swedish pornographers to market Swedish pornography by way of linking it to progressive Swedish female emancipation.

Coincidentally, however, both pornographers and politicians found a temporary common ground in claiming that pornography just responded to a "natural" need for sexual stimulation. This view, in its turn, followed from a new, de-dramatized view on sex, which commercial as well as counter-cultural actors could share. However, even if women and their sexuality were central in the debates, Swedish women's own voices are very hard to come by in the sources—other than in the probably staged interviews in the pornographic magazines.

Tellingly, pornography was also framed as a problem mostly in terms of how it affected the viewers and their morality. Even if women's lack of interest in pornographic consumption was debated, pornography was seldom problematized during the late 1960s as a product mainly for male consumption. Importantly, the working conditions for those involved in its production were not discussed during the time period.[71] While the social security and gender equality of the welfare state have prevailed in the Swedish imagination of the nation, manifested in later reforms such as free contraceptives, liberal abortion rights, and paid parental leave, its history as a pioneer in pornographic commercial production has this far often been left out.

NOTES

1. *Toronto Star*, October 11, 1972.

2. Carl Marklund and Klaus Petersen, "Return to Sender: American Images of the Nordic Welfare States and Nordic Welfare State Branding," *European Journal of Scandinavian Studies*, 2 (2013): 245–257.

3. The press material from the U.S. is mainly collected from *New York Times*, *Time* and *Washington Post*. The Swedish press material consists of press-clippings collected by Pressbyrån (the distributor of magazines in Sweden at the time) and by the Swedish Attorney General.

4. Although the Freedom of the Press Act stipulated that the year of printing should appear on all publications, the issues of *Private* lack such information. However, from other sources, we know that the two first issues were published in 1965, that issue number four and five were published in 1967 and that issue number 9 and 10 were published in 1968. See, Swedish National Archive, Attorney General Archive, Acts on common cases no. 315, 1967; Leif Silbersky and Carlösten Nordmark, *Såra tukt och sedlighet: En debattbok om pornografin* (Stockholm: Prisma, 1969); *Private* special edition 30th anniversary 1995; Carl Abrahamsson and Jan Axelsson, "*Private* Magazine: Sweden's Berth of Hardcore," in *The History of Men's Magazines*, vol. 6: *1970s Under the Counter*, ed. Dian Hanson (Cologne: Taschen, 2005), 19–41.

5. Benedict Anderson, *Imagined Communities: Reflections on the Origin and Spread of Nationalism*, 2nd ed. (London/New York: Verso, 1991); Nikolas Glover and Carl Marklund, "Arabian Nights in the Midnight Sun? Exploring the Temporal Structure of Sexual Geographies," *Historisk Tidskrift*, 3 (2009): 487–510.

6. Olle Krantz, "Small European Countries in Economic Internationalisation: An Economic Historical Perspective," *Umeå Papers in Economic History*, 26 (2006): 1–22; Stewart Oakley, *The Story of Sweden* (London: Faber, 1966).

7. Tom O'Dell, *Culture Unbound: Americanization and Everyday Life in Sweden* (Lund: Nordic Academic Press 1997).

8. Sten Ottosson, *Svensk självbild under kalla kriget: En studie av stats-och utrikesministrarnas bild av Sverige 1950–1989* (Stockholm: Swedish Institute of International Affairs, 2003); Carl Marklund, "A Swedish *Norden* or a Nordic Sweden? Image Politics during the Cold War," in *Communicating the North: Media Structures and Images in the Making of the Nordic Region*, eds., Jonas Harvard and Peter Stadius (Farnham: Ashgate, 2013), 262–287.

9. Lena Lennerhed, *Frihet att njuta: Sexualdebatten i Sverige på 1960-talet* (Stockholm: Norstedt, 1994); Frederick Hale, "*Time* for Sex in Sweden: Enhancing the Myth of the 'Swedish sin' during the 1950s," *Scandinavian Studies* 3 (2003): 351–374.

10. Ann-Sofie Nilsson, *Den moraliska stormakten: En studie av socialdemokratins internationella aktivism* (Stockholm: Timbro, 1991); Ulf Bjereld, *Kritiker eller medlare? En studie av Sveriges utrikespolitiska roller 1945–90* (Stockholm: Nerenius & Santérus, 1992); Sten Ottosson, *Sverige mellan öst och väst: Svensk självbild under kalla kriget* (Gothenburg: Univ., 2001).

11. Bo Stråth, *Folkhemmet mot Europa: Ett historiskt perspektiv på 90-talet* (Stockholm: Tiden,

1993); Mikael af Malmborg, *Den ståndaktiga nationalstaten: Sverige och den västeuropeiska integrationen 1945-1959* (PhD diss., Lund University, 1994); Jenny Andersson, *När framtiden redan hänt: Socialdemokratin och folkhemsnostalgin* (Stockholm: Ordfront, 2009).

12. Parliament of Sweden. Protocol from the Second Chamber, 1928, vol. 1, no. 3, 11.

13. Yvonne Hirdman, *Att lägga livet tillrätta: Studier i svensk folkhemspolitik* (Stockholm: Carlsson, 1989); Renée Frangeur, *Yrkeskvinna eller makens tjänarinna? Striden om yrkesrätten för gifta kvinnor i mellankrigstidens Sverige* (Lund: Arkiv, 1998); Christina Florin, Lena Sommestad and Ulla Wikander, eds., *Kvinnor mot kvinnor. Om systerskapets svårigheter* (Stockholm: Norstedts Förlag, 1999).

14. Nira Yuval-Davis and Floya Anthias, eds., *Woman, Nation, State* (Basingstoke: Macmillan, 1989).

15. Gail Dines, "King Kong and the White Woman: *Hustler* Magazine and the Demonization of Black Masculinity," *Journal of Violence Against Women*, 3 (1998): 291–307; Homi Bhabha, ed., *Nation and Narration* (London: Routledge, 1990).

16. Mark Goodall, *Sweet & Savage: The World Through the Shockumentary Film Lens* (London: Heartpress 2006); Frida Beckman, *Between Desire and Pleasure: A Deleuzian Theory of Sexuality* (Edinburgh: Edinburgh University Press 2013).

17. Lennerhed, *Frihet att njuta*; Hale, "Time for sex in Sweden."

18. Joe David Brown, "Sin and Sweden," *Time*, April 25, 1955.

19. "Letters to the editor," *Time*, May 16, 1955. See also, in the same section, the letter from Swedish sex education activist Elise Ottesen-Jensen where she opposes that Brown quoted her from a private conversation at a party. Also the Swedish press attaché wrote an answer in "Letters to the editor," *Time*, May 9, 1955.

20. Marquis Childs, *Sweden: The Middle Way on Trial* (New Haven: Yale University Press, 1980); Carl Marklund, "The Social Laboratory, the Middle Way, and the Swedish Model: Three Frames for the Image of Sweden," *Scandinavian Journal of History*, 3 (2009): 264–285.

21. "Comment in Oslo," *New York Times*, July 29, 1960. See also "Eisenhower talk arouses Sweden," *New York Times*, July 29, 1960; "Erlander criticizes," *New York Times*, July 29, 1960; "Norse premier irate" *New York Times*, July 31, 1960; see also Melvin Tumin, "Velferdsstat og moral. En granskning af 'Eisenhower-hypotesen,'" *Tidsskrift for samfunnsforskning*, 1 (1961): 1–17. When Eisenhower visited Sweden in 1962 as a private person, he apologized for his earlier statement. See "Eisenhower offers apology to Sweden," *New York Times*, July 30, 1962.

22. Werner Wiskari, "Rejoinder to Sweden's Critics," *New York Times*, October 23, 1960.

23. Gunnar Myrdal, "'But Paradise can be boring': The Swedish way to Happiness," *New York Times*, January 30, 1966.

24. See also Gunnar Myrdal, *Beyond the Welfare State: Economic Planning and its International Implications* (London: Duckworth, 1960).

25. Göran Therborn, ed., *En ny vänster: En debattbok* (Stockholm: Rabén & Sjögren, 1966).

26. See for example C. L. Sulzberger, "Foreign Affairs: Sex and Sense," *New York Times*, December 5, 1969; Tom Buckley, "Oh! Copenhagen!," *New York Times*, February 8, 1970.

27. Commission on Obscenity and Pornography, *Report of the Commission on Obscenity and Pornography* (New York: Bantam Books, 1970); see also Buckley, "Oh! Copenhagen!"

28. "'The silence' pornography or masterpiece?," ad in *New York Times*, February 24, 1964.

29. "Trailer for *Sweden: Heaven and Hell* (Luigi Scattini, 1968)," accessed April 7, 2015, http://rstvideo.com/trailer/sweden-heaven-and-hell/

30. "Trailer for *Sweden: Heaven and Hell.*"

31. Lena Lennerhed, ed., *Riv alla murar! Vittnesseminarier om sexliberalismen och Pockettidningen R.* (Huddinge: Institute for Contemporary History, Södertörn University, 2002); Carl Marklund, "Hot Love and Cold People: Sexual Liberalism as Political Escapism in Radical Sweden," *Nordeuropaforum—Zeitschrift für Politik, Wirtschaft und Kultur*, 2 (2009): 83–101; Nikolas Glover, "Kritiker, krämare och kramare: Kommentar till texter om den svenska synden," in *Sexualpolitiska nyckeltexter*, eds. Klara Arnberg, Pia Laskar and Fia Sundevall (Stockholm: Leopard, 2015), 395–403.

32. Anders Åberg, *Tabu: filmaren Vilgot Sjöman* (Lund: Filmhäftet, 2001).

33. Mariah Larsson, "Drömmen om den goda pornografin: Om sextio-och sjuttiotalsfilmen och gränsen mellan konst och pornografi," *Tidskrift för genusvetenskap*, 1–2 (2007): 93–111; Klara Arnberg, *Motsättningarnas marknad: Den pornografiska pressens kommersiella genombrott och regleringen av pornografi i Sverige 1950–1980* (Lund: Sekel bokförlag, 2010).

34. See for example "High court frees film held obscene," *New York Times*, May 18, 1971; "Court

clears Swedish film," *New York Times*, June 16, 1971; Murray Schumach, "Ironical Obscenity Issue," *New York Times*, July 16, 1971.

35. See for example "Supreme court to decide if free counsel must be offered to the poor in trials for petty offences," *New York Times*, February 23, 1971; "U.S. Appeals Court Overturns Ban on a Swedish Film on Love," *New York Times*, September 17, 1970.

36. Ad for *Language of Love* in *New York Times*, July 2, 1971, 25.

37. Hale, "*Time* for sex in Sweden"; Glover and Marklund, "Arabian Nights in the Midnight Sun?"

38. Werner Wiskari, "Sweden is Casual on Pornography," *New York Times*, November 5, 1967; "'Vänsterpolitik' i Sverige granskas i USA:s press," *Dagens Nyheter*, November 6, 1967; "USA-protester till kungen mot svensk flodvåg av porr," *Aftonbladet*, November 6, 1967.

39. "David Frost interviewing Olof Palme, 1969," accessed April 7, 2015, https://www.youtube.com/watch?v=yLfBDHsfMPI

40. Carl Marklund, "American Mirrors and Swedish Self-Portraits: US Images of Sweden and Swedish Public Diplomacy in the USA in the 1970s and 80s," in *Histories of Public Diplomacy and Nation Branding in the Nordic and Baltic Countries: Representing the Periphery*, eds. Louis Clerc, Nikolas Glover & Paul Jordan (Leiden: Brill, 2015), 172–194.

41. See also George Embree, "Kiss her, don't slap her, Sweden's censors advice," *The Washington Post*, November 30, 1963.

42. "David Frost interviewing Olof Palme, 1969."

43. "Porr-kriget rasar vidare. Pastor Imsen 'kläs av' i *Sexträffen*," *Expressen* March 21, 1969.

44. "I natt slog pastor Imsen till igen mot porrbutiker," *Expressen*, March 8, 1969, "Präst-bröderna det stormar om," *Expressen*, February 11, 1970; "Präst hotar porrförsäljare med stryk," *Expressen*, February 7, 1970; "'Guds gerilla' åtalas för stora porrkriget," *Aftonbladet*, August 11, 1970.

45. SOU 1969:38, Kommittén för lagstiftningen om yttrande- och tryckfrihet, *Yttrandefrihetens gränser: Sårande av tukt och sedlighet: Brott mot trosfrid* (Stockholm: Statens offentliga utredningar, 1969).

46. Parliament of Sweden. Proposition no. 125, 1970.

47. United Nations. 4. Protocol amending the Agreement for the Suppression of the Circulation of Obscene Publications, signed at Paris, on 4 May 1910, Lake Success, New York, 4 May 1949, *Treaty Series*, vol. 30, 3.

48. Commission on Obscenity and Pornography, *Report*.

49. Klara Arnberg, "Synd på export: 1960-talets pornografiska press och den svenska synden," *Historisk Tidskrift*, 3 (2009): 467–486.

50. Arnberg, "Synd på export"; Eric Schaefer, "I'll take Sweden: The Shifting Discourse of the 'Sexy Nation' in Sexploitation Films," in *Sex Scene: Media and the Sexual Revolution*, ed., Eric Schaefer (Durham and London: Duke University Press 2014), 207–234.

51. Arnberg, *Motsättningarnas marknad*, 109; 200–201.

52. David Hebditch and Nick Anning, *Porn Gold: Inside the Pornography Business* (London: Faber 1988), 120.

53. *Private*, 1 (1965), 21. Original in Swedish, translated by the authors.

54. See for example *Private*, 5 (unknown year), 10.

55. Marklund, "Hot Love and Cold People."

56. *Private*, 4 (1967). Original in English.

57. Klara Arnberg, "Under the Counter, Under the Radar? The Business and Regulation of the Pornographic Press in Sweden 1950-1971," *Enterprise & Society*, 2 (2012): 350–377.

58. Hebditch and Anning, *Porn Gold*, 139.

59. *Private*, 8 (unknown year), 19. Original in English.

60. *Private*, 6 (unknown year), 2.

61. *Private*, 9 (unknown year), 1. Original in English.

62. Lennerhed, ed., *Riv alla murar!*

63. *Private*, 9 (unknown year), 2-3. Original in English. See also Thomas Sjöberg, *Private med Milton och Milton* (Stockholm: Fischer & Co, 2002), 34.

64. Sjöberg, *Private med Milton och Milton*, 35.

65. See for example Swedish National Archive, Attorney General Archive, Acts on common cases, Supplement to no. 390, 1968.

66. Silbersky and Nordmark, *Såra tukt och sedlighet*, 26–27.

67. Carrie Pitzulo, "The Battle in Every Man's Bed: Playboy and the Fiery Feminists," *Journal of the History of Sexuality*, 2 (2008): 259–289.
68. *Private*, 7 (unknown year), 3. Original in English.
69. Tumin, "Velferdsstat og moral."
70. Glover and Marklund, "Arabian Nights in the Midnight Sun?"
71. Arnberg, *Motsättningarnas marknad*.

BIBLIOGRAPHY

Åberg, Anders. *Tabu: filmaren Vilgot Sjöman*. Lund: Filmhäftet, 2001.
Abrahamsson, Carl, and Jan Axelsson. "*Private* Magazine: Sweden's Berth of Hardcore." In *The History of Men's Magazines*, vol. 6: *1970s Under the Counter*, edited by Dian Hanson, 19–41. Cologne: Taschen, 2005.
af Malmborg, Mikael. *Den ståndaktiga nationalstaten: Sverige och den västeuropeiska integrationen 1945–1959*. Ph.D. diss., Lund University, 1994.
Anderson, Benedict. *Imagined Communities: Reflections on the Origin and Spread of Nationalism*. 2nd ed. London/New York: Verso, 1991.
Andersson, Jenny. *När framtiden redan hänt: Socialdemokratin och folkhemsnostalgin*. Stockholm: Ordfront, 2009.
Arnberg, Klara. "Synd på export: 1960-talets pornografiska press och den svenska synden." *Historisk Tidskrift*, 129:3 (2009): 467–486.
_____. "Under the Counter, Under the Radar? The Business and Regulation of the Pornographic Press in Sweden 1950–1971." *Enterprise & Society*, 13:2 (2012): 350–377.
_____. *Motsättningarnas marknad: Den pornografiska pressens kommersiella genombrott och regleringen av pornografi i Sverige 1950–1980*. Lund: Sekel bokförlag, 2010.
Beckman, Frida. *Between Desire and Pleasure: A Deleuzian Theory of Sexuality*. Edinburgh: Edinburgh University Press, 2013.
Bhabha, Homi, ed. *Nation and Narration*. London: Routledge, 1990.
Bjereld, Ulf. *Kritiker eller medlare? En studie av Sveriges utrikespolitiska roller 1945–90*. Stockholm: Nerenius & Santérus, 1992.
Brown, Joe David. "Sin and Sweden." *Time*, April 25, 1955.
Buckley, Tom. "Oh! Copenhagen!" *New York Times*, February 8, 1970.
Childs, Marquis. *Sweden: The Middle Way on Trial*. New Haven, CT: Yale University Press, 1980.
"Comment in Oslo." *New York Times*, July 29, 1960.
Commission on Obscenity and Pornography. *Report of the Commission on Obscenity and Pornography*. New York: Bantam Books, 1970.
"Court clears Swedish film." *New York Times*, June 16, 1971.
"David Frost interviewing Olof Palme, 1969." Accessed April 7, 2015. https://www.youtube.com/watch?v=yLfBDHsfMPI
Dines, Gail. "King Kong and the White Woman: Hustler Magazine and the Demonization of Black Masculinity." *Journal of Violence Against Women*, 4:3 (1998): 291–307.
"Eisenhower Offers Apology to Sweden." *New York Times*, July 30, 1962.
"Eisenhower Talk Arouses Sweden." *New York Times*, July 29, 1960.
Embree, George. "Kiss her, don't slap her, Sweden's censors advice." *The Washington Post*, Nov. 30, 1963.
"Erlander criticizes." *New York Times*, July 29, 1960.
Florin, Christina, Lena Sommestad, and Ulla Wikander, eds. *Kvinnor mot kvinnor. Om systerskapets svårigheter*. Stockholm: Norstedts Förlag, 1999.
Frangeur, Renée. *Yrkeskvinna eller makens tjänarinna? Striden om yrkesrätten för gifta kvinnor i mellankrigstidens Sverige*. Lund: Arkiv, 1998.
Glover, Nikolas. "Kritiker, krämare och kramare: Kommentar till texter om den svenska synden." In *Sexualpolitiska nyckeltexter*, edited by Klara Arnberg, Pia Laskar and Fia Sundevall, 395–403. Stockholm: Leopard, 2015.
Glover, Nikolas, and Carl Marklund. "Arabian Nights in the Midnight Sun? Exploring the Temporal Structure of Sexual Geographies." *Historisk Tidskrift*, 129:3 (2009): 487–510.
Goodall, Mark. *Sweet & Savage: The World Through the Shockumentary Film Lens*. London: Heartpress, 2006.
"'Guds gerilla' åtalas för stora porrkriget." *Aftonbladet*, August 11, 1970.

Hale, Frederick. "*Time* for Sex in Sweden: Enhancing the Myth of the 'Swedish sin' during the 1950s." *Scandinavian Studies* 75:3 (2003): 351–374.
Hebditch, David, and Nick Anning. *Porn Gold: Inside the Pornography Business*. London: Faber, 1988.
"High Court Frees Film Held Obscene." *New York Times*, May 18, 1971.
Hirdman, Yvonne. *Att lägga livet tillrätta: Studier i svensk folkhemspolitik*. Stockholm: Carlsson, 1989.
"I natt slog pastor Imsen till igen mot porrbutiker." *Expressen*, March 8, 1969.
Krantz, Olle. "Small European Countries in Economic Internationalisation: An Economic Historical Perspective." *Umeå Papers in Economic History*, 26 (2006): 1–22.
Language of Love. Advertisement. *New York Times*, July 2, 1971.
Larsson, Mariah. "Drömmen om den goda pornografin: Om sextio-och sjuttiotalsfilmen och gränsen mellan konst och pornografi." *Tidskrift för genusvetenskap*, 1–2 (2007): 93–111.
Lennerhed, Lena. *Frihet att njuta: Sexualdebatten i Sverige på 1960-talet*. Stockholm: Norstedt, 1994.
_____, ed. *Riv alla murar! Vittnesseminarier om sexliberalismen och Pockettidningen R*. Huddinge: Institute for Contemporary History, Södertörn University, 2002.
Letters to the editor. *Time*, May 16, 1955.
Letters to the editor. *Time*, May 9, 1955.
Marklund, Carl. "American Mirrors and Swedish Self-Portraits: US Images of Sweden and Swedish Public Diplomacy in the USA in the 1970s and 80s." In *Histories of Public Diplomacy and Nation Branding in the Nordic and Baltic Countries: Representing the Periphery*, edited by Louis Clerc, Nikolas Glover and Paul Jordan, 172–194, Leiden: Brill, 2015.
_____. "Hot Love and Cold People: Sexual Liberalism as Political Escapism in Radical Sweden." *Nordeuropaforum—Zeitschrift für Politik, Wirtschaft und Kultur*, 2 (2009): 83–101.
_____. "The Social Laboratory, the Middle Way, and the Swedish Model: Three Frames for the Image of Sweden." *Scandinavian Journal of History*, 34:3 (2009): 264–285.
_____. "A Swedish *Norden* or a Nordic Sweden? Image Politics during the Cold War." In *Communicating the North: Media Structures and Images in the Making of the Nordic Region*, edited by Jonas Harvard and Peter Stadius, 262–287. Farnham: Ashgate, 2013.
_____, and Klaus Petersen. "Return to Sender: American Images of the Nordic Welfare States and Nordic Welfare State Branding." *European Journal of Scandinavian Studies*, 2 (2013): 245–257.
Myrdal, Gunnar. "'But Paradise can be boring': The Swedish way to Happiness." *New York Times*, January 30, 1966.
_____. *Beyond the Welfare State: Economic Planning and its International Implications*. London: Duckworth, 1960.
Nilsson, Ann-Sofie. *Den moraliska stormakten: En studie av socialdemokratins internationella aktivism*. Stockholm: Timbro, 1991.
"Norse premier irate." *New York Times*, July 31, 1960.
Oakley, Stewart. *The Story of Sweden*. London: Faber, 1966.
O'Dell, Tom. *Culture Unbound: Americanization and Everyday Life in Sweden*. Lund: Nordic Academic Press, 1997.
Ottosson, Sten. *Sverige mellan öst och väst: Svensk självbild under kalla kriget*. Gothenburg: UnIV. 2001.
_____. *Svensk självbild under kalla kriget: En studie av stats-och utrikesministrarnas bild av Sverige 1950–1989*. Stockholm: Swedish Institute of International Affairs, 2003.
Parliament of Sweden. Proposition no. 125, 1970.
Parliament of Sweden. Protocol from the Second Chamber, 1928, vol. 1, no 3.
Pitzulo, Carrie. "The Battle in Every Man's Bed: Playboy and the Fiery Feminists." *Journal of the History of Sexuality*, 17:2 (2008): 259–289.
"Porr-kriget rasar vidare. Pastor Imsen 'kläs av' i *Sexträffen*." *Expressen* March 21, 1969.
"Präst hotar porrförsäljare med stryk." *Expressen*, February 7, 1970.
"Präst-bröderna det stormar om." *Expressen*, February 11, 1970.
Private issues 1–10 (1965–1968).
Private special edition 30th anniversary issue (1995).
Schaefer, Eric. "I'll take Sweden: The Shifting Discourse of the 'Sexy Nation' in Sexploitation Films." In *Sex Scene: Media and the Sexual Revolution*, edited by Eric Schaefer, 207–234. Durham, NC: Duke University Press, 2014.
Schumach, Murray. "Ironical Obscenity Issue." *New York Times*, July 16, 1971.
Silbersky, Leif, and Carlösten Nordmark. *Såra tukt och sedlighet: En debattbok om pornografin*. Stockholm: Prisma, 1969.

"'The silence' pornography or masterpiece?" Ad in *New York Times*, February 24, 1964.
Sjöberg, Thomas. *Private med Milton och Milton*. Stockholm: Fischer & Co, 2002.
SOU 1969:38, Kommittén för lagstiftningen om yttrande-och tryckfrihet. *Yttrandefrihetens gränser: Sårande av tukt och sedlighet: Brott mot trosfrid*. Stockholm: 1969.
Stråth, Bo. *Folkhemmet mot Europa: Ett historiskt perspektiv på 90-talet*. Stockholm: Tiden, 1993.
Sulzberger, C.L. "Foreign Affairs: Sex and Sense." *New York Times*, December 5, 1969.
"Supreme court to decide if free counsel must be offered to the poor in trials for petty offences." *New York Times*, February 23, 1971.
Swedish National Archive. Attorney General Archive, acts on common cases no. 315, 1967.
Swedish National Archive. Attorney General Archive, acts on common cases, supplement to no. 390, 1968.
Therborn, Göran, ed. *En ny vänster: En debattbok*. Stockholm: Rabén & Sjögren, 1966.
Toronto Star, October 11, 1972.
"Trailer for *Sweden: Heaven and Hell* (Luigi Scattini, 1968)." Accessed April 7, 2015. http://rstvideo.com/trailer/sweden-heaven-and-hell/
Tumin, Melvin. "Velferdsstat og moral. En granskning af 'Eisenhower-hypotesen.'" *Tidsskrift for samfunnsforskning*, 1 (1961): 1–17.
United Nations. 4. Protocol amending the Agreement for the Suppression of the Circulation of Obscene Publications, signed at Paris, on 4 May 1910, Lake Success, New York, 4 May 1949, Treaty Series, vol. 30.
"U.S. Appeals Court Overturns Ban on a Swedish Film on Love." *New York Times*, September 17, 1970.
"USA-protester till kungen mot svensk flodvåg av porr." *Aftonbladet*, November 6, 1967.
"'Vänsterpolitik' i Sverige granskas i USA:s press." *Dagens Nyheter*, November 6, 1967.
Wiskari, Werner. "Rejoinder to Sweden's Critics." *New York Times*, October 23, 1960.
_____. "Sweden is Casual on Pornography." *New York Times*, November 5, 1967.
Yuval-Davis, Nira, and Floya Anthias, eds. *Woman, Nation, State*. Basingstoke: Macmillan, 1989.

A Modicum of Social Value?
The Critical and Legal Discussion of I Am Curious (Yellow) *in America*

Ulf Jonas Björk

In May 1968, Swedish film director Vilgot Sjöman found himself testifying before a federal jury in New York City. At issue was his 1967 film *Jag är nyfiken—gul/I Am Curious (Yellow)*, which had been seized by the U.S. Customs Bureau earlier in the year because it was, in the words of one U.S. official, "the most explicit movie ever to be imported here."[1] Attorneys for Grove Press, the U.S. distributor for *Curious (Yellow)*, had called Sjöman and more than a dozen other witnesses to convince the jury that the film had artistic and social qualities that would redeem it from being classified as legally obscene and destined to be banned.

As it turned out, the New York trial was only the beginning of U.S. legal proceedings involving Sjöman's film; for the next several years, attempts to ban it would be made across America, and the question whether *Curious (Yellow)* had value would run through all the ensuing trials and court rulings. Outside the legal arena, it would also be a recurrent theme in critical assessments of the film. The purpose of this essay is to discuss how the value argument was settled in several of these court cases, to outline how critics viewed the film, and to show connections between the legal and the critical receptions of *Curious (Yellow)*. As the weighing of the explicitness of Sjöman's film against its other qualities was by no means a phenomenon unique to the United States, the essay also makes comparisons with how the film was received in its home country, Sweden, and it provides a longer perspective by showing how *Curious (Yellow)* has been remembered in both countries. To begin with, it is necessary to discuss the director's purpose for his film.

"All of Sweden into the Film"

Vilgot Sjöman was an established film director when in 1965 he began work on the project that would eventually yield *I Am Curious (Yellow)* and its companion film, *I Am Curious (Blue)*. He had started his career in films as an assistant to legendary Swedish director Ingmar Bergman, and his first four films closely followed the technical and narrative conventions of Bergman and other Swedish directors, although they also revealed

Sjöman's predilection for sexual themes. His second work, the controversial *491*, made him well-known in his home country when it opened in 1964.[2]

Sjöman followed *491* with two more films, *Klänningen/The Dress* in 1964 and *Syskonbädd 1782/My Sister My Love* in 1966. Possibly because reviews of the latter struck a theme of Sjöman being indebted to his mentor Ingmar Bergman, Vilgot Sjöman seemed determined to make a totally different film when he began working on the *Curious* films the same year that *My Sister My Love* was released.[3] He broached the subject over lunch with the actress who would be the star of *Curious (Yellow)*, Lena Nyman, and she enthusiastically recorded her impression of the project in her diary: "His new movie is going to be made in a new way. With a somewhat young company and going on forever. It will be freaky and nuts and we are going to get all of Sweden into the film."[4]

The second sentence of Nyman's diary entry provided a clue to Sjöman's ambition for his film: it was to be, as he explained in his testimony in New York, "a portrait of Sweden right now in the late '60s as I experienced my country" where "all kinds of ideas could be used, ideas that somehow reflected the conflicts and the climate of Sweden."[5]

To ensure that he would be able to pursue new directions in filmmaking, Sjöman secured promises from Sandrews, the theater chain that financed and would distribute his new film, that gave him "total freedom" to make "a film without a script," as he later put it. The absence of a script entailed improvising scenes together with his actors and also mixing fictional and documentary scenes. In addition, Sjöman wanted to follow in the footsteps of auteur film-makers such as Jean-Luc Godard, so *Curious (Yellow)* would partly be a film about film-making, with the director himself frequently appearing on camera and with the actors often being themselves and not the characters they play.[6]

As Sjöman started pondering the contents of *Curious (Yellow)*, a list of topics that he drafted included the items "Politics, Social Issues, Sex, Religion, Humanity, Gender Roles, the Welfare State, Violence and Non-Violence and Miscellaneous."[7] More succinctly, the director summed up the content of his film with the words "Sex and Socialism," and that turned out to be a rather apt summary of the eventual film, as two distinctive parts are evident. The socialism component consists of the camera following the protagonist Lena—played by Lena Nyman—as she walks around Stockholm with a microphone and poses provocative questions—about fascism in Spain, equality for women, non-violence instead of national defense, and whether socialism has failed and Sweden remains a class-based society. Her targets are real-life Swedes in all walks of life, such as subway travelers, conscripts into the army, police officers, trade union bosses, and vacationers coming back from Francoist Spain, so the interview scenes have an obvious documentary character.[8]

The "sex" part of Sjöman's film chronicles Lena's affair with menswear salesman Börje, played by Börje Ahlstedt. Their saga is told through a number of sexually explicit scenes, part of the director's determination to shatter taboos surrounding sexuality and to jettison what one Swedish reviewer called cinematic "pajama and sheet conventions."[9]

Curious (Yellow) in Sweden: Censorship Issues and Critical Appraisal

All films intended for public exhibition in Sweden had to be cleared by the government censors at the National Board of Film Censors, and the explicit nature of the sex scenes in *Curious (Yellow)* meant that the film might raise issues there. After a month-long process, the bureau announced that six scenes in the film were problematic and might have to be deleted before it could be cleared for theatrical release. However, because it thought that any decision to censor Sjöman's film might have wider implications for the overall work of the Board and film censorship in general, the bureau referred the matter to another body, the Film Review Council, for guidance and advice. The Council had been established in 1954 to allow for scrutiny by members of the public of the work of the Board, whose members were civil servants, and the Council's opinion should be solicited in cases where censorship might interfere with the artistic qualities of a film. After screening the film, the Council recommended that *Curious (Yellow)* be released without any censorship because of its artistic qualities and a "political and moral commitment that is unusual in Swedish films." The council's recommendation foreshadowed, in a sense, the discussion that would surround *Curious (Yellow)* in the United States. In the end, the three censors of the Board voted 2–1 to clear the film for exhibition to audiences fifteen and above, removing all impediments to the release of Sjöman's film in Sweden.[10]

Three days after *Curious (Yellow)* was cleared by the Board, the film opened in Stockholm and Gothenburg, Sweden's two largest cities. Newspaper reviewers in both cities treated the film with respect, an attitude reinforced, suggests film historian Anders Åberg, by the fact that they had access to a diary written by Vilgot Sjöman during the making of the film, a book that gave the film added intellectual weight. With the diary in the back of their minds, reviewers tended to focus their discussion on whether Sjöman had been able to follow the intentions set down in the book rather than on the explicitness of the sex scenes.[11]

To several critics he had. Mauritz Edström of *Dagens Nyheter* in Stockholm praised the film for its "simplicity and cogency" and its willingness to deal with political issues, and Jurgen Schildt of *Aftonbladet* also lauded its political approach. Writing for *Arbetet* in Malmö, Sweden's third largest city, Nils Beyer considered *Curious (Yellow)* an "experimental film or a play in film that you get a great deal of amusement out of."[12] The sex scenes did not seem to be of particular concern to reviewers in Sweden's three largest cities. Monica Tunbäck-Hanson, the reviewer at *Göteborgs-Posten*, saw something comical in them, although she questioned whether their multitude was "artistically motivated." To Edström, the "de-romanticized love" of the sex scenes was a challenge by Sjöman to "a nation of voyeurs" who generously supported "weekly magazines with centerfolds and restaurants with nudie shows."[13] Outside Sweden's largest cities, however, some critics were less charitable when it came to finding artistic qualities and social and political commentary in Sjöman's film: to the reviewer at *Falu-Kuriren* in central Sweden, the essence of *Curious (Yellow)* was "a plump broad and a vulgar guy illustrating, in a yawningly boring manner, a manual in sexual technique."[14]

Like the Stockholm film critics, some audience members interviewed by the newspapers in the Swedish capital tended to focus on Sjöman's political and social message, lauding the interview scenes and the director's "social criticism without flourishes."[15] In Gothenburg, however, the reaction was notably different, according to a reporter for *Göteborgs-Tidningen*, who noted "silent and shocked people" exhibiting "fear and disgust" and calling the film "a speculation in filth" as they were leaving the theater on opening night.[16]

Whatever weight critics and theater patrons assigned to the overall purpose of Sjöman's film, there is little doubt that its sexual content loomed large when it came to making *Curious (Yellow)* a media event, particularly in the Stockholm tabloids *Aftonbladet* and *Expressen*. The two provided daily coverage of the wrangling among the censors at the Board over "Sjöman's sex film," and the inevitable angle of their opening-night coverage was that theater patrons could "handle" the sex scenes and were not "shocked."[17]

Doubts About the Appeal Abroad

There were some indications early on that Vilgot Sjöman's biting criticism of Swedish society that was so appealing to Swedish critics might lose a great deal of its resonance as the film traveled abroad. Just before *Curious (Yellow)* opened in Stockholm, the Swedish Film Institute had hosted a symposium for international cinema critics about contemporary Swedish film, and Sjöman arranged for an advance showing of his film to that gathering. Stockholm newspapers covered the question-and-answer session that followed between the director and the foreign guests and also asked for short personal assessments from seven of them. A few of those who spoke with Sjöman and provided capsule reviews for the press liked the film, but the majority thought that its two components, sex and socialism, did not make for a cohesive film. A Soviet critic found the two parts "incoherent," and Peter Cowie, a British expert on Swedish film, could not see any relationship between them.[18] Three years later, Cowie, although by then more positive toward the film, suggested that its director's message and purpose may have little meaning for foreign audiences:

> Close-ups of sexual organs and such like, while not pornographically stimulating per se, are bound to give those very members of his audience Sjöman wants to provoke, the excuse to attack his film as unwholesome and depraved, thus diverting attention from what the director claims is the key issue in *I Am Curious*—namely, the absence of social and political responsibility in Sweden. This reaction to the film is even more pronounced abroad, for in many countries Sjöman's satire must seem outdated beside his sexual attitudes. The important scene showing the King about to abdicate and leave the country, for example, contributes a cruel and witty salvo to the Republic vs. Monarchy debate in Sweden, but it has no relevance in Germany or the U.S.A.[19]

Writing for the men's magazine *Se* a few weeks after the film had opened in Stockholm, TV producer and media critic Ulf Thorén was blunter in making essentially the same observation:

> Why not splice together a little 20-minuter from "I Am Curious (Yellow)," with all the naked butts and all the panting close-ups, and send this to happy little theater owners in Buenos Aires, Dallas and Beirut? The rest of the film is obviously totally uninteresting to foreign people.[20]

However enticing the sex in *Curious (Yellow)* was perceived to be to foreign theater owners and audiences, there were clear indications that Sweden's increasingly liberal attitude towards sex in the late 1960s had few counterparts abroad, particularly not in the United States. In a story published in November 1967, a correspondent for the *New York Times* interviewed Swedish Minister of Justice Herman Kling, who was quoted to the effect that Sweden's attitude toward pornography was more tolerant, and as evidence of that tolerance the minister noted that there had been no censorship of *Curious (Yellow)*, a film with "complete and prolonged nudity of both the male and the female stars in several scenes and sexual intercourse ... shown frequently."[21] A year later, another *Times* reporter returned to the topic, claiming that *Curious (Yellow)* had rendered censorship "dead" in Sweden and relating how pornographic pictures and magazines were openly displayed in Stockholm shop windows.[22]

The United States vs. I Am Curious (Yellow): First Trials

As noted in the introduction, the U.S. Customs Bureau in New York seized Sjöman's film when Grove Press sought to bring it into the United States.[23] (Reporting back to readers in Stockholm, a correspondent for Dagens Nyheter claimed that Sjöman would be "burned at the stake," an overreaching allusion to the practice of Customs of destroying banned films by burning them.[24]) A jury trial began in federal court in New York in late May 1968 after a judge had refused a request by Grove Press to clear the film through summary judgment.[25]

Before the jury was the question whether Curious (Yellow) was obscene in a legal sense, and in their deliberations jurors were instructed by Judge Thomas F. Murphy to consider three questions: did the film's dominant theme appeal to prurient interest, was the film patently offensive, and did it utterly lack social value? The three-part test proposed by Murphy was based on several recent rulings by the U.S. Supreme Court that had thoroughly changed obscenity case law in America within the span of a decade, during what legal scholar Richard F. Hixson calls "the most active and most chaotic obscenity years for the Court."[26]

The Supreme Court had first defined obscenity in the 1957 case Roth v. United States, which established that materials that are deemed legally obscene do not have First Amendment protection. It also suggested, however, that not every depiction of sex was necessarily obscene, because only sexually explicit materials "utterly without redeeming social importance" fell into the category of legal obscenity. Sex portrayals appearing "e.g. in art, literature and scientific works" did not.[27]

Nine years after Roth, in the Memoirs v. Massachusetts case, the Supreme Court reshaped the general definition into a three-part test that considered whether materials at issue appealed to prurient interest, were patently offensive, and were "utterly without redeeming social value"—essentially the test in Judge Murphy's instruction to the jurors in the Curious (Yellow) trial. Another ruling, a year later, Redrup v. New York, mandated that the three-part test be strictly followed and was, in the words of Hixson, "about as far to the left" as the Court would go in its attitude toward obscenity. In 1973, a more conservative court changed the community standards that were offended by obscene materials from national to local and substituted "lacks serious literary, artistic, political, or scientific value" for the Memoirs phrase "utterly without redeeming social value," thereby reversing what Hixson calls "the liberalization of obscenity protection under the Constitution."[28] It is worth noting, however, that even the 1973 Supreme Court ruling retained the value argument, although in modified form.

It was the more liberal Memoirs definition of value that faced Grove Press as its attorneys sought to overturn the customs ban in May 1968. Would the social criticism and satire and the experimental cinematic techniques of the director of Curious (Yellow) be sufficient reasons to counterbalance the film's sexual explicitness?

To make that case, Grove Press called a number of expert witnesses—film critics, psychiatrists, a minister, and author Norman Mailer, as well as Sjöman himself.[29] A general theme in the testimony was that the sex scenes were an integrated part of the film's overall content, showing that Lena's attitudes toward sex were in accordance with her attitude toward political and social issues and that they constituted an essential element in an honest and complete portrayal of a modern young woman. The experts also stressed that the film had broken new ground in the way it mixed documentary material with fiction and thus had artistic qualities. To Mailer, for instance, *Curious (Yellow)* was "a major work ... one of the most important motion pictures I have ever seen in my life."[30] The cross-examination of Sjöman by U.S. Attorney Lawrence W. Shilling was, according to a correspondent for *Expressen*, "downright hostile," producing "a revealing confrontation between the puritanical USA views of sexuality and Vilgot Sjöman's more realistic vision of young love in Sweden of today."[31] *Dagens Nyheter*'s New York correspondent related to readers how the attorney for Grove Press "in a monotonous voice" asked witness after witness to affirm that the sex scenes in *Curious (Yellow)* were "artistically warranted," explaining that the film had to have social value to avoid being judged obscene.[32] Even Shilling had driven home that aspect during his questioning of New York Customs Commissioner Irving Fishman, suggesting to him that the film's sexual content had to be "balanced or weighed" against "the social values or ideas of social value." Shilling had claimed that *Curious (Yellow)* lacked any such value, as it was merely "a series of bizarre sexual episodes, designed to shock and linked together by what can charitably be described as a soap opera." In the end, the jury accepted his argument, answering in the affirmative all three questions posed to them by the judge.[33]

In his denial of summary judgment for Grove Press earlier in the year, Judge Murphy had also touched on the value argument. He had viewed *Curious (Yellow)* and found it "repulsive and revolting, the sexual scenes having no relationship to the story line or plot—if there was one."[34] The judge then went on to dismiss the opinions of experts in affidavits submitted by Grove about the film's purpose: "If the film has a message, whether it is public poll taking on the social structure of the Swedish society or the advocacy of non-violence or anti–Francoism, I would suspect it is merely dross, providing a vehicle for portraying sexual deviation and hard core pornography."[35] The film, moreover, was "insulting to the American public" and "devoid of social value."[36]

After the New York jury had agreed with Murphy in the subsequent trial, it fell to the U.S. Court of Appeals for the Second Circuit to consider the value of *I Am Curious (Yellow)*. That court's ruling, by a three-judge panel, was 2–1 in favor of reversing the district court. Writing for the Majority, Justice Paul Raymond Hays first argued that sex was not the dominant theme of the film (although he seemed uncertain what exactly the main theme was, noting that even the experts testifying on behalf of Sjöman's work seemed unable to agree on that point). He found it even clearer that *I Am Curious (Yellow)* had social value, as "it is quite certain that 'I Am Curious' does present ideas and does strive to present these ideas artistically." It thus represented an "intellectual effort that the First Amendment was designed to protect."[37]

Hays was supported by Justice Henry Friendly, who in a concurring opinion also voted to reverse the district court. Doing so with reservations and "no little distaste," Friendly voiced his clear dislike of *Curious (Yellow)* and stressed that "redeeming social value" could not rescue a film "if the sexual episodes were simply lugged in and bore no relationship whatever to the theme." Still, he could not find that there was no connection whatsoever between the "serious purpose" of Vilgot Sjöman's film and its "sexual episodes and displays of nudity."[38]

The third member of the panel, Chief Justice J. Edward Lumbard, dissented vigorously. To Lumbard, sex was the main point of *Curious (Yellow)*, as a plot was "non-existent." Sjöman's purpose, argued the judge, was simply to shock audiences by breaking "sexual taboos and clichés," as the director had clearly stated when he testified in the trial court. The sexual acts in the film, more explicit than "anything thus far exhibited in this country," bore "no conceivable relevance to any social value, except that of box-office appeal," according to Lumbard.[39]

Redeeming Social Quality? Legal Cases Across the United States

The ruling by the Second Circuit Court of Appeals cleared the way for the importation of Sjöman's film into the United States, but whether *Curious (Yellow)* could actually be shown would continue to present challenges as it was distributed to theaters across the country. In contrast to Sweden, where the decision by the government censors meant that Sjöman's film was cleared for exhibition nationwide, the U.S. legal landscape presented a scenario where state and local governments had the power to determine what films could be shown in theaters. By November 1970, a year and a half after the federal appeals-court ruling, *Curious (Yellow)* had been banned in ten states (a figure that would rise to fifteen a year later), according to Edward de Grazia, one of the attorneys for Grove Press.[40]

Courts that declared the film legal had a fairly straightforward task, as the main point was establishing that there was social value in *Curious (Yellow)*. The New Jersey Supreme Court, for instance, did so by comparing the witnesses called by both sides. Experts summoned on behalf of Grove Press were "clearly more persuasive than that of plaintiffs and amply reflects the required 'modicum of social value,'" the court ruled.[41]

Judges upholding bans against *I Am Curious (Yellow)* were obligated to address the value argument as well, and they did so in elaborate ways. When Grove Press appealed a decision by the Maryland State Board of Censors to not license Sjöman's film for theatrical exhibition to the Maryland state Court of Appeals, that court in a 4–3 ruling declared the ban legal. Writing for the majority, Judge Thomas B. Finan found that the director's attempts "to use social questions to depict the restlessness of youth and its search for identity, against an intellectual ambience, were patently strained and contrived." The protagonist's "concern with social and political problems, so artificially depicted," did not supply "the redeeming social quality required to sustain the film."[42] To Finan, even Sjöman's mix of fact and fiction, so impressive to some of the critics who had testified in New York, was suspect, and he thought that "the sexual sequences appear artificially interjected into the film" and that "the many interviews seem a contrived ruse to give the movie social value."[43]

The Maryland court's suggestion that Sjöman had added political and social commentary merely to lend legitimacy to the explicit sex scenes was echoed in subsequent rulings by other judges. The Georgia Supreme Court ruled in 1971 that *Curious (Yellow)* so offended "all sense of decency" that "the fact that it contains some non-obscene matter does not preclude a finding that, considering it as a whole, it is utterly without redeeming social value."[44] The same year, the Arizona Supreme Court upheld the seizure of the film by law enforcement officials in Phoenix because "interspacing it with items of alleged redeeming social value" did not save *Curious (Yellow)* from being ruled obscene.[45]

Asked by Grove Press to invalidate law-enforcement actions in Youngstown, Ohio, that involved seizing copies of the film and arresting projectionists, a federal district court focused on both the film's protagonists and its audience. Taking to heart a local psychiatrist's view that *I Am Curious (Yellow)* was the story of "a severely disturbed person whose aberrant sexual behavior was symptomatic of her general sicknesses," Judge Frank Celebrezze thought that subjecting Youngstown residents to "twelve to twenty minutes of the sexual activities of two concededly abnormal persons" was so offensive that it came to dominate the film.[46] Dismissing the testimony of Grove Press witnesses who had stressed that depicting graphic sex was a component of Sjöman's artistic vision for *cinéma vérité* and thus had inherent artistic value, Celebrezze declared that *Curious (Yellow)* "was to be shown for general audiences not to museum curators, professors of the cinema and sophisticated reviewers of the cinema verite."[47] Those general audiences, moreover, had been lured to the theaters by marketing that played up the sex scenes and had come with "expectations of being titillated by pornography and being patently offended by depictions which go beyond anything ever shown in a film for general release."[48] The sex scenes, the main draw for theater patrons, had created "a psychology of titillation in the viewers causing them to fail to perceive whatever social value the movie may purport to purvey."[49] Thus, as audiences were unable to perceive social value because they were preoccupied with the sex scenes, the film had no such value.

In March 1970, the U.S. Supreme Court agreed to review whether *Curious (Yellow)* was obscene in an action that arose from the 1969 Maryland case. A month later, Justice William O. Douglas announced that he would recuse himself from the case because an article he had written had appeared in the Grove Press journal *Evergreen Review*. His absence opened up the prospect of a divided court, and that was the eventual outcome, as the remaining eight justices deadlocked 4–4 in their ruling in March 1971. As a consequence, the Maryland ban stood, and the issue of whether Sjöman's film was obscene remained unsettled.[50]

Critics Weigh Sex Against Value

The possible social value of *Curious (Yellow)* was not only a legal matter. Film reviewers at newspapers and magazines brought it up almost immediately after the film opened in New York theaters in March 1969. (A number of critics had already seen the film a year earlier during the court proceedings where they were called as expert witnesses or asked to provide affidavits, but their opinions of it then had not reached a wider audience.) Not surprisingly, given that they belonged to a category of experts who had been called to testify to the film's value on behalf of Grove Press, critics generally rejected the argument that Sjöman's film was obscene. It was not, wrote Joseph Morgenstern in *Newsweek*, "the tawdry sex-exploitation film that the government tried to pretend it was."[51] The reviewer for the *New York Times*, Vincent Canby, thought the sex scenes were "explicit, honest and so unaffectedly frank as to be non-pornographic—that is, if to be pornographic means to be offensive to morals."[52] Any "full-length portrait" of the film's protagonist, Canby suggested, had to include the sex scenes. Writing from Stockholm, *Look* magazine's reviewer Leonard Gross thought the "sad" way in which sex was depicted in *Curious (Yellow)* was used by its director "to make a political point: lack of commitment in affairs of state is as disastrous as in affairs of heart."[53]

The reviewer for *Look's* main rival, *Life*, used the appellate-court ruling that released the film as a starting point. Richard Schickel noted that "because its heroine's search for values includes a lot of political and social as well as sexual experiment and because of its earnest portrait of questioning, questing youth confronting the smug liberalism of an enlightened middle-class society" the film was neither dominated by sex nor lacking in social value.[54] Hollis Alpert, writing for the *Saturday Review*, even sought to downplay the sexual content of the film: "For one thing, there simply is not that much sex in the film. Oh, certainly the girl and boy of the film do make love frequently, and in a variety of positions and circumstances. They are seen in the nude, but not suggestively."[55] To Alpert, what was important about *I Am Curious (Yellow)* was "the evident purpose of Vilgot Sjöman to explore and say something, through cinematic methods, about the political and social climate of his country, Sweden."[56]

Alpert, Canby, and Gross were three of the more enthusiastic reviewers of the film. Other critics were less positive, although still treating it as a legitimate and valuable work of cinematic art. Morgenstern of *Newsweek* characterized it as "a slightly confused and confusing movie" that would bore its audience, and his nameless counterpart at *Time*, who thought the sex scenes "not much more erotic than the Fannie Mae cookbook," dismissed it as an "artistic failure" that was "too interminably boring, too determinedly insular and, like the sex scenes themselves, finally and fatally passionless."[57] Schickel of *Life* did not find the film boring but thought it lacked "heart."[58]

The reviews discussed above appeared in elite publications with a national readership, and it is possible that the response in the *Spokesman-Review* in Spokane, Washington, was more indicative of overall press reaction. It characterized the film as a "me-too skin flick" whose leading man and lady were "just not up to the good old American ideal" when it came to looks.[59] In other venues, such as Phoenix, Arizona, editorial policies dictated that X-rated films not be mentioned and let alone reviewed, so local papers there did not even report that police had raided a local theater that was showing Sjöman's film.[60]

"Sensational Box Office"

Whatever the critical and legal response to *Curious (Yellow)*, theaters showing Sjöman's film found audiences eager to see it. In part that may have been due to the legal controversies surrounding *Curious (Yellow)*, but, as Kevin Heffernan shows, it was also due to the film transcending several kinds of commercial cinema.[61] Public interest in *Curious (Yellow)* translated into what the trade publication *Variety* called "sensational" box-office revenue.[62] Three months after opening in New York, it was also showing or had been shown in Washington, D.C., Philadelphia, San Francisco, Boston, Los Angeles and Houston and had generated more than $1 million in ticket sales. *Curious (Yellow)* passed the $5 million mark in late October, and for two weeks in late November and early December 1969, more people went to see it than any other film in the United States.[63] Eventually, Grove Press would earn a total of $19 million from *Curious (Yellow)*, making it the most successful foreign-language film in U.S. history, a record it held until the 1990s.[64]

Curiosity about the film was by no means a big-city phenomenon, either. The *New York Times* noted that theaters in fifty-three cities had shown Sjöman's film by late November 1969, and *Variety* had observed three months earlier that *Curious (Yellow)* had not just appeared "in obvious and much publicized locations" such as New York, San Francisco, Los Angeles, and Boston but also in "such curious localities as Albuquerque, New Mexico, Virginia Beach, Va., Woodburn, N.Y. and St. Petersburg, Fla."[65] The manager of a drive-in theater showing the film in Richmond, Virginia, found that "traffic was backed up for miles" on weekends, and in San Antonio, Texas, a theater charging the unheard-of admission fee of $5 still sold out showings of *Curious (Yellow)*. In small-town Derry, New Hampshire, 5,000 people saw the film in its first week.[66]

Curious (Yellow) *in Hindsight*

Newspaper stories recollecting the sensation that Sjöman's film caused in New Hampshire and Virginia tend to focus less on the fact that *Curious (Yellow)* "ostensibly was supposed to have some kind of Swedish political statement," as one reporter put it, than on the film's sex scenes.[67] Sjöman's ambition for his film does still surface in some accounts looking back, such as the *New York Times'* 2006 obituary for the Swedish filmmaker, which characterized his 1967 creation as a "story of the social, political and sexual journey of a young Swedish woman" and noted "its documentary-style techniques, hand-held cameras and interpolation of real and made-up events," as well as its connection to the tradition of French directors such as Jean-Luc Godard.[68] More often, however, latter-day references to *Curious (Yellow)* tend to ignore the political and artistic aspects of the film in favor of the sex scenes. Newspaper articles mentioning Sjöman's film with a perspective of two decades or more routinely use terms such as "Swedish sex shocker," "sex documentary," "semi-pornographic," and "porn movie."[69]

Often, the sexual content of *Curious (Yellow)* is used to cast the film as a forerunner of the far more explicit productions that followed in the 1970s, such as *Deep Throat*.[70] A 2001 story in the *Dayton Daily News* about the city's local art theater's changing from being a venue for New Wave films and folk music concerts into a "porn palace" pinpointed the start of that transition to when its owners realized the appeal of "soft-porn fare" such as *I Am Curious (Yellow)*.[71] When the qualities that critics in 1969 held up as transforming *I Am Curious (Yellow)* into something more than a sexually explicit film are mentioned, it is typically in dismissive terms that echo the words of judges claiming that Sjöman's film lacked value. A 1993 article in the *Kansas City Star*, for example, dismissed the claim of Sjöman that the sex scenes were part of a larger whole, calling *Curious (Yellow)* "a banal Scandinavian skin flick masquerading as a serious work of art."[72]

In Sweden, latter-day assessments of the film tend to be less dismissive of its director's ambitions, but there, too, the sex scenes of *Curious (Yellow)* loom large, at least in retrospective. Announcing a 1992 television broadcast of the film, *Expressen* observed that its purpose was to be "critical of the Social Democratic establishment" but that "the sex scenes between Lena Nyman and Börje Ahlstedt overshadowed everything."[73] *Aftonbladet* claimed three years later that *Curious (Yellow)* was "first and foremost a political film" but that that part of the film "faded into the background because of the soon-to-be world-famous sex scenes."[74] When a DVD set with the *Curious* films was issued in 2005, *Hallands Nyheter* brought up the documentary interview scenes and Sjöman's criticism of Sweden's class structure, but ended with the claim that "what has received the most attention are the sexual provocations."[75]

As is evident from the reaction to *I Am Curious (Yellow)* in both Sweden and the United States in the 1960s, there is little doubt that the film crossed a threshold with its explicit depiction of sex. The sex scenes of the film generated attention to and publicity for it in its home country as well as the United States, and there were some similarities in the way Sjöman's film was received. In both countries, the issue arose whether the explicitness of *Curious (Yellow)* warranted censorship in some form. Also surfacing in the debate over Sjöman's film in both Sweden and the United States was to what extent its artistic values and purposes legitimized its sexual content. In the views of critics on both sides of the Atlantic, that was certainly the case.

In other respects, *Curious (Yellow)* was viewed differently in the two countries. In Sweden, Sjöman's ambitious attempt to combine sexual explicitness with social and political criticism and unconventional techniques of film-making had greater resonance with audiences, as they were familiar with the institutions and attitudes that the film attacked. As *I Am Curious (Yellow)* crossed the Atlantic, it faced viewers for whom the criticism had little relevance. The politics and social issues of a small country on the periphery of Europe were not universal enough themes to engage many audience members in the United States. Explicit sex scenes—and the controversy they caused—were, and they became the main legacy of one of the most successful foreign-language films in American motion-picture history.

Notes

1. Eric Sjöquist, "Fientlig stämning i salen då Sjöman vittnade," *Expressen*, May 23, 1968, 11; "Swedish Movie Is Seized By Customs for 'Obscenity'" (1968). *New York Times*, January 19, 29; "'Jag är nyfiken' fast i USA-tull," *Expressen*, January 20, 1968.

2. See Lena Lennerhed's contribution to this volume. See also Leif Furhammar, *Filmen i Sverige—en historia i tio kapitel och en fortsättning*, third edition (Stockholm: Dialogos förlag and Svenska filminstitutet, 2003), 303–04; Anders Åberg, "7 × 70 + 1 = Skandal," *Humanetten*, No. 9, Fall 2009, http://vxu.se/hum/publ/humanetten/nummer9/art0112.html; Jon Dunås, "Vilgot Sjömans paradoxala tabubrott," *Svenska Dagbladet*, April 6, 2004, 71.

3. Ulrika Knutson, "Han skapade svenska synden," *Veckans Affärer*, December 6, 2007, http://www.va.se/magasinet/2007/49/svenska-syndens-fader/ ; Mauritz Edström, "Sjömans självporträtt: Dagbok om filmen," *Dagens Nyheter*, October 11, 1967, 14; Anders Åberg, *Tabu: Filmaren Vilgot Sjöman*. Lund: Filmhäftet, 2001), 169–70; Furhammar, 304.

4. Knutson.

5. *I Am Curious (Yellow): The Complete Scenario of the Film by Vilgot Sjöman with over 250 illustrations*. (New York: Grove Press, 1968), 243.

6. Åberg, *Tabu*, 174–75, 184–85; Carl-Henrik Svenstedt, "Vilgot Sjöman, gul och blå," *Svenska Dagbladet*, October 10, 1967, 10; Director's introduction, *Jag är nyfiken—en film i gult/Jag är nyfiken—en film i blått*, DVD Recording (Home Vision Entertainment, 2003); Edström, "Sjömans självporträtt"; Bertil Behring, "Nyfiken Sjöman: Socialismens ideal—sviks de av kärleken," *Kvällsposten*, October 10, 1967, 16; Sverker Andreason, "Vilgot Sjöman," *Modern Swedish Cinema 1* (Stockholm: The Swedish Film Institute, 1974).

7. Åberg, *Tabu*, 176; Knutson.

8. Svenstedt; Behring; Mauritz Edström, "Vilgot kontra världen," *Dagens Nyheter*, October 7, 1967, 15

9. Ulla Swedberg, "Sjömans provokationer & notifikationer," *Göteborgs-Tidningen*, October 12, 1967, 4; Bo Petersén, "Han som sprängde männens sexvall," *Expressen*, October 10, 1967, 21.

10. Åberg "7 × 70"; "Vad censuren grubblar på," *Dagens Nyheter*, October 6, 1967, 22; "Eliza," "Sjömans film frisläppt—Skoglund protesterar," *Svenska Dagbladet*, October 7, 1967, 10.

11. Åberg, *Tabu*, 194–95.

12. Nils Beyer, "Vilgot Sjömans 'sexchock'—en oskyldig lek!" *Arbetet*, October 10, 1967, 11; Jurgen Schildt, "Vilgot Sjöman synar samtiden," *Aftonbladet*, October 10, 1967, 20; Mauritz Edström, "Sjömans inbrott i verkligheten—ilsket, skamlöst och kvickt," *Dagens Nyheter*, October 10, 1967, 10.

13. Monica Tunbäck-Hanson, "Från attack mot alla våra konventioner," *Göteborgs-Posten*, October 10, 1967, 16; Edström, "Sjömans inbrott."
14. Ragnar Liljedahl, "Politik och sexualteknik," *Falu-Kuriren*, November 8, 1967, 5.
15. "Chockar scener som denna? Nej, publiken tog det med ro," *Expressen*, October 10, 1967, 20.
16. "Jag är nyfiken blev en chock för åskådarna," *Göteborgs-Tidningen*, October 10, 1967, 13.
17. "Sjömans sexfilm fick klartecken," *Expressen*, October 7, 1967, 6; "Sjömans nya film blev ingen chock för publiken," *Aftonbladet*, October 10, 1967, 1; "Publiken tålde sexfilmen," *Expressen*, October 10, 1967, 1.
18. Edström, "Vilgot kontra"; "Sju utländska kritiker om Sjöman & Nyman," *Expressen*, October 10, 1967, 4.
19. Peter Cowie, *Sweden 2* (London: A. Zwemmer Limited, 1970) 213–14.
20. "Ulf Thorén har sett 'Jag är nyfiken—gul' och ger Vilgot Sjöman en snyting," *Se*, October 8, 1967, 20.
21. Werner Wiskari, "Sweden Is Casual on Pornography," *New York Times*, November 5, 1967, 27.
22. John M. Lee, "Danes and Swedes Are Moving Toward Greater Sex Freedom," *New York Times*, November 6, 1968, 44.
23. "Swedish Movie Is Seized."
24. "Sjöman på bål hot i USA" (1968). *Dagens Nyheter*, 22 January, 1.
25. "Grove Press Movie on Trial as Obscene," *New York Times*, May 21, 1968, 42; Kevin Heffernan, "A Prurient (Dis)Interest: The American Release and Reception of *I Am Curious (Yellow)*," in *Sex Scene: Media and the Sexual Revolution*, ed. by Eric Schaefer (Durham: Duke University Press, 2014), 107.
26. Richard F. Hixson, *Pornography and the Justices: The Supreme Court and the Intractable Obscenity Problem*. Carbondale: Southern Illinois University Press, 1996), 20; "'I Am Curious' Found to Be Obscene Film," *New York Times*, May 24, 1968, 36.
27. Fredrik Schauer, *The Law of Obscenity* (Washington, D.C.: The Bureau of National Affairs, Inc., 1976) 36–37; Susan Elkin, "Casenote: Taking Serious Value Seriously: Obscenity, Pope v. Illinois, and an Objective Standard," *University of Miami Law Review* 41 (1986–87): 859–60; Edward John Main, "The Neglected Prong of the Miller Test for Obscenity: Serious Literary, Artistic and Political Value," *Southern Illinois University Law Journal* 11(1986–87): 1159–60.
28. Hixson 1998, 478–79; Elkin 1986–87, 860
29. Excerpts from the testimony of eight witnesses—film critics Stanley Kauffmann of the *New Republic* and John Simon of the *New Leader*, the Rev. Howard Moody of New York's Judson Memorial Church, psychiatrist Tom Levin of Albert Einstein College of Medicine, Commissioner of Customs Irving Fishman, the Rev. Dan M. Potter of New York's Protestant Council, and Mailer—are in "Trial Transcripts," *Jag är nyfiken—en film i gult/Jag är nyfiken—en film i blått*, DVD Recording (Home Vision Entertainment, 2003); according to *Dagens Nyheter*, Grove had notified the court that it had some 30 expert witnesses ready, and at least six more are named or alluded to in other newspaper accounts; Sven Åhman, "Federal domstolsjury såg 'Nyfiken-gul,'" *Dagens Nyheter*, May 21, 1968, 21; "Sjöman vittnade om Nyfiken-gul i USA-domstol," *Sydsvenska Dagbladet Snällposten*, May 24, 1968, 8; Eric Sjöquist, "Nu har Vilgot Sjöman fått hela rätten riktigt nyfiken: Älskar amerikaner på balustrader som Lena Nyman?" *Expressen*, May 23, 1968, 11.
30. "Trial Transcripts."
31. Sjöquist, "Fientlig stämning."
32. Åhman.
33. "'I Am Curious' Found"; "Trial Transcripts"; Eric Sjöquist, "'Nyfiken-gul' fälld igen: 'Anstötlig och liderlig,'" *Expressen*, May 24, 1968, 16.
34. *United States of America v. A Motion Picture Entitled "I Am Curious (Yellow),"* (1968) 285 F. Supp. 472.
35. *Ibid.*, 472
36. *Ibid.*, 472
37. *United States of America v. A Motion Picture Entitled "I Am Curious (Yellow)"* (1968) 285 F. 2d 200
38. *Ibid.*, 201.
39. *Ibid.*, 203.
40. Fred P. Graham, "Court Ban Urged on 'I Am Curious,'" *New York Times*, November 11, 1970, 29; Edward de Grazia, Edward and Roger K. Newman, *Banned Films: Movies, Censors and the First Amendment* (New York: R.R. Bowker Company, 1982) 197–303.

41. *Joseph P. Lordi v. UA New Jersey Theatres* (1969) 108 N.J. 31.
42. *Wagonheim v. Maryland Board of Censors* (1969) 255 Md. 307.
43. Ibid., 307.
44. *Evans Theatre Corporation v. Slaton* (1971) 227 Ga. 381.
45. *NGC Theatre Corporation v. John Mummert* (1971) 107 Ariz. 489.
46. *Grove Press v. Flask* (1970) 326 F. Supp. 586
47. Ibid., 586.
48. Ibid., 585–86.
49. Ibid., 586.
50. "High Court Lets Stand Maryland Ban on 'Curious,'" *New York Times*, March 9, 1971, 24; "Douglas Abstains from 3 Rulings," *New York Times*, April 28, 1970, 30; "Justices Agree to Review 'I Am Curious (Yellow),'" *New York Times*, March 24. 1970, 23; "New Rules for Obscenity?" *Time*, May 11, 1970, 84.
51. Joseph Morgenstern, "Curiouser and Curiouser," *Newsweek*, March 24, 1969, 114.
52. Vincent Canby, "Screen: 'I Am Curious (Yellow)' From Sweden," *New York Times*, March 11, 1969, 42.
53. Leonard Gross, "After Nudity, What, Indeed?" *Look*, April 29, 1969, 82.
54. Richard Schickel, "It Hides Nothing But the Heart," *Life*, March 21, 1969, 12.
55. Hollis Alpert, "On Being Curious Twice," *Saturday Review*, March 15, 1969, 54.
56. Alpert.
57. "Dubious Yellow" *Time*, March 14, 1969, 98; Morgenstern.
58. Schickel.
59. Doug Floyd, "Clean Consciences and Dirty Movies," *The Spokesman-Review* (Spokane, Wash.), August 28, 2000, A1; see also Jackson's chapter in this volume.
60. Dewey Webb Death, "The Naked Dessert: Under Every Rock?" *Phoenix New Times,* February 5, 1992, 30.
61. Heffernan, 106.
62. "'Curious' Packs 'Em in 2 N.Y. Spots," *Variety*, March 12, 1969, 9.
63. "50 Top-Grossing Films," *Variety*, October 29, 1969, 11; "Top Grossers for May," *Variety*, June 11, 1969, 12; "50 Top-Grossing Films" *Variety*, December 3, 1969, 11.
64. "'Like Water for Chocolate' Tops Records" *Houston Chronicle*, July 13, 1993, 3.
65. "'Curious' Now in 21 Markets," *Variety,* 20 August 20, 1969, 8; "Passaic Court and Theater Chain Agree on Ban of 'I Am Curious,'" *New York Times*, November 26, 1969, 40.
66. Tami Plyler, "Theaters again Making Comeback in Derry," *New Hampshire Union Leader*, 13 September 13, 1994, 5; Bob, Polunsky, "No 'Mystery' Why Film Isn't Here," *San Antonio Express-News*, August 29, 193, 3H; Frank Douglas, "Life at X-rated Drive-in Seems Shocking Only at First Blush," *Richmond Times-Dispatch*, 5 October 5, 1986, B1.
67. Plyler.
68. Douglas Martin, "Vilgot Sjöman, Filmmaker Without Taboos, Dies at 81," *New York Times*, 11 April 11, 2006, B7.
69. Death; Steve Persall, "Sarasota Film Fest Needs Patron Saints," *St. Petersburg Times*, July 20, 1993, 6B; Claudia Puig, "'Tiger' Cuts Through Foreign-film Reluctance," *USA Today*, March, 22, 2001, 1D; Carl Cunningham, "'Jackie O': Pop Goes the Opera," *Washington Post*, March 17. 1997, D7.
70. Shawn Levy, "Closer, Deeper look at 'Throat,'" *Oregonian*, February 18, 2005, 32.
71. Jim De Brosse, "Theater's History More than Dirty Movies," *Dayton Daily News*, July 29, 2001, 1C.
72. George Gurley, "Midtown's Dim View of a Bright Idea," *Kansas City Star*, January 21, 1993, C1.
73. "Sexscenerna alla minns," *Expressen*, December 22, 1992, TVE1.
74. Jan Olov Andersson, "Dagens film," December 21, 1995, 11.
75. Malin Henriksson, "Nyfiken-filmerna ges ut på dvd," *Hallands Nyheter,* November 17, 2005, 22.

REFERENCES

Åberg, Anders. "7 × 70 + 1 = Skandal." In *Humanetten*, 9, 2009, http://vxu.se/hum/publ/humanetten/nummer9/art0112.html.
_____. *Tabu: Filmaren Vilgot Sjöman*. Lund: Filmhäftet, 2001.
Åhman, Sven. "Federal domstolsjury såg 'Nyfiken-gul.'" *Dagens Nyheter*, May 21, 1968.
Alpert, Hollis. "On Being Curious Twice." *Saturday Review*, March 15, 1969.

Andersson, Jan Olov. "Dagens film." December 21, 1995.
Andreason, Sverker. "Vilgot Sjöman." In *Modern Swedish Cinema 1*. Stockholm: The Swedish Film Institute, 1974.
Behring, Bertil. "Nyfiken Sjöman: Socialismens ideal—sviks de av kärleken." *Kvällsposten*, October 10, 1967.
Beyer, Nils. "Vilgot Sjömans 'sexchock'—en oskyldig lek!" *Arbetet*, October 10, 1967.
Canby, Vincent. "Screen: 'I Am Curious (Yellow)' From Sweden." *New York Times*, March 11, 1969.
"Chockar Scener som denna? Nej, publiken tog det med ro." *Expressen*, October 10, 1967.
Cowie, Peter. *Sweden 2*. London: A. Zwemmer Limited, 1970.
Cunningham, Carl. "'Jackie O': Pop Goes the Opera." *Washington Post*, March 17. 1997.
"'Curious' Now in 21 Markets." *Variety*, 20 August 20, 1969.
"'Curious' Packs 'Em in 2 N.Y. Spots." *Variety*, March 12, 1969.
De Brosse, Jim. "Theater's History More than Dirty Movies." *Dayton Daily News*, July 29, 2001.
de Grazia, Edward, and Roger K. Newman. *Banned Films: Movies, Censors and the First Amendment*. New York: R.R. Bowker Company, 1982.
Director's introduction. *Jag är nyfiken—en film i gult/Jag är nyfiken—en film i blått*, DVD Recording (Home Vision Entertainment, 2003).
"Douglas Abstains from 3 Rulings." *New York Times*, April 28, 1970.
Douglas, Frank. "Life at X-rated Drive-in Seems Shocking Only at First Blush." *Richmond Times-Dispatch*, 5 October 5, 1986.
"Dubious Yellow." *Time*, March 14, 1969.
Dunås, Jon. "Vilgot Sjömans paradoxala tabubrott." *Svenska Dagbladet*, April 6, 2004.
Edström, Mauritz. "Sjömans inbrott i verkligheten—ilsket, skamlöst och kvickt." *Dagens Nyheter*, October 10, 1967.
_____. "Sjömans självporträtt: Dagbok om filmen." *Dagens Nyheter*, October 11, 1967.
_____. "Vilgot kontra världen." *Dagens Nyheter*, October 7, 1967.
"Eliza." "Sjömans film frisläppt—Skoglund protesterar." *Svenska Dagbladet*, October 7, 1967.
Elkin, Susan. "Casenote: Taking Serious Value Seriously: Obscenity, Pope v. Illinois, and an Objective Standard." In *University of Miami Law Review* 41, 1986–87: 859–60.
Evans Theatre Corporation v. Slaton (1971) 227 Ga. 381.
"50 Top-Grossing Films." *Variety*, October 29, 1969.
Floyd, Doug. "Clean Consciences and Dirty Movies." *The Spokesman-Review* (Spokane, Wash.), August 28, 2000.
Furhammar, Leif. *Filmen i Sverige—en historia i tio kapitel och en fortsättning*, third edition. Stockholm: Dialogos Förlag and Svenska filminstitutet, 2003.
Graham, Fred P. "Court Ban Urged on 'I Am Curious.'" *New York Times*, November 11, 1970.
Gross, Leonard. "After Nudity, What, Indeed?" *Look*, April 29, 1969.
"Grove Press Movie on Trial as Obscene." *New York Times*, May 21, 1968.
Grove Press v. Flask (1970) 326 F. Supp. 586
Gurley, George. "Midtown's Dim View of a Bright Idea." *Kansas City Star*, January 21, 1993.
Heffernan, Kevin. "A Prurient (Dis)Interest: The American Release and Reception of *I Am Curious (Yellow)*." In *Sex Scene: Media and the Sexual Revolution*, edited by Eric Schaefer. Durham, NC: Duke University Press, 2014.
Henriksson, Malin. "Nyfiken-filmerna ges ut på dvd." *Hallands Nyheter*, November 17, 2005.
"High Court Lets Stand Maryland Ban on 'Curious.'" *New York Times*, March 9, 1971.
Hixson, Richard F. *Pornography and the Justices: The Supreme Court and the Intractable Obscenity Problem*. Carbondale: Southern Illinois University Press, 1996.
"'I Am Curious' Found to Be Obscene Film." *New York Times*, May 24, 1968.
I Am Curious (Yellow): The Complete Scenario of the Film by Vilgot Sjöman with over 250 Illustrations. New York: Grove Press, 1968.
"Jag är nyfiken blev en chock för åskådarna." *Göteborgs-Tidningen*, October 10, 1967.
"'Jag är nyfiken' fast i USA-tull." *Expressen*, January 20, 1968.
Joseph P. Lordi v. UA New Jersey Theatres (1969) 108 N.J. 31.
"Justices Agree to Review 'I Am Curious (Yellow).'" *New York Times*, March 24. 1970.
Knutson, Ulrika. "Han skapade svenska synden." *Veckans Affärer*, December 6, 2007. http://www.va.se/magasinet/2007/49/svenska-syndens-fader/.

Lee, John M. "Danes and Swedes Are Moving Toward Greater Sex Freedom." *New York Times*, November 6, 1968.
Levy, Shawn. "Closer, Deeper look at 'Throat.'" *Oregonian*, February 18, 2005.
"'Like Water for Chocolate' Tops Records." *Houston Chronicle*, July 13, 1993.
Liljedahl, Ragnar. "Politik och sexualteknik." *Falu-Kuriren*, November 8, 1967.
Main, Edward John. "The Neglected Prong of the Miller Test for Obscenity: Serious Literary, Artistic and Political Value." In *Southern Illinois University Law Journal* 11, 1986–87: 1159–60.
Martin, Douglas. "Vilgot Sjöman, Filmmaker Without Taboos, Dies at 81." *New York Times*, 11 April 11, 2006.
Morgenstern, Joseph. "Curiouser and Curiouser." *Newsweek*, March 24, 1969.
"New Rules for Obscenity?" *Time*, May 11, 1970.
NGC Theatre Corporation v. John Mummert (1971) 107 Ariz. 489.
"Passaic Court and Theater Chain Agree on Ban of 'I Am Curious.'" *New York Times*, November 26, 1969.
Persall, Steve. "Sarasota Film Fest Needs Patron Saints." *St. Petersburg Times*, July 20, 1993.
Petersén, Bo. "Han som sprängde männens sexvall." *Expressen*, October 10, 1967.
Plyler, Tami. "Theaters again Making Comeback in Derry." *New Hampshire Union Leader*, September 13, 1994.
Polunsky, Bob. "No 'Mystery' Why Film Isn't Here." *San Antonio Express-News*, August 29, 1993.
"Publiken tålde sexfilmen." *Expressen*, October 10, 1967.
Puig, Claudia. "'Tiger' Cuts Through Foreign-film Reluctance." *USA Today*, March, 22, 2001.
Schauer, Fredrik. *The Law of Obscenity*. Washington, D.C.: The Bureau of National Affairs, Inc., 1976.
Schickel, Richard. "It Hides Nothing But the Heart." *Life*, March 21, 1969.
Schildt, Jurgen. "Vilgot Sjöman synar samtiden." *Aftonbladet*, October 10, 1967.
"Sexscenerna alla minns." *Expressen*, December 22, 1992.
"Sjöman på bål hot i USA." *Dagens Nyheter*, 22 January, 1, 1968.
"Sjöman vittnade om Nyfiken-gul i USA-domstol." *Sydsvenska Dagbladet Snällposten*, May 24, 1968.
"Sjöman's nya film blev ingen chock för publiken." *Aftonbladet*, October 10, 1967.
"Sjömans sexfilm fick klartecken." *Expressen*, October 7, 1967.
Sjöquist, Eric. "'Nyfiken-gul' fälld igen: 'Anstötlig och liderlig.'" *Expressen*, May 24, 1968.
———. "Fientlig stämning i salen då Sjöman vittnade." *Expressen*, May 23, 1968.
———. "Nu har Vilgot Sjöman fått hela rätten riktigt nyfiken: Älskar amerikaner på balustrader som Lena Nyman?" *Expressen*, May 23, 1968.
"Sju utländska kritiker om Sjöman & Nyman." *Expressen*, October 10, 1967.
Svenstedt, Carl-Henrik. "Vilgot Sjöman, gul och blå." *Svenska Dagbladet*, October 10, 1967.
Swedberg, Ulla. "Sjömans provokationer & notifikationer." *Göteborgs-Tidningen*, October 12, 1967.
"Swedish Movie Is Seized By Customs for 'Obscenity.'" *New York Times*, January 19, 1968.
"Top Grossers for May." *Variety*, June 11, 1969, 12; "50 Top-Grossing Films" *Variety*, December 3, 1969.
"Trial Transcripts." *Jag är nyfiken—en film i gult/Jag är nyfiken—en film i blått*, DVD Recording (Home Vision Entertainment, 2003).
Tunbäck-Hanson, Monica. "Från attack mot alla våra konventioner." *Göteborgs-Posten*, October 10, 1967.
"Ulf Thorén har sett 'Jag är nyfiken—gul' och ger Vilgot Sjöman en snyting." *Se*, October 8, 1967.
United States of America v. A Motion Picture Entitled "I Am Curious (Yellow)," (1968) 285 F. Supp. 472.
United States of America v. A Motion Picture Entitled "I Am Curious (Yellow)," (1968) 285 F. 2d 200.
Wagonheim v. Maryland Board of Censors (1969) 255 Md. 307.
"Vad censuren grubblar på." *Dagens Nyheter*, October 6, 1967.
Webb Death, Dewey. "The Naked Dessert: Under Every Rock?" *Phoenix New Times*, February 5, 1992.
Wiskari, Werner. "Sweden Is Casual on Pornography." *New York Times*, November 5, 1967.

Many of Your Finer Nudie Films
Saga Film, Swedish National Cinema and Seventies Transnational Erotic Film

KEVIN HEFFERNAN

Introduction

In the 1984 comedy *Splash* (Ron Howard), landlocked mermaid Madison (Darryl Hannah) is captured by scientists and imprisoned in a U.S. government research facility. In an improvised rescue attempt, the sympathetic Dr. Walter Kornbluth (Eugene Levy) attempts to convince the Army guards that Madison's human boyfriend Allen (Tom Hanks) and his brother Freddie (John Candy) are two long-awaited ichthyologists from the Stockholm Institute. When a suspicious and unexpectedly bilingual guard begins to pepper them with questions in Swedish, a desperate Freddie blurts out, "*Hej raring. Jag har en tolvtum ... tumspenis*" ("Hey, babe. I have a twelve inch ... inch penis").[1] The guard bursts out laughing and lets them into the lab. When they get past the checkpoint, Allen asks Freddie how he was able to speak Swedish to the guard. Freddie replies, "Well, lemme tell ya something. Many of your finer nudie films come from Sweden. Well, after you see 'em four or five hundred times, this stuff starts to sink in."

This joke from a 1980s Hollywood film condenses many contradictory American impressions of a Swedish national cinema. First, Freddie mouths the widespread contemporary opinion that most Swedish films screened in America were at that time, or had been for a decade or so, endlessly re-released sex films whose audience is composed of lonely, unattached men. Second, erotic films from Sweden were seen as having higher production values and more tasteful content than American hardcore grindhouse fare (note the use of "finer nudie films" instead of "better porno movies"). Finally, the dialog expresses the anachronistic and contradictory notion that these films have been screened in Swedish with English subtitles or even screened without subtitles to the blithe unconcern of the raincoat crowd.

As Eric Schaefer has shown, from the late sixties to the dawn of the home video era, Sweden, along with its neighbor Denmark, played a huge role in the international erotic imagination.[2] After the establishment of a domestic hardcore erotic cinema in the U.S., however, sex films from Sweden and other European countries often played the same role in American exhibitors' schedule as their cousins in the horror genre, namely as second features on double bills. This did not keep Swedish and American investors and filmmakers from proffering a modified, transnational iteration of "Swedish sin" to worldwide porn moviegoers in which international casts and locations, the use of journeyman filmmakers, and narrative and stylistic motifs still coalesced into a recognizable Swedish erotic national cinema. One Swedish production firm, Sture Sjöstedt's Saga Film, came to specialize in international co-productions and often deployed American talent, both behind and in front of the camera, to offer a variation of "your finer nudie films [...] from Sweden" to a world audience. I will trace out the relationship between a contested and ambivalent "Swedish" erotic cinema and the role of international finance and distribution in two of American director Joe Sarno's projects for Saga Film, *Butterflies/Butterfly* (1975) and *Fäbodjäntan/Come and Blow the Horn* (1978), and I will conclude with a brief sketch of some of the factors which led to the decline of this branding of a specifically Swedish approach to the sex film.

Film Style and the Marketing of a Swedish National Identity

In addition to Schaefer's essay, "I'll Take Sweden," and some of the works in this volume, several works of recent English-language scholarship have attempted to chart the role of eroticism in the international reception of a broadly-defined Swedish national cinema. Tino Balio's *Foreign Film Renaissance on American Screens* traces the reception of Ingmar Bergman's 1950s films against the background of the post-war art theater, changes in film journalism, and America's growing fascination with existential philosophy. The stark, minimalist aesthetic of Bergman's films and their often brutal, high-voltage dramatic situations rooted in sexual anxiety seemed to cement in many Americans' minds a brooding, pessimistic Swedish national character.[3] A similar tension between enlightenment and titillation in Sweden's own efforts to use the cinema for comprehensive sex education is meticulously detailed in Elisabet Björklund's *The Most Delicate Subject*,[4] and Jack Stevenson's *Scandinavian Blue* attempts a synoptic account of post-war commercial erotic Danish and Swedish cinema in their native cultural, industrial, and artistic contexts and provides along the way some amusing sideswipes at provincial America's bewilderment when confronted by these movies.[5]

Each of these works proceeds from a set of assumptions about the nature of a national cinema. First, this national cinema somehow exists in the context of overarching cultural concerns unique to the country which produces it, and those concerns can, to a greater or lesser degree, be comprehended by other nations to whom the movies are distributed and shown. Second, film style, mood, and tone can evoke these cultural concerns and allow for a highly mediated but empathetic response to them, especially in outstanding examples, such as the films of Ingmar Bergman. Finally, each commercial national cinema draws upon indigenous and sometimes self-referential aesthetic conventions, stock characters, plots, performers, and popular genres which are often invisible and unknown to popular overseas audiences but which constitute crucial information for seeing these films through the eyes of their contemporary domestic audience.

Mariah Larsson, in her 2010 essay "Practice Makes Perfect?" adds a much-needed nuance to any informed view of a Swedish erotic national cinema in her account of the crucial role international finance and co-productions played in the Swedish sex film of the 1970s. Notions of authenticity become problematized when we realize that "these films seem to eradicate national differences while simultaneously playing on national stereotypes."[6] She singles out the contribution of American director Joe Sarno to both that studio's output and to that of a number of other companies in Sweden between 1968 and 1978.[7] In fact, I would argue that the American Joe Sarno did as much to develop the conventions and motifs of Swedish sex films as did native sons Torgny Wickman and Mac Ahlberg by deftly using the "national stereotypes" of film style and tone as seen in the art cinema of Bergman and other auteurs. Between *Jag, en oskuld/Inga* (1968) and *Come and Blow the Horn,* Sarno's Swedish sex films, many of which were produced and/or financed by Saga Film with an eye toward the international market, sustained and refined a set of stylistic, thematic, and narrative tropes which provided a template followed by native erotic film directors and identified many of his movies as "Swedish" and "finer nudie films" even when they featured American actors or were filmed in other European countries.

There are several reasons why Joe Sarno was the ideal emissary to bridge the gap between the American and Swedish sex film markets. First, his American films seem to have been successful at the Swedish box office (see below). Second, Sarno's films were blocked, acted and shot in a self-consciously (some critics said pretentiously) European style, often using Bergman's own favorite composition, the two-shot West, seen below in a scene from *Inga*.

This aesthetic trope served several functions. First, aping the style of a recognized European auteur was a possible hedge against obscenity prosecution in America during a time in which films were subject to such sanctions if they did not possess "redeeming social, artistic, or educational value." Second, many sexploitation movies and imported

Bergman-like compositions in *Inga* (Joe Sarno, 1968). Monika Strömmerstedt and Frida Dagheim. Frame grab.

art films could receive profitable bookings at American drive-in theaters during a time in which these categories were diffuse and permeable; thus, Sarno's films could be booked in a greater number of situations if they looked like both art films and sexploitation. Finally, shooting a scene in this way was a dramatically effective way of executing pages of dialog without repeated camera setups, a fact that could not have been lost on auteur Bergman, who brought the technique from the stage to the film studio, where his budgets were consistent but modest.

Two of the earliest Swedish box-office smashes in the sixties new wave of erotic cinema were Mac Ahlberg's *Jag—en kvinna/I, a Woman* from 1965 (U.S. release, 1966) and Sarno's *Inga* from 1968. *I, a Woman* treats the urban space of Stockholm as a character in its own right, a deeply ambivalent zone of consumerist and sexual utopia on one hand and a possible site of alienation and predation on the other. This location had great significance for both domestic and international audiences: The peeling away of Sweden's film censorship over the decade of the 1960s coincided with rapid economic growth which brought unprecedented numbers of women into the work force and occurred near the end of a massive century-long migration of population from rural areas to major metropolitan centers or *storstadsområden* such as Stockholm. Between 1900 and 1960, the national population living in urban areas had grown from around one third to 85 per cent of the entire population.[8] The urban population had grown so fast in the postwar period that in 1965, the Social Democratic government began the seven year-long *Miljonprogrammet*, or Million Dwellings Program, a plan to fund the construction of a million new urban apartments which would be paid off by owners and dwellers over a thirty year period.[9] Sweden's adoption of a comprehensive model of sex education and the widespread availability of contraception, were partly a response to the massive overcrowding and housing shortages in the *storstadsområden* and the need to bring more women into the work force in a time of labor shortage.[10]

A tectonic shift in population patterns and its resulting cultural dislocation,[11] a rapidly changing urban environment,[12] a youthful population coming of age after being raised with a liberal, permissive attitude about sex and gender roles,[13] and a seismic change in the economic and social role of women[14] all provided not just the social anxieties necessary for a sensationalized exploitation cinema focused on youthful sex but its dramatic structure, dominant iconography, and themes as well. We can see all of these elements in inchoate form in *Inga*. While Americans imagined Sweden as a modern, enlightened, sexually permissive urban space, domestic audiences were more likely to see in parts of *Inga* the deeply ambivalent contrast between the urban consumerism of Stockholm and a nostalgic view of the slower, pastoral realm of the country. This theme, established in mainstream Swedish cinema as early as Arne Mattsson's *Hon dansade en sommar/One Summer of Happiness* (1951), was to become one of the strongest markers of national identity in Swedish film eroticism, as I will discuss below.

Inga, a co-production between Swedish studio Omega Film AB and the American independent Cannon, was released in the U.S. in 1968 and was the breakout role for Swedish sex starlet Marie Liljedahl, who was the next in line of a series of Nordic softcore actresses who would achieve marquee status over the next few years and which had begun with Essy Persson in *I, a Woman*. The film tells the story of the title character, a sixteen year-old virgin who comes to the country to live with Greta, her aunt who is an obsessive consumer of high fashion (she wears a different ultramodern ensemble in every scene) and who is supporting Karl, a young writer who is beginning to chafe at her financial and sexual manipulation of him. Greta is rapidly spending all of her late husband's money on Karl and expensive consumer goods, so she puts in motion a plan to groom Inga as a mistress for Einar, the lecherous scion of a monied family, in exchange for a stipend from Einar's family. Over the course of the film, the outsider Inga begins to destabilize all of the relations around her as she and Karl become aware of an intense mutual attraction and her desires become more urgent, which the film dramatizes in two discreetly staged masturbation sequences[15] which Sarno later told film historian Mike Vraney were unsimulated with only camera operator Sarno and actress Liljedahl present on set.[16] The visual style of the film alternates between rigorously staged Bergmanesque interior tableaux shot in very long takes which create an atmosphere of physical and emotional claustrophobia and highly lyrical exterior passages set in the country landscape and at a seaside dock where a sailboat promised to Karl by Greta comes to symbolize to him both her control of him and his means of escape.

In the late 1960s, several Swedish feminists and sociologists expressed grave concern that the supposed move to reciprocity and equality between men and women as the result of women's greater presence in the urban workplace and as consumers was having the unintended but highly predictable effect of urging women to use their economic power to become dedicated consumers of beauty and fashion products that would turn them into objects of consumption for men.[17] This is one of the major themes of *Inga*, even though Stockholm is seen only once and spoken of a few times in the film. In adjacent scenes, Greta buys Karl the sailboat to keep him beholden to her, and then she takes Inga on a shopping trip to Stockholm as part of a grooming process to turn Inga into both a consumer of fashion and an object of consumption for Einar. The shopping montage is scored with a sprightly musical theme and was of a piece with similar montages in Swedish sex films of this period. However, Sarno later complained that the "marching band music" (as he called it) the producers laid under the movie compromised much of the allusiveness and ambiguity he had worked hard to give the film in its cinematography and performances.[18] Stockholm is also present off-screen when, on a later afternoon, Greta introduces Inga to Mildred and Ingrid, two young women who she knows serve up virgins to their vulturine friend Gunnar for defloration. She sends Inga off on an afternoon bike ride with the two after telling her that the decadent louche Einar cannot see her because he is spending the day in Stockholm. The film ends with both Inga and Karl rejecting their respective roles as objects of consumption and consummating their authentic desire for each other in another scene of discreetly filmed but, according to Sarno, unsimulated sex which ends with Inga's (and, presumably, Marie Liljedahl's) onscreen orgasm. The two then flee the community in the sailboat, leaving Greta alone at the film's conclusion.

These themes and motifs became the coin of the realm in many of the Swedish softcore films designed for international audiences over the next several years. Two films showcasing Marie Liljedahl's Swedish nymphet heartthrob successor, Christina Lindberg, repeat and vary the formula. *Maid in Sweden* from 1971, produced and released by *Inga's* financier Cannon, is a virtual remake of the earlier film, in which Lindberg plays a young woman from the provinces, named Inga, who comes to Stockholm to visit her sister Greta and is pursued by both her sister's lothario boyfriend Casten and by Björn, a moody young artist. Many of the sex scenes are structured around the Sarno-esque moment of a woman standing in a doorway watching another couple *in flagrante delicto* and experiencing arousal and/or an enraged sense of betrayal. The movie's location shooting, thematic contrast between Stockholm and the northern provinces, shopping montages, emphasis on pot smoking and the counterculture, and soundtrack compromised by a voice double for Lindberg, show how some of these elements had by then coalesced into a recognizable form.

Anita (1973), directed by Sweden's then-reigning erotic auteur, Torgny Wickman, tells the story of a teenager from the inland town of Katrineholm who runs away to Stockholm after she has been humiliated and shunned for her uncontrollable sexual acting out. There, she cruises bus stations, construction sites, and storefront shops for compulsive, anonymous sex in a *Miljonprogrammet*-era hellscape of contractor demolition, cavernous foundation digs, and brutalist municipal high-rise buildings widely despised by many Stockholm residents at the time of *Anita*'s principal cinematography.[19]

After a particularly demeaning interlude, she meets Erik, a young psychology student who takes her to a student house occupied by artists, musicians, and writers located in a quiet, verdant area on the south shore of the Saltsjön Bay. There, in a third space removed from both the provincial Katrineholm where Anita's military father holds court, and the alienated, anonymous space of Sergels torg in central Stockholm,[20] Erik, who is both a new incarnation of the sensitive lover Karl from *Inga* and a mouthpiece for the compassionate, therapeutic discourse of healthy sex expressed by clinicians Inge and Sten Hegeler found in Wickman's earlier sex education features, *Ur kärlekens språk/Language of Love* (1969) and *Mera ur kärlekens språk/More About the Language of Love* (1970), engages her in a long, talking cure. Eventually, the two end up as a conventional monogamous couple, canoodling in a 19th century church at the film's end.

Anita was a co-production between Swedish Filmproduction and Alpha France. The French company stipulated that hard-core inserts using a body double for Lindberg be filmed for all of the movie's sex scenes so the movie could be booked in their chain of

Anita cruises constructions sites. Christina Lindberg and Arne Ragneborn in *Anita* (Torgny Wickman, 1973). Courtesy Klubb Super 8.

hardcore theaters in France. This circulation of transnational Swedish sex films in multiple versions with different levels of explicitness would come to characterize the second wave of Swedish porn in the mid-seventies. In 1975, independent U.S. distributor Lee Hessel's Cambist Films released the hardcore version into American theaters under the title *Anita, Swedish Nymphette*. Wickman's film is both a commercial domestic film tempering its often morbid erotic spectacle through an engagement[21] with social anxieties about the changing space of Stockholm, the role therein of displaced women from the provinces, and juvenile delinquency,[22] and a profitable export pandering to curious audiences deeply conflicted about Swedish female "emancipation."

In her essay on the financing and production of the Swedish sex film of the 1970s, Larsson describes Sture Sjöstedt's Saga Film as "the most transnational of the Swedish porn production companies" in its use of international talent on both sides of the camera and its ambitious and successful program of international co-production.[23] In fact, if we expand the definition of a national cinema to encompass production financing and distribution advances, Saga Film emerges as the most ambitious, prolific, and longest-running erotic filmmaking concern in Scandinavia. In 1951, Sjöstedt opened the Hollywood Theater in Stockholm as a specialty house programming documentary films and cartoons. By the end of the decade, television had colonized this programming niche, and the company's growing circuit of theaters began to specialize in screening American, French, and German nudie films during that cycle's popularity in 1959–63, and this lucrative programming strategy continued as black-and-white American sexploitation films proliferated in the middle of the decade and Sjöstedt formed Saga Film to book his imports into other theaters. According to Per Sjöstedt, Joe Sarno's early New York–based erotic dramas such as *Sin in the Suburbs* (1964), *The Bed, and How to Make It* (1966), and *Anything for Money* (1967), had been among the most successful imports Sture Sjöstedt had booked into his flagship Hollywood Theater and into other movie houses through the company's distribution subsidiary.

In 1969, the Sjöstedt family moved to Rome, and Sture offered several Italian producers distribution advances to secure Scandinavian rights to many mainstream films, including the *Trinity* western films, netting the company millions of dollars in revenue. Meanwhile, *Deep Throat* (Gerard Damiano, 1972) played for three years at the Hollywood Theater. Although Saga kept its mainstream distribution and adult exhibition divisions separate, money from the Italian films was invested in porn co-productions with Monarex and other German and American companies, including the three Joe Sarno films shot in Germany with Marie Forså in 1973 and 1974 (see below).

In 1977, Sture's son Göran started Hemvideo, the first adult video company in Sweden, and in spite of Sture's initial skepticism, Hemvideo's releases of Saga's adult titles became the most lucrative activity of their adult division. By the late seventies, Saga Film was investing heavily in American adult films both to provide a stream of product to Hemvideo and as a tax shelter against Sweden's very high marginal corporate income tax rate.[24] Saga invested in New York adult film producer and director Chuck Vincent on some of his most successful and inventive films, including director Larry Revene's *Sizzle* (1979) and *Fascination* (1980) and Vincent's own *Games Women Play* (1980) and *Roommates* (1981). Acting as liaison with Saga Film, Sture's son Per partnered with Vincent and Revene in the company Lunarex, which produced some of the most ambitious hardcore films of the period, many of which featured international locations, beginning in 1980 with *Bon Appétit* and *That Lucky Stiff*. The connection between Vincent, Revene, and Saga produced films with high production values, major stars, and scripts and performances consonant with more conventional low-budget features, all of which made softcore versions perennial favorites on late-night cable television.[25] Lunarex and Saga Film were still financing innovative adult entertainment after home video had rendered the original theater circuit obsolete: The company produced the first block of performer-turned-director Candida Royalle's groundbreaking *Femme* series of porn videos for women and couples, including *Christine's Secret*, *Urban Heat* (both 1984), *Three Daughters* (1986), and *Rites of Passion* (1987).[26] Although Swedish sin was no longer a hot topic, Swedish money from Saga Film continued to finance what could be called aspirational adult films possessing many of the characteristics of style, humor, and sophistication that were once crucial aspects of the Swedish sex film brand.

The Star System, Genre and Authorship: Butterflies *and* Come and Blow the Horn *as Swedish Erotic Cinema*

During hardcore cinema's second wave of popularity in late 1970s, French stars such as Brigitte Lahaie and Marilyn Jess, American stars such as Vanessa Del Rio, Annette Haven, and Leslie Bovee, and Danish porn power couple Bent and Bie Warburg were crucial to the financing and successful international distribution of theatrical porn films. However, the star system in the pornographic film industry is the site of multiple and contradictory discourses of the adult industry's own industrial organization and division of labor, the aesthetic unity of films in the porn genre, and the broader culture's ambivalent fascination with celebrity. In America, a high-output adult film industry whose diffuse distribution and exhibition activities were separate from the larger film industry made the investment in stars, which would require high salaries and labor devoted to promotion and publicity, a high-risk endeavor with little promise of return. For the early part of the 1970s, the most well-known American performers in the X business, sold on their anatomical assets or specialized sexual skills, were less in the mold of their contemporaries in post-studio Hollywood than in the tradition of notorious and/or novelty performers in the classical exploitation film of the 1930s through the 1950s.

In Scandinavia, Denmark's "animal lover," the zoophile Bodil Joensen, who appeared in many loops and features with the beloved animals from her farm, was a film celebrity in this mold. However, in Denmark and Sweden, hardcore cinema was often integrated into a larger mainstream entertainment business. This enabled films such as Denmark's *Bedside* and *Zodiac* film series to make use of known faces and names from film and television in order to secure their successful booking into mainstream theaters and, later, on television, even if the conventional thespians did not take part in the explicit sex.[27] European audiences accepted the often obvious hardcore inserts added to sex scenes starring professional actors, particularly male leads, as an acceptable trade-off for the films' ability to maintain character portrayal and achieve a unified tone in the transitions between narrative-driven scenes and their relatively brief scenes of explicit sex.

Given the fierce and unremitting physical demands placed on pre–Viagra male porn performers, their ranks were relatively small. It is therefore surprising that three of the most prolific American porn performers of the 1970s and 1980s, Harry Reems *né* Herbert Streicher, Rob Everett *aka* Eric Edwards, and Jamie Gillis, were also ambitious actors with multiple credits in Off Broadway stage productions. Reems' periodic sojourns to

Sweden in 1974 through 1976, however, had less to do with his acting skills than with the notoriety he had unwillingly achieved as the defendant in a federal obscenity trial prosecuted by the U.S. Department of Justice in the conservative venue of Memphis, Tennessee. Soon after the release of *Deep Throat*, Reems was charged with conspiracy to commit interstate transport of obscene materials along with the film's financial backers from the Colombo crime syndicate. This was an ambitious effort by prosecutors to make an example of Reems/Streicher and send a message to so-called above-the-line creative personnel in porn that they could be dragged into court and prosecuted for obscenity along with financers, distributors, and exhibitors. While on trial and later after conviction but awaiting appeal, Reems took his case to the public through TV interviews, a lecture tour, and the support of Hollywood celebrities such as Warren Beatty, Jack Nicholson, and Louise Fletcher. After the incoming Presidential administration of Jimmy Carter departed from his Republican predecessor's zeal in using pornography as red meat for conservative voters, his conviction was overturned in 1977, a new trial was ordered, and the charges were eventually dropped. This was the signal that the industry had been awaiting, and for this and a number of other reasons, the American porn industry flourished for the rest of the decade with high-budget feature films, a new commitment to a more conventional star system, and a growing crossover to a more diverse audience of straight couples.[28]

The broadly-defined Swedish porn films in which Reems starred during this period, *Butterflies*, *Justine och Juliette/Swedish Minx* (1975), and *Bel Ami* (1976) were all released in the U.S. in 1977 by American distributors seeking to capitalize on the publicity surrounding Reems' legal exoneration. In fact, Leisure Time Booking's 1977 American one-sheet for *Butterflies* re-imagined the female characters alluded to in the film's title not as fragile beings held captive by the selfish and manipulative Frank, the character played by Reems (more on this below), but as winged female *amoretti* lifting the mustachioed actor to safety from his Memphis captors in an image that could well be titled "The Apotheosis of Harry Reems."

Thus, hard-working Off Broadway actor Herb Streicher—who reluctantly, even accidentally, became the first American male porn celebrity under a gag name devised by *Deep Throat*'s director—saw his "name" above the title in three very well-made and widely released European films in 1977, but his "stardom" and pay scale were commensurate with those of novelty performers famous for scandal or notoriety rather than those of mainstream contemporary movie stars in Europe or the U.S.

Reems' female co-star in all three of his European films, Swedish Marie Forså, made her starring debut in 1973 in Sarno's three features filmed in Germany and produced by Saga Film, German company Monarex, and Swedish distributor Gebe Film, *Der Fluch der schwarzen Schwestern/The Devil's Plaything* (1973), *Vild på sex/Bibi* (1974), and *Butterflies*. In addition, she played the lead role in Mac Ahlberg's *Flossie* (1974). Much of the running times of these films displayed her restrained but effective acting skills, fluency in several languages, and very attractive and minimally made-up freckled face and body.

This occurred just as the European box-office success of the Danish *Zodiac* films, which began in that year with *I jomfruens tegn/Danish Pastries* ushered in the period of maximum instability between porn and mainstream film industry stardom. Forså attempted to negotiate the delicate process of establishing herself as a star in films with hardcore content, agreeing to engage in onscreen sex, but refusing to allow explicit views of the action into a film's final print. In addition, for films sold primarily on their hard-

The apotheosis of Harry Reems. Poster for *Butterflies* (Joe Sarno, 1974).

core content, she was billed as "Maria Lynn." These stipulations were designed to facilitate an ultimately unsuccessful attempt to cross what seemed to be a narrowing strait between the porn and mainstream film industries. By the time the films released as *Butterflies*, *Swedish Minx*, and *Bel Ami* appeared in the U.S., Forså was playing a supporting role to her male American co-stars in the films' promotion. In the U.S., Forså never became a marquee name in either porn or drive-in sexploitation bookings where her films were screened in softcore versions, both because she declined to be explicitly filmed engaging in sex and because her successful porn films could never be connected with her roles in softcore films. In other words, her American star persona fell victim to the Swedish sex film's more open and ambiguous discourses of film stardom.

Butterflies made extensive use of both the Bavarian forest and the ultramodern apartments and nightclubs of Munich. Although it was shot in English by an American director and featured American adult film actors as male leads, it is both one of the definitive Swedish erotic films and a testament to the heartiness and versatility of the distinguishing features of the Swedish sex film formula. In *Butterflies*, Denise (Marie Forså) grows stifled by both the parochial farm community in which she has grown up and her relationship with the gentle but unadventurous student Freddy (Eric Edwards, billed under his given name, Rob Everett). She fills her farmhouse bedroom with fashion magazines and strikes modeling poses in the mirror, dreaming of escape. One morning, she leaves the farm and hitchhikes to Munich. After a comic interlude featuring a sweaty, jowly, walrus-like middle-aged lingerie salesman, she meets wealthy night-club owner Frank (Harry Reems), who takes her to his apartment in Munich and ensconces her in the bedroom, even as his live-in girlfriend Marina seethes in resentment and drinks brandy in the living room before he kicks her out. Ruth, Frank's club manager, takes Denise shopping for clothes and keeps her busy while the sociopathic lothario continues his conquests at the apartment and the nightclub. As Frank grooms Natasha, her replacement, Denise grows more angry and despondent. Eventually, she confronts him in the club and later strips naked in front of him in the apartment, rejecting her once longed-for status as objectified commodity, throwing all of the clothes Ruth has brought her into a pile and putting on her dress from the beginning of the film. The ambiguous last shot of the film shows her hitchhiking on the side of the road, perhaps to a new city, perhaps home to Freddy and her aunt's farm.

Many of the themes and stylistic tropes that had come to characterize Swedish erotic cinema are present in *Butterflies*: The journey from country to city (here Munich stands in for Stockholm) and back again, the urban space as consumer utopia and site of women as objects to be consumed (like most Swedish porn, *Butterflies* contains nightclub dancing scenes that border on the baroque), the sensitive male lover and his doppelganger, the narcissistic lecher. Like the protagonists of *I, a Woman*, *Inga*, *Maid in Sweden*, and *Anita*, Denise in *Butterflies* ultimately rejects the role into which men have attempted to cast her.

The early, bucolic scenes of *Butterflies* show Denise and Freddy running and making love on the rolling hills of grass, in the pine forest, and near a river, and the scenes are shot with a telephoto lens which provides a shallow depth of field with flowers and grass in the foreground, lending a diffused blur to the image.

This represents a newer version of Swedish lyrical eroticism, or perhaps a new set of national stereotypes, which Sarno had adapted from *Elvira Madigan*, Bo Widerberg's 1967 film based on a 19th century incident of a female tightrope walker and an Army colonel who fall in love and run away together, fleeing their responsibilities and hiding in the countryside before ultimately killing each other in a murder-suicide pact. Widerberg's film became famous for the almost delirious pictorialism of its outdoor sequences shot with telephoto lenses in dappled afternoon sunlight as the two lovers play out their brief life together. *Elvira Madigan*'s final image is a freeze-frame of Hedvig, the female protagonist, letting a butterfly in her hands go free at the moment her lover Sixten shoots her to death, providing Sarno's later film with a title as well as a thematic and stylistic template. The butterfly Denise in Sarno's movie is probably Forså's best role and most engaging performance, but the permeability of porn and mainstream stardom she had hoped to exploit would prove to be temporary. In both the U.S. and Europe, *Butterflies* was released in hardcore and softcore versions, but even in the soft version, Forså's unsimulated sex with both Everett and Reems is visible for a few frames.

If *Butterflies* problematizes the categories of both a Swedish national erotic cinema and a hardcore porn film, *Come and Blow the Horn* is a straightforward attempt to make an unapologetically explicit film in Swedish using a Swedish cast and location and telling a story using a specifically Swedish set of cultural references. The idea for the film came to Göran and Sture Sjöstedt after Hemvideo customers wanted to hear the breathless sex talk of porn scenes in their native language.[29] *Come and Blow the Horn* was written and directed by Joe Sarno under the pseudonym "Lawrence Henning" and is set during the midsommar, or summer solstice, celebration on a farm in the Lake Siljan and Dal River areas of Dalarna in central Sweden. As is common during summers in Dalarna, farm owner Maude has opened her home to visitors, a couple, Björn and Agneta, who have just returned from missionary work in Africa. Maud's daughter Britt and her boyfriend

An homage to Bo Widerberg. Marie Forså and Eric Edwards (as Rob Everett). Frame grab from *Butterflies* (Joe Sarno, 1974).

Karl are also staying at the farm for the celebration, and Olle, the farmhand, is taking care of the animals. The outsider to the group, an eccentric young woman from the area, named Monika, claims to be an orphaned Laplander and the reincarnation of a village priestess who led Viking-era pagan fertility rituals, the actual historical antecedent to the modern midsommar celebration.[30] Monika has found an old, rusty horn, which she claims was used by the village priestess to summon the women to sexual arousal when she saw a ship on the horizon bringing the men home from sea voyages. For much of the film, Monika's prankish blowing of the horn in the fields and on the hillsides causes the women of the group to become so sexually aroused that they immediately initiate sex with the nearest man, creating both abandon and torment for the repressed Björn. On the actual midsummer's night, though, the matriarch Maude presses a horn on the wall of her farmhouse into service and blows it during the perpetual midnight sun, first leading the three other women to have sex together in Britt's room and finally to reconstitute the two heterosexual couples and form a polyamorous triad between herself, Monika, and Olle at film's end while the folk melody "Polska från Äppelbo" plays on the soundtrack.[31]

From one perspective, *Come and Blow the Horn* continues many of the pastoral motifs of the Swedish countryside seen in *Inga*, *Elvira Madigan*, *Anita*, and *Butterflies*. In this, the film is partaking of a widespread Swedish view (alien to many Americans) that the countryside and its people are a lusty, passionate lot with no patience for the repressed conservatism of the bourgeoisie in cities and towns. Sociologist Sondra Herman writes:

> Scandinavian ruralism has prevented prudery from taking hold. Casual about nudity in the bath or at the beach, accepting sexuality much as they accept and appreciate physical culture, the Scandinavians like to remind visitors that "nature is our real religion." With a deep, almost mystical reverence for the woods, the high grass fields, and the shrouded lakes, the Swedes create an atmosphere about their lives that makes sexual double standards and old-fashioned morality quite ridiculous.[32]

The horn in *Come and Blow the Horn* is, of course, the classic pornographic trope of the magic talisman which initiates sexual activity and moves the narrative forward, but the highly literate Sarno sets this motif alongside an intricate network of musical and floral symbolism. An instrumental rendition of the song "Midsommarblomster" plays under the opening credits, and Swedish filmgoers are invited to recall the song's lyrics about young people placing seven kinds of flowers under their pillow on the night of the solstice in the hope of dreaming of their true love. Also, the purple geranium flower of the song's title is increasingly associated with the character of Maude near the end of the film as she begins to realize that she herself is the reincarnation of the priestess in charge of the midsummer rituals.

On the other hand, the film is a hilarious send-up of the very idea of a culturally "authentic" Swedish national pornographic cinema, a parody of what a manifesto calling for just such a cinema would look like. The middle section of the film, in which the monogamous heterosexual couples are fragmented and reassembled with Maude and Olle into an expedient series of groups and couplings, is scored with festive traditional arrangements of songs for the indigenous Dalarna folk dance of the *hambo* in three-quarter time. This creates a highly incongruous comic tone, even though Monika has already recited pages of dialog linking modern celebratory Dalarna traditions with more primal origins. But most spectacular is *Come and Blow the Horn*'s skewering (literally) of the tradition of the maypole. After Monika has provided the summer guests (and the viewer) with the information that the maypole had its origins in phallic ceremonial stones used in ritual sex by the village priestesses, the film's midpoint presents a scene which has given *Come and Blow the Horn* cult status for years on home video. Since the woman blowing the horn cannot feel its effects, Britt blows the horn so Monika can masturbate while she feels its power. Maude, left alone in her kitchen, becomes overwhelmed with desire and re-enacts the phallic maypole ritual with an enormous pork and veal *falukorv* sausage, a piece of Scandinavian charcuterie that is over a meter long and over ten centimeters in diameter. Here, the filmmakers are having tremendous fun translating some of the generic tropes of the porn genre into cultural traditions "relevant" to Swedes. This, of course, has the effect of drawing attention to the fact that the overwhelming majority of Swedish erotic films are transnational in character and that if national borders on them were closed, only national stereotypes would remain.[33]

Conclusion

The Swedish sex films of the hardcore era exhibit contradictory, hybrid discourses of national identity, genre, and the star system. Through films produced in Sweden as well as investment in international production and distribution to both theatrical and ancillary markets, the Swedish film industry was vitally engaged with important changes in transnational adult cinema. As Larsson notes, American directors such as Sarno, Charles Kaufman, and the highly underrated Paul D. Gerber *aka* David Reberg played a major role in many films which became exemplars of "Swedish" sexploitation and porn.[34] Sarno's female-centered erotic outsider narrative which made its Scandinavian debut in *Inga* was repeated and varied by transnational Swedish sex films with financing and locations from countries such as West Germany and the U.S., and films such as Sarno's *Kärlekson/Love's Island*, *Come and Blow the Horn*, and Wickman's *Ta mej i dalen/ Practice Makes Perfect* which self-consciously deployed supposedly culturally specific "Swedish" elements for the domestic audience, frequently did so in a mode of parody or burlesque.

In 1975, the sell-by date of "Swedish sin" had passed, and Swedish features were typically used by adult exhibitors in the U.S. as program filler in a fallow period during which the production branch of the American porn industry waited for the outcome of legal challenges to its activities. In lieu of promoting the appeal of highly charismatic female performers such as Marie Forså, Bie Warburg, or Christa Linda, American financiers and distributors sent New York-based porn talent to Europe to provide stateside appeal for films made in Sweden. By this time, the international success of *Emmanuelle* (Just Jaeckin, 1974) had provided a new model for upscale erotic feature film entertainment (what Andrews calls "aspirational soft-core" cinema),[35] and a number of Swedish sex movies, such as Mac Ahlberg's *Flossie* and Gerber's *I lust och nöd/Liz* (1976), were modeled on, and in the latter case promoted as successors to, the Sylvia Kristel blockbuster. But during this period and well into the 1980s, Sture Sjöstedt and Saga Film were important participants in "your finer nudie films" produced in the U.S. by skilled auteurs such as Chuck Vincent, Larry Revene, and Candida Royalle. These filmmakers continued the broadly-defined "Swedish" trend of sex films and videos with high production values which could be profitably sold initially to drive-in theaters and eventually in the mid–1980s to cable TV and video markets in softcore versions. By this time, Saga Film was awash in money from domestic video releases of the Scandinavian and American porn they had financed and mainstream European features to which they had retained home video rights in Sweden, and the American porn theater was poised on the brink of two year-long videotape-led extinction. At this point, a loyal American fan of Swedish erotic cinema could be flawlessly played by John Candy as a backwards-looking, lonely, single, good-hearted oaf, and most of America would get the joke.[36]

NOTES

1. Many thanks to Mariah Larsson for providing me with the Swedish dialog from this scene, which in American release prints is translated in a subtitle.
2. Eric Schaefer, "'I'll Take Sweden': The Shifting Discourse of the 'Sexy Nation' in Sexploitation Films" in Eric Schaefer, ed. *Sex Scene: Media and the Sexual Revolution* (Durham and London: Duke University Press, 2014), 207–233.
3. Tino Balio, *The Foreign Film Renaissance on American Screens, 1946–1973* (Madison, Wisconsin: University of Wisconsin Press, 2010), 130–144.
4. Elisabet Björklund, *The Most Delicate Subject: A History of Sex Education Films in Sweden* (PhD diss., Lund University, 2012).
5. Jack Stevenson, *Scandinavian Blue: The Erotic Cinema of Sweden and Denmark in the 1960s and 1970s* (Jefferson, North Carolina: McFarland and Company, 2010).
6. Mariah Larsson, "Practice Makes Perfect? The Production of the Swedish Sex Film in the 1970s" *Film International*, 8:6 (2010), 43.
7. Larsson, "Practice Makes Perfect," 45.
8. Torvald Gerger, "Investigations into Migrations of Manpower" *Human Geography*, 50:1 (1968), 27.
9. See Thordis Arrhenius, "Preservation and Protest: Counterculture and Heritage in 1970s Sweden" *Future Anterior: Journal of Historic Preservation, History, Theory, and Criticism*, 7:2 (Winter 2010), 108–110.
10. See Maurice Wilkinson, "An Econometric Analysis of Fertility in Sweden, 1870–1965" *Econometrica*, 41: 4 (July 1973), Nathanael T. Lauster, "A Room of One's Own or Room Enough for Two? Access to Housing and New Household Formation in Sweden, 1968–1992" *Population Research and Policy Review*, 25:4 (Aug., 2006), 329–351.
11. The recruitment of unskilled, generally politically conservative rural workers into the urban workforce created significant disruption in both labor organization and consensus-building efforts of the Social Democratic Party. See Ulf Himmelstrand and Jan Lindhagen, "The Rejected Status-Seeker in Mass Politics: Fact and Fiction: Status-Rejection, Ideological Conviction, and Some Other Hypotheses about Social-Democratic Loyalty in Sweden" *Acta Sociologica*, 13:4 (1970): 213–236, 214–217.
12. See Arrhenius, "Preservation and Protest," 113–123.
13. The deep ambivalence and outright resentment with which some responded to this state of affairs is discussed in Elina Haavio-Manilla, "Convergences Between East and West: Tradition and Modernity in Sex Roles in Sweden, Finland, and the Soviet Union" *Acta Sociologica*, 13:1–2 (1971): 114–125, 120.
14. Analyses of the responses to the increasing economic independence of women in Sweden and the changing family structures which followed can be found in Joachim Israel and Rosmari Eliasson, "Consumption Society, Sex Roles, and Sexual Behavior" *Acta Sociologica*, 14:1–2 (1971): 68–82, 70–71 [Social psychologist Israel was one of the panel of clinical experts featured in Wickman's *Kärlekens XYZ/XYZ of Love* (1971)], Sondra R. Herman, "Sex Roles and Sexual Attitudes in Sweden—A New Phase" *The Massachussetts Review*, 13:1–2 (Winter-Spring 1972), 59–62, and Ursula Henz and Jan O. Jonsson, "Union Disruption in Sweden: Does Economic Dependency Inhibit Separation?" *International Journal of Sociology*, 33:1, (Spring, 2003): 3–39, 5–11.
15. An excellent analysis of this aspect of *Inga*, as well as an enumeration of the ways in which *Butterflies* extends many of its themes and approaches, can be found in David Andrews, *Soft in the Middle: The Contemporary Soft Core Feature in its Contexts* (Columbus, Ohio: Ohio State University Press, 2006), 66–70.
16. This aspect of the film's production is discussed on the commentary track of the Retro-Seduction DVD release of *Inga* from 2006.
17. See Israel and Eliasson, "Consumption Society," 72–73 and Herman, "Sex Roles," 60–63.

18. Several of the issues Sarno took with aspects of *Inga's* post-production can be heard on the commentary track of Retro Seduction's 2006 DVD release of the film in which Sarno discusses the movie with Mike Vraney of Something Weird Video, sexploitation film pioneer David Friedman, and former genre film distributor Sam Sherman.

19. An account of some of these protests and their relation to the changing urban policies of the period can be found in Arrhenius, "Preservation and Protest."

20. Many thanks to Mariah Larsson for helping me identify the section of Stockholm in which these scenes in *Anita* were shot.

21. Larsson points out that sex films "with a message" were part of the characteristic approach Inge Ivarson's Swedish Filmproduction Investment AB took to the sex film genre during the transition to hardcore. See "Practice Makes Perfect?," 46.

22. See Björn O. Ahlander, "Juvenile Delinquency in Sweden" *Acta Sociologica*, 3:2–3. Essays in Honor of Torgny T. Segerstedt Presented on His Fiftieth Birthday (1959)

23. Larsson, "Practice Makes Perfect?," 46.

24. A detailed history of Saga Film's activities in adult and mainstream film and video was provided by Per Sjöstedt in an interview with the author, July 2014.

25. The collaboration between Vincent, Revene, and Per Sjöstedt was recounted by Larry Revene in an interview with the author, September 2014.

26. An exhaustive history of the financing, production, and distribution of the Femme video line was provided by Candida Royalle in an interview with the author, June 2014.

27. See Mariah Larsson, "Contested Pleasures" *Swedish Film: An Introduction and Reader*, ed. Mariah Larsson and Anders Marklund (Lund: Nordic Academic Press, 2010) and Kevin Heffernan, "From Sex Entertainment for the Whole Family to Maturepix: *I jomfrueus tegn* and Transnational Erotic Cinema," forthcoming.

28. The crucial importance of the Harry Reems trial to a wary adult film industry contemplating its next move was described by Larry Revene in an interview with the author, September 2014.

29. The overwhelming majority of American adult movies had been released by Saga in unsubtitled English since the nudie movie days, and many German adult films were released in their English-dubbed versions without subtitles. Per Sjöstedt, interview with the author, July 2014.

30. The practices and origins of the Swedish midsommar celebration is detailed in J.G. Frazer, *The Golden Bough*, vol. 1, rev. ed. (Cambridge: Cambridge University Press, 1951), 67–69.

31. The traditional and contemporary music heard on the soundtrack of *Come and Blow the Horn* is listed on the fact sheet for the film at Swedish Film Institute's Swedish Film Database located at http://www.sfi.se/en-GB/Swedish-film-database/Item/?itemid=5028&type=MOVIE&iv=PdfGen [Accessed October, 2014]

32. Herman," Sex Roles," 50.

33. For further discussion of the film, see Mats Björkin's contribution to this volume.

34. See Larsson, "Practice Makes Perfect," 46.

35. Andrews, *Soft in the Middle*, 7.

36. I would like to thank Shawn Wilson and the staff of the library of the Kinsey Institute at the University of Indiana for their generosity during my research visit in 2014. Per Sjöstedt, Candida Royalle, Larry Revene, Anton Holden, Michael Bowen, and Casey Scott patiently answered many of my questions and shared their experience and expertise during the researching and writing of this essay. Finally, Joan Hawkins provided delightful hospitality and scintillating conversation during my visit to Bloomington.

REFERENCES

Ahlander, Björn O. "Juvenile Delinquency in Sweden." *Acta Sociologica*, 3:2–3. Essays in Honour of Torgny T. Segerstedt Presented on His Fiftieth Birthday (1959).

Andrews, David. *Soft in the Middle: The Contemporary Soft Core Feature in its Contexts*, Columbus: Ohio State University Press, 2006.

Arrhenius, Thordis. "Preservation and Protest: Counterculture and Heritage in 1970s Sweden." *Future Anterior: Journal of Historic Preservation, History, Theory, and Criticism*, 7:2 (2010): 108–110.

Balio, Tino. *The Foreign Film Renaissance on American Screens, 1946–1973*. Madison: University of Wisconsin Press, 2010.

Björklund, Elisabet. *The Most Delicate Subject: A History of Sex Education Films in Sweden*. Ph.D. diss., Lund University, 2012.

Frazer, J.G. *The Golden Bough*, vol. 1, rev. ed., Cambridge: Cambridge University Press, 1951.
Gerger, Torvald. "Investigations into Migrations of Manpower." *Human Geography*, 50:1 (1968).
Haavio-Manilla, Elina. "Convergences Between East and West: Tradition and Modernity in Sex Roles in Sweden, Finland, and the Soviet Union." *Acta Sociologica*, 13:1–2 (1971): 114–125.
Heffernan, Kevin. "From Sex Entertainment for the Whole Family to Maturepix: *I Jomfruens tegn* and Transnational Erotic Cinema," forthcoming.
Henz, Ursula, and Jan O. Jonsson. "Union Disruption in Sweden: Does Economic Dependency Inhibit Separation?" *International Journal of Sociology*, 33:1 (2003): 3–39.
Herman, Sondra R. "Sex Roles and Sexual Attitudes in Sweden—A New Phase." *The Massachusetts Review*, 13:1–2 (1972): 59–62.
Himmelstrand, Ulf, and Jan Lindhagen. "The Rejected Status-Seeker in Mass Politics: Fact and Fiction: Status-Rejection, Ideological Conviction, and Some Other Hypotheses about Social-Democratic Loyalty in Sweden." *Acta Sociologica*, 13:4 (1970): 213–236.
Inga. Commentary track. Retro-Seduction DVD, 2006.
Israel, Joachim, and Rosmari Eliasson. "Consumption Society, Sex Roles, and Sexual Behavior." *Acta Sociologica*, 14:1–2 (1971): 68–82.
Larsson, Mariah. "Contested Pleasures." In *Swedish Film: An Introduction and Reader*, edited by Mariah Larsson and Anders Marklund, 205–213. Lund: Nordic Academic Press, 2010.
Larsson, Mariah. "Practice Makes Perfect? The Production of the Swedish Sex Film in the 1970s." *Film International*, 8:6 (2010): 40–49.
Lauster, Nathanael T. "A Room of One's Own or Room Enough for Two? Access to Housing and New Household Formation in Sweden, 1968–1992." *Population Research and Policy Review*, 25:4 (2006): 329–351.
Revene, Larry. Interview with author, September 2014.
Royalle, Candida. Interview with author, June 2014.
Schaefer, Eric. "'I'll Take Sweden': The Shifting Discourse of the 'Sexy Nation' in Sexploitation Films." In *Sex Scene: Media and the Sexual Revolution*, edited by Eric Schaefer, Durham, NC: Duke University Press, 2014: 207–233.
Sjöstedt, Per. Interview with author, July 2014.
Stevenson, Jack. *Scandinavian Blue: The Erotic Cinema of Sweden and Denmark in the 1960s and 1970s*. Jefferson, NC: McFarland, 2010.
Wilkinson, Maurice. "An Econometric Analysis of Fertility in Sweden, 1870–1965." *Econometrica*, 41:4 (1973): 633–642.

About the Contributors

Anders Wilhelm Åberg is a senior lecturer of film studies at Linnaeus University, Sweden. He is the author of *Tabu: Filmaren Vilgot Sjöman* (2001), as well as several articles on European art cinema and children's film. His current research focuses on Swedish children's film and nationalism. Other research interests include intermedial aspects of contemporary television fiction, as well as film, health and the environment.

Klara Arnberg is a researcher at the Department of Economic History at Stockholm University. Her research concerns the history of pornography, advertising, and consumption. She has published in *Entreprise & Society*, *Sexuality & Culture*, and *NORA: Nordic Journal of Feminist and Gender Research* and *Journal of Homosexuality*. She is co-author of a book about moral panics, with Tommy Gustafsson, and has co-edited two volumes of key Swedish sources in gender history and in sexuality history.

Bengt Bengtsson holds a Ph.D. in cinema studies from Stockholm University. His 1998 dissertation, "Ungdom i fara: Ungdomsproblem i svensk spelfilm 1942–62," was about youth problems in Swedish films. Between 1999 and 2014 he was assistant professor at University of Gävle. His is currently researching Swedish television, film archives, film criticism, regional film, and the works of Arne Mattsson.

Ulf Jonas Björk is a professor and chair of the Department of Journalism and Public Relations at Indiana University–Indianapolis, where he teaches media history, writing, and communications law. He has published a number of articles and book chapters about the image of Sweden in American mass media, and the influence of U.S. mass media and popular culture in Sweden.

Mats Björkin is a senior lecturer in film studies at Gothenburg University. His research concerns the interactions between media technologies, nature, and human beings. Among his published articles are "Reconstructing Past Media Ecologies: The 1960s generation in Sweden" in the *European Journal of Communication* (2015) and "Peer-to-Peer File-Sharing Systems: Files, Objects, Distribution" in *Cultural Technologies: The Shaping of Culture in Media and Society* (2012).

Elisabet Björklund is a senior lecturer in film studies at Linnaeus University in Växjö and a postdoctoral researcher at the Department of History of Science and Ideas at Uppsala University. She earned her Ph.D. from Lund University in 2013, with the dissertation "The Most Delicate Subject: A History of Sex Education Films in Sweden" (2012). She is the author of "'This Is a Dirty Movie'—*Taxi Driver* and 'Swedish Sin'" in the *Journal of Scandinavian Cinema* (2011).

Lars Diurlin is a doctoral candidate in film studies at Lund University. His dissertation project concerns the Swedish experimental filmmaker Peter Kylberg. He was the managing director of the Fantastic Film Festival in Lund, Sweden, from 2007 to 2009, and worked at Atlantic Film from 2009 to 2010.

Tommy Gustafsson is a professor of film studies at Linnaeus University, Sweden. He is the author of *Masculinity in the Golden Age of Swedish Cinema: A Cultural Analysis of 1920s Films* (2014), and the co-edited *Nordic Genre Film: Small Nation Film Cultures in the Global Marketplace* (2015) and *Transnational Ecocinema: Film Culture in an Era of Ecological Transformation* (2013), both with Pietari Kääpä.

Kevin Heffernan teaches media history and culture in the Division of Film and Media Arts at Southern Methodist University, in Dallas, Texas. He is the author of *Ghouls, Gimmicks and Gold: Horror Films and the American Movie Business, 1952–1968* (2004), and he is writing a book tentatively titled *From Beavis and Butt Head to Tea Party Nation: Dumb White Guy Politics and Culture in America*.

Anu Koivunen is a professor of cinema studies at Stockholm University, currently studying the aesthetics of intimacy in Jörn Donner's films (1963–1973). Her publications include "Uncanny Motions: Facing Death, Morphing Life," in *Discourse: Journal for Theoretical Studies in Media and Culture* (2014), "Force of Affects, Weight of Histories in Love Is a Treasure (2002)" in *Carnal Aesthetics* (2013), and *Performative Histories, Foundational Framings: Gender and Sexuality in Niskavuori Films (1938–1984)* (2003).

Maaret Koskinen is a professor of cinema studies at Stockholm University, and a board member of the Swedish Film Institute. Her publications include *Ingmar Bergman Revisited: Cinema, Performance and the Arts* (ed., 2008), and *Ingmar Bergman's* The Silence: *Pictures in the Typewriter, Writings on the Screen* (2010). Her recent work focuses upon Swedish feature film in a transnational light and the cultural adaptation processes in an intermedial context.

Mariah Larsson is a senior lecturer in film studies at Linnaeus University. Her areas of interest include film and sexuality, national and transnational cinema, and popular culture. Recent publications include "Making Love Detumescently: Some Preliminary Notes on the Body Language of the Penis," in *Kosmorama* (2014), and "Joe Sarno and Historiography: Some Thoughts on *The Sarnos: A Life in Dirty Movies*," in the *Journal of Scandinavian Cinema* (2013).

Lena Lennerhed is a professor of the history of ideas at Södertörn University in Stockholm, Sweden. She has published books and articles about sex education, sexual liberalism, sex reform, and abortion in the 20th century. Recent publications are "Sherri Finkbine's Choice. Abortion, sex-liberalism and feminism in Sweden in the 1960s and 1970s," in *Women's History Magazine* (2013), and "Sexual Liberalism in Sweden" in Gert Hekma & Alain Giami (eds.), *Sexual Revolutions* (2014).

Arne Lunde is an associate professor of Scandinavian studies and of cinema and media studies at UCLA. He is the author of *Nordic Exposures: Scandinavian Identities in Classical Hollywood Cinema* (2010) and has also published in *Journal of Scandinavian Cinema, Film International, Film Quarterly*, and *The Moving Image*. His current research includes a book project on the films of Ingmar Bergman of the 1940s and 50s inside the Swedish studio system.

Anders Marklund is a senior lecturer in film studies at Lund University. His research interests relate to Swedish, Scandinavian, and European cinema. He is the co-editor of *Swedish Film: An Introduction and Reader* (2010), and the founder and principal editor of *Journal of Scandinavian Cinema*. His publications include "Dark Memories in the Provincial Worlds of Ingmar Bergman's Fanny and Alexander and Federico Fellini's Amarcord" in *IMAGES* (2013).

Carl Marklund is a postdoctoral researcher at the Center for Baltic and East European Studies at Södertörn University. He has a Ph.D. in history from the European University Institute. His publications include "Hot Love and Cold People: Sexual Liberalism as Political Escapism in Radical Sweden" in *Nordeuropaforum* (2009) and he is the co-editor of *The Paradox of Openness: Transparency and Participation in Nordic Cultures of Consensus* (2014).

Per Vesterlund is a senior lecturer in film studies at Gävle University, and is currently working on a project about Harry Schein. He is the co-editor of *Svensk television—en mediehistoria* (2008) and of *Citizen Schein* (2010).

Index

Numbers in **_bold italics_** refer to pages with photographs.

A-produktion 63
Åberg, Anders (Wilhelm) 118, 203
abortion 11, 18, 38, 120, 121, 186, 187, 195
Abramson, Hans 43
Ace in the Hole 65
adult cinema 6, 229
Advisory Council *see* Film Review Council
Agaton Sax and the Byköping Feast see *Agaton Sax och Byköpings gästabud*
Agaton Sax och Byköpings gästabud 176
Ahlberg, Mac 2, 75, 76, 133, 176, 218, 219, 224, 229
Ahlgren, Stig 64
Ahlmark-Michanek, Kristina 43–44
Ahlstedt, Börje 51, 54, 202, 210
Ahnsjö, Sven 143, 147
Alfred 119
Alfred Nobel see *Alfred*
All About Eve 65
All These Women see *För att inte tala om alla dessa kvinnor*
Allen, Woody 2, 15
Alpert, Hollis 13, 209
Alpha France 221
Älskarinnan 50, 119
American International Pictures 14
Anderson, Benedict 90, 186
Andersson, Bibi 163
Andersson, Bo **_120_**
Andersson, Harriet 11, 12, 13, 14, 15, 38–39, **_39_**, 41, 43, **_43_**, 44
Andersson, Lars Gustaf 177
Andrée, Ulf 173
Anger, Kenneth 82
Änglagård 87
Änglar, finns dom? 173
Anita see *Anita—ur en tonårsflickas dagbok*
Anita—ur en tonårsflickas dagbok 221, **_221_**, 222, 226, 228
Ann and Eve see *Ann och Eve—de erotiska*
Ann och Eve—de erotiska 4, 61–72, **_66_**, **_68_**, **_69_**
Ansikte mot ansikte 18
Ansiktet 16, 17, 64

Antonioni, Michelangelo 39, 41, 67
Anything for Money 222
The Apartment 42
Arlach, Heinrich 79
Arnberg, Klara 74, 146
Arne (pseudonym) 87
art cinema, 16, 18, 31, 38, 40, 41, 42, 44, 61, 62, 65, 67, 70, 71, 77, 218; *see also* arthouse
arthouse 11, 12, 16, 17, 18, 87; *see also* art cinema
As the Naked Wind from the Sea see *... som havets nakna vind*
Att älska 4, 37–44
Att angöra en brygga 174
auteur 11, 18, 21, 38, 39, 40, 50, 51, 61, 62, 71, 76, 154, 202, 218, 219, 221, 229; *see also* authorship
authorship 4, 49, 50, 52; *see also* auteur
Axelman, Torbjörn 64

Babb, Kroger 3, 11, 13–15
Bad Seed see *Rötägg*
Bäddat för lusta 176
Balio, Tino 15, 16, 217
Bamse 63
Bamse—The Teddy Bear see *Bamse*
Bara en mor 1, 30
Bardot, Brigitte 43
Barrow, Clyde 193
Baxter, Les 14
BDSM 131, 134
Beatty, Warren 224
Beaudine, William 3, 13
The Bed, and How to Make It 222
Bed of Lust see *Bäddat för lusta*
Bedside films 77, 223
Bel Ami 76, 224, 226
Bellis, Aina 161, 162
Bergenblock (no first name) 109
Bergenstråhle, Johan 176
Bergfelder, Tim 18
Berglund, Anita 86
Berglund, Anne-Marie 4, 74–75, 77–82, **_80_**
Bergman, Ingmar 1, 2, 3, 5, 11–18, 21–25, 29, 31, 37, 38, 39, 40, 41, 50, 51, 56, 63, 64, 70, 75, 87, 117, 118, 119, 123, 126, 144, 146, 153–

163, 170, 173, 188, 201, 202, 217, 218–220, **_218_**
Bergman, Marie 86
Bergström-Walan, Maj-Briht 147
Berne, Robert *see* Ahlberg, Mac
bestiality 2, 5, 118, 123, 131, 193
Beyer, Nils 54, 63, 203
Bibi see *Vild på sex*
Bison Film 71
Björklund, Elisabet 217
Björnstrand, Gunnar 64
Black Power 129
Black Sun see *Mannen i skuggan*
Blomgren, Bengt 1
Blushing Charlie see *Lyckliga skitar*
Boheman, Erik 187
Bon Appétit 222
Böök, Fredrik 90
Bordwell, David 22–23, 29, 31
Bourdieu, Pierre 154
Bovee, Leslie 223
Brandhild, Arne 176
The Bread of Love see *Kärlekens bröd*
Breaking Point 176
A Brief Survey of Film in Sweden, Presented to Gimbels Visitors by Gimbels and SFI 173
Brown, Joe David 170, 171, 186
Brusendorff, Ove 37
Buñuel, Luis 122
Buried Treasure 79, 81
Butterflies 6, 217, 223–228, **_225_**, **_227_**
Butterfly see *Butterflies*

Cambist Films 222
Canby, Vincent 208–209
Candy, John 216, 230
Cannon 219, 220
Capra, Frank 33n39
Carter, Jimmy 224
Casablanca 24–25, 29
Cavani, Liliana 75
Celebrezze, Frank 208
The Chameleons see *Kameleonterna*
Chans 122
Christian Democratic Unity/Christian Democrats 116, 121

235

Index

Christine's Secret 223
Cinema Ordinance 117, 160
cinéma vérité 51, 208
Citizen Kane 14, 65, 155
Clouzot, Henri-Georges 43
The Cold War 186, 194
Collmar, Lars 116, 122
Collsiöö, Jan **190**
Come and Blow the Horn see *Fäbodjäntan*
Constance 78
Corman, Roger 14
Cornell, Jonas 173
Cowie, Peter 174, 176, 204
Crisis see *Kris*
Crist, Judith 17
Criterion 14–15, 16
Crowther, Bosley 12–13
Curtiz, Michael 24
Cybulski, Zbigniew 39

Dagheim, Frida **218**
Dahlström, Leif 70
Damiano, Gerard 77, 222
Danish Pastries see *I jomfruens tegn*
Davidsson, Katarina 77, 79
Davis, Arthur 17
Davis, Helen 17
Dear John see *Käre John*
Deep Throat 77, 80, 210, 222, 224
de Funès, Luis 175
De Geer, Carl Johan 189
de Grazia, Edward 207
Del Rio, Vanessa 223
Denmark/Danish 2, 21, 30, 37, 74, 77, 79, 133, 141, 142, 173, 187, 191, 216, 217, 223, 224
The Devil's Eye see *Djävulens öga*
The Devil's Plaything see *Der Fluch der schwarzen Schwestern*
The Devil's Wanton see *Fängelse*
Dietrich, Marlene 18
Dirty Diaries 78
Dirty Fingers see *Smutsiga fingrar*
Ditte—Child of Man see *Ditte Menneskebarn*
Ditte Menneskebarn 30
Djävulens öga 17
documentary 4, 6, 49, 87, 130, 189, 202, 206, 210, 222
Dom kallar oss mods 2, 130
Donner, Jörn 4, 37–44, **39, 43**
Douglas, William O. 208
The Dress see *Klänningen*
Driver dagg, faller regn 86
Dybeck, Richard 92

Ecstasy 13
Edenborg, Carl-Mikael 78, 81
Edgren, Gustaf 86
Edlund, Lennart 109–111
Edström, Mauritz 116, 122, 203
L'Éducation d'Orphélie 78, 82
Edwards, Eric 223, 226, **227**
8½ 65
8 mm film 129, 131
Eisenhower, Dwight D. 15, 187, 194

Ekbladh, Gunnar 148
Ekborg, Lars 14
Ekman, Hasse 71
Ekman, Mikael 1
Ekström, Per Olof 12, 26
Elmquist, Bernt 79
Elthammar, Olof 147–148
Elvira Madigan 63, 226–228
Embassy Pictures 17
The Emigrants see *Utvandrarna*
Emmanuelle 229
Eriksson, Göran O. 49
Eriksson, Wiktor 87
Erixon, Sigurd 93
Erotikon 42
Eveready Harton in Buried Treasure see *Buried Treasure*
Everett, Rob see Edwards, Eric

Fäbodjäntan 4, 6, 79, 86–96, **92, 94**, 217, 218, 223, 227–229
The Face see *Ansiktet*
Face to Face see *Ansikte mot ansikte*
Fahrenheit 451 51
Fängelse 17–18
Fången 79
Faris, Daniel 12, 14
Fascination 222
Fellini, Federico 16, 41, 64, 65, 67
feminism 44, 74, 75, 76, 77, 78, 82, 154, 165n10, 175, 194, 220; see also women's movement
Femme 77
La Femme est une femme 41
Femme series 223
Fenix 79, 81
Film Classics Inc. 12
film policy 5, 62, 71, 72n2, 153, 160; see also Swedish Film Institute; Swedish film reform
The Film Research Group 5, 142–150
Film Review Council (Advisory Council) 117, 127–131, 133, 160, 203
Filmcentrum 177
Filmforskningsgruppen see The Film Research Group
Filmgranskningsrådet see Film Review Council
Finan, Thomas B. 207
Fishman, Irving 206
Fletcher, Louise 224
Flossie 76, 79, 80, 224, 229
Floyd, Calvin 74, 176
Der Fluch der schwarzen Schwestern 224
Flynn, Errol 18
folkhemmet ("the people's home") 119, 122, 186; see also the Swedish model; the Swedish welfare state
För att inte tala om alla dessa kvinnor 18, 40, 64
The Forgotten Ones see *Los Olvidados*
Forså, Marie 79, 222, 224, 226–227, **227**, 229

Forssell, Lars 52
The 400 Blows see *Les Quatres Cents Coups*
491 2, 5, 38, 40, 42, 50, 51, 70, 116–124, 126, 128, 130, 158, 159, 173, 202
Från pussar till porr 21
Från spex till sex 173
Franco, Francisco 56, 57, 202, 206
Frank, Jack 79
freedom of expression 49, 50, 170; see also freedom of speech; Yttrandefrihetsutredningen
freedom of speech 5, 122, 123, 126, 142, 150; see also freedom of expression; Yttrandefrihetsutredningen
Freud, Sigmund 25, 50, 52, 56–59, 80
Friberg, Gösta 79
Fridolinski, Alex see Vibenius, Bo A.
Friedman, David 11, 13, 14
Friendly, Henry 206
Fröken Julie 3, 21, 23, 25, 26, 29, 63
From the Lives of the Marionettes see *Ur marionetternas liv*
Frost, David 190, **190**
Frustration see *Skepp till Indialand*
Fuck/Blue Movie 170n33
Furhammar, Leif 64, 126, 134, 143, 144, 148, 149, 159, 160

Games Women Play 222
Gamlin, Yngve 1
Garbo, Greta 14
gay 16, 192; see also homosexuality
GeBe Film AB 79, 224
genitals 2, 29, 62, 106, 111, 123; see also hardcore
Gerber, Paul D. 229
Gillis, Jamie 223
Glover, Nikolas 172
Godard, Jean-Luc 39, 41, 202, 210
Göransson, Bengt 160
Gordon, Michael 42
Görling, Lars
Gottlieb, Sidney 22, 26, 27
The Graduate 29, 30
grindhouse 11, 12, 65, 216
Gross, Leonard 208, 209
Grove Press 201, 205–209
Guilt see *Tillsammans med Gunilla måndag kväll och tisdag*
Guldbagge 119, 165n31
Gurley Brown, Helen 44
Gustaf VI Adolf (Swedish king, 1950–1973) 189, 204
Gycklarnas afton 16

Häggbom, Råland 130
Hakim, Gaston 13, 14
Hale, Frederick 170
Hale, Wanda 17, 41
Halldoff, Jan **120**
Halliday, Bryant 11, 16
Hallmark Productions 13–14

Index

Hallo Baby 176
Hamnstad 18
A Handful of Love see *En handfull kärlek*
En handfull kärlek 119
Hanks, Tom 216
Hannah, Darryl 216
Happy Family see *Den k... familjen*
Här har du ditt liv 163
Här kommer bärsärkarna 63–64
hardcore 6, 49, 62, 65, 74, 75, 76, 77, 79, 81, 87, 95, 101, 106, 154, 157, 169, 176, 177, 206, 216, 221–222, 223, 224, 227, 229; see also genitals
Harvey, Cyrus, Jr. 11, 16
Haven, Annette 223
Hays, Paul Raymond 206
Hays Code 22, 24, 29, 31; see also Production Code
Hazelius, Artur 89, 90, 92
Hearst, Randolph 155
Hederberg, Hans 121
Hedling, Erik 18
Hedman, Werner 74
Heffernan, Kevin 16, 17, 209
Hegeler, Inge 221
Hegeler, Sten 221
Hellbom, Olle 26
Hellström, Gunnar 122
Hemvideo 222, 227
Henning, Lawrence see Sarno, Joe
Henning-Jensen, Bjarne 30
Here Is Your Life see *Här har du ditt liv*
Herman, Sondra 228
Hessel, Lee 222
Hets 12, 18
Hickox, Douglas 65
Hiltunen, Leena 86, 87, **92, 94**
Hiroshima, Mon Amour 41
Hitchcock, Alfred 22, 26
Hixson, Richard F. 205
Hjertén, Hanserik 70
Höglund, Gunnar 1, 71
Hollywood 11, 12, 14, 18, 24, 33*n*39, 53, 118, 161, 216, 223, 224
Hollywood (theater) 222
Un Homme et une femme 63
homosexuality 2, 117, 118, 119, 120, 121, 127, 132, 133, 141; see also gay; lesbianism
Hon dansade en sommar 3, 4, 12, 21–24, 26, 30–32, 37, 61, 62, 70, 86, 134, 173, 219
Höök, Marianne 67
HotMen CoolBoyz 78
House of Angels see *Änglagård*
Howard, Ron 216
Humphrey, Daniel 12, 14, 16–17
Hyltén-Cavallius, Gun 171, 176

I, a Woman see *Jeg—en kvinde*
I, a Woman, Part II see *Jag—en kvinna 2*
I Am Curious (Blue) see *Jag är nyfiken—blå*
I Am Curious (Yellow) see *Jag är nyfiken—gul*

I jomfruens tegn 224
I løvens tegn 74, 79
I lust och nöd 229
I rök och dans 1, 12
Ibsen, Henrik 12, 44, 88
Idestam-Almquist, Bengt 63
Illicit Interlude see *Sommarlek*
imagined community 1, 90
In the Sign of the Lion see *I løvens tegn*
incest 2, 17, 62, 154
Inga see *Jag, en oskuld*
Inkräktarna 176
Intrator, Jerald 14
The Intruders see *Inkräktarna*
Isberg, Linnea 78
Israel, Joacim 230*n*14
It Rains on Our Love see *Det regnar på vår kärlek*
It's a Wonderful Life 33*n*39
Ivarson, Inge 71, 76, 79, 231*n*21

Jacobsson, Ulla 12
Jaeckin, Just 229
Jag är nyfiken—blå 2, 4, 49, 50, 51, 53, 54, 55, **56**, 58, 120, 189, 201, 202, 210
Jag är nyfiken—gul 2, 4, 6, 49, 50, 51, 53, 55, 58, 73, 119, 120, 130, 134, 158, 170, 189, 201–211
Jag—en kvinna 2 65
Jag—en kvinna see *Jeg—en kvinde*
Jag, en oskuld 2, 65, 71, 75, 132, 218–221, **218**, 226, 228, 229, 230*n*15
Janssen, Claes 147
Janus film 3, 11, 15, 16–18
Jarl, Stefan 2, 130
Jeg—en kvinde 2, 75, 133, 219, 226
Jerneman, Per Trygve 105–108
Jess, Marilyn 223
Jet Film 129
Joensen, Bodil 223
Jonsson, Bo 172–174, 176, 178–179*n*30
Jörgensen, Knud 79, 86
Josephson, Erland 18
Jungfrukällan 17, 118, 159
Just Once More see *Chans*
Justine and Juliette see *Justine och Juliette*
Justine och Juliette 76, 224, 226

Den k... familjen 79
Kaeyér, Karl 102–105, 107
Kameleonterna 64
Kaplan, Nelly 75, 82
Kär lek—så gör vi. Brev till Inge och Sten 176
Käre John 1, 170, 173
Kärlekens bröd 61
Kärlekens XYZ 230*n*14
Kärlekson 79, 229
Kaufman, Charles 229
Kaufmann, Anette 27, 28
Kennedy, John F. 158
Kenton, Earle C. 14
The Kiss on the Cruise see *Kyssen på kryssen*

Kissinger, Henry 163
Klänningen 202
Kling, Herman 189–191, 194, 204
Klubb Super 8, **80, 188, 221**
The Knack ... And How to Get It 171
Knight, Arthur 13
Knutsson, Gunilla 174, 176
Kohner, Paul 161–162
Koskinen, Maaret 18, 128
Krantz, Leif 70
Kris 18
Kristel, Sylvia 229
Kulick, Don 134
Kurosawa, Akira 16
Kutchinsky, Berl 187
Kvinnolek 65, 132
Kvinnors väntan 16, 17, 18
Kyssen på kryssen 72*n*24

Lagercrantz, Olof 151*n*17
Lahaie, Brigitte 223
Lamarr, Hedy 13
Lamb, John 3
Lang, Maria 63
Language of Love see *Ur kärlekens språk*
Larsson, Mariah 87, 130, 175, 217, 231*n*21
Lasseby, Stig 176
Léaud, Jean-Pierre 15
Lehman, Peter 82
Leisure Time Booking 224
Lelouch, Claude 63
Lennerhed, Lena 38, 126, 175
lesbianism 2, 11, 18, 65, 77, 111, 130, 132, 141; see also homosexuality
Lester, Richard 171
Levine, Joseph E. 17
Levy, Eugene 216
Lidblom, Dick 108–112
Liljedahl, Marie 61, 65, **66**, 219, 220
Liljeson (no first name) 105–106
Linda, Christa 229
Lindberg, Christina 220, 221, **221**
Linder, Erik Hjalmar 122
Lindgren, Göran 170
Lindgren, Lars-Magnus 1, 170, 173
Lindqvist, Jan 2
Lindqvist, Torbjörn 79, 91
Linnaeus, Carolus 90
Lippe, Morton 15
Liz see *I lust och nöd*
Ljungberg, Rune 176
Ljuvlig är sommarnatten 63
Löthwall, Lars-Olof 176
Love Mates see *Änglar, finns dom?*
Love Play—This Is Our Way see *Kär lek—så gör vi. Brev till Inge och Sten*
Lovely is the Summer Night see *Ljuvlig är sommarnatten*
Love's Island see *Kärleksön*
Lubitsch, Ernst 42
Lumbard, J. Edward 206–207
Lunarex 222, 223
Lundkvist, Artur 54

238 Index

Lust, Erika 77
Lyckliga skitar 119
Lynghøft, Lisbeth 78
Lynn, Maria *see* Forså, Marie

Mackendrick, Alexander 65
Mad Men 2, 5, 155–158, 164
Mae, Fannie, 209
The Magician see Ansiktet
Maid in Sweden 220, 226
Mailer, Norman 119, 205–206
Malacca 119
Malle, Louis 41
Malmkjær, Poul 37
Malmsten, Birger 13, 61
A Man and a Woman see Un Homme et une femme
Mankiewicz, Joseph L 65
Mannekäng i rött 65
Mannen i skuggan 71
Mannequin in Red see Mannekäng i rött
Mannering, Edward *see* Ahlberg, Mac
Manns, Torsten 175
Marklund, Carl 172
Marmstedt, Lorens 17
Marx, Karl 56
masochism 15, 52, 55, 57, 58, 59n21, 127, 133
masturbation 2, 38, 79, 80, 104, 105, 113–114n41, 118, 127, 130, 132, 220, 229
Mateos, Julián **69**
Mattsson, Arne 3, 4, 12, 21–24, 26–32, 61–72, 72n24, 86, 134, 173, 219
Meineche, Annelise 133
Mekas, Jonas 177
Mera ur kärlekens språk 130–133, 221
Midsummer 1, 25, 26, 32n22, 89, 95, 228
Miljonprogrammet 219, 221
Miller, William Ian 27
Million Dwellings Program *see* Miljonprogrammet
Milton, Berth, Sr. 192–194
Minerva Film 65
Miss Julie see Fröken Julie
The Mistress see Älskarinnan
Mixed-Up Women see One Too Many
Molly see Molly—familjeflickan
Molly—familjeflickan 76, 80
Mom and Dad 3, 13
Monarex 222, 224
Monika—The Story of a Bad Girl see Sommaren med Monika
Monroe, Marilyn 15
Montelius, Ragnar 148
Mördaren—en helt vanlig person 63
More About the Language of Love see Mera ur kärlekens språk
Morgenstern, Joseph 208, 209
Muller, Eddie 12, 14
Mulvey, Laura 175
The Murderer—A Perfectly Ordinary Person see Mördaren—en helt vanlig person
Murphy, Thomas F. 205–206
Music in Darkness see Musik i mörker
Musik i mörker 17
My Sister, My Love see Syskonbädd 1782
Myrdal, Gunnar 187, 189

The Naked Night see Gycklarnas afton
När kärleken kom till byn 22
Näsström, Gustaf 89
National Board of Film Censors 2, 5, 76, 116–119, 122, 123, 126–135, 143, 148, 150, 158–160, 188, 202, 203, 204
Nattlek 75, 170
Nattvardsgästerna 50, 119
Nea 75
Nichols, Mike 29
Nicholson, Jack 224
Night Games see Nattlek
Night Is My Future see Musik i mörker
The Night Porter see Il portiere di notti
Niklas and the Figure see Niklas och figuren
Niklas och figuren 173
Nilsson, Maj-Britt 13
Nordgren, Erik 14
Nordisk Tonefilm
Nutley, Colin 87
Nyberg, Börje 132
Nyman, Jack 141
Nyman, Lena 4, 49–51, 53–54, **56**, 57–58, **120**, 202, 210
Nymark, Leif **120**
nymphomania 17, 18, 193

obscenity (law) 2, 4, 6, 50, 74, 75, 116–119, 121, 123, 126–130, 189, 192, 201, 205–208, 218, 224
Olin, Stig 18
Olofsson, Darwin 171
Los Olvidados 122
Omega Film 65, 219
Den onda cirkeln 63
One Summer of Happiness see Hon dansade en sommar
One Swedish Summer see …som havets nakna vind
One Too Many 14
Only a Mother see Bara en mor
Ormens ägg 18
Orwell, George 154
Ottesen-Jensen, Elise 196n19

Palm, Sture 129
Palme, Mårten 165n13
Palme, Olof 5, 153–158, 160, 162, 163, 165n13, 186, 190, **190**, 191, 193
Palme, Ulf 1
Pecker Island see Buried Treasure
Penley, Constance 81
Pentecostal Movement 116, 121, 150, 191

Persona 18, 56
Persson, Annika 53–54, 57
Persson, Essy 2, 219
Pethrus, Lewi 116, 121
Petré, Gio 61, 65, **68**, **69**
Pettersson, Axel Hakon 108–111
Pettersson, Hilma Martina 105–106, 108
Pillow Talk 42, 44
Pink Prison 78
Pitzulo, Carrie 193
Poe, Edgar Allan 14
Polanski, Roman 133
Porr i skandalskolan 176
Port of Call see Hamnstad
Il portiere di notti 75
Practice Makes Perfect see Ta mej i dalen
Price, Vincent 65
Prison see Fängelse
Private 6, 185, 191–193, 195n4
Production Code 2, 11, 22, 53; *see also* Hays Code
Puzzy Power 77, 78

"Quality film" 71, 159, 163, 168, 169
Les Quatres Cents Coups 15
Qvist, Per Olov 26

Rabal, Francisco 65, **68**
Ragneborn, Arne **221**
Raid in the Summer see Strandhugg i somras
Rain Follows the Dew see Driver dagg, faller regn
Rapport från Stockholms sexträsk 176
Reberg, David *see* Gerber, Paul D.
Reems, Harry 80, 223, 224, **225**, 226–227
Det regnar på vår kärlek 18
Report from the Stockholm Sex Jungle see Rapport från Stockholms sexträsk
Repulsion 133
Resnais, Alain 41
Revene, Larry 222, 229
RFSU 145
Riefenstahl, Leni 16
Rites of Passion 223
Robin Hood *see* Idestam-Almquist, Bengt
Roommates 222
Roos (no first name) 105–106
Rötägg 22
Roud, Richard 41
Royalle, Candida 77, 223, 229
Rubin, Gayle 127, 131, 134

Sabrina 42
sadism 133, 134
Saga Film 6, 217–218, 222–224, 229
Sahlberg, Gardar 173, 175
Sams 74, 176
Samuelsson, Kurt 116
Sandrews 25, 39, 170, 202
Sarno, Joe 2, 4, 6, 65, 75, 79, 86, 87, 88, **92**, **94**, 95, 96, 132, 217–

220, *218*, 222, 224, *225*, 226–227, *227*, 228–229
The Sarnos: A Life in Dirty Movies 87
Sarris, Andrew 41
Såsom i en spegel 159
Sawdust and Tinsel see *Gycklarnas afton*
The Scandal School see *Porr i skandalskolan*
Scattini, Luigi 188, 189
Scener ur ett äktenskap 165n10
Scenes from a Marriage see *Scener ur ett äktenskap*
Schaefer, Eric 13, 21, 38, 76, 101, 112, 216, 217
Schein, Harry 5, 64, 67, 75, 123, 128, 141, 142–150, 151n17, 153–164, *157*, 166n32, 168–177
Schickel, Richard 209
Schildt, Jurgen 70, 122, 203
Scorsese, Martin 2
The Second Coming of Eve see *Porr i skandalskolan*
Secrets of Women see *Kvinnors väntan*
Segerstedt, Torgny 143, 144, 148, 150
Sellier, Geneviève 40
Selznick, David O. 12
Semitov, Vladimir 26
The Sensual Woman 133
Serling, Rod 17
The Serpent's Egg see *Ormens ägg*
The Seven Year Itch 42
The Seventh Seal see *Det sjunde inseglet*
sex education 38, 40, 43, 105, 121, 147, 172, 193, 196n19, 219; films 2, 3, 13, 76, 123, 130, 132, 189, 217, 221
Sex Purchase Act 3
Sexual Freedom in Denmark 3
SFI see Swedish Film Institute
Shilling, Lawrence W. 206
A Ship Bound for India see *Skepp till Indialand*
Silbersky, Leif 193
The Silence see *Tystnaden*
Sima, Jonas 58
Sin in the Suburbs 222
Sjöberg, Alf 1, 3, 12, 21–23, 25–26, 30, 32n18, 63
Sjöman, Vilgot 2, 4, 5, 6, 38, 39, 40, 42, 49–59, *56*, 64, 70, 116, 118–120, *120*, 123, 126, 130, 146, 158, 159, 170, 173, 175, 177, 189, 201–211
Sjöstedt, Göran 227
Sjöstedt, Per 222
Sjöstedt, Sture 217, 222, 227, 229
Sjöström, Victor 86
Det sjunde inseglet 16
Skepp till Indialand 12
Skoglund, Erik 117–118, 127–133, 135, 143, 150
Smith, Gudmund 143
Smultronstället 16, 64
Smutsiga fingrar 71

Söderström, Karl Helge 108–111
Softcore 2, 49, 65, 76, 78, 87, 170, 176, 219, 220, 223, 226, 227, 229
...som havets nakna vind 1, 71
Sommar och syndare 63
Sommaren med Monika 1, 2, 3, 11–15, 31, 173
Sommarlek 3, 12, 13, 16, 21, 23, 25, 28, 29
En söndag i september 38, 39
Sörenson, Elisabeth 70
Sound of Näverlur 91
Span, Anna 77
Splash 216
stag film 74, 81, 101–104, 112
Statens biografbyrå see National Board of Film Censors
Stevenson, Jack 37, 217
Stigsdotter, Ingrid 18
Stiller, Mauritz 42, 86
Stockholm's Nude Centre 129
Strandhugg i somras 1
Streicher, Herbert see Reems, Harry
Strindberg, August 21, 25, 32n18
Strömmerstedt, Monika *218*
Summer Interlude see *Sommarlek*
Summer with Monika see *Sommaren med Monika*
Summers and Sinners see *Sommar och syndare*
A Sunday in September see *En söndag i september*
Sundgren, Nils Petter 21, 22, 30
Sundholm, John 177
Sundquist, Folke 12
Svedlund, Doris 17
Svensk Filmindustri 5, 16, 17, 62, 117, 123, 159, 161, 162
Svezia, inferno e paradiso see *Sweden: Heaven and Hell*
Sweden: Heaven and Hell 188, *188*, 189
The Swedish Association for Sexuality Education see RFSU
Swedish Family Games see *Sams*
Swedish Film Institute 2, 3, 5, 62, 64, 67, 71, 75, 77, 87, 123, 128, 141, 142–146, 148–149, 153, 155, 156, 159–164, 168–177, 204
Swedish film reform 123, 141, 143, 150, 153, 157, 169, 171; see also film policy; Swedish Film Institute
Swedish Filmproduction Investment AB 221
Swedish Minx see *Justine och Juliette*
The Swedish model 171, 187; see also folkhemmet, the Swedish welfare state
Swedish Nymphette see *Anita—ur en tonårsflickas dagbok*
Swedish welfare state 40, 119, 122, 142, 186, 187, 189, 194, 195, 202; see also Swedish model; Swedish welfare state
Sweet Smell of Success 65
Syskonbädd 1782 120, 202

Ta mej i dalen 229
Taboo see *Tabu*
Tabu 120
Tallroth, Tore 172, 173
Taxi Driver 2, 3
Tchaikovsky, Pyotr 13
Tengroth, Birgit 64
Terrafilm 17
That Lucky Stiff 222
Theater of Blood 65
Theslöf, Georg 26–27
They Call Her One-Eye see *Thriller—en grym film*
They Call Us Misfits see *Dom kallar oss mods*
Thirst see *Törst*
This Country Life see *Ta mej i dalen*
Thomas, Jack 15
Thorén, Ulf 204
Three Daughters 223
Three Strange Loves see *Törst*
Thriller—A Cruel Picture see *Thriller—en grym film*
Thriller—en grym film 76, 176
Through a Glass Darkly see *Såsom i en spegel*
Thulin, Ingrid 155, *157*, 158, 161
Thunberg, Lars 122
Till glädje 18
Tillsammans med Gunilla måndag kväll och tisdag 130
Times Film Corporation 12, 16
Timm, Mikael 156, 164
To Go Ashore see *Att angöra en brygga*
To Ingrid, My Love, Lisa see *Kvinnolek*
To Joy see *Till glädje*
To Love see *Att älska*
Tomas (no last name) 86
Torment see *Hets*
Torn, Bert see Ahlberg, Mac
Törst 17, 18
Trankell, Arne 143
Trinity films 222
Troell, Jan 174
Truffaut, François 15, 51
The Truth see *La Verité*
Tumin, Melvin 194
Tunbäck Hanson, Monica 203
The Twilight Zone 17
Tystnaden 2, 17–18, 31, 38, 40, 70, 118, 123, 126, 128, 144, 146, 151n2, *157*, 159–160, 170, 173, 188

Uden en trævl 133
Ullmann, Liv 18, 162–163
Ur kärlekens språk 2, 3, 71, 75, 76, 123, 130, 132, 173, 175, 189, 221
Ur marionetternas liv 18
Urban Heat 223
Utvandrarna 174

Vallquist, Gunnel 52
Veckända i Stockholm 4, 74, 77–79, *80,* 81–82
Vennberg, Karl 122
La Vérité 43

240 Index

Vesterskov, Knud 78
Vibenius, Bo A. 76, 176
The Vicious Circle see *Den onda cirkeln*
Vidal, Gore 155
The Vietnam War 2, 158, 163, 193
Vild på sex 224
Vincent, Chuck 222, 229
Vinterhed, Kerstin 49, 57
Virgin Spring see *Jungfrukällan*
von Sydow, Max 17, 161
von Trier, Lars 77
Vraney, Mike 220

Waiting Women see *Kvinnors väntan*
Wallenberg, Louise 158
Wallin, Emil Sigfrid 108-111
Warburg, Bent 223
Warburg, Bie 223, 229
Warhol, Andy 73n33, 82
Warrick, Ruth 14
Weekend in Stockholm see *Veckända i Stockholm*

Weidenhayn, Ergon Percy 108-109, 111
Weiss, Peter 165n10
Welles, Orson 65, 155
When Love Came to the Village see *När kärleken kom till byn*
Wickman, Krister 153, 160
Wickman, Torgny 2, 71, 75, 123, 130, 173, 176, 218, 221, *221*, 222, 229, 230n14
Widegren, Kajsa 78
Widerberg, Bo 39, 63, 64, 161, 226-227, **227**
Wild Strawberries see *Smultronstället*
The Wild Vikings see *Här kommer bärsärkarna*
Wilder, Billy 42, 65
Williams, Linda 21, 22, 24, 29, 33n34, 33n39, 101, 112
Winchell, Walter 13
Winter Light see *Nattvardsgästerna*
Wiskari, Werner 187
Without a Stitch see *Uden en trævl*

Wolodarski, Peter 166n32
A Woman Is a Woman see *La Femme est une femme*
Woman of Darkness see *Yngsjömordet*
women's movement 76, 77, 123; see also feminism
World War II 22, 112, 156
Wyatt, Justin 41

XYZ of Love see *Kärlekens XYZ*

Yes, Count the Possibilities see *Kvinnolek*
Yngsjömordet 62
Yttrandefrihetsutredningen 150; see also freedom of expression; freedom of speech

Zentropa 77
Zetterling, Mai 75, 170
Zodiac films 74, 77, 223, 224
Zorn, Anders 92, 93

www.ingramcontent.com/pod-product-compliance
Ingram Content Group UK Ltd.
Pitfield, Milton Keynes, MK11 3LW, UK
UKHW050534150426
5217IPUK00026B/1925